UNSCRIPTED™

LIFE, LIBERTY, AND THE PURSUIT OF ENTREPRENEURSHIP

MJ DeMARCO

International Best-Selling Author of The Millionaire Fastlane

AMARYLLIS BUSINESS

An imprint of Manjul Publishing House

AMARYLLIS
BUSINESS

An imprint of Manjul Publishing House Pvt. Ltd.
• C-16, Sector 3, Noida, Uttar Pradesh 201301, India
Website: www.manjulindia.com
Registered Office:
• 2nd Floor, Usha Preet Complex,
42, Malviya Nagar, Bhopal 462 003 - India
Distribution Centres
Ahmedabad, Bengaluru, Chennai, Hyderabad,
Kochi, Kolkata, Mumbai, Noida, Pune

Unscripted: Life, Liberty, and the Pursuit of Entrepreneurship
by MJ DeMarco

English edition first published in the USA by
Viperion Publishing Corporation 5513 W 11000 N Suite 161
Highland UT 84004

This English edition first published in India in 2026 by
Amaryllis Business – an imprint of Manjul Publishing House Pvt Ltd

ISBN 978-93-7317-135-7

Printed and bound in India by Repro India Ltd.

The information presented herein represents the view of the author as of the date of publication. This book is presented for informational and entertainment purposes only. Due to the rate at which economic and cultural conditions change, the author reserves the right to alter and update his opinions based on new conditions. While every attempt has been made to verify the information in this book, neither the author nor the publisher, or their affiliates/partners assume any responsibility for errors, inaccuracies, or omissions. At no time shall the information contained herein be construed as professional, investment, tax, accounting, legal, or medical advice. This book does not constitute a recommendation or a warrant of suitability for any particular business, industry, website, security, portfolio of securities, transaction, or investment strategy.

THE STORIES

Many of the stories and excerpts in this book are sourced from The Fastlane Forum, an entrepreneurial community I founded in 2007. Although edited for clarity, they are real stories from real people.

In the last ten years, I've had the privilege to interact with over 30,000 entrepreneurs in over 500,000 posts totaling millions of visits—from millionaires to aspiring entrepreneurs to lifelong employees taking the startup leap. The Fastlane community has been instrumental in making this book happen. But more importantly, it has given thousands of people around the world the tools and social permission to live the *UNSCRIPTED*™ dream.

THE RESOURCES

The Discussion Forum:

http://www.theFastlaneForum.com

Book Website:

http://www.getUnscripted.com
http://www.theMillionaireFastlane.com

Social Media:

Facebook.com/goUnscripted
Facebook.com/TheMillionaireFastlane
Twitter.com/MJDeMarco

TABLE OF CONTENTS

MEANING AND PURPOSE (MP)

FASTLANE ENTREPRENEURSHIP (FE)

KINETIC EXECUTION (KE)

THE FOUR DISCIPLINES (4D)

PART FIVE: A NEW DAWN... NEVER WORK AGAIN

HAS LIFE REGRESSED INTO PAYING BILLS AND LIVING FOR A WEEKEND?

****** PREFACE ******

You weren't born to slave nine-to-five, Monday-through-Friday, pay bills and then die. When life's final moment arrives, what will your spirit sing? Regret and remorse? Or peace and happiness?

Take a moment and forecast your life's trajectory to your deathbed. And be honest. Will you mourn lost time and the things you didn't do? Places you didn't see? Will your life review be all work and zero legacy? If your future forecast looks bleakly uninspiring and not worthy of your family's history books, you have a chance to change it—right here and right now.

Elderly people nearing the end of their lives often wish they could take a time machine back to their youth and chat with their younger selves. Once there, they would tell their younger selves their life wisdom and regretful warnings that only decades of experience could reveal. By changing the past, they hope to change the future, which has become today. Sadly, what usually remains is a life haunted by the ghosts of dead dreams which have long died.

After selling my Internet company in 2007 and retiring young in my thirties as opposed to old in my sixties, I set off to tackle the "younger self" question as it pertained to life and business. If I could go back and speak to twenty-year-old me, someone who consistently struggled, what foresight would I share? What "wisdom" did I need slapped in my face? What did my failures unearth? And more importantly, how could *other people* benefit from this wisdom?

After three years of self-reflection, the rough draft made *Moby Dick* look like a novella. Yes, my many mistakes and their learnings filled page after page. But even more revealing, I ended up with a book unlike anything else available—a book completely contrary to mainstream thought. In other words, happiness wasn't found doing what conventional wisdom embraced—*but doing exactly the opposite.*

While there are countless books on finance, navigating life, and starting businesses, none of them told the *real story*. Instead, these books pushed feel-good fairy tales and Wall Street fantasies—prepackaged templates that baked-in mediocrity and forsaken dreams. Chances are you've read these books and wondered the same as I: *Are there really multimillionaires living the rock-star life because they wage-slaved Monday through Friday while penny-pinching their way to a balanced portfolio of mutual funds?* Or is that CNBC financial guru with the orange face and annoying voice really rich because of what she overtly *preaches* or what she covertly *practices*? And my favorite: Can I really live the dream selling Amway while alienating my friends and family in the process?

During production, publishing "experts" warned that my book would never sell. Those same experts also said I was committing the ultimate author sacrilege: I wasn't pushing readers into a "back-end sales funnel", ya know, so I could sell you a coaching seminar costing as much as a Cadillac.

Well, I didn't give a shit.

I was writing from my heart. Not for fame, fortune, or some egocentric motive that could catapult me into the privileged world of gurus and seminar hustlers.

In 2011 after a year-long editing marathon, I finally self-published *The Millionaire Fastlane* with limited distribution and no fanfare. And by "no fanfare," I mean I didn't hire a PR firm to hack the best-seller list with a phony launch scheme. I didn't benefit from any quid-pro-quo endorsements from "influencers" or "thought leaders." I spent virtually nothing on advertising. The mainstream media ignored me. Bloggers ignored me. The "start-up" clique rolling the hallowed streets of Silicon Valley ignored me. But you know who didn't ignore me? Readers tired of average advice from average books promoting an average life.

As months passed, the book sold in steady chunks. Dozens of sales turned into hundreds, then thousands, then tens of thousands. Soon, sales exceeded $1 million and then $2 million. Language licensing and translations followed: Korean, Japanese, Italian, and more. My Twitter feed blew up with readers who couldn't put the book down…

Might be the best book I've ever read.

Brilliant business wisdom.

Listening to your book is blowing my mind.

And many more.

Despite what many deemed a cheesy "get rich quick" title and an ugly cover, the book hit number one on Amazon in multiple categories and on multiple occasions. While the book never hit *The New York Times* best-seller list, it has sold more than most of them. Mind you, the average self-published book pulls in about $900 in retail sales.

In the end, I shocked readers by "coming clean"—serving up a comprehensive road map for financial success, one based on indisputable mathematics, regardless of time, circumstance, or economics. Readers got the tough-love truth about entrepreneurship, self-made wealth, the hypocrites who preach it, and even happiness.

As *Fastlane* spread worldwide, readers begged: "We want another book!" *Fastlane* was resurrecting dreams and changing lives. While writing two books in the same genre was not my intent, I *knew* another book lived in me, because the greatest con of the century exposed in *Fastlane* was only growing stronger. And in its wake, it was destroying critical thought and personal responsibility and, ultimately, murdering dreams. While *Fastlane* unmasked the myths of wealth, it really hinted at something more: an esoteric reality hidden in the fabric of society; a cultural underbelly threading something insidiously deceptive—*a sociological scheme sentencing your life to an existence of blind obedience, resigned mediocrity, and abandoned dreams.*

You see, if you fail your dreams, it won't be because you lacked effort or enthusiasm; it will be because your life was sold into a Machiavellian system where your lifetime role was already *SCRIPTED* for an uninspiring performance. You've been unwittingly cast to play a rigged carnival game masquerading as life, which few win and many lose…

UNSCRIPTED: Life, Liberty, and the Pursuit of Entrepreneurship is your pen to rewrite a future that's already been written. Don't wait for life's twilight to dream about time machines; it exists in this moment.

Your younger self is here.

Right now.

And it's excited for the opportunity—the opportunity to resurrect your dreams and change the history that awaits.

INTRODUCTION

Un • script • ed (adjective)
"...Not following a prepared script"
(Merriam Webster Dictionary)

Life. Liberty. And the pursuit of entrepreneurship. It's awaking in the morning and pinching yourself black-and-blue—that OMG, this is my life, and it's freaking awesome. You live in your dream house, but there's no mortgage. No alarm clock, no boss, no bills. No claims on the day's time other than what you choose. It's making more money before breakfast than you made for an entire week at your last job. It's a crazy expensive car parked in your garage, a victorious symbol that your dreams no longer sleep in fantasies, but are awake with reality.

Make no mistake, this life exists.

I know, because it's been mine for nearly 20 years.

And in a few short years, it can be yours as well. That's right, you won't need 5 decades of thankless jobs, mind-numbing frugality, and patient investing with our trusted friends on Wall Street.

Unfortunately, you've been *SCRIPTED* to believe that such a life is out of your reach, or only possible for a certain type of person. Someone with a certain college degree, a certain amount of VC funding, or a certain contact list of connected friends from Stanford. I'm here to tell you, that none of it's true.

While I've been an entrepreneur most of my life, I'm no one special. You won't read about me over at Tech Crunch or in some Silicon Valley newsletter. While I've been an Internet entrepreneur since the old "you've got mail" AOL days, I've never been funded by venture capitalists, never had a payroll with more than 5 people on it, and never studied computer science at school. Despite this, I've been able to create profitable businesses that create the type of *UNSCRIPTED* life I've described above. We're talking about five- and six-figure monthly profits with valuations in the millions. Although I've had two successful "exits", don't let that scare you; it's just a welcome (and sometimes unexpected) side effect of the process.

Now, you probably noticed this book is LONG. I mean like, super long. There's a reason for this.

I'm not one of these "book a month" authors who writes about a trendy marketing tactic that becomes ineffectively overused within a year.

I'm not an author who writes 200 pages of filler about one concept when only four paragraphs are enough. In other words, I didn't spend 3 years writing this book to enlarge my income streams—*I wrote it to change your life.* And in order to change your life, a lot needs to be said. Yes, this goes beyond starting a business and making some side cash— it's about reclaiming life-and-liberty through the pursuit of entrepreneurship.

If you don't know, let me break it to you: *Slavery still exists.* Except today's contemporary slavery is called the *SCRIPT*—an implied social contract whereas a gilded cage is exchanged for voluntary indebtedness and lifelong toil, a price sacrificed by a non-redeemable fifty-years of Monday through Friday, an invisible servitude in which freedom is only promised by the arrival of life's fading twilight. *UNSCRIPTED* is your blueprint into an awakening of abundance, freedom, and happiness; a keystone to unleashing a life few dream of.

- In Part 1, I will identify the problem that has haunted you since you've been old enough to have a job. You have sensed it, felt it, and now, you fear you're living it.
- In Part 2, I will expose the greatest con of the century and detail exactly how it has stolen your dreams, and if you allow it, it will steal your life. To defeat a thief, you have to understand the thief.
- In Part 3, I will unveil the high-definition vision of what is possible once your mind is free from the cultural doctrines ruling the game.
- In Part 4, the bulk of this book, I will reveal the definitive blueprint to *UNSCRIPTED* Entrepreneurship, a detailed framework that will show you how to start a business that just doesn't keep the bill-paying treadmill circulating, it breaks it— and then it changes your life forever.
- In Part 5, I will detail the greatest passive income system in existence where work becomes optional. Yup, you will learn how to never work another day in your life, where to find it, and how to get started immediately.

If you haven't read my first book, *The Millionaire Fastlane*, don't worry. *UNSCRIPTED* stands alone. I wouldn't have published it if I didn't think it could change lives. Question is, *will you allow it to change yours?*

First, if you have a great job, a chummy relationship with your boss, and are just thrilled with your 401(k), congratulations. I give you mad props. You're winning a rigged game. You're that dude who wins the giant stuffed elephant at the traveling carnival. How you tossed those plastic rings around the beer bottles, I'll never know. However, in light of your superpowers, this book probably isn't for you.

Second, I don't believe you can change your life by reading another "financial freedom" book that worships IRAs, stock-market investing, and soul-suffocating frugality. Do you really want to read another biblical-sized lecture idolizing the compound-interest fantasy? Hit Amazon and you'll find ten gazillion books on such crap. This book's title is *UNSCRIPTED*, not "be like fucking everyone else on the planet."

Third, *UNSCRIPTED* is for you if your life has become hopeless and dissatisfying. It's for you if you're held hostage by a weekday and the bribery of its paycheck. If you're sick of the suck, and tired of the tiresome: the break-room gossip, the organizational politics, the managerial ass-kissing, and whatever else boils when multiple human beings are tossed in a box and tasked with corporate minutia, I have your escape.

UNSCRIPTED is for you if you crave autonomy and the creative license to pursue work that matters. It's for you if you're a youngster who'd rather live richly young—travel, nice cars, free time—versus waiting to live richly old: wheelchairs, arthritis, and bridge. It's for you if you have X-ray vision and can see what your parents cannot—that life's formulaic template has become dated and flawed.

But most importantly, *UNSCRIPTED* is for you if you've been an aspiring entrepreneur far too long, someone who can't turn a corner, turn a break, or turn a profit. Someone who might already own a business, but like a job, it steals time and just barely keeps the bills paid until next month. If you're someone who would rather hear the discomforting truths from a multimillionaire over another broke blogger peddling in fantasies and narcissistic feel-good platitudes, I have your escape.

Finally, *UNSCRIPTED* is for you if you're willing to risk changing yourself. Everyone wants change, but few want to change their choices. This book will be tough because life is tough. Uncomfortable truths, belief challenges, and ego-shattering revelations lie ahead. Some will assign *UNSCRIPTED's* blunt and insulting tone to themselves and miss the point entirely. If you think I'm a rude, politically incorrect asshole, please, return to your safe space and ask for a refund. Your opinion changes nothing about my reality, but I'm hoping mine changes yours. I didn't write *UNSCRIPTED* to coddle and protect the status quo that's been suffocating your dreams. Disruptive change doesn't come from some mental masturbation that sparks one day and flames-out the next—it comes from the depths of your heart and soul. If you're open to the red pill, I have your escape.

So, if I haven't been clear, let me be now: *UNSCRIPTED is not something you try, it's something you live.* If you're ready for the challenge, get ready for a shit-your-pants revelation that everything you've been taught and told is bullshit. Legendary bullshit. We're talking stuff that would make Ponzi feel out-scammed and out-lied. Don't be mistaken, *UNSCRIPTED* is NOT about paradigm shifts. I hate that phrase. A paradigm shift doesn't keep a sinking Titanic afloat. The problem is the paradigm itself. The problem is that you've allowed the paradigm to set the rules, call the shots, and dictate the decisions. The problem is, you've allowed ordinary thinking preached by ordinary people to produce exactly that—an ordinary life. *The paradigm shift is realizing that the paradigm is shit.*

PART 1

THE DISSONANCE... IS SOMETHING WRONG?

BUYER'S REMORSE.

PART 1: Author's Objective:

CONFESSION

To give clarity to the subtle whispers that have canvassed your life in pursuit of a confession: "something" in your life does not feel right.

1010101010101010101010101010101010101010101010101010101010101010101010101010101010101010101010 10101010

CHAPTER 1

1010101010101010101010101010101010101010101010101010101010101010101010101010101010101010101010 10101010

TALES FROM THE SCRIPT: A MONDAY STORY

How in the hell could a man enjoy being awakened at 6:30am
by an alarm clock, leap out of bed, dress, force-feed, shit, piss,
brush teeth and hair, and fight traffic to get to a place where
essentially you made lots of money for somebody else and
were asked to be grateful for the opportunity to do so?
~ Charles Bukowski, Author

SAME SHIT, DIFFERENT DAY

♬ ♬ How the hell'd we wind up like this? ♬ ♬
♬ ♬ why weren't we able ♬ ♬
♬ ♬ to see the signs that we missed ♬ ♬
♬ ♬ and try an' turn the tables ♬ ♬

Fuck.

It's Monday morning, 5:15 a.m.

For the third time, my iPhone is screaming that Nickelback song I once loved, but now hate. Another snooze and I'll be late.

Yes, it's time to wake up.

After cursing myself for not changing that damn song to something by Metallica, I yank myself out of bed, slightly hungover from the night before. I dread the day—actually no, the week—to come. Needing a jump start, I stumble into the shower, hoping for a clean perspective. No luck. The forthcoming day rivals getting a colonoscopy. As I lynch-tie my neck and arm my suit, regret and resignation ravage my soul.

Something is not right.

Perhaps it's the $800 suit. Perhaps it's the credit card that paid for the suit. Perhaps it's the stinking realization that my weekend highlight was watching two mediocre football teams play in the Las Vegas Bowl. Perhaps it's the morning darkness and the stark reality that my short Cancun vacation is still months away.

Unfortunately, this is no time for a Jesus moment.

With moments to eat, I grab an artificially colored bowl of sugar-coated grain. With one eye on the clock and another on the meal plan pinned to the refrigerator—the one I'm supposed to follow religiously for the next eight weeks—I blame Toucan Sam for my first transgression.

Minutes later, I lumber to the driveway and wriggle into my car, sealing myself in the frigid cabin. My breath shivers a cloud. "Ugh," I groan. Even my new Mercedes C-Class and its fifty-seven payments remaining has lost its luster. I back out of my driveway and head to the freeway.

For the next hour, I sit trapped, fender-to-bumper in my little box, with thousands of other people like me. What I don't know is that my fellow commuters, some appearing more successful than I, are not happy either. Like me, they've failed their diets, failed their purpose, and failed their dreams. As a result, they've bribed their misery with more expensive boxes adorned with softer leather, shinier chrome, and fancier gadgets—boxes branded by prestigious insignia such as Lexus, Audi, and BMW.

Their mission, like mine, is appeasement: to bribe themselves into believing that they are different from the other 20,000 souls enslaved by the same paradigm imprisoning me.

Two miles and twenty minutes less from my life, I wonder, *Is a sheep who drives a Mercedes to the slaughterhouse still a sheep?*

Another hour drains before I arrive at my workplace where I pay seven bucks for the privilege to park near my building, a towering glass skyscraper that ironically, pierces the sky like a crystal dagger. As the orderly mob herds into the atrium, solemn yet caffeinated, I begin my day with a lie.

"Good morning," I greet the receptionist as I rush into a crowded elevator.

As I ascend to the sixtieth floor with my fellow inmates, I have seconds to meditate: "For the love of God, why can't it be Friday?" No time for fantasies, the doors slide open where purgatory awaits—a colossal floor featuring dozens of paneled cubes segregated into cells. Like a prison, each cell is customized to its occupant and decorated with family photos, knick-knacks engraved with biblical proverbs and unheeded platitudes, or an occasional art project from a child, yet to be cursed.

Quickly, I lipstick the pig: "OK, at least I have a job." It's a nice try, but I can't hoodwink my heart; gratitude shouldn't feel like death row at San Quentin.

I arrive at my cube, floor my satchel, and thunk to my seat.

Odd.

Manny, my cubicle neighbor who starts his day an hour earlier than I, has not arrived. In fact, his desk has been wiped clean.

Then I see it.

Sitting atop my inbox and ominously stamped CONFIDENTIAL is a large manila envelope from corporate.

Shit, this can't be good.

The last "confidential" love letter I received doubled my health insurance costs because Congress passed some fucked-up law that no one bothered to read. I dreadfully tear open the envelope.

Apparently Manny was fired this morning for not doing his job. Well, actually his job was being done, just not by him. Supposedly, Manny deviously outsourced his duties to IT workers in China, allowing him to surf Reddit and watch funny cat videos all day. The clandestine operation scammed for months.

According to the corporate dispatch, Manny was "let go" and his work temporarily off-loaded to me. Company courtesy reads like an offer from Don Corleone: My work will expand one hour per day and one Saturday a month for the next three months—for the same exact pay. OMFG. And no, they're not kidding.

Suddenly, I *feel* a scene from *Star Wars* involving a trash compactor. The air thins and my eyes gloss over as a suffocating cloud forms above Cubicle 129A. I clench my teeth so tight that my capped molar breaks in half; at least my dentist will be happy. Rage follows. Then bitterness and betrayal. I'm not sure who I'd like to strangle: my boss, my coworker, or myself.

WTF has my life become?

Is this why I went to college for five years?

This wasn't my plan!

As I pout like a child without my lollipop, temporary insanity gives way to functional logic: Grin and bear it. I'm trapped. I can't quit. I have bills—credit cards, a mortgage, a fancy car, student loans to the tune of 50G—and no savings. And then there's Amanda—my uptown, uptight girlfriend who demanded an engagement ring six months ago. Throw in a biological clock ticking at warp speed and our relationship is like riding the bumper cars at the county fair. "This job is everything," I reason. "Without it, I'm shitting bricks without a diaper."

For the next four hours, I sit in my cube, poking into my computer, suffering though the minutiae of purchase orders, past-due invoices, and IERs—internal escalation reports—the corporate world's version of schoolyard demerits. As my day drags on and I realize four more days of this insufferable hell awaits, and half my Saturday, I stomach a depressing truth: My dreams are dead. *The consolation prize for them has become a car and a weekend.*

For the rest of my day, I slag through work, eyeballing the clock like a dog salivating for a bone. Tick by tick, minute by minute, the clock widens the incongruence gnawing at my brain. With each passing, a part of my soul dies. And yet each moves me closer to the day's freedom.

Ten hours earlier, time ordered me awake, and now, time orders me to leave.

I hop back into my car, joining the others who endured a similar soul-suffocating day. I'm relieved it's over and a lifeboat awaits: It's Monday, and Monday means NFL Football. I crack the day's first smile, one that disappears seven minutes later. There's an accident on the I-90 freeway and I won't be home for another two hours. And I'll miss most of the game.

At home, defeated and demoralized, I drop-kick myself to the couch and crack open a cold Budweiser. It tastes like chilled piss. One sip and it's clear: don't use a butter knife when a chainsaw is needed. Four shots of Jack Daniels later and it's mission accomplished.

The room is spinning.

I'm lost to the television and catch the final ten minutes of the Steelers/Broncos game—a blowout not worth watching.

Channel flipping through alternate realities, I pay homage to the television: I can anonymously watch the lives of those suffering the same doldrums as me or interestingly, those who have been lucky and escaped it.

As I toast the death of my dreams, a *Law and Order* rerun gives way to an infomercial narrated by an overexcited dude with a bad British accent. He's selling a fat-squashing spandex compression girdle. Apparently, ten-years of custard donuts has a ten-second fix, assuming you don't get naked with the fool you fooled. As the hucksters and their "fat-choking bustier" bellow on, I slowly fade and pass out—not into a deep sleep but a shallow oblivion void of rejuvenation.

Hours seem like minutes, abruptly shattered by a morning noise…

♫ ♫ How the hell'd we wind up like this? ♫ ♫
♫ ♫ why weren't we able ♫ ♫
♫ ♫ to see the signs that we missed ♫ ♫
♫ ♫ and try an' turn the tables ♫ ♫

Fuck.

It's time to do this again…

CHAPTER 2

CARELESS WHISPERS: GUILTY SOULS HAVE NO RHYTHM

None of us will ever accomplish anything excellent or commanding except when he listens to this whisper which is heard by him alone.
~ **Thomas Carlyle, Philosopher**

THAT "SOMETHING" IS INDEED SOMETHING…

This story was my story. While I've adapted and embellished it to contemporary life, it's ghostwritten by my experience. Replace the iPhone with an alarm clock, a Mercedes with a Mitsubishi, and a cubicle with a limousine cab and you have it: a familiar story repeated by millions, day after day, year after year. While my story might not resemble your day, many walls can cage a prison. I had many: a warehouse, the front seat of a cargo van, a data-entry cubicle, and—how could I forget—a filthy kitchen in a Chinese restaurant. Your prison could be a nondescript office in a skyscraper, a suburban precinct, or a hospital operating room. Even esteemed professionals, doctors and lawyers, have found that the most comfortably respected prison is still, well, a prison.

However, what's important are not the walls that frame your story but the sense that *something* is wrong. A careless whisper guilts your soul; a heartfelt pleading bemoaning regret and restlessness; a guttural dissonance which you've camouflaged by the mundane and the mediocre. If you're young, perhaps you haven't felt this *something* yet, but you've seen it. For example, take this post at The Fastlane Forum:

> I'm nineteen, finishing my second year of college. As I sit around the table with my family and spin the spaghetti around my fork, it's clear.

> My mother has been working fifteen years at a job she hates. My father has a masters degree in electrical engineering where he's worked at NASA making military hardware. He has been laid off several times and gone unemployed for months at a stretch. He works now, but I noticed something...
> They are not happy. The life is sucked out of them.
> No passion. No dreams. No goals.
> Just the same thing.
> Every.
> Single.
> Day. [1]

Like this student observed, many of these *somethings* are tangible. They can sit in front of you as two parents dead to the world. My *something* was framed on a wall: two business degrees that cost me five years and $40,000—yeah, the ones that got me that great ten-dollar-an-hour job slinging pipe in the Chicago slums. Your tangible *something* could be your garage, the one with the twenty-three horsepower riding mower, surely jeering the neighbors envious, and yet, you're still unfulfilled and unhappy. Or worse, it's an air mattress in your parents' basement, the one you bought for camping that's become a temporary bed, at least until you can "figure things out" before your thirty-third birthday.

The other *somethings* are intangible and resonate as white noise—a nagging chorus of dissonant emotions continually whispering life's swill.

If you're younger, one of these whispers could be shame pacified by faux fame: you've earned rock-star status on Xbox Live, but in the real world, you haven't earned jack.

Another whisper could be the sting of insignificance: if you were suddenly kidnapped and beamed to planet Romulus, no one outside your family would give a shit other than your roommate, who really isn't missing you—he just misses your half of the rent payment.

Other whispers are weekly appointments with anguish: the arrival of Sunday night and its awaiting Monday feels like hide-and-seek with the grim reaper. Or perhaps the whisper is contempt salted with guilt: you hate your job, your boss, and your company, but damn, that paycheck is instant amnesia.

If you're older, the whispers likely stew as frustration: You did everything right in life as recommended and directed by authority, and yet, no matter how much you work, save, and scrimp, getting ahead is impossible. Some urgent expense always looms—the dog needs shots, the car needs tires, or the kids need cash for a school project.

Other whispers echo as disbelief and skepticism: the bank paid seven cents in interest last year and, at the rate your 401(k) is growing, you'll retire by the twenty-fourth century.

And then there's perhaps the most haunting whisper: regret. You were going to do something with your life. Be rich. Famous. A CEO. Independently successful. A parent who spends time with their kids beyond throwing a pizza on the dinner table and calling it a night. Yup, you were going to be accomplished, proud, and happy. But now it's all a dead dream sitting atop a stack of bills, atop a desk, atop a mediocre life.

Every something tormenting your daily humdrum hints of a great deception. Clues to a ruse. An imminent awareness that only needs its confession: *You're living, but you aren't alive.*

Your heart beats, but there is no pulse.

Your mind is poisoned, but the toxicology is clean.

Your soul has been stolen, but there are no thieves.

Suspicion swells while incongruity gnaws.

Yes, this wasn't the life you signed up for.

This wasn't your plan.

Something is wrong.

Your soul will resonate its desires or discontent when faced with quiet or minimal distraction; for example sleeping, showering, or during a massage.

How are you responding to your soul's voice? Is it denied? Ignored? Muzzled with the intense demand of meaningless work? Distracted by a television? Honored?

CHAPTER 3

THE MODERN DAY MATRIX: THE SCRIPT

When a well-packaged web of lies has been sold gradually to the masses over generations, the truth will seem utterly preposterous and its speaker a raving lunatic.
~ **Dresden James, Author**

WHAT IF I TOLD YOU...

Something is indeed something. For most people, it's dismissed as life's background noise. Others hear the whispers and bury it with weekend merriment. For the rest of us who aren't easily manipulated, we question it. We seek its source, challenge its presence, and ask, "What the hell is going on?"

My first hint that something was wrong with the world happened as a struggling young entrepreneur in Chicago. At the time, I had a menial job as a limousine driver, which paid my bills and funded my crazy business ideas. Because the job required a special license granted by the city, I had to drive downtown to take a test for its qualification. I arrived early with time to blow, so I grabbed a coffee and seated myself at a cafe window. As I gazed out into the commuter swarms navigating the Monday morning rush, I noticed something: Everyone moved with an eerie robotic efficiency, indifferent and obtuse. The variety of faces, no matter the age, race, or gender, were uniformly vacant and resigned, each etched with a stone-faced glower as if they've walked the walk a thousand times.

As the organized freneticism mesmerized me, the street rush slowly faded into an obscure moving fog. Unique individuals with goals, dreams, and aspirations;

sons, daughters, wives, husbands, all suddenly blurred into a single collective as if one organism compelled by instinct. Did any part of the sum question why they were on a frozen street at 6:30 a.m.? And why would they repeat the same insanity for the next four days? Was anyone pursuing their dream, or were they pursuing what culture programmed them to pursue?

The sudden realization struck me—and frightened me: it was not free will at work, but conditioned instinct, like a bee buzzing to the hive or an ant marching to an anthill. Moreover, dress or implied social hierarchy played no relevance: three-piece suits, jeans, work overalls—the horde behaved as if controlled by a single puppet master.

As I reflected on the scene, I knew I could never—and would never—be normal as prescribed by cultural routine. That day sealed my fate as an entrepreneur—either one who'd eventually succeed or one who would fail and die trying. Lucky for me (and you), entrepreneurship was the snips that clipped the puppet master's strings.

In the 1999 hit movie, *The Matrix*, Neo is given a choice: swallow the blue pill and continue living a mediocre ignorance, or swallow the red pill and jolt awake to a free but imperfect truth. Within the film's dark dystopia, *The Matrix* represents the default operating system for the human species, a virtual reality enslaving us to a parasitic machine race. While comatose and imprisoned, the machines feed our minds with a simulation designed to keep us oblivious, distracted, and obedient to the system draining our humanity.

Well…

What if I told you that our world suffers from the same deception—a deception orchestrated not by artificial intelligence but by *conventional intelligence*? A deception of unchallenged and outdated wisdom, a dream-killing dogma tyrannized by stale traditions, narrow beliefs, and cultural conformity? A deception that represents the greatest con of the civilized world—a ruse that feigns freedom and comfort, when in truth, its sole purpose is economic slavery and human homogenization, a servitude system where you become an instrument, not of inspiration or aspiration but of perspiration and desperation.

What if I told you that this deception has infiltrated your mind and embedded itself as your default operating system, an autonomous program shadowing your entire life, from cradle to grave, from career to companionship, a presumptuous, yet unwritten rulebook by which all decisions are weighed, regardless of consequence to heart or soul?

What if I told you that this operating system has granted you an inauthentic life of someone else's design? A life you did not choose. A life meticulously preplanned and preordained to follow a predictable blueprint of mediocrity. A life where dreams are forsaken for a television and a paycheck. A life consecrated by an obsolete template, decreed by authority, sanctified by education, certified by media, and obfuscated by government. A life serving to die versus living to serve.

What if I told you you've become an unwitting participant in an obligatory game, one victim in a genocide of dreams, a pawn institutionally directed by the rank doctrine that every human must go to college, get a job, get married, have kids, use credit cards, finance a car, mortgage a house, stare at the latest smartphone (further entrenching your obedience), save and cheapskate your paycheck while entrusting it to Wall Street, all while you continue feeding the bloodthirsty parasites drunk on your life force?

What if I told you that all your whispers, the despondence, the uneasiness, is your soul knocking on the door of consciousness, pleading to be heard?

Get red-pilled my fellow human being…

You aren't living by free will; you're living by a SCRIPT.

> ? ***Sunday evening is the litmus test for a SCRIPTED existence—how do you feel about the impending Monday? Excited? Or dour and cheerless?***

PART 2

THE SCRIPT... ENGINEERING YOUR INVOLUNTARY SLAVERY

SEEMS LEGIT.

PART 2: Author's Objective:

AWARENESS

To expose the cultural expectations and societal mores that have framed your current existence, and done so without your knowledge or consent. To defeat the enemy, you have to know the enemy.

CHAPTER 4

THE INAUTHENTIC LIFE: TRAPPED BY "OTHER PEOPLE'S" THINKING

> The problem is not people being educated. The problem is that they are educated just enough to believe what they've been taught, but not educated enough to question what they've been taught.
> ~ **Author Unknown**

THE PARADIGM IS SHIT...

The *SCRIPT*. It's not an instruction booklet given at grade school or map stapled to your college degree. It's not seen or touched, but it is there. Like the air you breathe, it's invisibly omnipresent.

My downtown trip featuring a horde of caffeinated zombies highlights the typical plight of a first-world human, regardless of country or culture: Forced awake, drag yourself out of bed; drive, train, or walk to a tolerated job; and exist on autopilot—eight hours a day, five days a week, for the next fifty years. Like a scuffed record repeating its track, today plays like yesterday, which will play exactly like tomorrow. As a result, life's paycheck becomes a weekend where the workweek's postponements are reclaimed, a layaway earmarked for fun or relaxation, a respite to recharge your soul from the strain of the transaction.

What few know is, we've been programmed for this existence, a willful modern-day slavery. You see, like an operating system on a computer, the *SCRIPT* runs the show. Give it life's helm and accept my sympathies. It will command how you think, work, play, vote, save, invest, retire—and how you die.

In a 2005 commencement speech at Stanford University, Steve Jobs said, "Don't be trapped by dogma—which is living with the results of other people's thinking." Steve Jobs was referring to the *SCRIPT*: an inescapable gospel of cultural presumptions woven by "other people's thinking"; a browbeaten pantheon of provincial beliefs and sanctified social mores.

So ask yourself, is this *your* thinking? Or *other* people's thinking?

Go to college and earn a degree, regardless of cost, demand, or economics. Finance your commodified education with an indiscriminate appetite for student loans, notwithstanding the five "preapproved" credit cards you've already accepted. Graduate with empty credentials and a useless degree making you no different from millions with the same degree. Leave the cloistered world of university saddled in debt—either yourself, your parents, or both. Get a job so you can officially join the privileged ranks of a time prostitute—trading huge blocks of your life's time bank, five days of seven, in exchange for little pieces of paper called money. Slave all day, usually repeating monotonous tasks, so you can pay for the education you just finished, the clothes you just dressed, the car you just drove, and the apartment you just left. Use credit cards to live conveniently: Starbucks for breakfast, Chipotle for lunch, and Chick-fil-A for dinner. Party hard at the club. Buy rounds of drinks, trying to impress strangers and women out of your league. Buy overpriced bottles of vodka, hit the VIP room, and try impressing them more. Rack up debt unrestrained; after all, it's celebration time—you graduated!

Grow older.

Climb the corporate ladder. Wake up, hit snooze, and wake up again. Get into a routine: work, traffic, *Seinfeld* reruns, sleep. Repeat four times this week. Work overtime and show your corporate overlords that you're willing to do whatever it takes. Schmooze your boss, the one with the bad suit and the bad breath. Hate your job, tolerate your coworkers, but love your paycheck. Get a pay raise and a promotion. Buy a cool car, a cool condo, and some cool clothes. Live a fabulous weekend enriched by spirited drinking and escapism entertainment. Work hard, play harder. Spend unrestrained—after all, YOLO!

Grow older.

Follow fashion: Prada, Louis Vuitton, Chanel. Follow pop culture: LeBron, Miley, TMZ. Follow popular television drama: *Game of Thrones, Breaking Bad, The Walking Dead*. Follow the lives of fake people on fake television shows portrayed as reality. Worship celebrities and athletes. Adopt celebrity opinions and their politics because they're famous. Pay your taxes. Pay your bills: your mortgage, your car payment, your cable bill, your homeowners' association fees. Continue stacking debt—after all, you work hard and deserve it.

Grow older.

Vacation two weeks every year, but only when the overlords permit. Charge the latest and greatest stuff: Dr. Dre owns noise-canceling headphones; P. Diddy owns this; Lady Gaga owns that. Spend to feel accomplished. Spend to feel good, at least until Monday arrives or the bill that Monday must pay. Spend to fill a void you can't explain. Feel cornered: by a job, a mortgage, a car, a credit card, and by an existence. Feel freedom drip away while medicating the truth with more distraction: more consumer debt and more fictional escapes.

Grow older.

Hear your biological clock ticking. Worry you're still single. Date a friend. Date a coworker. Start online dating: Tinder, Match, eHarmony. Meet your mate. Marry your mate. Spend a fortune on a six-hour wedding, one that takes six years to pay off.

Continue working. Continue spending. Continue distraction. Continue dreading your Sunday night. Dread Monday more. Dream about quitting. Dream about traveling the world. Dream about waking up when you want to wake up. Dream about greatness, something more meaningful than the meaningless of paying bills and repeating. Dream about dreams long dead.

Grow older.

Have kids. Raise your kids. Get responsible. Change your debt perception. Start retirement planning. Follow the advice of obnoxious radio personalities, like the one with the orange tan and the popped collar. Take financial advice brokered by broke brokers. Learn how to get rich from people who aren't rich. Save 10 percent of your paycheck, max your 401(k), contribute to an IRA and an indexed mutual fund. Invest everything saved into the stock market, hope for 10 percent, and pray to avoid a crash.

Save for your child's college education. Work harder and longer. Get out of debt. Make a budget. Follow a budget. Clip coupons. Cancel the movie channels. Cancel the cable subscription. Stop drinking Starbucks. Stop eating Chipotle. Bag a lunch. Stop going to the movies, stop shopping name brand, and stop shopping period. Stop dreaming about sports cars because every dime must be coveted and handed to Wall Street. Settle for less, stop enjoying, stop living, and start dying.

Grow older.

Trust you'll be able to retire by sixty-five. Trust you'll be alive by sixty-five. Trust Wall Street. Trust compound interest, hoping it gives you 10 percent a year despite zero interest rates for the last decade. Trust the economy always has a job for you. Trust your house continually appreciates. Trust the mainstream media while believing their objectivity. Trust the drug companies. Trust the food you're eating is healthy. Trust the USDA food pyramid, the FDA, and its board of pharmaceutical executives. Trust your obese doctor. Trust your government representatives.

Wither older.

Insist that your kids get good grades so they can get into a good college and, like you, get a good job so they can repeat the same death march you can't escape. Teach your kids the difference between "pipe dreams" and "reality."

Continue working. Continue aging in indifference. Repeat, set to autopilot, and patiently wait while chained to the worst partners ever partnered: hope and time. Hope the stock market grew your portfolio. Hope inflation hasn't ravaged your portfolio. Hope compound interest yields the projected returns promised by the fiscal sycophants. Hope your money hasn't been hyperinflated away by blank-check politicians. Hope Social Security still exists. Hope there's enough money left to win the free time you've never had and always dreamed of.

Wither older.

Feel regret. Remorse. Your bucket list is full and your time bank is near empty. Your portfolio shares a similar state of emptiness. Hit sixty-five. Come to the unpleasant truth that hope and time haven't yielded the promised 10 percent per year. Delay retirement. Delay the wife's retirement. Delay for more work, more saving, and more frugality.

Unfortunately, time doesn't give a shit. Time doesn't care that you were promised a carefree retirement because you trusted six decades to an index fund. Time doesn't care that you're years away from a dream cruise. Time doesn't care that you worked for sixty years, spent a fortune bolstering the economy, and paid a king's ransom in taxes. Time doesn't care what was promised and not delivered.

Because time says it's time to die…

Before retirement, before the bucket list, before resolving the regret…

Welcome to the *SCRIPT*…

Manufactured by conventional wisdom…

Distributed by institutionalized indoctrination…

And swallowed with blind faith…

Wake up…the product being manufactured is you.

> ***Herds are organized for economic purposes: slaughter, shearing, milking. Herd with the crowd and you will get predictable results designed for the crowd.***

HOW I ESCAPED MANUFACTURED MEDIOCRITY

I've been fortunate.

Unlike most youngsters, my *SCRIPTED* programming was stalled by a viral seed of doubt. But it didn't start that way. As expected, environment and circumstance kick-started the process. I was raised in a dysfunctional lower-middle-class family, a fertile garden for *SCRIPTED* roots. By my early teens, the bedrock had been laid: get good grades, get into a good college, graduate, and get a good job.

My dreams of an extraordinary life suffered an early death with the death of my parents' marriage. Dad bailed for the drinking and swinging single life and left my high-school-educated mom with three expensive tyrants. That's when I learned about "real life": no new clothes, no first-run movies, and no Sizzler. Settling for less was life. And that's when I gave up thinking that life would be anything but ordinary. Back then, a popular television program, *Lifestyles of the Rich and Famous*, reinforced a *SCRIPTED* theme: Fantastic dreams were for the rich and famous—celebrities, pro athletes, and rock stars. I couldn't sing, my gut swallowed my waist, and I certainly wasn't Sinatra's second coming. Circumstances cultivated the seed, and *SCRIPT* indoctrination was underway.

And then something happened. And it changed everything.

I don't remember my age, but I was old enough to ogle sports cars and sixteen-year-old girls. While rolling over to the ice cream parlor, hoping to further inflate the tire around my stomach, I spotted a Lamborghini Countach parked outside—my dream car. I froze in a drooling, wide-eyed trance. My appetite, forgotten. My shyness, spurned. Overcome with adrenaline, I kissed my comfort zone good-bye and asked the young owner what he did for work.

His response?

He said he was an entrepreneur—specifically, an inventor.

And at that moment, while accosted by this gorgeous piece of machinery, something clicked: *I became aware that dreams were not just for athletes, rocks stars, and Hollywood actors but also for entrepreneurs. And those dreams could happen young.*

Wham.

The *SCRIPT*'s viral threat was born. The incident planted a rogue code and seeded my entrepreneurial DNA, a path that grew into more than a random career choice—it became an awareness and a defense to the biggest scams of the century.

In the years that followed, I nurtured this seed while the *SCRIPT* failed its assimilation.

As a teenager, I practiced neighborhood entrepreneurship, albeit failingly (more on that later). In high school and college, I studied entrepreneurship extensively on my own—my school offered no such curriculum. Story after story, my research confirmed the truth: Successful entrepreneurs were among the few who lived extraordinarily, both in material and spiritual abundance. Mind you, back then business start-ups weren't glorified by weekly reports of billion-dollar liquidation events from upstart garage projects and ramen noodle diets.

By the time I graduated college, having suffered through a mélange of "how to be a good employee," I was further "all-in" on entrepreneurship, knowing I could never lynch a tie five times a week. Life, liberty, and the pursuit of entrepreneurship would not be my job. *It would be my life*. However, looking back, I wasn't prepared for what awaited: a world that sung the same song from every radio where lowering the volume is as difficult as bending steel with your bare hands. Continue onward and let the truth be your mute.

> **?** ***What presumptive rules, social mores, and cultural norms have you followed without question? And have those constructs given you the life you dreamed?***

CHAPTER 5

CONVENTIONAL WISDOM: THE ROAD TO A CONVENTIONAL LIFE

Is there any point in public debate in a society where hardly anyone has been taught HOW to think, while millions have been taught WHAT to think?
~ Peter Hitchens, Journalist and Author

CONVENTIONAL = ORDINARY = MEDIOCRITY

The *SCRIPT*'s most powerful weapon is its implied social contract—a social contract inked by conventional wisdom dispensed by conventional people living conventional lives. And anytime you comply with the social mandates, you endorse the contract.

However, the jig doesn't end there. Dig deeper and the *SCRIPT* packs a more insidious truth: an institutional army of parasites, profiteers, and conspirators who feed off *SCRIPTED* hosts. Deep Throat had it right—follow the money. The official definition? *The SCRIPT is conventional wisdom directing a conventional life, dispensed by either a compromised party of convention or a profiteering party of prejudice.*

Now, when I say conventional wisdom, I'm not referencing uncommon sense, like gambling your entire paycheck at the roulette table or driving after nine margaritas. Nope, I'm talking about the unchallenged social standards and assumptive dogma driving the human experience within any first-world culture. Take for example the following statements, all representing either prescriptive or assumptive *SCRIPTED* doctrine:

- To succeed in life, you need a college degree.
- A college graduate earns X more dollars than someone who doesn't.
- Comfort and security start with a good job at a good company.

- Starting a business is risky.
- To get rich, you should pinch pennies and eliminate all unnecessary expenditures.
- To grow wealth, you should faithfully invest your saved pennies into the stock market, preferably in a low-cost indexed mutual fund.
- To retire rich, be patient through the decades and let "compound interest" work its magic.
- Wealth is measured by your bank account and the material possessions it buys: the house where you live, the car you drive, the clothes you wear.
- Your home is a great investment.
- Monday through Friday is for work; Saturday and Sunday are for play.
- Retirement happens at sixty-five or, if you're a hard worker and a good investor, fifty-five.
- The trusted instruments of wealth accumulation are IRAs, 401ks, and a well-diversified portfolio, namely indexed mutual funds.
- If you want to make more money, go back to school and get an advanced degree.
- Money doesn't buy happiness.
- Good things come to those who wait.
- Follow your passion, do what you love, and you'll never work another day in your life.
- Time is money.

Each of these statements (or any derivative phrasing) is what I call *SCRIPT*Speak. On any given day, at any given website, you're perpetually bludgeoned over the head with this bunk like no one has heard it before.

If this advice has you stuck in a shithole, take heart. You aren't to blame as much as you think. The fact is, your current situation might not have been your plan, but it's the *SCRIPT*'s plan. Your college thanks you. Your bank thanks you. Your government thanks you. Your retail stores, restaurants, and corporations thank you. Hollywood thanks you. Wall Street's minions—their brokers, their bankers, and their CNBC personalities—thank you. And moving forward unchanged, they will thank you until you've worked your last hour and invested your last dime.

You see, like Steve Jobs, who wasn't trapped by the dogma of conventional wisdom, the rich get richer because the rich aren't bound by the *SCRIPT—they're the ones profiting from it.*

The proliferation of *SCRIPT*Speak is not random. It is either autonomically regurgitated by a *compromised party* or meticulously orchestrated by a *prejudiced party.* No matter who's the parrot, you should listen to neither.

THE COMPROMISED PARTY OF CONVENTION (THE CROWD)

A *compromised party* is someone who holds the *SCRIPT* as their life's operating system. Compromised parties can be friends, family, coworkers, and authority figures: teachers, coaches, and guidance counselors. As such, *SCRIPT* propagation is parroted; the compromised party was taught X, Y, and Z as a youngster, and now, as an adult, they will convey the same beliefs because it's the only reality they know. The nine-to-five, paycheck-to-paycheck, live-for-a-weekend is their life, and it shall become yours.

As a result, you're another cow to be milked, no better than a soldier ant given his marching orders by the queen. When it comes to *SCRIPT*Speak from the *SCRIPTED*, ask yourself this: *If I accept average advice from average people living average lives, can I expect to be anything but average?*

THE PROFITEERING PARTY OF PREJUDICE (THE MONEY)

Like a compromised party, a *prejudiced party* also disseminates *SCRIPTED* doctrine. However, whereas a compromised party parrots platitudes simply because they think it's best for you, a prejudiced party profits from *SCRIPT*Speak.

For example, a typical prejudiced party writes articles about how a *SCRIPTED* existence will yield future fortunes. As such, they profit from the sale of books, financial products, seminars, and various other fee-based products or services.

For example, in December of 2015, a MarketWatch.com article led with the headline, "How time can turn $3,000 into $50 million."[2] In this perfect example of *SCRIPTED* horseshit, the author begins his fantasy with the statement, "I can't say I've done it, but I'm going to show you how you could."

Awesome. And let me show you how to jump out of an airplane without a parachute. Oh yeah, I haven't done it, but don't worry, you'll be in front of me to soften the blow when your ignorant butt splatters on the concrete.

But wait, this shit gets better.

The author goes on to say that the illustrious fifty-million-dollar fantasyland happens with regular, 12 percent market returns. Obviously in his *SCRIPTED* Neverland, Madoff is legit and so are his returns. In any event, the author is involved in multiple ventures that profit from *SCRIPTED* doctrine, namely a "wealth management" and an "investment advisory" firm. Prejudiced party, ya think? Lock, stock, and barrel.

"NO! I AM THE BOSS OF ME!"

Daddy: *I love your Lego castles. Are you going to be a king when you grow up?*

Billy: *Nah, I wanna live in a trailer next to the steel mill. When I grow up, I'm gonna be scrubbing the castle's toilets.*

First, let me say I have nothing against dirty work.I wrote, "scrubbing toilets" because it's a chapter from my life. Yes, I had a job cleaning shit stains, which incidentally was a job I held *after* college. If only I could have scrubbed those shitters with my two business degrees...

Anyway, how would you react if your child aspired to scrub toilets? Perplexed? Concerned? Fib and correct him: "You can be anything you set your mind to"?

The truth is, our children don't dream about mediocrity and uninspired living.

Had my son answered like this, I'd ask him why he felt that way. Would living in a trailer and scrubbing toilets make him happy? If so, it's the end of the story. But I doubt any child in recorded history has ever answered the "when you grow up" question with a tale of trailer-park living and shit-scrubbing labor.

When you were a kid and an adult scolded you to do stuff you didn't like, you'd assert, "No! I am the boss of me!"

You see, before the *SCRIPT* clawed into you, you were once free. Pure and unmolested. You'd wake up happy and excited about the day. As a kid, you had fantastic dreams and unstoppable visions powering an optimistic future. You wanted to be the next DiCaprio, the next Hemingway, the next Jordan, the next Elvis, the next Picasso, the next great something—if not worldly, then locally, as a gourmet chef, a brave firefighter, or a respected policeman. Whatever your dreams, you acted on them on the playground, in books, or by Halloween costume. Dreams were alive and teeming with probability.

And then *something* happened.

You grew up.

Suddenly you were no longer the boss of you. You were issued into an educational system that happened, not surprisingly, Monday through Friday—the perfect, practiced assimilation to what was foreshadowed. And suddenly the reality of your friends, family, and peers became yours.

With no explanation and no event to mark the shift, everyone encouraging your dreams suddenly changed their stories. Be realistic. Grow up. That's impossible. Stop daydreaming about this and that. Reality became a picture painted by the brush strokes from everyone around you who lived in unremarkable mediocrity.

What happened?

The *SCRIPT*—modern civilization's impermeable intranet where dreams are killed and life routinizes into the mundane and trivial—got into your head. And the rest becomes history: the worthless degree, the debt stockpile, the contemptible job, the weekend bribe, the elderly retirement...

? ***WHO or WHAT has become "the boss of you?" A pile of student loan debt? A job, a car payment, or a mortgage? Unwritten expectations from family or peers?***

CHAPTER 6

THE SCRIPTED OPERATING SYSTEM: THE WEB OF SERVITUDE

The ideal tyranny is that which is ignorantly self-administered by its victims. The most perfect slaves are, therefore, those which blissfully and unawaredly enslave themselves.
~ **Dresden James, Author**

THE FRAMEWORK FOR OBEDIENCE

A spider weaves a web for one purpose: to ensnare prey for consumption later. Like a spider, the *SCRIPT* also weaves a web, an operating system that's programs your mind to accept a voluntary slavery destined for obedience and economic servitude.

The *SCRIPTED* operating system (OS) codes itself with a distro. (In computing, a "distro" is a software collection which distributes an operating system to end users.) The *SCRIPT*'s distro is responsible for dissemination, then assimilation. And like all software programmed for a purpose, the *SCRIPTED* OS also has its purpose: to manufacture you into a *M.O.D.E.L. Citizen* tamed to its precepts.

Your defense is knowledge.

Life, liberty, and the pursuit of entrepreneurship is the offense.

Here is the *SCRIPTED* OS decoded:

THE SEEDERS:

Like a torrent hosted within a computer system, seeders write and enforce *SCRIPTED* doctrine. As described earlier, seeders are compromised or prejudiced parties.

THE HYPERREALITIES:

The *SCRIPT*'s illusions, the hyperrealities reinforce your obedience and captivity through deception, distortion, or diversion.

TEMPORAL PROSTITUTION:
Seeders and their hyperrealities sanctify a criminal trade for your most precious asset: your time.

THE LIFE PATHS:
The illusion of free choice and deciding your slave owner: Door *A*, the Sidewalk; or Door *B*, The Slowlane. Both lead to the slaughterhouse. Neither makes you the boss of you.

DISTRACTION:
If you're distracted, the *SCRIPTED* OS stays hidden. *M.O.D.E.L. Citizenship* becomes a foregone conclusion.

M.O.D.E.L. CITIZENSHIP:
You unwillingly become a *SCRIPTED* servant who is (M)ediocre, (O)bedient, (D)ependent, (E)ntertained, and (L)ifeless and who then becomes a seeder, a compromised party propagating the *SCRIPTED* OS.

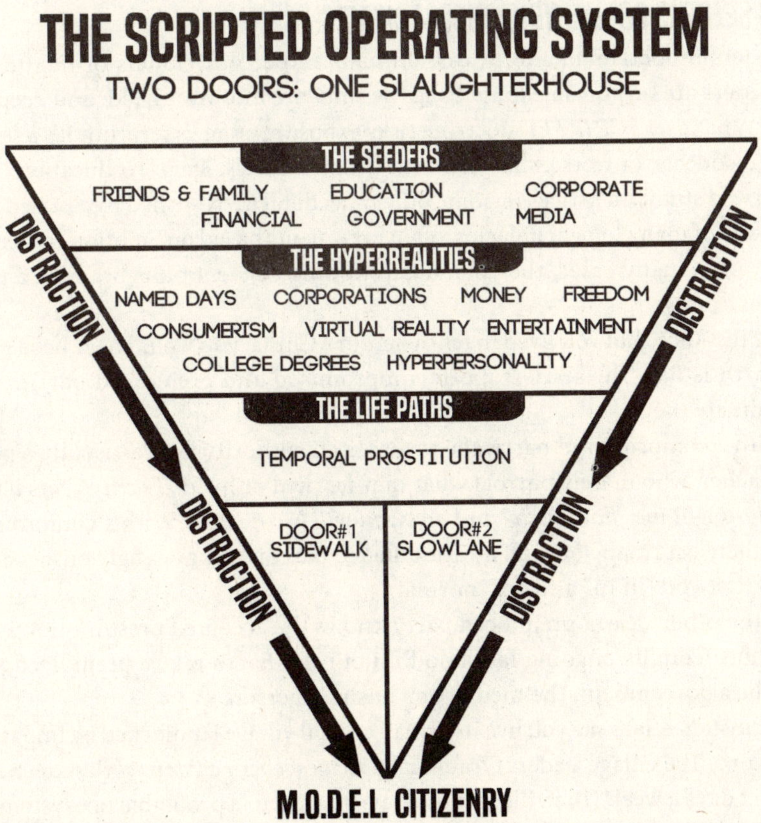

CHAPTER 7

THE SEEDERS: OUR LIFE SUCKS, YOURS SHOULD TOO

We are not taught to be thinkers, but reflectors of our culture. Let's teach our children to be thinkers.
~ Jacque Fresco, Futurist

THE 6 SEEDERS CODING YOUR INDOCTRINATION

Seeders indoctrinate and/or disseminate. Either individuals or institutions, seeders are responsible for getting the software into your head, and keeping it there. Whenever *SCRIPTED* doctrine risks exposure or faces scrutiny, it's a seeder's job to reeducate, or worse, shut down the debate entirely. Such "reeducation" could be a flawed study, an article, or some other anecdotal item pushed by a biased party using one of many logical fallacies, often arguments based on emotion rather than fact. And in many cases, the person questioning convention is branded a quack or an extremist.

For instance, had you lived in tenth-century China, you would have been taught the Earth is flat. The seeders, both compromised and prejudiced parties, then disseminate the lie.

With a compromised party, the seeder is an authority figure, usually a parent or a teacher, who merely parrots what they learned or lived. *Twenty years ago my teacher taught me "flat Earth" and now you will learn it too.* With a compromised party, there isn't malicious intent. The afflicted party is unknowingly miseducating you so that you "fit in" and are "normal."

In the other case, a prejudiced party knows the accepted presumption is a lie yet profits from its ongoing falsehood. In our flat-Earth tale, a prejudiced party could be a government, the media, or a businessperson.

For instance, let's say you live in a small coastal village landlocked by impassable mountains. The village leaders tyrannically suggest every citizen work sixteen-hour days, six days a week. The village plutocrats, thanks to a profitable tax system, live lavishly and work sparingly. They also know the truth—the Earth is not flat—but through benevolent, state-sponsored education, they teach the lie: "The Earth is flat, and sailing away is 'dangerous and risky.'"

But trouble brews. Outside town lives a young boatman who dishonors the village chieftains and claims the Earth is round. Behind his outlandish claim is another claim: he says he's successfully sailed the ocean and found a better way of life. Upon hearing such blasphemy and knowing its threat to the village's economic prosperity, the leaders (who control the media) publish news stories smearing the boatman as a crazy lunatic. Others label his reports as "fake news". As such, the villagers dismiss the boatman and remain pliant to the cultural system their leaders have ordained, not knowing a better life is just a short easterly sale.

Our world suffers a similar scenario, thanks to six seeders who have made the *SCRIPTED* OS as ubiquitous as Instagram narcissism.

Those seeders are:

THE SEEDERS

FRIENDS & FAMILY — EDUCATION — CORPORATE
FINANCIAL — GOVERNMENT — MEDIA

#1) FRIENDS AND FAMILY: OUR LIFE SUCKS, SO YOURS SHOULD TOO.

I studied finance at college. Not because I enjoyed math, but because my family instructed, "The money is in finance." My uncle was a successful Fortune 500 financial executive so instead of studying entrepreneurship, I was steered into depreciation formulas, standard deviations, and portfolio theory. After four expensive years, I earned a finance degree, despite being a creative, left-handed, crayon-the-wall deviant who loved math as much as a prostate exam.

After earning the accolade and hating every class, I had a gut check: "Shit, I can't do this for the rest of my life, even as a 'fallback' for entrepreneurial failure." So I stayed and got another degree, one better suited for entrepreneurship: marketing.

In every case, the *SCRIPT*'s epidemiology starts with family.

As a child, you're as defenseless to imprinting as a toddler is to his stinky diapers. Its first upload comes from your parents because they too are living by the same *SCRIPT*. They want what *they think* is best for you, and unfortunately, what's best in their eyes is "normal" and "safe." Take for example these two accounts posted at The Fastlane Entrepreneur Forum:

> **(1)** When I was a youngster, I saw a Porsche and my dad had a new Toyota Camry. I asked my dad, "Why does the guy driving the Porsche have a better car than us?" My father told me it's because he was lucky. So I thought, "OK, I hope I grow up lucky."[3]

(2) I was in Subway for lunch when a Lamborghini rolled by, eliciting a lot of head turns and chatter. At the next table, I overheard a son ask his dad how to get a Lamborghini. The conversation went like this: "Well son, a Lamborghini is a lot of money! If you want to get one, you'll have to work hard in school, get into a good college, and get a good job at some place like Microsoft. By the time you're my age you would be able to afford one. And that, my son, is how successful people do it." [4]

While these two examples glorify flashy cars as a success standard, they represent more: To a child, these cars personify dreams, much like when I was young. Unfortunately, after your parents squash your childhood dreams—you'll never own a Lamborghini unless you're lucky—you're hit with life's *SCRIPTED* bullshit: get good grades so you can get into a good college so you can get a good job, work hard, finance a house and a car, and live exactly like we do.

But it doesn't stop at family.

Friends and colleagues are also potent seeders. Yes, the ones who are broke and miserable. The ones voicing such concerns as "that's a bad idea" or "that's not realistic." For these naysayers, their accomplishments are few while their excuses are plenty; the American Dream is dead and something else blows the blame: the economy, the boss, the evil globalists, the evil Republicans, the evil Democrats, or the sun shining in late June.

Unless you have carefully cultivated your friends and coworkers, chances are they don't want you succeeding beyond their own success. Ever tell your peers you got a new job? Notice the likes and congratulations. But tell them you quit your job to go after your dream? #Stinkface. Unfurl the umbrella for the hellstorm about to rain. You'll be bludgeoned with dire warnings and caveats.

Translation?

SCRIPT divergence is unacceptable. You must be like us. You must stay within the lines of the nine-to-five model. Speak of anything outside the formula and watch the spaghetti fly. Watch friends drop. Watch loved ones doubt you, or worse, disown you.

Unfortunately, in Asian and Indian cultures the *SCRIPT* has a choking grip and a higher price for deviation. In multiple instances, young immigrant students have vented frustration on my forum because they hate the path they've been forced to take, but their parents insist because of cultural expectations.

Parent says, "Be a doctor!" Child says, "No, that doesn't make me happy!" Take for example this forum comment:

Long story short, I dropped out of school to start a business. Now I am looking for a job just to pay the bills while I chip away at my mission. However, my parents don't believe in my ideas. I don't have a problem

> with all the scrutiny and the yelling, but the tables have turned. My parents are more emotionally involved. My mom is depressed and says I need to be realistic; otherwise, I am going to end up a loser at a dead end. My father says, "Look what you're doing to your mom; she is lost because you did not finish your degree and get a job with a big company." Now I am this horrible deadbeat son. Like many immigrant families, it's get a degree and a nine-to-five with a huge corporation or be a loser. [5]

Sad that *SCRIPTED* noncompliance means being labeled a loser. Or worse, family banishment. Parents are not encouraging dreams. Instead, we're smothering our kids with sacrosanct traditions and antiquated templates for living. The truth is, some parents would rather enjoy the prestige of having their kid be a miserable doctor ready to jump off a cliff over a happy human being.

> ***If the people in your family or peer group are NOT happy and living a life you would like to lead, their life advice should be considered cautiously.***

#2) EDUCATION: GET IN LINE, RAISE YOUR HAND, FOLLOW INSTRUCTIONS

If friends and family are a *SCRIPTED* vise, education is the crank. As the crank screws tighter, so does the *SCRIPT's* mental machinery. The truth is, *we're being indoctrinated, not educated.*

As soon as you're old enough to hold a crayon, you're taught that "work" or "things I'd rather not do" start Monday and end Friday, while "play" is reserved for the weekend. By the time you graduate from college, you'll suffer through 650 weeks in seventeen consecutive years of Monday-through-Friday conditioning, a regimen accounting for nearly 100 percent of your sentient life, in which it's clear: for each of the next 2,600 weeks of your life (fifty years), you must surrender five days into the system, while two are for you. Good deal?

Next, the educational system conditions you to accept an authoritative structure requiring permission: At 8:00 a.m., you need to be in homeroom; math is at nine and gym at ten. Eat lunch at noon. Ask permission to piss. Do as you're told, stay in a single-file line, and don't talk unless asked. At work, you do the same. You follow instructions. Do as you're told. Unplanned absences are frowned upon. Any weekday freedom requires permission: personal days, vacations, or an early recess to watch your kid's baseball game.

In high school and throughout college, the *SCRIPTED* worldview targets its primary nemesis: *critical thinking.* Instead of exposing our kids to free thought, educational institutions are now full-fledged indoctrination camps pushing ideological agendas from ideological administrators. Critical thinking is being systematically destroyed where two opposing viewpoints are no longer debated. Instead, students are blustered with opinions and partisan doctrine presented as facts or established rules of normalcy.

For instance, in 2014, a Connecticut high school blocked Internet access to conservative websites, such as the National Rifle Association, Christianity.com, and the National Right to Life. The message? You cannot think for yourself; we will think for you. I'm not advocating Jesus or guns—I'm advocating critical thinking and the freedom to examine both sides *so you can decide for yourself.*

When issues are presented through a *SCRIPTED* firewall, no matter if it's a domineering Catholic nun with a wooden stick or a Marxist professor wearing an ugly sweater vest, critical thinking is conveniently destroyed. And guess what? The *SCRIPT* doesn't want you thinking critically.

Educational propagandists and their thought police, however, are not limited to just state-run institutions—they could be private or theological. Regardless, the war for your child's mind has no safe harbor. Statistics reveal a whopping 72 percent of American colleges and their faculty promote a state-centric collectivism (over individualism) while stifling divergent thought.[6] The university system, once an intellectual crossroad for ideas, is now the largest confirmation bias on the planet, where mass cast opinions are sheathed in "safe spaces" as undebatable truths.

Another *SCRIPTED* failing is failure itself.

In school, failure is a bad thing. Marked by a bloody F and a parental beatdown, failure is admonished. Fail and you're grounded! No TV, no iPad! Is it any shock that straight-A students make great employees while the C-students are the guys hiring them? The A-students do as they're told, follow rules unquestioningly and stay within the lines. Meanwhile, C-student and future billionaire Johnny is a ninth grader's newest BFF—he's underneath the bleachers selling his older brother's *Playboys* at twenty-five dollars a pop.

Education's final nail in the *SCRIPTED* OS is a disturbing ethos of victimology and the normalization of averageness, as if these things were virtues. Competitive drive is being suppressed and gagged. Our public schools (and some parents) are grooming our kids to be a dithering, over-medicated and over-coddled band of wimps who throw tantrums when their sippy cups go empty. Today, we protect feelings. We praise when no praise was earned. Because you simply exist, you are entitled. And if you're not granted entitlement, you're a victim. Firm discipline (where's that Catholic nun with the stick when you need her?) has been replaced by "time out" and flowery negotiations.

For example, this is an actual letter sent home with students from a Michigan elementary school, a preemptive warning that your child's competitive drive must be stifled and, of course, his or her feelings protected:

> The purpose of the day is for our school to get together for an enjoyable two hours of activities and provide an opportunity for students, teachers and parents to interact cooperatively. Since we believe that all of our children are winners, the need for athletic ability and the competitive "urge to win" will be kept to a minimum. The real reward will be the enjoyment and good feelings of participation. [7]

Ahh, "good feelings of participation"—God knows life is filled with those, right? Merely "participate" at work and you get fired. How's that for good feelings? Oh, and the "urge to win" or "out compete" someone who doesn't give a shit? Surely that has no use in real life, eh? I wish I was making this up.

Similarly, a Rhode Island middle school pushed the mediocrity mandate by trying to cancel their traditional honors night because rewarding students who do well is "exclusive."

After an uproar from some parents, they backtracked. One of those parents rhetorically asked a local reporter, "How else are they supposed to learn coping skills, not just based on success but relative failure?" His daughter affirmed the same when she indicated she worked harder during the semester in an effort to not miss this year's event.[8] Perhaps next year, the Rhode Island school can honor the students who thought their homework sucked and played *Call of Duty* for four months straight. You see, there was a time when working hard earned a trophy on stage; now you get them for showing up with your hands in your pockets.

Educational institutions and their *SCRIPTED* tentacles are now manufacturing entire generations of brain-dead adults who never failed in their entire life and have a wall of participation trophies to show for it. Their greatest accomplishments are caricatures in the virtual versus the real world. They're brainwashed to believe that life is fair and it will protect your feelings. Hard work, optional. Competing, optional. Going above the call, optional. Many fear phone and face-to-face communication, opting for more impersonal methods, such as texting, Snapchatting, and Instagramming. Others hyperventilate and get "triggered" at the slightest criticism or divergent opinions that intrude on their preselected and prescreened world.

For example, in May 2014, Condoleezza Rice, former U.S. Secretary of State and a member of the Stanford University faculty, was scheduled to deliver the commencement speech at Rutgers University. Students protested, apparently not liking her political orientation and Iraq War involvement. After backlashes, she rescinded.[9] Similarly, in 2017, Milo Yiannopoulos, a British journalist and writer at Breitbart news, attempted to bring his controversial (and often offensive) opinions to California Berkeley. Students didn't protest, they rioted; burning property, smashing windows, and overall, acting like a bunch of petulant children who didn't get their juice boxes. Yes, the university that birthed the free speech movement is now trying to kill it.

The truth is, these snowflakes shit their Pampers when anything threatens their coddled lexicon—a contrary viewpoint, an opposition idea, or anything divergent to their sequestered safe spaces. Yes, when free speech doesn't agree with my zero years of real life experience, it's time to hurl some bricks through windows.

Sad, but college campuses have degenerated into expensive brainwashing clinics for *SCRIPTED* groupthink, a petri dish incubating mollycoddled adults ill-equipped to question their puppetmasters who thread their strings.

Bottom line, not only is the *SCRIPT* teaching our kids to think inside the box of conforming mediocrity, but it's imbuing them with the false expectation that they can plow through life doing the minimums: show up, text, post selfies.... Do so and you can win all that life has to offer. The awakening is, indeed, rude.

#3) CORPORATE SEEDERS: BE ALL YOU CAN BE

Whereas the education seeder teaches us to be good little employees, the corporate seeder tells us why: *so you can afford all the goodies we make and be happy.*

Corporate advertising makes it clear: happiness, success, or fulfillment is just one credit card swipe away.

Want the best a man can get? Buy Gillette.

A breakfast of champions? Eat Wheaties.

Be all you can be? Join the Army.

Relentlessly pursuing perfection? Buy a Lexus.

The good folks over at Harley-Davidson say, "American by Birth, Rebel by Choice"—yes, the rebellious life is yours for sixty easy payments and mostly driven on the weekend, LOL. Never mind your 610 credit score, the $114 in your retirement account, or your crappy sales job at the cell phone store—you're such the rebel!

Unfortunately, by the time we hit grade school, the *SCRIPT*'s corporate seeder has us believing happiness and social hierarchy are determined by brand consumption. Fun and excitement are found in a bowl of Apple Jacks or a McDonald's Happy Meal. You can't just watch the new *Star Wars* movie; you have to own all the action figures.

By high school, you learn that if Johnny's parents drive a BMW, well then, Johnny's rich. If Brooke Adams, the most popular girl in school, sees you wearing off-brand shoes from Payless, it's social suicide. Unless you're one of the cool kids wearing Abercrombie, don't bother asking her out. Even in my own experience with teenage gift buying, it's Beats headphones or nothing at all. Yeah, I'd rather not enjoy music than be seen wearing something else. You see, the *SCRIPT* teaches our children that their popularity and "coolness" are driven by consumption: what they wear and what they drive.

This sad reality was witnessed in 2014, when college student Elliot Rodger went on a killing spree in Santa Barbara, California, and cut six innocent lives short. In his public ramblings, he made it clear that *SCRIPTED* dogma was to blame: Expensive consumer goods—Ray-Ban shades, Armani clothing, and a BMW—should have provided him with happiness and female companionship as advertised. When it didn't, anger and betrayal boiled. And a sickening rampage followed. Of course, the *SCRIPT* doesn't create sociopathic killers, but in this case, it contributed.

Aimed straight at our kids, the *SCRIPTED* message is clear: Adult success is correlated to buying shit. Flash your credit card, finance your rock star life, and show up styling. Do so and happily-ever-after is your reward.

#4) THE FINANCIAL SEEDER: TRUST THOSE WHO CANNOT BE TRUSTED

I was told recently that a friend of a friend wrote a book on how to get rich. According to my buddy, the book details the usual financial orthodoxy involving Wall Street, frugality, and three-quarters of your life. The problem is, my friend knows this guy well. Very well. And guess what? He's not rich. Not even close. And yet here he is, the proverbial blind leading the blind. If you want to become a champion swimmer, shouldn't your coach know how to swim?

Every nine-seconds, a new personal finance book is published. OK, I made that stat up, but I'm guessing there are a bazillion books on retirement, personal finance, and investing. And no matter who the author, these books always dance the same dingbat dance: "Work hard and long, save and invest for decades, and one day you'll be rich."

You see, *this explains why most people over sixty-five are multimillionaires.*

#MicDrops

NOT.

According to US Census data, the median average income for near-retirees is only $2,146 a month. Additionally, according to the 2014 Retirement Confidence Survey, a whopping 60 percent have saved less than $25,000.[10]

I guess theory doesn't work out in practice.

Behind the avalanche of money books lurks the *SCRIPT* and its financial seeder, the multitrillion-dollar financial industry consisting of banks, government, financial funds, and investment houses, including the mediums bolstering them.

Their job?

To entice your fiscal future into the grip of hope-and-pray—three uncontrollable and unpredictable markets: the job market, the stock market, and the housing market. That's right, anchor your retirement to Wall Street, a bunch of untouchable bankers, and a Ponzified Social Security scheme propped up by a perpetual printing press called a government.

Meanwhile, your bank pays you .01 percent interest on your savings, and the financial seeders of the *SCRIPTED* fantasy get fabulously wealthy managing your money while charging hefty fees for the privilege. The goal is your undying belief that your life savings are in good hands. When you find out it isn't, it's too late. You're too old, or worse, dead.

#5) GOVERNMENT: THE SANTA CLAUS FOR ADULTS WHO LIVE LIKE CHILDREN

There will never be a more wretched hive of scum and villainy. Washington DC, your government, is the insatiable mother ship of *SCRIPTED* doctrine. In the old days, we had a representative government where citizens took temporary leave from their profession to serve political office. Back then, government was "by the people, for the people"; today, it's "by the few, for the few." And crawling within the legislative halls are over 10,000 lobbyists, who spend an average of $3 billion annually, each greasing a special-interest agenda.[11]

Meanwhile, millions of *M.O.D.E.L. Citizens* are unknowingly trapped in a servitude system designed to enrich government and power. The battlefront for this high-stakes game plays out in a political duopoly that feigns citizen representation. One party promises freebies; the other promises freedom—but neither can be trusted. The joke's on you. No matter the promises, your vote is merely symbolic in determining where power shifts and consolidates among special interests and oligarchs.

Listen to politicians and they'll campaign *SCRIPTED* platitudes that make you seethe with envy, anger, or both: Those evil business owners, surely rich through nefarious means, aren't paying their fair share and need to be penalized for their obscene profits. Oh, and you're poor because someone else is rich. Never mind that the last time you opened a book, brick phones were technological marvels. But don't worry, the government is here to institute moral and just order!

In 2011, amidst thunderous applause, Barack Obama stood straight-faced at a campaign podium and said, "If you own a business—you didn't build that." Conservatives jumped on the gaffe like flies to dung while progressives dismissed the statement as selective paraphrasing. On whatever side of the political spectrum you sit, the *SCRIPTED* message is clear: you owe the government gratitude for their benevolence; whether it's in-context (roads, bridges or fire departments) or out-of-context (businesses built from your sweat and tears), good ole Uncle Sam loves you (and your money) and their help is paramount to your success.

And then there's my favorite *SCRIPTED* scam propped up by…who would guess? The Federal Reserve. They have a knack for conducting studies. Yes, the money-printing wart of the government wants you to know that "a college degree is worth X dollars over your lifetime!" In 2014, *The Economist* reported that student-loan debt exceeded $1.2 trillion dollars. This debt cannot be bankrupted away. It must be repaid with tax-producing work. And work produces economic growth, which produces more consumption and more taxes.

Is it any coincidence that the manufacturing process for *M.O.D.E.L. Citizens* cements in college? For the uninformed, college is a leather-lined conveyor belt straight into the *SCRIPTED* slaughterhouse.

You see, when you participate in a *SCRIPTED* economy—paying a fortune for a college degree, financing a thirty-year mortgage, buying a bunch of crap you don't need—you bankroll government. After 9/11, in response to the new terrorist threat, President George W. Bush infamously suggested that Americans "go shopping" because, by all means, if you want to defeat religious radicals, a new Ford Mustang could be the silver bullet we've been looking for. The government knows consumption powers the *SCRIPTED* machine—whether it's war, votes, $47,000 TSA iPad apps, or a huge industrial contract priced at 300 percent over market. Make no mistake, we are being collateralized.

#6) MEDIA: WE'RE OBJECTIVE IN OUR SUBJECTIVITY

Noam Chomsky once said, "The smart way to keep people passive and obedient is to strictly limit the spectrum of acceptable opinion, but allow very lively debate within that spectrum." No words better describe the *SCRIPT*'s mouthpiece, the media. From the local news to the national press agencies, to Internet newspapers to talk radio, the illusion of this tainted water is, you pick the flavor.

Decades ago, the media once objectively reported the news and let you judge. Yes, journalism was real. Since then, Bernstein and Woodward have regressed into Olbermann and O'Reilly. Now journalists are *SCRIPTED* propagandists in the business of public relations—censoring, distorting, and crafting whatever "news" befits their agenda. News channels no longer objectively report but have become unconfessed spokespersons for the political duopoly, fire-walling truth and stoking the fires of our biases.

With a fully co-opted media, we now live in an ineptocracy controlled by an oligarchy. The least able to produce elect the least able to lead who then confiscate the production from a diminished pool of producers. In return, laws, which aren't read, debated, or understood, are passed benefiting the power structure. Mistruths and misdirections are spouted from both sides of the aisle as a matter of public policy—and the media doesn't give a shit. Politicians, from world leaders to the city councilman, lie and hem-haw daily—and again, the media doesn't give a shit. Collective heads are buried in asses while the ineptocracy demands news over the First Lady's dress or some pissing royal baby born across the pond. While Rome burns and the arsonists roam free, the headline of the day has degenerated into candid paparazzi pics of Kim Kardashian's ass or who was, or who wasn't, invited to the latest celebrity wedding. Meanwhile, genocide to the likes of Hitler 2.0 is occurring in the Middle East, but gosh golly, who can pay attention when *Two Broke Girls* is having their season finale?

Puhleeze, move along folks, nothing to see here.

The media mouthpiece seeds for other seeders, a nonstop torrent of propaganda that makes Joseph Goebbels grin in hell. Hit your favorite financial website and you'll read it: They'll tell you that the secret to wealth and a cushy retirement is hope-and-pray—fifty years invested into stocks, bonds, or whatever asset class is bubbling du jour. Other websites regurgitate Buffettisms *ad nauseam*, as if Warren

Buffett's empire isn't about entrepreneurship, but about logging onto eTrade and buying one hundred shares of General Electric. And the worst of the rabble, the "thrifty millionaire" stories that make me want to rip my head off and throw it in a Cuisinart.

Unlike family, the media's complicity in the grand scheme is prejudicial. There's no money in hard truths, but fantasy buys eyeballs; it buys votes; it buys stuff emulating the fantasy; and most importantly, it funnels money into the Wall Street casinos. The *SCRIPTED* narrative is profitable to everyone in the chain, from stakeholders to the corporate advertisers to the governments that tax the activity and its outcome.

As in the movie's *Matrix*, your *SCRIPTED* life is integral to the machine's survival. By chasing the next greatest gadget and the next greatest weekend high, you intravenously tap yourself into the belly of the beast. Yes, the rat race needs rats. The slaughterhouse needs lambs. Question is, are you willing to sell your soul for a weekend and television?

?

What seeders are currently influencing your life?
Are their motives in your best interest? Or theirs?

CHAPTER 8

HYPERREALITY: YOUR ILLUSIONARY CAPTORS

Those who are able to see beyond the shadows and lies of their culture will never be understood, let alone believed, by the masses.
~ **Plato, Philosopher**

REMOVING YOUR BLINDFOLD

After I sold my first company, I bought a red Corvette. At the time, I thought it was a unique car, rare among millions. Except it wasn't. My brain simply convinced me it was. As a proud new owner, I suddenly saw Corvettes everywhere. Women are annoyingly familiar with this phenomena: buy an expensive Louis Vuitton and hit the mall; suddenly every woman appears to own one.

This mental phenomenon is known as an *observational bias*, and it's a brain function known as your *reticular activating system*, or RAS. Your RAS has many critical functions, one being a filter. At any moment, your brain is swamped with billions of pieces of data. If you're reading this on a train, your brain is flooded by a barrage of sensory input: the people around you, their clothes, their look, the cute girl four seats up, the odor of the guy seated next to you, the sound of the tracks, the lighting in the cab, the seat against your butt, the discomfort of your suit—the list is endless. Because your brain must process these data, your RAS makes quick judgments about what it should and shouldn't see.

Once you're made aware of something, like owning a Corvette, your brain stops filtering Corvettes and filtered data are suddenly seen. My Corvette's cognitive distortion wasn't that they were more frequent on the road, it was my RAS no longer ignored them.

So what does your RAS have to do with the *SCRIPT*? Well, since your RAS sees once it's made aware, *awareness holds the key for transforming subconsciousness to reality.*

The *SCRIPT*'s illusions flow through its seeders: media, family, educational institutions, and the rest. However, the *SCRIPT*'s real power isn't from its seeders; *it is from the false realities cast by its seeders.* And because your brain is überlazy and unaware of the falsities, you become complicit in the scheme. Yes, your brain, in its glorious attempt for efficiency, is largely undermining your ability to live an extraordinary life.

Because your brain deficiently perceives reality, what follows is a great cascade of false conclusions causing misguided beliefs. Misguided beliefs cause misguided actions. Misguided actions produce unwanted results. And unwanted results create dissatisfaction.

A dramatic life shift requires a dramatic mind shift. Right now, your lazy brain is a *SCRIPTED* ally. Once your RAS is nudged, the blindfold drops. *SCRIPTED* doctrine whitelists from your firewall, and suddenly actual reality becomes clear. This paves the way to rewriting injurious beliefs and social contracts not written in stone but written in reflective shadows.

Once your brain is exposed to the secrets behind a magician's tricks, the appearance of magic disappears. As does the magician's power to deceive.

THE SCRIPT'S SHADOWED CONVENTIONS: HYPERREALITY

Misperceived reality is best hyperbolized in the ancient story, "The Allegory of the Cave," by Greek philosopher Plato. The tale is about several prisoners held captive in a cave their entire lives. The prisoners are chained in such a way they cannot move their heads or legs, forced to forever stare at a cave wall. Behind them, a fire blazes high above. Stationed behind the prisoners and in front of the fire is a depressed walkway and a parapet wall. On the walkway hidden behind the parapet, several puppeteers upcast various figurines, objects, and shapes, casting shadows on the prisoners' wall. The prisoners cannot see the puppeteers or the objects passing behind them, only their walled shadows. Because these shadows are the only reality the prisoners know, they are misperceived as real and substantive, despite the reality that schemes behind them.

This ancient story told more than 2,000 years ago is just as relevant today.

You see, the *SCRIPT* is also a collection of shadows, simulations, and cognitive distortions—a collection of authentic fakes and mental alchemy designed to keep us chained in a cave, mesmerized by a pseudo reality. And instead of shadows cast by puppeteers, the *SCRIPT* has its seeders. The truth is, the *SCRIPT*, you, I, and the entire civilized world revolve around a web of wizardry called *hyperrealities.*

Wikipedia defines hyperreality as the "inability of consciousness to distinguish reality from a simulation of reality, especially in technologically advanced postmodern societies." Furthermore, a "hyperreality is seen as a condition in which what is real and what is fiction are seamlessly blended together so that there is no clear distinction between where one ends and the other begins."[12] In other words, we are interacting with simulations instead of truths.

For example, Las Vegas is a hyperreality. Each casino presents a hyperreal experience where you feel like a king, a pharaoh, or a sheik—at least as long as your money lasts. Unfortunately, *SCRIPTED* hyperrealities aren't as obvious as Las Vegas. Unless you activate your RAS and train your brain to *see* hyperreality, the *SCRIPTED* shadows are perceived as real. Awareness gates the bridge to defiance.

CONVENTIONAL ILLUSIONS: THE SCRIPT'S 9 HYPERREALITIES

Nine primary hyperrealities underwrite the *SCRIPT*, each culturally iconic. These are the fables of *SCRIPTED* doctrine. The weapons of mass distraction. The Jedi mind tricks. These hyperrealities surround our existence and cannot be avoided. Our goal is to swivel your head around from the cave wall, expose the reality behind the shadowed projections, and activate your RAS.

THE HYPERREALITIES

NAMED DAYS CORPORATIONS MONEY FREEDOM
CONSUMERISM VIRTUAL REALITY ENTERTAINMENT
COLLEGE DEGREES HYPERPERSONALITY

HYPERREALITY #1: NAMED DAYS

I'm alone in darkness. As a stiff chill drafts my neck, I'm about to be scared out of my wits. It's Tuesday morning and I'm in a movie theater watching the newly released horror flick *Saw*. The theater is empty, not because the movie sucks but because everyone else is busy—busy trading life away in exchange for little pieces of paper called money. And ironically, while I piss my pants in fear for the next two hours, my business makes enough money to pay for the movie twentyfold. Meanwhile, outside the theater darkness lies the true horror of the day: Millions of people have killed their Tuesday and willfully postponed their life until the weekend. I'm not sure what's scarier, the mass murder of Monday through Friday or the murders in the movie I'm about to watch.

Long ago, your first day at school birthed the hyperreality "named days."

Think "Monday through Friday" and what do you feel? Anguish? Maybe a little discomfort? How about the word "Saturday"? Or "Friday night"?

Named days order the week by titles, Monday through Sunday, carrying with it the implication that Monday starts work and Friday ends it, while the weekend reserves play. The fact is, named days are a hyperreality, one the industrialized world has perfected to perfection.

Beneath the named-days scheme is a man-made illusion your mind has made real—*the illusion that your life's limited and precious time must be systematically segregated by days, with each day's title designating whether work or play is expected.*

The truth behind the shadow? There is no celestial reason or natural phenomenon behind a seven-day week cycle. The Earth simply takes twenty-four hours to rotate on its axis, and the Earth has no idea if that rotation happens on Sunday or Thursday. If aliens orbited Earth, Monday through Sunday wouldn't be recognized. Nope, their supercomputers would identify one planetary rotation equals twenty-four hours and one revolution around the sun is another 365 twenty-four hour sequences.

For every creature on Earth, named days don't exist. Your dog Rex doesn't know the difference between a Sunday and a Tuesday, other than you might spend more time with him on Sunday. His Sunday *feels* exactly the same as a Monday.

The mathematics are real; named days are not. In other words, *the entire scheme is an artificial interval to institute order.* Monday is an illusion. Sunday equals Thursday. The Earth is indifferent, with the exception of one creature: humans.

HYPERREALITY #2: CONSUMERISM

Consumerism is *the myth that consumption can produce success or happiness.* Despite that Vogue magazine, despite that Audi commercial, despite that banner ad, you are not what you own, *but you can be owned by what you own.*

If the *SCRIPT* was a jail cell, consumerism and the debt it creates are its bars of incarceration. That house with the thirty-year mortgage, that car with the seven-year loan, that boat, and that degree—all backbreaking expenses that can paralyze your existence. Consumerism, materialism, or "stuff" is the ubiquitous hyperreality that dominates the world's economic engine, and it will dominate yours if you cannot pierce its shadow.

Megacorporations spend trillions annually to create consumer hyperrealities—or in marketing speak, "brands"—all designed to communicate a fabricated perception. BRAND X says you're wealthy, BRAND Y says you're fashionable, and BRAND Z says you're rugged. If you drive a Toyota Prius, the advertised perception is practicality or thriftiness. A Lamborghini advertises "wealth," which may or may not be factual.

When I bought my first Lamborghini, the hardest part of the purchase wasn't the price tag; it was succumbing to a hyperreality. From a utilitarian standpoint, a car gets you from point A to point B. My Lamborghini was 5 percent car and 95 percent hyperreality. But in the real world, people cannot make the distinction. For example, whenever I valeted my hyperreality at a night club, I immediately bypassed the line and got into the club. Had I driven my Toyota and valeted, I'd receive no such treatment. Nope, get to the end of the line, buddy! In the Lambo, I am presumed rich and noteworthy; in the Toyota, I wait with the rest of the proletariat. Reality is ridiculously distorted. My car changes nothing about me—not my looks, height, or the nine bucks in my wallet—but it changes perception.

The consumer hyperreality cons the ladies as well.

See those expensive red-bottomed stilettos? Depending on who you ask, some will say you're classy. Affluent and stylish. Visit some gossip blogs and they'll accuse you of being a well-paid escort. Whatever the message, it's not real but simply a crafted perception. Drop these prestigious brands in a post-apocalyptic world where survival is the priority and their influence is stripped down to utility. What's left is a means for transportation and an uncomfortable height-enhancing shoe.

Consumerism's job is to trick you into thinking utility is not enough. The off-brand jersey from Target won't do—you need the Nike. Instead of safely driving from point A to point B in a Honda, you need the Infiniti adorned in triple-stitched leather. The *SCRIPTED* seeders are spending trillions brainwashing us that utility is for chumps; we must also cast a shadowy statement. Just because you bought the most expensive basketball shorts at the pro shop doesn't mean you can dunk like LeBron. Consumer proxy doesn't change reality.

HYPERREALITY #3: A COLLEGE DEGREE

My first day at college, I arrived late. My roommate (whom I never met until then) had already unpacked his side of the dorm room. On his wall hung a poster featuring a seaside mansion with a five-car garage filled with exotic cars. Above the garish picture in bold lettering was the statement "**Justification for Higher Education.**" I laugh thinking about it now. The fact is, for most college grads, "higher education" is not getting them five-car garages but five figures of debt and a job waiting tables at the seaside diner.

The "college degree" hyperreality is two-pronged. First, it is *the stale idea that intelligence and financial wealth require a college degree, regardless of cost, and more so, a life without one is forever underscored by underemployment and underachievement.*

In a recent report, one of ten college graduates (graduates!) thought Judge Judy was on the Supreme Court.[13] Intelligence? Similarly, a nonpartisan student group asked random Texas A&M students several basic history questions, such as "Who won the Civil War?" and "Who is the vice president?" Shockingly, all the students got some of the questions wrong, yet all of them knew who Brad Pitt's wife was.[14] Even if these results are due to selective editing, the travesty can't be whitewashed: These institutions aren't educating our youth but instead creating *SCRIPTED* idiots.

The hallowed halls of academia no longer teach intelligence and common sense. Such critical survival skills have been swallowed by such crap as "Feminist Perspectives: Politicizing Beyoncé" (thanks Rutgers[15]) and "Critical Theory on Sexuality" (Occidental College[16]).

As for success and/or financial wealth, think about the last three items you bought. Upon handing over your cash, did you ask the sales clerk if the inventor had a college degree? And if he did, what if it was a philosophy degree and not an engineering degree? The last time you were at Walmart trolling the aisles and reading labels, did you look for a disclaimer revealing the manufacturer's college credentials? How about the last book you bought at Amazon? Before you clicked "Add to Cart," did you specifically check the writer's college transcripts?

The fact is, *a college degree is not a prerequisite to consumption.* You buy what you want without regard to credentials. But listen to *SCRIPTED* seeders and they'll warn otherwise. *SCRIPTED* authorities drill into our kids that success is a veritable improbability without a college degree. Political "think tanks" unleash report after report claiming mathematical truths: "People with college degrees earn more over their lifetime than their non-degreed counterparts." #RollsEyes

For example, the latest such report came from the New York Federal Reserve in September 2014, where they indicated that a college degree is worth more than $300,000 over the graduate's life. First, this study used data beginning in 1970. That alone should make you chuckle.

Second, the report didn't indicate sampling. If you sample one hundred failing or below-average high school students who aren't going to college and compare them to one hundred well-adjusted B students who trail blaze to college, yeah, there's a statistical difference.

The fact is, students who perform well in high school are likely to go to college—the underperforming students typically don't and go into more vocational careers. The sampling bias in these studies is virtually impossible to eradicate unless researchers can persuade parents to keep their book-smart teens away from college.

And third, don't you find it unusual that the Federal Reserve, the money-printing arm of the government, has taken such a great interest in promoting college degrees? In fact, one look at their website and it seems they've devoted a lot of time to persuading citizens that college degrees are worth the price. Things that make you go hmm…

Another common college fallacy pops up on my forum every so often. When someone asks, "Should I go to college?" a parrothead is guaranteed to say "A degree is a good backup plan." #SMH #EnjoyBartending

Your degree as a "backup plan" is as good as a shovel in your garage. Just ask the millions of unemployed and underemployed graduates who are waiting tables just how strong that safety net is—about as thick as the paper the degree is printed on.

The college hyperreality's second prong is *the notion that spending a fortune on a degree in whatever you're passionate about, say marine biology or astronomy, guarantees that there's a job waiting for you after graduation—and that your degree entitles you to it.* When your parents asked you, "What do you want to be when you grow up?" no one said the likelihood of a job in that field was a long shot. As a parent, you nod your head, smile, and affirm that your kid can be anything he wants, despite market demand, economics, and a culture that has vilified job-creating businesses. But guess what? If there are no businesses and no entrepreneurs—society's redheaded whipping boys—there will be no jobs. Such an oxymoronic position is akin to loving babies but hating mothers.

The truth is, we're sending an entire generation of kids to college to earn degrees they can't use for jobs they can't get. Meanwhile, student-loan debt tops a trillion, collegiate coffers have enlarged to the point where football coaches are salaried in the millions, and thousands of well-educated youngsters are lined up at the job fair competing for jobs they could have gotten fresh out of high school.

Again, the reality is different from the hyperrealistic version. A college degree doesn't produce jobs out of thin air. It entitles you to NOTHING. I repeat, NOTHING.

My significant other is a nurse who recently had a good story exposing college's dual-pronged hyperreality. Her curse is working with surgeons and unwittingly hearing the intricate details about their lives. Anyhow, she noticed many aren't happy in the medical profession and yet are obstinately grooming their kids for the same existence. She hears stories about prepubescent kids being shuffled into advanced pre-college studies. She hears stories of rigorous extracurricular, after-school schedules that end at supper and resume until bedtime. The doctors reason, "My child must score well on the SATs and have a well-rounded entry application so he can get into a prestigious college." Never once has she heard "this is what my kid wants." Do we really want our kids taking classes they hate so they can pursue a career they also will hate?

The hidden *SCRIPTED* agenda behind college is economic indebtedness—to get you enslaved into the nine-to-five "named-days" work cycle, regardless of cost, job economics, and circumstances. A college degree has been arrogated as a holy grail, an accolade no longer worthy of the title. Now, before you steam your panties, especially if you're an engineer, doctor, or attorney, let me be clear: I am NOT advocating that everyone skips college. A college degree reflects specific-practice knowledge.

For example, I recently had elbow surgery and my surgeon had extensive education. His degree(s) indicated minimum training, and yeah, I'm damn glad he had it. But here's the hook: I picked my surgeon NOT based on his college degree but based on peer recommendations and his existing track record. When twenty pro athletes—cumulatively earning more than $100 million a year—trust this surgeon, you've got the right one. A degree might get you in the door; performance gets you cooking in the kitchen.

The degree hyperreality is closest to truth in highly regulated fields, such as medicine, law, and engineering. Government mandates minimum standards, and yes, that's a good thing. However, the farther you move away from these fields and into more pedestrian endeavors, the college degree hyperreality grows more shadowy.

Simply put, *people want what they want*—and if you have what they want, they aren't going to care about your college days. If you're bleeding to death and need a tourniquet, you're not stopping the guy offering one and asking, "Wait a sec, didn't you fail Biology 101 at Arizona State?"

HYPERREALITY #4: HYPER-PERSONALITY

It's Saturday night in North Scottsdale and I'm eating dinner at a trendy Japanese restaurant. The venue is packed and excitement fills the air. In my day, places like this were called meat markets. In my sight line, adjacent to my corner table sit six beautiful young ladies, probably a generation or two after mine. As the waitress shuffles between them, taking their chocolate martini and sake orders, it's clear this is a "girls' night out." Over the next hour, I witness just how prevalent—and sad—hyper-personality has become.

Before dinner, during dinner, and after dinner, not one, not several, but every woman at this table was preoccupied and smitten with her smartphone. It was as if the smartphone was being dined and real conversations with real friends was the distraction. Of course these ladies giggled and talked amongst themselves, but it was never a minute away from a smartphone peek, a keypad swaddle, or a social media selfie opportunity.

This story demonstrates how powerful hyper-personality has become, not just to young people, but to anyone with a smartphone glued to their face. *Hyper-personality is a person's public image, a facade projected by fame or social media, a carefully crafted mirage that does not represent the real, humanized version of the individual.*

In fame's case, the hyper-personality is often revered or worshiped. As such, their opinions are regarded as cult gospel. With social media, where individuals post the Photoshopped highlight reels of their life, the hyper-personality becomes an unreasonable and unsustainable capstone extrapolated from speciously curated snapshots of time. And in many cases like my girls-night story, *the expression of the hyper-self becomes more important than the true self.*

When renown is involved, the hyper-personality and its perception become the communicative front. For instance, would you believe I'm a hyperreality? When someone writes me and says, "You're my idol" or "You're a GOD!" (Yes, I've received email with those subject lines), they're perceiving and interacting with me as a hyper-personality, not the real me. Some fans think I have a crystal ball capable of predicting anything, anytime, anywhere. MJ, is this a good idea? Should I drop out of college after three years? Such is the magic of hyper-personality, but again, such magic is an illusion.

When someone calls themselves a "guru," they raise themselves to a hyper-standard, a perception of omnipotence. This is why I hate the word "guru." I have no crystal ball or a super-success secret. While my odds might be better than the average Joe, they're not sure things. I fail at business, make mistakes, fart, trip down stairs, and make poor decisions. I am human, just like you.

Another example of hyper-personalities is famous personas.

Can you imagine Warren Buffett losing money? He makes bad investments. He is wrong on a lot of things. And yet, when the "Oracle of Omaha" speaks, people melt to their knees and lick the lint between his toes. Same goes when a famous face walks into a restaurant. People react as if they're seeing Elvis reincarnated. Oooohhhs, ahhhhhss, followed by, ohh, the restaurant has comped your dinner.

Just like named days, these folks are hyperrealities, but they're no different from you. Celebrity perception is a Saturday. Yourself? Meh, a boring Tuesday. The fact is, they eat, breathe, and shit stinky poop, just like you. They get divorced, go bankrupt, make mistakes, and yes, they even pick their nose. They are human.

And yet the *SCRIPTED* worship these celebrities (and their opinions) to staggering levels of idolatry. It's actually frightening. For instance, in early September 2014, the Young America Foundation uncovered some disturbing data regarding hyper-personality. They took to the streets of George Washington University and interviewed random college students. When asked about recent events involving a nude-photo hacking scandal, a shocking twenty-nine of thirty were able to identify one or more celebrities involved. Sadly, when asked to name which anniversary of a major national event was approaching (September 11), only six of thirty could do so. Worse, only four of thirty could name one of the journalists beheaded by ISIS in Iraq.[17]

The media casts our biggest shadows. Because the media exalts hyper-personalities, they get treated differently than the *SCRIPTED*. When Ray Rice, the star running back for the Baltimore Ravens, was caught on video punching out his fiancé, he originally returned to the team. When he first took the field during preseason, fans cheered rabidly from the sidelines while knuckleheadedly sporting their Ray Rice jerseys. Such idiocy can only come from people jaggedly blinded by hyper-personality. Clearly, fantasy football points from running backs are more important than reality knockout points from wife sluggers.

Social media is another offender.

If hyper-personality was a day, it'd be Halloween, and social media the mask. With easily accessible social media tools—Facebook, Instagram, Snapchat—crafting our own fakery is so easy a caveman could do it. As a result, we've created a swath of people who have carefully crafted an illusion of importance that has systematically poisoned the will and desire to actually do the hard work that importance demands. By meticulously curating and photoshopping what we socially advertise, each of us becomes a powerful shadow caster, erecting a staged phantom while hiding the dirt underneath. By sharing only life's highlights and cloaking the rest, we cast a pseudo reality.

Sure, Becky's new Acura and the ten pictures Facebooked will certainly draw a horde of likes and comments, but know what isn't posted? Becky's coupon book with seventy-two payments at $500 a month, struck at 12 percent interest. And Joe's Caribbean vacation photos received ninety-two likes and thirty-two raving comments. Not shocking, Joe didn't post his last credit card statement, which paid for the trip, the one with the huge balance that will take twenty-two years to pay off because he can only afford the minimum payments.

Ever tried online dating? Welcome to hyper-personality—people post *what they want to be*, not what they actually are. Those smoking-hot pictures of Ryan, that guy you can't wait to meet tonight? He's a Photoshop expert and has cleverly twiddled away thirty pounds of fat, right after using the blur tool, erasing unsightly wrinkles aging his face.

What's advertised on social media smoking our smokescreens is a fabrication. If you're using it as a measuring stick for peer comparison, fluffy white clouds will go dark, leaving you feeling unworthy and depressed. So, the next time a stranger posts "lifestyle" photos on Instagram and you feel a tinge of insecurity, try remembering these people don't give one fuck about you. Nope, zero fucks are given. And yet, you care about them? Hyper-personality has you dwelling on the lives of others, instead of dwelling on your own.

HYPERREALITY #5: VIRTUAL REALITY

Virtual reality is a captivating and addictive simulation of an alternate reality exploiting a series of enticement heuristics: competition, goal achievement, faux improvement, and positive feedback loops. Virtual reality (VR), much like its sibling hyper-personality, plays on our desires to feel worthy and respected—while doing so with comfort and ease, void of risk and public humiliation.

Video games (Xbox, PlayStation), online realities (*Minecraft*, *Second Life*), and mobile gaming (*Angry Birds*, *Game of War*, and *Pick My Nose*) are VR examples that millions choose over reality. OK, I made up *Pick My Nose*, but that's how ridiculous this crap has become. The numbers for *Minecraft* sales are a staggering fifty-four million copies—that's nearly the entire population of Italy or 1,100 Yankee Stadiums jam-packed with fans.

The VR predilection is so disturbing that in 2014, Business Insider reported that Kim Kardashian's mobile game was grossing over $700,000 PER DAY.[18]

Holy fuckery.

Of course, such fuckery couldn't escape my investigation as I wondered, "What the hell do people do on a Kim Kardashian game that warranted the movement of $21 million per month?" Well…they buy fake purses, fake clothes, and fake jewelry so they can achieve some sort of fake VIP status. Yeah, hyperrealities within hyperrealities. Folks, you can't make this shit up. (Although it was later reported she *only* made $100 million on the game, darn, fire the maid!)

Virtual reality's allure and subsequent grip emerges by tickling your feedback loop while simultaneously playing to your lazy brain. Using a psychological laundry list of addiction tactics, virtual reality mesmerizes us with faux rewards, flimsy achievements, shallow confidence, and various other digital enticements. Your brain is then stimulated with a forged positive reinforcement loop. Worse, it's stimulated with little or no effort. Why hit the dojo every day for black-belt training when you can just sit on the couch, grab some Cheetos, and press the "ON" button?

There's a war for your mind and your money. Unchecked and unaware, your brain laps it up like a thirsty dog. Once hooked, it lays the groundwork for behavioral responses that border on the insane: camping out on sidewalks, declining nights out with friends because you just gotta hit that next level; or worse, letting it become the most important thing in your life—because it is your life. Take this comment reported by a forum user:

> I was at a party once with a guy who spent half the night checking his phone just to make sure his Clash of Clans army was being built on time. WTF![19]

The *SCRIPT* has armed virtual reality with all the latest psychological weaponry hoodwinking you into a state of entertained distraction—so entertainingly distracted that you share your addiction on Facebook. Which reminds me...for the love of God, stop sending me game requests. No, I'm not interested in helping you build your fake farm, your fake army, or your fake city. But I am interested in unfriending you.

Anyhow, the problem with virtual reality is not entertainment. I love playing a good first-person shooter every so often. The problem is when it goes beyond entertainment and virtual life supplants real life. Know anyone like that?

Make life your game: you acquire experience points, gold, money, cars, assets, liabilities; you weigh decisions, act, not act, solve problems, and overall, manage yourself as a player. And yet, instead of seeing life as a game to be won, the *SCRIPT* has confiscated your player avatar and made you the one to be gamed.

HYPERREALITY #6: ENTERTAINMENT

The entertainment hyperreality is an emotional or intellectually irrational investment in an entertainment format—sports, television, movies—where the investment becomes either an impassioned part of your identity or an erroneous belief about reality.

Like many, I enjoy watching sports as much as playing them. In particular, I'm a big NFL guy. However, I'm not so big into it that it's an impassioned piece of my identity.

In early 2016, the Arizona Cardinals (my hometown team) got slaughtered in the NFC Championship game. I was upset for about ninety-seconds. I didn't cry or beat up my girlfriend. And I certainly didn't lose any sleep over it.

At the end of the day, the game was just entertainment. I have zero emotional attachment to the outcome because my life is more important.

Unfortunately, I can't say the same for most folks, where entertainment is an escape and a medium for meaning. Scan the bleachers after a devastating loss and you'll see people sobbing their eyes out like a Hummer ran over their puppy. Such emotional fallouts are compliments of the entertainment hyperreality—an irrational emotional investment into something where it becomes wired into your identity.

Going back to that Cardinals game, when the defeated team returned to Phoenix, two fans greeted them at the airport. One of them actually had a Cardinal Super Bowl 50 logo TATTOOED on his forearm.[20] This is an extreme case where entertainment has completely consumed a life. I wonder…how much meaning does life lack if your forearm is tattooed with a sporting event that will be forgotten three weeks later?

Oh, and ever listen to the clowns commenting on sports radio? "Duh, I think Coach Bill Belichick should have passed more and ran Tom Brady on more bootlegs…." Oh really? I'm sorry, and who are you? Oh yeah, just some random peabrain who's never played football in his life. Please grace us with your opinion.

And my favorite. After a team wins or loses, the all-inclusive use of "we"—as if you are a part of the team and contributed to their performance. "Duh, we really played well last night and I think next week will be a really tough game for us."

We? Us? Since when did the New England Patriots put pizza-eating plumbers on the payroll for lounging in the recliner while watching a game? You don't belong to a team because you homestead in a geographic area. Just ask any St. Louis Rams fan.

This same type of irrational attachment happens with movies and television.

Did you see the long-awaited *Star Wars: The Force Awakens?* You probably loved it, like most of the world. I thought it sucked ass. And I'm a big *Star Wars* fan. Heck, my books pop *Star Wars* lines often. But in the case of *The Force Awakens*, I watched it like any other movie: from a cinematic and plot perspective. How good is the story? Is the "science fiction" believable with respect to science? I didn't let emotional investments sway me from honesty. From a story angle (not to mention science), it was just a plot retread with zero scientific believability. Youthful nostalgic emotions didn't cloud my honesty. Seriously, if the sun was sucked dry in the Star Wars universe, life on Earth would go on as if nothing happened. I can suspend disbelief, not my entire brain.

Anyhow, I know this sounds like I'm a curmudgeon who doesn't like fun, but that wouldn't be true. I love entertainment—*it just isn't woven into my life's purpose.* That's important, because I've been there when it was. I've wasted too much precious time on this shit—time I'll never get back.

When I was younger, I medicated my dissatisfaction in every episode from *Star Trek: The Next Generation*. Darmok and Jalad at Tanagra! There! Are! Five! Lights! My apologies to non-Trekkies, but the obsession bordered on the ridiculous as I still remember this crap twenty-five years later! Likewise during the nineties, the Chicago Bulls had Michael Jordan and the television had me. I never missed a game. I got angry and depressed after losses, punched walls, and spent fortunes on NBA shirts—yeah, I was emotionally invested like it actually impacted my life. It was so bad I scheduled my world around it. Date with a gym hottie? Nope, raincheck—Jordan is battling Patrick Ewing tonight.

If yin is the emotional side of the entertainment hyperreality, then yang is *intellectual irrationality.*

For instance, thanks to Hollywood scriptwriting, are you one of millions who believe that a Macintosh PowerBook computer, circa 1996, can save the world from an alien race that has traveled trillions of miles across the galaxy? *Independence Day*, 1996. Heck, in *Batman Begins*, apparently the standard for achieving superhero status is simply a few pull-ups in a subterranean prison. Watch a dozen Hollywood comedies and you'll think you're superhuman. You can have unprotected sex with old flames, strangers at truck stops, and hookers in Harlem and yet be totally immune from herpes, chlamydia, or unplanned pregnancy. Commandeer a police cruiser in Las Vegas, skydive off the roof of a casino, and even commit felony breaking and entering, and by golly, there are no consequences—just shits and giggles.

These hyperrealities are so powerful that youngsters imitate and decide careers based on them. Compliments of the hit TV show CSI, most high schoolers actually think crime scene investigators interrogate suspects and routinely get into gun battles down at the marina. As a result, the demand for CSI degrees has more than doubled.[21]

And then there's reality television.

How long can the travesty continue before the zombies figure out these shows aren't real? Cleverly edited and stoked for ratings, reality TV is about as real as the breasts at a pricey Vegas night club. All of it dramatic illusion, but most believing it's a legitimate microcosm of life. In a 2014 article on Deadspin.com, Floyd Mayweather actually confesses to the Nevada State Athletic Commission that his reality TV show *All Access* is completely fake. Scenes, manufactured and scripted. That marijuana joint? Fake. That thirty-one-minute-long bout? Fake.[22]

Think YouTube is different? Those funny videos with millions of views? Fake. One regrettable look at the comments reveals people are clueless. Many of these life portraits are more shadowed manipulations on the wall, nebulous realities, and clever Photoshops making us more malleable to the *SCRIPT* and less malleable to the real world.

HYPERREALITY #7: MONEY

Money.

It's why you're probably reading this book. Give a hundred-dollar bill a good stare. Note your feelings. Feel a tinge of freedom? Choices, power, or security? While these feelings might be real, their origins are based on another mirage. Money, the world's dominant hyperreality, is *a mutually shared belief that physical money (a stack of paper bills) or virtual digital money (a number on a computer screen) is valuable and that the person possessing it is equally valuable.*

In ancient cultures, such value expressions could be feathers in a headdress, a tribal age, the size of a flock, or the number of emerald stones possessed. The object is irrelevant; *it's only valuable because our society mutually agrees it is.* In essence, it's a worthless shred of paper with pictures of dead guys. Or it's pixels, a digitized number on a computer screen. In either case, our culture has universally agreed that these representations hold transactional value, just like we believe Monday is for work and Saturday is for play.

The next time you're watching a post-apocalyptic movie, note how hyperrealities fall apart. Paper money becomes worthless and used as toilet paper. Fuel becomes better than gold. For example, in the 1992 movie *Waterworld*, one of the worst movies ever made, dirt becomes a currency. In *The Book of Eli*, water and books are valued commodities. And of course, named days disappear—every day is another day to survive.

Unfortunately, if the belief (or the system upholding it) crumbles, so does the hyperreality. History has countless examples of money becoming kindling for the bonfire: the Zimbabwe dollar, the Weimar mark, and the Hungarian pengo are just a few. Iceland even flirted with such disasters as recently as a few years ago. Money is just another shadow on a cave wall, a projection agreeably accepted as real.

HYPERREALITY #8: FREEDOM

Joseph Goebbels, the minister of propaganda for Nazi Germany and history's biggest liar, knew big lies needed repeating to be believed. The repetition created a *consensus fallacy*—the idea that if many people believe something, some position, or some ideology, it must be true. Consensus fallacies are how common ideas escape critical thinking and become hyperrealities, such as Earth is the center of the universe.

The most fraudulent hyperreality running rampant in the First World is freedom itself—*the perception that we come into this world free and unencumbered, a sovereign person born with inalienable rights that cannot be co-opted, confiscated, or subjugated by any laws, customs, or beliefs.*

Not true. Not for you, me, or anyone else.

The truth is, we are livestock. Hosts for a diabolical purpose. Free-range slaves. Like free-range chickens, we roam free in our container (a country), provided the illusion of freedom, but we are still held captive for our eggs—our economic impact. If you leave, you need permission (a visa) and your leave is limited to whatever the visiting container (country) allows, usually ninety days.

You see, ever since your parents signed your birth certificate, you've become government collateral. Corporatized by our country, we're not sovereign individuals free from governance, we're corporations—corporations subject to taxation, regulation, registration, licensing, and a whole host of authoritative mandates. You, the corporation, are owned by the government. Everything you own, and everything I own, is also owned by the government.

Yes, you read that right. Everything. And the *SCRIPT*? It's merely the custodian of the collateral through its hyperrealistic advancement through childhood indoctrination, commercialization, media manipulation, and social engineering. Now, I realize this borders on conspiracy-theorist screed, but I assure you everything is incontrovertible fact as much as the sun setting in the west.

With *SCRIPTED* doctrine fully entrancing the populace, unquestioned and undoubted, your government enjoys lifetime benefits through your corporate self's economic output in the form of labor and consumption. This drives taxation and/or dependent constituents who love voting as much as they do consuming. And with an unlimited supply of voting and consuming human collateral, the government can continue to print money today to pay off printed money yesterday. Perhaps this is why the Federal Reserve is so interested in promoting "a college degree is worth $20 gazillion."

Money truly is no longer backed by gold but backed by blood—you—and the *SCRIPT* administrates the chattel. In 1933, President Franklin Roosevelt paved the way for currency backed by human collateral over physical collateral, such as gold. When you hear the phrase, "backed by the full faith and credit of the US Government," what you're really hearing is, "backed by United States citizens." Our money system is financed on our backs, and the *SCRIPT* keeps fish in the pond while the collateral fattens the system. And while we're technically *free* to make choices, we're NOT really *free* in terms of sovereignty.

I realize these are quite the leaps. Enslaved over free? Everything I own is not really mine? Thankfully you don't need to believe it because, frankly, most won't. And that's OK because you don't need to buy the slave argument to win the *UNSCRIPTED* life. This section (or this book) isn't about sovereignty, straw-man personas, the fiat banking system, or some argument about birth certificates as it pertains to admiralty law. It's about taking the blindfold off and asking the tough questions. Like, if confiscating 100 percent of your economic output constitutes slavery, at which point does it cease to be slavery? 80 percent? 50 percent? 39.6 percent?

So here's the candid truth about freedom and the stuff we think we own.

In 2014, I paid cash for a house in beautiful Fountain Hills, Arizona. I own it free and clear, with no mortgage or bank involvement. Liberating, eh? But the truth is, I really don't own it. The government has given me equitable title, which means I'm free to *use* it as long as I play by their rules. In effect, my home is leased from the government (the State of Arizona) and my yearly property taxes are the lease payment. If I refuse to pay my property taxes, the state will repossess what seemingly is mine. And the amount of the delinquency is immaterial—twenty bucks or twenty-thousand, it doesn't matter. Don't pay and say bye-bye to your crib. Heck, in Pennsylvania, a woman lost her house when it sold at auction for an unpaid six-dollar tax bill![23]

Ownership? Not exactly.

The same holds true for your car. Cancel your insurance, your driver's license, and remove your license plate. How long will it take before you are pulled over, arrested, and your car towed? In my birth state of Illinois, you'd last about thirteen minutes. Licensing is simply a co-opted freedom sold back to you by your friendly neighborhood bureaucrat.

Here is another story exposing the freedom hyperreality. After I moved, my mail got mixed up and was not forwarded. As a result, I underpaid my state tax and the account went delinquent. By the time I heard about the underpayment, the State of Arizona was threatening asset seizure. Here is the exact verbiage from their personal love letter to me, known as the Final Demand before Enforced Collection:

> The Department of Revenue is preparing to take action against you. These actions might include tax liens and/or the levy or seizure of your bank account, wages, and other assets.

Oh, and the amount I underpaid? A whopping $144.78—the current price tag for having your life confiscated.

Things aren't any better at the federal level. Stop paying your income taxes and have tea ready for the IRS. Take a spin on the tax roulette wheel and see how long it takes to have assets and bank accounts seized. Every year, the US Department of the Treasury holds approximately 300 public auctions. Here are the Treasury Department's exact words, from its website:

> We sell property forfeited as a result of violations of federal law enforced by the Department of the Treasury or nonpayment of Internal Revenue Service taxes. A wide variety of merchandise is available, including automobiles, aircraft, boats, real estate, jewelry, electronics, wearing apparel, industrial equipment, and miscellaneous goods.[24]

Again, all facts—not anti-government conspiracy rhetoric. Everything you own, from your diamond wedding ring to that hideous Affliction shirt you shouldn't be wearing, is available for repossession. Don't play by the rules sustaining the *SCRIPTED* system, and watch freedom disappear. Sovereignty is an illusion. Liberty is free-range. Of course *UNSCRIPTED* is NOT about dodging taxes or driving without car insurance. We simply seek to understand and acknowledge the game, while learning how to legally avoid it.

HYPERREALITY #9: CORPORATIONS

Enron. Worldcom. Comcast. Monsanto. Goldman Sachs.

These corporations likely gut a negative response. And yeah, it's probably well deserved. Surf Reddit for a few minutes and you'll find there's no love lost for the world's primary business formation, the corporation.

In 2011, on HBO's *Real Time with Bill Maher*, senator and presidential candidate Bernie Sanders said, "Corporations are not people."[25] Likewise, Elizabeth Warren cheered in her senatorial campaigns the tried-and-true populous claptrap, "Corporations are not people!" And of course the sheep gave it booming applause.

Such corporate contempt from the political establishment with regard to corporations usually involves two things: (1) its "personhood" in the eyes of the law; and (2) its electoral and legislative influence of elections through special-interest lobbying and political action committees (PACs), compliments of the *Citizens United* Supreme Court ruling. Both arguments have merit, as corporate cash-mucking elections and legislative processes aren't really good things. Nonetheless, their primary thesis, "Corporations are not people," is entirely false—both in the eyes of the law and in their unadulterated form. Underneath this erroneous worldview is another hyperreality: *the perception that corporations are evil, faceless, monolithic superstructures born from nothingness and responsible for every sin in the free world.*

The reality? Underneath the corporate veil, cranking the gears, aren't monkeys, robots, or artificial intelligence but people: managers, employees, corporate executives, and shareholders. *And these people are capable of every sin imaginable.* Corporations are evil and greedy? No, *people* are evil and greedy!

Think of it this way: If an errant drive-by shooting strikes you in the leg while walking the dog, who are you angry at? The car? Or *the people in the car shooting?* The car is directed by its occupants, just like a corporation.

Corporate distrust is warranted, but the guile is displaced. Moving down the corporate chain, shareholders elect the executives. And those shareholders aren't bigwigs living in ivory towers; they're common people investing for retirement: husbands, wives, Grandma and Grandpa. Your landscaper. Your bartender. They all link the corporate chain and they probably don't know it.

Log on to your E-Trade account and buy a share of Apple Corporation. Congratulations, you, already a corporation, are now a part of another corporation, a shareholder, who gets a vote on directing corporate policy. Anyone who owns a stock, pension shares, IRAs, or retirement funds is entangled in the corporate system! When Grandma invests her pension into an ETF or a mutual fund, she is buying corporate shares that make business decisions to the benefit of Grandma shareholder. And when Grandma's shares appreciate, she's happy and bakes peach cobbler.

As for corporate ancestry, humans give birth to them and the process is entirely gender neutral. Human corporations birth corporate corporations. Behind these corporations are multiple faces who dictate policy, and such policy merely flows downstream.

Including my corporate self, I own four other corporations. If you buy a book from my corporation and decide it's stinking garbage and want a refund, you get your money back, no questions asked, because *I decided* that to be the policy. My corporation is neither altruistic nor greedy. The law says it's separate and its own person; however, it's really just a paper filing with the state, one executing my desires.

The ultimate proof that corporations reflect owner beliefs and/or intent came from the landmark Supreme Court case *Burwell v. Hobby Lobby.* In this case, a Christian-owned business refused to comply with health-care mandates involving contraception. The court ruled the owners of closely held companies could project their beliefs onto their corporation. Once again, don't get mad at the car—get mad at the people driving the car.

So the next time the jackasses at Comcast treat you like trash, Comcast the corporation is not treating you poorly; it's management—people—who are treating you poorly, starting at the top. Somebody decided you were less important than profit. Somebody decided you get shitlisted while "That's not our policy" is the answer to your problem. You see, corporations are people, and the corporation is just another shadow on a cave wall. Shadows are not this issue—it's the people casting them.

? ***Which hyperrealities play a predominant role in your life? And will awareness change how you will interact with them in the future?***

CHAPTER 9

TEMPORAL PROSTITUTION: TRADING GOOD TIME FOR BAD

Lost time is never found again.
~ **Benjamin Franklin, Statesman**

SELL YOUTHFUL TIME NOW; BUY ELDERLY TIME LATER

In finance, "the time value of money" is as fundamental as salt and pepper are to cooking. The gist of "time value" is that money TODAY is more valuable than money TOMORROW. When these calculations are made, future money is discounted and valued less. This is why $10,000 today is more valuable than $11,000 ten years from now.

So why is TIME not discounted the same way?

This misuse of time value rolls out the red carpet for our last and crowning hyperreality, which frames the two *SCRIPTED* OS life-paths: *temporal prostitution—the subordination of time to money; the presumption that time is unlimited and can be fecklessly traded, squandered, and dishonored, while money is piously coveted as a limited resource.*

THE LIFE PATHS

TEMPORAL PROSTITUTION

Like most *SCRIPTED* hyperrealities, the truth has been blissfully whitewashed. While time's infinite existence might have a spiritual truth to it, mortality changes the science. Once our limited existence is plotted atop an unending string of time, time becomes hyperreal, neither infinite nor abundant. This self-deception makes commodifying time acceptable, like a worthless trinket bought and sold at a swap meet.

Philosophically, what is time to you? An age measurement? A way to keep appointments? Unfortunately, time is merciless and it doesn't care how you define it, how you see it, or how you treat it. It's the undisputed killing champion of the world, racking up over a hundred billion wins and zero losses. No army and no earthly disaster can claim the same. You can't escape time's ravenous siphon, and yet everyone merrily pisses it away without hesitation.

At its core, your existence feeds on time just like food and water. *Life is rationed by time.* Like cotton weaves a shirt or water fills a pool, your life rations embody the breadth of your existence. Nonrefillable and nonrefundable, time is a fuel tank that perpetually burns, permanently sealed from measurement or manipulation. And while your total life rations are unknown, their daily dispensaries are not.

Each of us is gifted with twenty-four hours or 86,400 seconds per day. No one gets more; no one gets less. How you honor (or dishonor) these life rations marks the difference between being further entrenched into *SCRIPTED* dogma or escaping it.

For instance, know anyone who spends most of their free time in front of a video game? How about the poor sap who spends two hours waiting in line for a free hamburger? Few people explicitly work for three bucks per hour, but give them a freebie or a savings opportunity at that same rate and you'll have tents lined around the building. Do you think billionaires are pissing their time away on a blog, arguing with strangers on the other side of the country about how some fictional HBO character shouldn't have been killed off?

Temporal prostitution is one of the greatest tragedies of humanity.

My first temporal-prostitution "WTF moment" was a job I had at Sears Roebuck as a five-dollar-per-hour stock clerk in the drapery department. Talk about a sixteen-year-old's nightmare. I was probably the only teenager in the world who could carry on a conversation about valances. Anyhow, Ed Guerro was my crotchety supervisor who was your classic hawkeyed micromanager. He demanded perfection and cursed everything I did: the towels are folded wrong; those toasters aren't stacked properly; or my favorite, if you need to piss, wait for lunch or piss your pants.

It was at Sears where I learned that in order to make $500, I had to swap one hundred hours of my life, and swap them under the constant surveillance of Ed Guerro.

This was important. Back then, my hobby was car stereos, and a 300-watt Rockford Fosgate amplifier with a $500 price tag had my interest. My audio system, already amped and stacked with dual twelve-inch subwoofers, shook the street with thunderous force. My neighbors hated me, and I salted their anger by not rocking to Neil Diamond but to 2 Live Crew. However, in my rebellious mind, they didn't hate me enough. My shit needed to thump harder, and that new Fosgate amplifier would, indeed, volumize the thumpings.

But there was a problem…

I hated my job. And I hated Ed.

This was a watershed moment because I noticed trading time for money sucked, but it also held another truth few grasp: The things I wanted, specifically my amp, really didn't cost money; *they cost me fragments of my life.* The price tag for my amplifier wasn't $500; it was one hundred hourly life rations joyously spent with dickhead Ed. Suddenly, a few extra decibels of bass didn't seem worth it.

The life-ration concept is uniquely demonstrated in the 2011 movie *In Time.* In the movie, humans have their forearms timestamped with a countdown death clock, which ticks toward the end of life. With a quick glance, anyone can see how many life rations they have left to breathe. In this dystopia, work is not paid with money but with more life rations—time added onto your death clock. Working one day might earn you two. While the movie wouldn't win an Oscar, it exposed some great revelations with respect to how we use our time.

First, just because your death clock isn't visibly stamped on your forearm doesn't mean it isn't there. Like air, it exists—you just can't see it. This invisible time bomb perpetually ticks toward death, bleeding every second of your life's rations. And nothing can stop it—not the $4 million you saved for the last forty years, not your MBA, not your granite countertops. We are relentlessly pursued by time with death as its final goal. It has no mercy and often, has no just cause.

So ask yourself. If a death clock suddenly became visible and advertised your life rations for easy viewing, say your smartphone, would you spend your time differently? Would you be OK sitting at a desk five days a week, doing a job you hated? Would you spend two days camped outside at Best Buy, hoping to save two hundred bucks on a curved television? How about buying into a financial scheme that promised freedom only after 90 percent of your life's rations have bled dry? And more importantly, what remaining time on your death clock would deliver the much-needed head smack that screamed, "OMG, my life is too precious to be squandered on a sidewalk waiting to save ten bucks." Six weeks? Months? Years?

Second, under *SCRIPTED* rule, how many life rations are you trading today to earn freedom tomorrow? When we project the same "time value of money" principle to time, we come to the same conclusion: *Free time today is better than free time tomorrow.* Youthful time sold today (working five days a week) so you can buy elderly time later (retirement in your twilight) is a bad bet.

Think how ridiculous this is. You work Monday through Friday, or you spend five life rations just so you can earn two. Five for two. Would you accept this negative rate of return in the financial world? Hey, invest five life rations and I'll give you two back as payment? Oh and BTW, *you won't get back your original investment.* Remember, time spent can never be reclaimed or refilled, so it's **not** an interest payment; *it's an immediate loss of principal* and a dismally negative rate of return.

Gone means gone. In the *In Time* world, negative returns wouldn't fly; no one would work because it pays better not to! And yet, in our invisible-death-clock world, it's perfectly accepted.

In the end, our fate is sealed. However, what isn't sealed is the *type of time* you can enjoy among your life rations. Within your time bank, there are two time types you can manipulate: (1) *free time* and (2) *indentured time*.

Free time is the time you own, and it's the only time that's important. No one has a claim on it. You do what you want: sleep in, write, read, whatever warms your heart. Follow *SCRIPTED* protocol and you're locked into a shitty deal where free time is automatically presumed to exist only on the weekends, at least until retirement at some godforsaken age a gazillion years later. Retirement might as well mean "the flash of free time before I die."

Conversely, indentured time is time *someone else owns*: school, studying, work, traffic, your biz, etc. So if your workday consists of nine hours at the office, two hours in traffic, two hours in dress/undress, and one hour in unwind time, how much free time do you really have? Assuming eight hours for sleep, add up the work-related time, and your free time amounts to a pitiful two hours per day for a workday. Effective use of your life's rations?

> ***Under temporal prostitution, the things you buy cost more than just money—they cost future fragments of your life, transforming FREE time into INDENTURED time.***

Consider this: Two lives, Bob and MJ, each equally granted seventy-five years of life. Both get the standard twenty-four-hour day. The difference between the two is how time is honored or dishonored. Bob invests his life's work in a system where time is prostituted. He experiences sixty-three years of indentured time while enjoying only twelve years of free time: three health-challenged years after retirement and nine years in his lazy youth. He never writes that book he dreamed of. He never scuba dives in the Caribbean because his cardiologist recommended against it. He never took that two-month Mediterranean cruise. He never watched his son win the lacrosse championship. Never, never, and never. But hey, don't worry—he's saved quite the portfolio and was featured on Business Insider's front page as a model for portfolio wealth; never mind that he destroyed one wealth in pursuit of another.

Live poor and die rich. It's *SCRIPT*ably diabolical.

MJ, on the other hand, invests his life's work in a system that honors time. He experiences twenty-three indentured years while enjoying a whopping forty-two years of free time, mostly experienced after he retired in his thirties. "Never" is not in his vocabulary, but "when," "where," and "how" are.

Who do you think will have lived a life rich in experiences: friendship, art, travel, contribution, and spiritual fulfillment? When the life rations drip their last drip and the death clock taps the grim reaper on the shoulder, what will your human spirit resonate—regret, or peace?

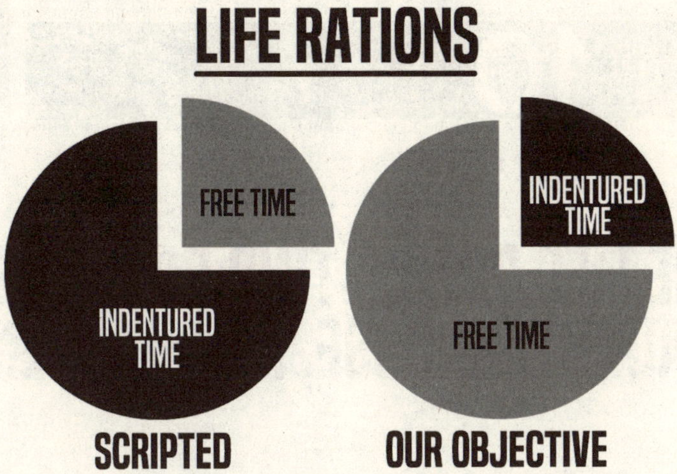

Temporal prostitution is the path to the dark side, and it doesn't require a throaty mask—but it does have an evil emperor. Allow the *SCRIPT* to write the rules and you'll accept the worst trade mankind has ever foisted on intelligent beings: the horrendous "sell good time today so you can buy bad time tomorrow," where 71 percent of your adult life is routinely dismissed in favor of an elderly promise called retirement.

OMFG!

And people lap this crap up like it's raining lottery tickets during a prosperity gospel. Only temporal prostitution perfected by the *SCRIPTED* OS can lipstick the worst travesty of humankind and make it as routine as a daily shower.

The average lifespan consists of 2.3 billion seconds. The average currency value traded per HOUR is $220 billion, nearly 11,000% more. Time is scarce, money is not.

CHAPTER 10

THE LIFE PATHS: TWO DOORS, ONE SLAUGHTERHOUSE, NO DIFFERENCE

The individual has always had to struggle to keep from being overwhelmed by the tribe. If you try it, you will be lonely often, and sometimes frightened. But no price is too high to pay for the privilege of owning yourself.
~ **Friedrich Nietzsche, Philosopher**

THE ILLUSION OF CHOICE: WHO WILL BE YOUR SLAVEMASTER?

Temporal prostitution is the escort. Holding your hand with a wink and a smile, it leads to one of two doors, a *SCRIPTED* offer you can't refuse. Two choices where two paths lead to two different lives. Both paths promise happiness, but don't be fooled. It's another *SCRIPTED* illusion diabolically engineered to keep you on the path to *M.O.D.E.L. Citizenship*. You see, no matter which door you choose, their roads converge to the same regretful destination riddled in deferred dreams, lifelong work, and broken promises. Your choice is meaningless because both choices lead directly into the *SCRIPTED* slaughterhouse.

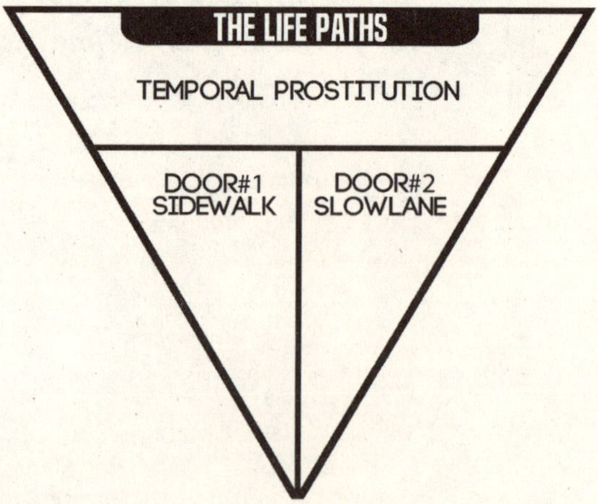

Getting to choose your leash and the slaveowner who pulls it, still makes you a slave.

Once you expose the life paths and determine which one applies to your life, you can better plan your escape.

DOOR #1: THE SIDEWALK (TRADE TOMORROW FOR TODAY)

The Path:	The Sidewalk
The Promise:	Happiness through consumption
The Leash:	Consumption and entitlement
The Collar:	Debt and dependence
The Slavemaster:	Corporations and/or government
The Rat Race:	Consume, debt, work (or vote), repeat

THE "PAY FOR IT LATER" CULTURE

Know anyone living large, and yet they're always complaining about money? You know the type, friends who forget their wallet and can't pay their restaurant tab? Or worse, they order five glasses of wine, and yet they want to evenly split the bill though you drank nothing? Welcome to Door #1, the *Sidewalk*. For the unknowing masses, it's an attractive red-carpeted causeway; for the *SCRIPT*, it's the carotid artery right into the *M.O.D.E.L. Citizen* slaughterhouse.

Anyone can be a Sidewalker: lawyers, cashiers, entrepreneurs, truck drivers, doctors, engineers, the McDonald's manager and the cashier he manages. The Sidewalk is an equal-opportunity meat grinder, immune to race, education, achievements, titles, and income. The path to the Sidewalk has only one prerequisite: *Live to consume.*

The Sidewalk is the *SCRIPT's* paycheck-to-paycheck, pay-for-it-later plan, promising happiness through consumption, both material acquisition and hyperrealistic absorption. In return for temporary, short-lived comfort—the financed car, the vacation to Tahiti, the trendy wardrobe, the nights on the town in the VIP section—the future is forsaken for fleeting thrills, which must be repaid tomorrow by longer lurches of pain. The Sidewalk is much like that old drinking quote: "When you drink more than you should, you're just borrowing happiness from tomorrow."

Unfortunately, "tomorrow" is continually postponed until the pain compounds into an inescapable work mandate. Or worse, you become just another government-greased serf, whose vote can be bribed with the mere mention of "free stuff" just so long as someone else pays for it.

The common thread among Sidewalkers is they always live "one something" from broke: one paycheck, one business deal, one gig, one album failure, one welfare check, one contract. Unrestrained spending is often justified with cutesy acronyms, such as YOLO, TGIF, or FML. Unfortunately, YOLO's price doesn't live once; it lives and grows on your Visa card.

As such, a Sidewalker has no financial plan other than a relentless pursuit of cash to fund a lifestyle built on credit and yesterday's paycheck. And since a Sidewalker's financial plan is about as real as Santa Claus in mid-June, the fiscal future becomes a tenuous gamble reliant on guaranteed employment, government entitlements, and unlikely "easy money" crapshoots: casino gambling, lottery tickets, frivolous lawsuits, and various other free-money fairy tales.

Take for example the bankrupt athlete who earned over $50 million during his career. How could he go broke? Again, when consumption is life's banner, it's like being tailed by a hungry bear who drinks time and eats money. And once the real career fizzles, the consumption bear catches up.

This is what makes Sidewalkers unique. They can be impoverished apartment dwellers or seemingly affluent suburban homeowners. The *SCRIPT* doesn't care about gilded cages. Net income is merely a speed dial on the hedonic treadmill, a ticket for instant gratification and consumption—whatever is earned is spent.

Time isn't safe either.

Temporal prostitution is a way of life. Always needing to work and always loathing the obligation, Sidewalkers routinely waste time in superfluous hyperrealistic proxies: sports, television dramas, Internet comment wars. You see, the Sidewalker doesn't play the game of life; he spectates. He comments. He opines. He heckles the million-dollar athlete from the cheap seats. Culturally plugged in, Sidewalkers can shoot the shit by the water cooler for hours, dispensing a wide variety of opinions: who the Dallas Cowboys should have drafted; how George R.R. Martin should have written *Game of Thrones*; and how dare Showtime cancel *Dexter*? Instead of being the best he can be, the Sidewalker aspires to be the best copy of someone else: a famous person, a fictional character, or some other person not annexed by the *SCRIPT*.

CONSUMPTION, CORPORATIONS, AND DEBT, OH MY!

Bottom line, walk through Door #1 and you will be leashed by consumption, collared by debt, and owned by corporations. Simply put, your stuff owns you.

This "stuff" could be your mortgage, your car loan, your credit card debt, your addiction to some stupid HBO drama, your government freebies. No matter what it is, you are owned by your shit, which is owned by your debt, which is either owned or profited by a corporation. So you work for a corporation, everything you buy comes from a corporation, everything you watch is produced by a corporation, and the debt you owe is held by a corporation. Ah yes, as Sidewalkers say, the rich get richer.

Of course, none of this has been done with your consent. The Sidewalk is innocently introduced with college. If you're one of the fortunate who graduated debt-free, congratulations. You've escaped a snare. If you were like me, I financed my education with the government, who not shockingly, hands out student debt like candy from a white, windowless van. And then the *SCRIPT*'s meathooks claw into you. For the next four or five years, college teaches you consumption without production. While learning, you consume expensive textbooks, housing, clothes, sundries, food, drink, liquor, and whatever looks and feels good on campus. And don't forget those pre-approved credit cards, an enticing avalanche the moment you roll into the student union. Aren't those banks generous? Again, you are being groomed for consumption, the idea that it's OK to consume in excess of production and that such excess can be paid later. Meanwhile, those "losers" who skipped college and avoided consumption's snake pit are working while avoiding six-figured debt.

After graduation, the consumption mentality continues as hedonistic pleasure and peer one-upmanship. Armed with a new job, new money, and a pile of credit cards, projected success through ego-driven extravagance and conspicuous brand consumption is expected. I know because I fell for the same trap: I deserve to be rewarded for all the hard work in college! And now, because I have a job and a paycheck, I'm going to show the world how successful I am. Throw in social media and it's consumption's perfect storm.

Usually the ruse begins with a new car, of course financed. I remember my last week before college graduation: four friends bought new cars simply as a reward for getting a job—and this was before their first day on the job!

Then it follows with a new wardrobe (financed) because, gosh golly, you can't drive your Beemer in some off-label rags from Target. Or worse, your job requires a $2,000 suit for every day of the week. Of course, no consumption escapade is complete without the latest iPhone, iWatch, or iToilet, financed by any of your half-dozen credit cards. And if you're fortunate to get hired for a job paying better than average, consumption hits overdrive with a townhouse or a condo in Wrigleyville—again, all financed, but this time over thirty years.

At this point in your *SCRIPTED* existence, you're probably feeling pretty good about yourself. Unfortunately, it's short-lived with an expiration date, usually the moment the bills come due, the newness wears off, or the job wears thin.

Underneath the *SCRIPTED* delusion is the idea that success can be bought at a mall, parked in a garage, or cashed on a Friday. Few realize that every dollar owed shortens the leash and tightens the collar around their neck.

My firsthand experience being short-leashed and tight-collared happened after I graduated. I was miserable five days a week, working a dead-end construction job. But the money was good. Fresh off some bad advice—"fake it until you make it"—I bribed my weekday misery with a sports car, one I couldn't afford and had no business owning. The car payments siphoned most of my paycheck. I no longer could afford moving out from under my mother's wing. But damn, I looked good! And for a few weeks, I actually felt successful.

Epic fakery.

The problem with my car extravagance wasn't the payments but *the consequences of the payments*: It trapped me in a job I hated, a job that sapped my spirit and quarantined my entrepreneurial pursuits. Consumption stole my power to make choices—to be free. I wanted to quit but couldn't. I had debt and it siphoned all my time. Temporal prostitution, anyone?

Consumption's self-administered Sidewalk trap goes beyond consumption vanity. Looking stylish, you will probably attract a mate, one who has fallen in love with your wonderful public persona fashioned by your consumption mindset. Jenny thinks you look "hot" in a suit. She loves the Audi convertible and your loft in Buckhead. You're getting older, and you think she's fabulous in bed. The *SCRIPT* says, "Get married," because you know, most of your friends are already married and you feel left out. After dating a year or two, you decide to strap on the ultimate consumption accelerator: marriage and a litter of kids.

Game over.

SCRIPTED life becomes nearly a lock because *children necessitate consumption*. Let me repeat that: Children necessitate consumption, where it's no longer a fashionable choice but a requirement. You need to buy diapers, food, health care, and the latest video game—and you do it for at least eighteen years. Congratulations, you are the *SCRIPT*'s new best friend.

So the next time you're sowing your oats unprotected with some Tinder hookup or sitting in the finance office at the car dealer signing a contract, picture Admiral Ackbar heckling in the background: "Wait, it's a trap!"

And please understand, I'm not anti-marriage or anti-children; I am anti-consumption and anti-making-stupid-decisions-before-you've-fully-matured-into-the-person-you-will-become. Trust me, your twenty-two-year-old self will be an unrecognizable stranger to your thirty-two-year-old self—as will the person you attract. Marriage and children could be the most important part of your human experience. It's worth waiting until you've discovered your true self, where you can give your spouse and kids everything you've got, not just a kiss on the cheek and a weekend.

DOOR #2: THE SLOWLANE (TRADE TODAY FOR TOMORROW)

The Path:	The Slowlane
The Promise:	Freedom later through investing
The Leash:	Deprivation
The Slavemaster:	Time and Wall Street
The Collar:	Hope
The Rat Race:	Save, work, invest, wait, repeat

CHANGING THE LEASH AND THE COLLAR...

After a few years (or decades) of Sidewalk living, you might come to your senses. Once you're responsible for children, it hits that blowing $1200 on bottle service at the club isn't smart. One look at your credit card balance and your retirement prospects, and you might conclude mistakes were made. Overall, you're a fighter and refuse living with the debt collar. Such suspicions will lead to an investigation, and unfortunately, that investigation leads to the *SCRIPT*'s Door #2, *The Slowlane.* In fact, the *SCRIPT* is counting on it.

Generally speaking, The Slowlane appears to be a responsible choice because it's pitched by culture, media, and a trillion-dollar financial industry. Like the Sidewalk, the Slowlane makes promises: Miserly saving and investing today will lead to freedom tomorrow. In other words, incarcerate 90 percent of your adult life in a job/Wall Street scheme so you can hope to enjoy the last 10 percent.

The Slowlane is the presumption that decades of gainful employment circumscribed by thrifty living, tortuous saving, and regimented stock market investing will somehow make you a happy millionaire. The financial priesthood and the mainstream mouthpieces have made it clear: if you want a secure retirement and a millionaire portfolio by sixty-five, sacrifice now and put those sacrifices into the stock market.

Behind the theory is this backward idea that patience, or *time*, can make you wealthy. But wait, didn't we just say time is wealth? Yup; it's like a diet encouraging you to chop off your legs just so you can brag you lost weight. And then, once you've chopped off most of your life and all that remains is a wealthy octogenarian living on fumes, you can finally retire and hit that bucket list. Does selling five decades of youthful time so you can buy ten elderly years sound smart? If so, I have a bridge…

DEPRIVATION AND HOPE

At the heart of the Slowlane is a reasonable idea: *stop consuming.*

However, applied within the *SCRIPTED* OS, stop consuming means stop living. Specifically, start depriving yourself. Settle for less. Lower your expectations. Defer spending, defer experiencing—vacations, restaurants, movies—and defer life until retirement.

While the Sidewalker is leashed and collared by consumption and debt, the Slowlaner is leashed and collared by deprivation and hope. I call it the HOPE, STOP, and WAIT plan.

Sadly, changing paths does nothing but change your corporate master. Whereas a Sidewalker is broadly owned horizontally through a variety of corporations (banks, media, consumer products), the Slowlaner is vertically owned by just one corporate master. Your new corporate owner? Wall Street.

You see, whenever you put your financial future into Wall Street's hands, you're essentially saying, "Hope and time is my plan for financial freedom." For the plan to actually work, think about all the stars needed to align perfectly:

Hope I have a job—not just a job but a good job.

Hope the economy gives me that good job for the next fifty years.

Hope the stock market yields 10 percent a year and doesn't crash.

Hope the housing market doesn't implode and erase my equity.

Hope I'm alive by retirement.

Hope I'm healthy.

Hope the government doesn't hyperinflate my savings or the currency in which it is denominated.

Hope the government can continually fund a bankrupt Social Security program.

Yes, you are collared by hope, imprisoned by time, and owned by Wall Street.

But the leash is worse. Before you can test the plan, it requires the stingy leash of deprivation. Every dollar must be pinched, coveted, and invested. Expenses cut to bare minimums: Cancel the movie channels. Clip coupons. Buy your wardrobe from Goodwill. Ride the SuperShuttle from the airport to save eight dollars, even though it adds two hours to your ride. Stop going to first-run movies and wait for the DVD dollar rental. Stop vacationing. Stop ordering expensive wine at restaurants. (Restaurants? You shouldn't be at a restaurant, dummy. Save that cash; it could be worth $1,000 in fifty years!)

Stop this, stop that. Stop living and start dying.

HOPE, STOP, and WAIT. Sounds great, eh? The people profiting from the ruse tell you it is. The Slowlane is a multitrillion-dollar industry lickspittled by famous authors and radio personalities, financial planners, money managers, and a whole gauntlet of prejudiced parties. Not surprisingly, these fiscal prostitutes *don't get rich practicing their advice, they get rich teaching it.*

Pick up any book about personal finance and you're likely to read a 200-page mind-fuck about being cheap. Of course, these books don't overtly say, "Be cheap," but hide behind slippery phrases like "the simple life" or "frugal living." Some bloggers make a living on the entire concept, as if dumpster-diving for expired meat behind the Safeway is so brilliant. Regardless of the words beating you stupid, the concept is ridiculous and oxymoronic.

Scarcity does not create abundance. Replacing fiscal poverty with experiential poverty is like replacing your dietary protein with carbs and expecting muscle. And yet millions of people mistakenly believe that the menu of extraordinary living has "settle for less" listed as an entrée. It doesn't.

Think about it from the seeder's perspective. If you sold ten million books on how to pinch a penny from your ass, do you think you'd care about the stock market? Likewise, if you had $1 billion under management at your hedge fund, do you think you'd care about returns? *Win, lose, or draw, you make bank.*

Nonetheless, the beat goes on: One hundred dollars saved every month could be worth $5 million after fifty years! Inflation? Stock market crashes? Life expectancy? Survivor biases? Zero percent interest rates? Currency devaluation? My friends, pay no attention to probable reality because, just like lotteries, probable reality plays no role in feel-good fantasies! You're going to be rich!

Sadly, Slowlaners snort this BS like free cocaine in a billionaire's penthouse. And once again, temporal prostitution is saddled up and ridden toward death. There is no freedom without vitality. Six feet under is not freedom, and neither is a hip replacement and a wheelchair. Time, Wall Street, the economy, the job market, the housing market, government incompetence—these things are no better than rolling the dice at Caesars Palace, and at least there you'll feel like a king while snagging a free buffet.

Folks, if anyone says you need four or five decades to *earn* your freedom, close the browser, unsubscribe, or ask for a refund. The *SCRIPT* wants you to HOPE, STOP, and WAIT because by the time you discover winning this rodeo is like snake eyes at the craps table, it's too late.

Many who struggle financially have a strong work ethic—the problem is their "hard work" is being channeled in an ineffective and outdated system.

Which SCRIPTED door best represents your current life path? And will it lead to your desired dream life?

CHAPTER 11

DISTRACTION: THE MINISTRY OF ENTERTAINMENT

What the mass media offers is not popular art,
but entertainment which is intended to be consumed
like food, forgotten, and replaced by a new dish.
~ **W.H. Auden, Poet**

MOVE ALONG, NOTHING TO SEE HERE

((((((DDDDDDDDDDDD))))))

Hear that? Those are the Ds coming your way: Dread. Dissatisfaction. Depression. Disquiet. Discontent. Disillusionment. All predictable consequences for either door, the disharmonious emotional whispers onward to your final destination: *M.O.D.E.L. Citizenship.*

But before embarking, we'd like you to forget about those Ds. Instead, we want you comfortable. Entertained and humored. So here's one of the *SCRIPT's* many red herrings: a movie…

You see, both *SCRIPTED* paths cannot survive without their ministry of entertainment: distraction. While we're blissfully preoccupied watching our funny movie while stuffing our face with genetically modified food and being herded toward the slaughterhouse, our minds are being melted into submission.

Pay no attention to what's outside the rail car. Negative interest rates? Here's a cat playing with a ball of yarn. Twenty-trillion in government debt? Check out the celebrity dresses worn at the Oscars! Stock market crumbling? Sign this petition to stop HBO from canceling The Sopranos. Middle East genocide? Meh, did you hear Katy Perry's new album?

You see, if you're too plumply entertained in hyperrealistic distraction, you're no threat—no threat to the paradigms and certainly no threat to the meat grinder awaiting. Just sit back, relax, and focus on your movie because this train is leaving.

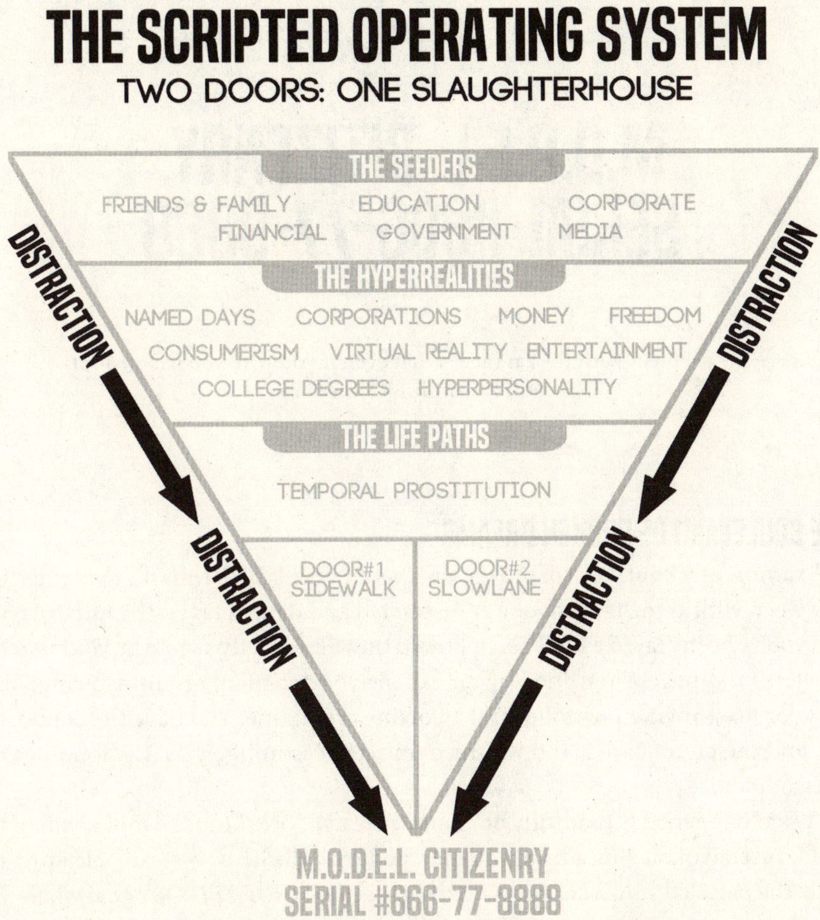

Unfortunately, distraction's objective is not to keep you entertained. It's to grind life into mediocrity. Autopiloted inertia—when both *SCRIPTED* paths seem inescapable and reversing appears impossibly painful. While season twenty-two of "whatever show is hot" rolls on, inside your spirit withers. Dreams fade. Life mulls into the trivial and mundane. The pending suicide mission is resigned as fate. Suddenly, instead of talking about goals and dreams, you're talking about how much the Lakers suck this year. Distraction is the medicating cocktail that lets us swallow our ignorant resignation that life will be ordinarily destined for a weekend and a once-a-year vacation. Meanwhile, the clickety-clack of the train tracks count down the years to the last and final stop...

M.O.D.E.L. Citizenry.

CHAPTER 12

M.O.D.E.L. CITIZENRY: SERIAL #666-77-8888

The problem with the rat race is that even if you win, you're still a rat.
~ **Lily Tomlin, Comedian**

THE BOULEVARD OF BROKEN DREAMS

Examine any boulevard of broken dreams and the *SCRIPT* marks the centerline. Deep within the taproot of our distracted and denied Ds rests a hurtful truth that you've been played a fool. You followed the rules exactly as told by your parents, teachers, and peers—outlined by an expensive education, an uninspiring job, a slow- or no-growing portfolio, and a flowing credit line. You have the condo, the car, and the credit cards, and yet freedom seems as unlikely as a T-bone steak at a vegan picnic.

What happened is painfully obvious: Instead of breaking the mold, you fit the mold. Instead of blazing a trail, you marched with the herd. Instead of leading the pack, the pack led you. *M.O.D.E.L. Citizenry* is the *SCRIPTED* OS's goal where you become a part of an indentured class concocted by either Sidewalk or Slowlane paths, the final consequence of being pawned in a rigged game that has few winners.

As the *SCRIPT's* newest manufactured *M.O.D.E.L. Citizen*, life is:

- **(M)EDIOCRE**: Life has regressed into an unremarkable yet comfortable ordinariness, where thriving is not an objective, but surviving.
- **(O)BEDIENT**: Free-thinking is dead; you follow popular opinion and trust your government and the news organizations fanning the flames of your biases.
- **(D)EPENDENT**: You're a debt serf owned by an army of corporations: product and service producers, Wall Street, government—or worse, you are owned by time.

- **(E)<u>NTERTAINED</u>**: Your entertained and humored mind distracts the heart to the point where your soul is no longer heard.
- **(L)<u>IFELESS</u>**: Dead at twenty-five but not buried until seventy-five. Goals, nonexistent. Optimism, scant. Dreams, murdered.

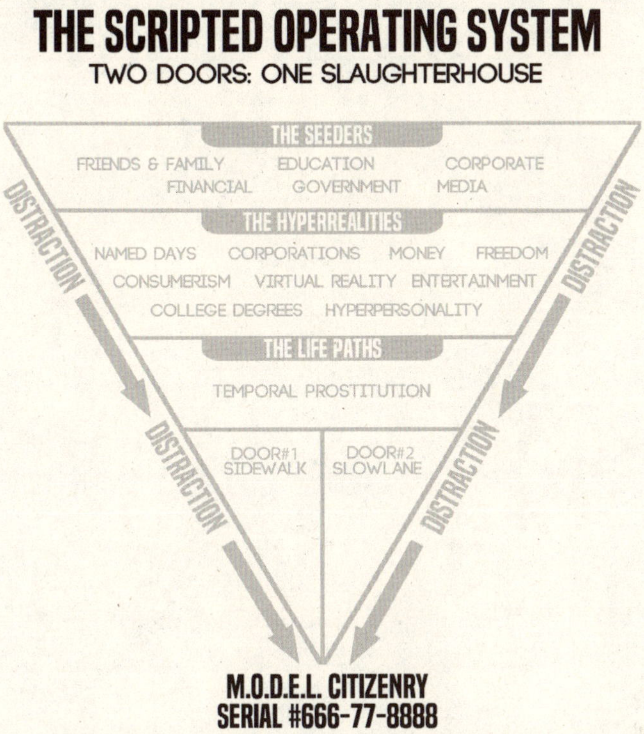

This *SCRIPT* is real. If you're thinking I'm Alex Jones 2.0., my guess is that the heat isn't hot enough. You see, the *SCRIPTED* OS works its deceit like that poor frog who dies in a boiling pot of water. No one willingly jumps into boiling water; we become suckers to the scheme by comfortably playing in lukewarm water while the heat slowly rises, optimally while showing the latest Hollywood movie while promising free popcorn.

The *SCRIPT* works its madness similarly. No one aspires to a mediocre life framed by a spiritual suicide. To stomach the heat, the temperature rises slowly, month by month, year by year, until the momentum is too strong to reverse—or worse, you're too old to fight.

No matter which road is taken, the outcome is the same: we're livestock held hostage by a corporate cartel—a variety of banks, media conglomerates, Wall Street money managers, and the ultimate parental corporate duo, your job and your government.

Fuck that shit. It's time to own yourself.

PART 3

THE ALTERNATIVE... LIVING UNSCRIPTED

THE ROAD LEAST TRAVELED MEETS THE MOST TRAVELED.

PART 3: Author's Objective:

VISION

To illustrate what is possible when your life is free from *SCRIPTED* expectations, and how to start crafting your own vision of that existence.

CHAPTER 13

THE UNSCRIPTED LIFE: "FUCK YOU"

Wealth consists not in having great possessions,
but in having few wants.
~ Epictetus, Philosopher

DESCRIBING INDESCRIBABLE: THE 5 "FUCK YOU" FREEDOMS

In Hollywood's *The Matrix*, the world is fooled by a neural simulation while carnivorous machines feed on our life force. Similarly in our world, government feeds on our economic output, our consumptive impetuses, and our consensus ignorance. Corporations play the foot soldiers, herding the unwashed into the machine's mouth while the hyperrealities keep us entertained and distracted.

Hopefully your blinders are off and you see the paradigm of compliance. Hopefully you're awake and now know that you've been sold a bullshit story by a bunch of bullshitters whose only goal is to keep you knee-deep in bullshit. And unlike a fictional movie, cleansing yourself from the bullshit isn't as easy as swallowing a red pill. You can't stop using money, paying your taxes, or interacting with a hyperdistracted world. However, the good news is that the *SCRIPT* has an escape through *UNSCRIPTION*—a life-changing subset of thought and action underwritten by entrepreneurship.

What can *UNSCRIPTED* do for you? Tough question. Word-smithing an *UNSCRIPTED* existence free from *M.O.D.E.L. Citizenship* is like trying to capture the "oohs and ahhs" of the Grand Canyon with a late-seventies Polaroid. Like a near-death experience, words cannot accurately express *UNSCRIPTION*. All I can do is paint a picture from my experience, and hope you can use it to craft a vision for yourself.

As for that picture, I suppose now would be a good time for me to shamelessly brag about all my "stuff"—you know, the garage full of European supercars, the imported exotic Ming Dynasty vases, and my haute couture wardrobe complete with leather-embroidered dragons and silken flaming swords. Oh, and let's not forget my favorite gadget: my wifi-enabled refrigerator with an authentic Monet embedded in the door.

But you know what? I won't do any such thing. You see, I don't own any of this crap. The truth is, *UNSCRIPTED is about what you don't have versus what you do have.*

UNSCRIPTED is self-actualized freedom by exclusion and excommunication. Don't confuse this with minimalism or being a waitstaff-stiffing cheapskate. *UNSCRIPTED* entrepreneurs live well by choice, not by necessity. "Well" is whatever you want, whether Teslas are preferred over Toyotas or Ferraris over Fords. I'm not here to define your fulfillment picture. I won't tell you that you need $100 million or $1 million to make it happen. My happiness is not yours. I'm only here to give you the blueprint for making it happen, and making it happen as fast as possible.

With that said, if I had to paint *UNSCRIPTED* with one color, it would be the color of "fuck you." Yup, fuck you.

Being charged an arm and leg for a mortgage? Fuck you. I'll pay cash.

Need to work next weekend and miss the kid's playoff game? Fuck you. I quit.

Stock market sinking and threatening retirement? Fuck you. The stock market doesn't fund my retirement.

Can't go on vacation until someone gives permission? Fuck you. I leave tomorrow.

Can't wear that cool outfit on casual Fridays? Fuck you. I'm wearing only underwear all day.

Don't like how your kids are being educated? Fuck you and your school. I'm homeschooling my kid.

Don't like your 2 percent pay raise? Fuck you. I'll make 200 percent more next year.

As "fuck you" implies, *UNSCRIPTED* is about pure, unadulterated life and liberty. Life means owning your time and thoughts while curating your existence. *It is not just to be, but to become.* The "fuck you" of liberty has five primary freedoms. They are:

1. **Freedom from work**
2. **Freedom from scarcity and fiscal constraint**
3. **Freedom from hyperrealistic influence**
4. **Freedom from hope and dependence**
5. **Freedom from ordinary and routine**

#1) FREEDOM FROM WORK

I successfully executed an *UNSCRIPTED* plan in multiple instances, and hence, I don't need to work another day in my life. Indentured time has been eliminated. I don't need to write books, start another company, or wake up by force every weekday morning. Theoretically, I retired nearly thirty-five years early. Still, every day is payday. Every day is Saturday. Every day is owned—every second and every hour are mine. Fundamentally, I am as rich in time as Bill Gates or any other billionaire.

You see, to be free from the necessity of work is like releasing a caged bird and unleashing the world as your playground. This liberation opens you to experimentation. Spontaneity. Clarity of action and purpose without fiscal measurement, interference, or influence. In other words, my life's work honors my soul, not some third-party "thought leader" in a position of authority.

Take this book, for instance. What do you think crucifying the trillion-dollar financial industry will do to my book sales? I'll make an educated guess that no one in the financial world would dare recommend *UNSCRIPTED*, let alone review it favorably. You see, if book sales (or money) were my driving influence as an author, I'd tell you that the best investment is a 401(k) and a Vanguard mutual fund. I'd tell you MLM is the best business model and everyone should do it. One opinion is the voice of necessity, a compromised integrity in lieu of putting Benzes in the garage, and the other is the voice of *UNSCRIPTION*.

And yet I still work. Why? Because it's a part of my life's meaning and purpose. Because it's my choice and not a force-fed exhibition, work rarely feels like work. Yeah, it's fun. And get this…I still earn a full-time CEO salary for a part-time effort. *UNSCRIPTION* transforms the world into one simple choice: Will you? Or won't you?

#2) FREEDOM FROM SCARCITY AND FISCAL CONSTRAINT

In early 2014, I dropped seven figures-plus on a beautiful home in Fountain Hills, Arizona. I could do a "cribs" video and talk about its many great amenities, but doing so is tantamount to *SCRIPTED* douchebaggery. Instead, I'd like to talk about what it doesn't have…

It doesn't have a mortgage. I told the bank "fuck you" and paid cash. Outside of maintenance and operating expenses, such as insurance and utilities, my basic living expenses can be paid with an income considered poverty in most states. No rent payment, no mortgage payment, no interest payment, no private mortgage insurance—never again, for life.

Likewise, it doesn't have cars in the garage with payments attached. I don't need leases or loans. Nope, whatever cars are parked are paid for. Some have tremendous miles and make no statements in traffic other than that I need to get from point A to point B. Others may come and go and are very expensive, Italian, rarely driven, and symbolic of the *UNSCRIPTED* path I've taken. What would your life look like without house or car payments?

And my favorite feature of homeownership? My home is free from the Gestapo HOA, better known as your trusty neighborhood homeowners' association. If you're not familiar with HOAs, they are composed of multiple jackasses posing as humans, telling you what you can and cannot do with your house. Want to paint your house? You need permission. Fly a flag on your front steps? Permission. Don't get permission and get fined or, worse, have a lien slapped on your house. I cannot tell you how happy I am knowing some loser cut from the varsity football team forty years ago can't tell me the appropriate trim height for my bushes.

But perhaps my favorite liberation is escaping the financial straitjacket while giving scarcity the middle finger, including the authors and bloggers who pitch it. Ah, the beauty of not being mind-fucked by money. It means dinner is a nice steak found at a nice steakhouse—not roadkill you found on Interstate 10. It means liberated shopping at "Whole Paycheck" with smug impunity, price and sale considerations ignored—not hauling a wad of coupons so thick that George Costanza would drop his jaw. It means flushing the toilet every shit—not rationing flushes every six dumps because, OMG, you'll save eighty-nine cents on every flush! And my favorite: the exhilaration of walking into Starbucks and buying whatever you want without hearing lectures about compound-interest tables and how much that five-buck coffee would grow if you just saved it while waiting for the invention of warp-drive.

#3) FREEDOM FROM HYPERREALISTIC INFLUENCE

One day I climbed into my truck and caught a glimpse of some papers jammed in between the seat and the center console. Now, if you ever hitched a ride in my car, you'd conclude that I'm a slob, or at least, I chauffeur one. Riding shotgun is like box seats at the county landfill without the Cracker Jack. Anyway, after starting the engine and lifting an eyebrow at the trash in my passenger well, some official-looking papers caught my eye. I grabbed them and took a look. OMG. What I found was an emotional mixed bag: First, shock, then happiness, and then fear. Buried in those papers, buried in my car was a check for $11,000. The check sat lost in my car for weeks, not cashed, not missed, and not needed. Shocking? Yes. Happy? You bet. I can't tell you how incredible it is to be debt-free without need, want, or desire. The fear? The check totally slipped my mind. Alzheimer's is a family friend, and let's just say, my memory rivals a Commodore 64.

The takeaway? Had I been bewitched by the consumer hyperreality, that $11G would have been spent the minute it hit my hands. If my priority was slaughtering the Joneses or some flamboyant Instagram playboy, I would have spent my millions on a bunch of junk that screamed, "Hey, look at me and my cool stuff!" The lesson is, I haven't pissed away my freedom playing the consumer con game. I didn't capitulate to the latest in German engineering and didn't buy the latest iPhone only to have it replaced a year later. Instead, that $11K was parked in a seat crevasse and never thought about again.

Perhaps my favorite hyperrealistic immunity is from trivial distraction. In June of 2014, Yahoo's front page announced that breakout pop star Iggy Azalea's video "Fancy" surpassed a hundred million views. At the same time, sectarian war broke out in Iraq. Ukraine was on the verge of a Russian invasion. And yet, Yahoo had nary a peep. As for the urgent matters that besiege the American idiocracy, namely Iggy's hundred million views, I'm proud to admit I was not one of them. The very definition of *UNSCRIPTED* means not being influenced by *SCRIPTED* trivialities. Pop culture, celebrity worship, and pro athletes are "no contest" to the life I'm leading.

For example, ask me who won the Stanley Cup last year. I don't know. And if you told me, I wouldn't remember. Why? Because I don't give a fuck. I don't care that some millionaire athlete threw an interception and lost the football game in the fourth quarter. While I respect pro athletes for their process, I pay attention to their livelihoods as much as they pay attention to mine. My life is too short, too important, and too valuable to get wrapped up in *SCRIPTED* zombification.

And finally, another hyperrealistic immunity is its bullshit detector. You see, when Dillion, a long-lost friend, sends me a Facebook message crusading for some "ground-floor opportunity" that's gonna make him rich, the BS thermometer spits mercury. His words are peppered with phony platitudes, excited emoticons, and stories of free BMWs that aren't really free but leased. Funny and sad, but no worries—I'm immune because I know the difference between entrepreneurship and a direct sales job in a network marketing company. I know the difference between leading the charge and being led by a charge. I know the difference between the *SCRIPTED* seeking shortcuts and the *UNSCRIPTED* targeting those seeking shortcuts.

But my *UNSCRIPTED* immunity doesn't end there. Rid of influence, I'm a human shield impervious to *SCRIPTED* dogmatisms and their ubiquity. It's like walking the planet uninfected amidst a zombie pandemic.

Oh gracious, look there: Another financial article authored by a non-millionaire telling me how to become a millionaire. In the *SCRIPTED* Xanadu, it's perfectly acceptable, like taking fitness advice from a fat dude who hasn't seen a gym since the Bush administration. But the fairy tales and unicorns have just started. Look, it's another financial guru dispensing another fiscal hypocrisy of "do what I say, not what I do." I chuckle. I shake my head. And then my humanity hits me with sadness—people buy the lies and pay for it with their lives.

#4) FREEDOM FROM HOPE AND DEPENDENCE

UNSCRIPTED means unbinding from hope and dependence as a financial plan.

It's a simple truth: "Fuck you" freedoms cannot be ascribed by dependence or hope. The source is irrelevant. Living in your parent's house? Dependent. Living off the government's nipple? Dependent. Is your lifestyle tied to a job and the income it provides? Sorry, dependent. Is your retirement locked into a fifty-year marriage with Wall Street? Or how well the stock market performs? Again, sorry—dependent.

Within the *SCRIPTED* OS, the holy trinity of retirement planning is tied to three unpredictable and uncontrollable markets: the job market, the stock market, and the housing market. In other words, follow the *SCRIPT* and your financial future is resigned to the gambles of dependence. *Adopt conventional thinking in this area and I guarantee, you will live conventionally.*

The truth is, the *UNSCRIPTED* don't rely on these markets for creating wealth. Nope, none of them. Less than 2 percent of my net worth comes compliments of any of these markets. As I write this, I own a few stocks, and it's only because they pay dividends. Being free from market shenanigans means something I hold very dear: I can give them the big "fuck you." Stock market up? Down? Who the hell cares! I don't give a shit because the stock market is not my vehicle for wealth. And the ultimate irony? I don't own an IRA or a 401(k)—traditionally espoused retirement vehicles—and yet I retired decades early. Oh lord, how could that be? You see, the *UNSCRIPTED* understand the difference between the uncontrollable limited leverage (depend on the job/stock/housing market for decades and pray to God) and controllable unlimited leverage (invest in a business system I create and control).

#5) FREEDOM FROM ORDINARY AND ROUTINE

A final *UNSCRIPTED* liberation is to be pardoned from the death sentence of ordinary and routine. As I mentioned, one of my meaningless jobs after college was driving limousines in the Chicago suburbs. While that sounds glamorous, it wasn't. The only difference between me and a taxi driver was six feet of legroom, a shelf full of liquor, and a privacy door, or as I call it, the porn door. Anyhow, this "meaningless" job wasn't so meaningless after all. For most days, I partook in the race of rats, with me as their driver. I saw routine on a daily basis.

One of my usual customers was an executive who would fly out Monday morning and return Thursday night. Despite driving this man nearly every week, we rarely spoke other than trip-pertinent information. Rarely a greeting, never a conversation, only a word or two, sometimes sprinkled in with a nod. Misery and scorn etched his morning face whenever I picked him up at his Barrington mansion. During rides to the airport, chats on his brick phone were occasional, the conversations callous, sometimes ruthless.

Then one Monday morning after I picked him up, something different happened. *He broke routine.* He actually engaged me in a cheerful conversation. He learned I had two business degrees and was an aspiring entrepreneur. I learned he was a lawyer with a wife and two kids. During the thirty-minute drive to the airport, I wondered, "Why now is Mr. Misery talking to me?" As I drove into the airport, I found out why: he was meeting his wife and kids in Hawaii for vacation.

Welcome to routine—err, I should say, breaking routine.

UNSCRIPTED is liberation from cultural norms and patterns of existence that don't serve your happiness. Such patterns are the traffic commute: the ride on the bus, the train, or the drive in the car. The nine to five, Monday through Friday, and the Sunday blues scarred by foreboding and discontent. The once-a-year vacation, the one that finally allows you to break, speak to a stranger, and crack a smile. The daily routine of waking up at 5:00 a.m. to a song you once loved, knotting a tie, working as you're told, driving home, microwaving dinner, watching the latest flavor of reality TV, and then repeating endlessly till your funeral.

Freedom from ordinary releases you from the cognitive clutter of *SCRIPTED* standards by which you are measured: your car, your job, your college degrees, your house, your social media posts, and yes, even your appearance. If you're one of the 5,000 people that follow me on my personal Facebook page, you'll notice something unusual: I rarely post anything. No politics, religion, or sports team crap. No gym photos or pictures of my healthy meal. The truth is, I care more about the real me than a crafted, social media me—so real me gets my attention.

In a similar vein, when you're unbound from ordinary, societal norms can't tell you how to dress or groom. *You own your own style.* As I write this, my hair is halfway down my back. Yes, it's that long and I haven't lost it.

"Madam…can I get you a drink?"

I hear that a lot when I dine out. From behind, I've been mistaken for a woman. When the server faces me and sees a man, hilarity ensues. The girlfriend finds it amusing. I don't. The point is, I haven't cut my hair because I don't need to cut my hair. There's no employee handbook I have to follow, giving me the freedom to roll like Axl Rose, minus the shrilly voice and goofy hip gyrations.

Likewise, I don't own a tie—why would I waste money on something I hate wearing? Heck, I don't even own an expensive shirt. My day-to-day attire is gym clothes. The last time I had a public speaking gig? I showed up in jeans and a T-shirt. I wear what's comfortable. If the audience wants to ignore me because my shoes aren't Ferragamo and my suit isn't Armani, well that audience would be in the wrong room and listening to the wrong speaker.

The *UNSCRIPTED* TLDR? Do, wear, buy, live, and pursue whatever you want. It's a beautiful way to live. But, will you even make it to the starting line? Let's find out.

? ***Try imagining an existence rich in the five freedoms. What would you be doing and where? What would you NOT be doing, wearing, or watching?***

CHAPTER 14

"FUCK THIS" BEFORE "FUCK YOU"

You can avoid reality, but you cannot avoid the consequences of avoiding reality.
~ **Ayn Rand, Author**

THE BEGINNING OF THE END: THE "FUCK THIS" EVENT (FTE)

Ever since *The Matrix* was released in 1999, the "red pill" has become symbolic for many things: transformation, awakening, knowledge, freedom, and the not so obvious, the painful road of unplugging from ordinary. As much as I'd like to be writing about rainbows, I cannot. Jim Rohn, the legendary motivational speaker, once said, "We must all suffer one of two things: the pain of discipline or the pain of regret." At some point, you will face the same choice: a life *in* hell, a *SCRIPTED* hyperreality fated by the treadmill of mediocrity; or a walk *through* hell, the red-pill reality of discipline, unpaid sacrifice, and dang it, a ton of failure.

The "fuck this" event (FTE) is your first step into this hell.

And no, it won't be a leisurely stroll through a blooming wheat field with a triumphant Hans Zimmer melody orchestrating the background. Cigars won't be lit and champagne won't be popping. Instead, the "fuck this" event is a traumatic moment, epiphanic, and painful. It's a pejorative mental breakthrough, one that sounds like any of the following: "No more!" "I've had it!" or "I can't live like this!" The FTE smacks you when the pain of the status quo finally exceeds the anticipated pain of its escape—the point of no return where nothing else matters. If awareness was a slow boil leading to this book, the FTE is a sudden flash burn of WTFU and GTFO.

In a June 2014 essay penned for *Worth* magazine, Mohamed El-Erian explained his reasoning behind his resignation as CEO of the investment firm PIMCO. In his essay, he cited his daughter for the reason. When El-Erian asked his daughter why she wouldn't brush her teeth and do as told, she produced a list of twenty-two milestones her father missed due to his workload. From her first day at school to a first soccer match to a Halloween parade, the list was exhaustive, enough to cause El-Erian to rethink his priorities. He wrote, "Talk about a wake-up call... I felt awful and got defensive: I had a good excuse for each missed event! Travel, important meetings, an urgent phone call, sudden to-dos... But it dawned on me that I was missing an infinitely more important point."[26]

Unfortunately, and unlike Mr. El-Erian, your FTE won't be accompanied by a $100 million nest egg and a twenty-two-point list from your ten-year-old daughter but something more disruptive. Like a curt letter from human resources that euphemistically says, "Thank you for the last fifteen years, but your services are no longer required; security will escort you out of the building." The FTE could come from a rickety cot with a spring piercing your spine: you're stranded by weather at an airport thousands of miles away from home, a revelation that once again, your child lacks a father and your wife lacks a husband. And let's hope your FTE doesn't come from an oncologist's office: a negative biopsy, a relieved reminder that you have one life and it might be over quicker than expected.

While my "fuck this" event was more than twenty years ago, it forever seared my mind. I was twenty-six, four years removed from college and working as a chauffeur in Chicago. My workday started like the other six days before it. It was an ungodly hour for a morning drop at O'Hare Airport. This morning was worse. The client for tow was Ruth Stafford, an old leathery hag from the Hillary Clinton school of fashion—she wore the same burgundy floral pantsuit on every trip. I'd guess Ruth deployed this ensemble no matter the occasion. Funeral? Wedding? Jazzercise? Floral pantsuit. We nicknamed the perpetual-pantsuit lady "Ruth STIFFord" because she'd tip one dollar, regardless of conditions. Drive Ruth through a nuclear apocalypse or the eye of a hurricane and, well, enjoy your buck, kiddo. Throw in a heavy snow forecast and what's left is a grueling day foreshadowed.

Anyhow, twelve hours and hundreds of gridlocked miles later, I was still working. By nightfall, a steady snow turned into a blinding blizzard. After I delivered my last client home, I tried to do the same, but the blizzard had other ideas. Roads were closed. Visibility, spotty.

Frustrated, I pulled the limousine to the shoulder of the road and parked.

I faced myself in an eerie silence. Ashamed. Disquieted. Hopeless. My cold socks, damp from hauling luggage all day, heckled my anguish. The disheartening truth was clear: Wipe me from the face of the planet and no one outside family would care. I was a nobody. My two business degrees, a waste. My impressive college GPA, earned years earlier, didn't mean jack. My dead-end job was just a merry-go-round keeping the bills paid until next month.

As I sat there, dazed and deadened by the sullen rhythmic hum of the windshield wipers, I confessed: My life was a train wreck and I was sick of the failure in the mirror. I was sick of cursing the alarm clock at 4:00 a.m. I was sick of chauffeuring drunk bachelors, spoiled prom-brats, and corporate executives. I was sick of enduring cold winters and humid summers while watching my life rot away in traffic. I was sick of being outcasted by my friends as we had nothing left in common—they talked about their jobs, cars, and two-bedroom townhouses; I talked about my entrepreneurial dreams. I was sick of my life's movie—a movie that no one would want to watch—and despite my preparation, the *SCRIPT* was still camped in the director's chair.

And that's when I considered ending my life. And that's when everything changed. *Something* needed to change…and that something was me.

> ***FTE's are memorable and often unmistakable. If you are unsure of yours, more than likely you have not had one.***

FAKING "FUCK THIS"

As you're reading, you might be thinking, "I've already had my 'fuck this' event!"

If true, congratulations. Unfortunately, most people *think* they had a "fuck this" event but haven't. What really happened was a "fuck this" moment—a temporary, irritating slap to the face, but nothing forceful enough to get you off your ass.

It's like that old folktale about the lazy dog lying in a gas station. Day after day, the dog lies there whimpering and moaning. After hearing the dog whimper every visit, a customer asks the clerk, "Hey, what's wrong with the dog?" The clerk responds, "Oh, he's just lying on a nail and it hurts." Confused, the customer asks, "Then why doesn't he get up?" The clerk retorts, "I guess it just doesn't hurt bad enough."

The truth is, you will have many moments in life that seem like "fuck this" events, but they aren't. A fake FTE is temporary, sometimes lasting only hours, sometimes days. *A true FTE shifts interest to commitment.* It pummels excuses into submission. It's unbalancing where nothing else matters and priorities shift: Xboxes are thrown in the attic; cable TV is canceled; and credit cards are paid. You see, most people are "interested" in entrepreneurship, financial freedom, and success—but most never commit. Why? *It just doesn't hurt bad enough.*

There's only one way to tell the difference between a fake FTE and a real FTE. A fake FTE has four threats and any one of them will send you right back to the *SCRIPT.* A real FTE has no threats; to breathe or not to breathe isn't a conscious choice—it just happens.

THREAT #1: MEDIOCRE COMFORT

A real FTE doesn't care about mediocre comfort. *Give a man an OK job that pays just enough to provide mediocre comfort and I'll show you a man that will keep his job indefinitely.* This is by design.

In 1926, in an interview published by *World's Work* magazine, industrial titan Henry Ford confesses why he reduced his workers' labor load from six days and forty-eight hours to five days and forty hours, all while keeping pay the same. He said:

> It is the influence of leisure on consumption which makes the [five day workweek] so necessary. The people who consume the bulk of goods are the people who make them. That is a fact we must never forget, that is the secret of our prosperity.

He continued:

> The people with a 5-day week will consume more goods than the people with a 6-day week. People who have more leisure must have more clothes. They must have a greater variety of food. They must have more transportation facilities. They naturally must have more service of various kinds. This increased consumption will require greater production than we now have. Instead of business being slowed up because the people are 'off work', it will be speeded up... This will lead to more work. And this to more profits.[27]

Still accepted, the modern five-day, forty-hour workweek is a *SCRIPTED* tool for obedience, keeping you occupied, clothed, and fed, and it's just enough to keep weekends earmarked as a leisurely celebration officiated by consumption. As long as your head stays slightly above water, the weekend bribe continues while the red pill swirls around in your mouth like a Jolly Rancher.

I see this every day, and no, I'm not exaggerating. While my first book created some life-altering "fuck this" events for my readers, in all honesty, it also created many failed "fuck this" moments. Hit the "Introduction" section at TheFastlaneForum.com and you'll witness page after page of them.

- *I'm so excited to begin!*
- *In thirty days, I will post everything I've done!*
- *Good-bye job! Hello entrepreneur!*

And then, bam! Twenty-four hours later, they're gone, never heard from again. Their grandiose declaration, meaningless. Instead of a true *SCRIPTED* disconnection, they reconnect: back to their job, their existing paradigm, and their spectacular weekend. The problem is, these people *like* the idea of entrepreneurship as much as they like the idea of winning free money. But they don't honor the effort or expectation required to make it real. For example, I had a college buddy who always talked entrepreneurship. Let's call him Willie.

Willie gets a job helping him fund his entrepreneurial dreams—you know, so he can "pay bills" and meet his obligations. After getting a decent-paying job, Willie starts accumulating surplus cash. Instead of saving it or investing it into his business, he buys a new Jeep and a townhouse in a hot city district. The next thing you know, Willie is job-trapped, as it's needed to fund his lifestyle. From the moment of his first paycheck, mediocre comfort ensues, justified and entrapped by "I have responsibilities." Willie's entrepreneurial dreams pay the price. But hey, at least he has a nice Jeep with only forty-five payments remaining.

Translation #1? Willie is owned by his junk and the mediocre comfort it provides. He isn't willing to risk or sacrifice comfort in hopes of something better.

Translation #2? Willie doesn't need entrepreneurship as much as he needs comfort. And entrepreneurship doesn't need him.

Similarly, a lot of fathers on my forum expressed concern that their teenage children have zero interest in entrepreneurship. Even the teenage boy in my life isn't interested in entrepreneurship and it doesn't surprise me. Why? Because they haven't experienced a shitty boss, a shitty job, or a shitty commute. When you experience how much the system sucks firsthand, the desire appears. *Warning people about a hot fire doesn't work—they need to feel the burn for themselves.*

The problem in these instances is *mediocre comfort*—enough of it that it prevents you from getting up off the nail. The nice car, the regular paycheck, the fun weekend of football games—all of it keeps you at the poker table with the same strategy, the same bets, and the same cards. In the end, nothing changes but the passage of time. At some point, you have to decide: What's more important? Your *UNSCRIPTED* dreams? Or watching the Yankees third game on a ten-game home stand? Your long-term happiness? Or your drunken stupors at the lake on Saturday afternoon?

THREAT #2: YOUR GUARDED PRIDE AND EGO

A real FTE overcomes an insulated ego. I was a C-student in high school, but in college I earned two business degrees, won scholarships, and graduated near the top of my class. Despite such accolades, I was willing to do anything to make my entrepreneurial dreams happen. That included washing dishes, driving cabs, mopping floors, and flipping burgers. You see, I wasn't "too good" not to do the dirty work. My dreams were stronger than my pride and ego.

If you're "too cool" and fear what your friends and family might think because you're waiting tables down at the Applebee's, you're probably not cut from an entrepreneurial cloth.

I once tweeted that if you're not willing to take a minimum-wage job, you're not willing to be an entrepreneur. Entrepreneurs can go weeks, sometimes months, without getting paid. Are you willing to make that sacrifice? *If you aren't willing to work for the minimum, how can you expect to work for nothing?*

My forum is crammed with people too proud, too cool, and too good to work a shit job. Some are even too cool to get a real job. And you know what? These proud souls will never succeed as entrepreneurs, let alone get out of the gates of a *SCRIPTED* existence. Had I been "too cool" to run a limo company for an absentee owner, I would have never learned the inside scoop about the business leading to my first successful company. The plague of "too cool" was seen during Ashton Kutcher's acceptance speech at the 2013 Teen Choice Awards. He said:

> I believe that opportunity looks a lot like hard work... When I was thirteen, I had my first job with my dad carrying shingles up to the roof. And then I got a job washing dishes at a restaurant. And then I got a job in grocery store deli. And then I got a job in factory sweeping Cheerio dust off the ground. And I've never had a job in my life that I was better than. I was always just lucky to have a job. And every job that I had was a stepping stone to my next job, and I never quit my job until I had my next job. And so opportunities look a lot like work.[28]

Epic speech, no doubt.

Epic crowd reaction, not so much.

As Mr. Kutcher voiced this life wisdom, the crowd didn't care to hear it. No raucous applause. No standing ovation. The crowd of mostly teens, surely mesmerized by Ashton's hyper-personality, sandwiched his "hard work" speech with crickets. Chirp chirp. Of course being sexy and cool was met with screams and catcalls. Clearly our youngsters are more interested in "big breaks" and "overnight success" than they are about sweeping floors and washing dishes.

THREAT #3: I HAVE RESPONSIBILITY

Are you "in deep"?

"In deep" is a phrase I use when I hear someone deeply entrenched in *SCRIPTED* living. It refers to someone who is so overwhelmed with responsibility, debt, and consumption that *SCRIPTED* disconnection is nearly impossible. Their burdens have them paralyzed, and only a real FTE can change it.

For example, every so often during an interview, I'm asked if I have any advice for someone with four ex-wives, seventeen kids from six different women, nine credit cards, two new cars, and a bad job. Really? Not sure I have any advice, at least the type of advice you'd want to hear. How about keep your damn pants zipped? Quit buying shit with money you don't have? Make better choices? With such a *robust* personal resume, this person doesn't have a money problem—*he has a decision-making problem.* And until that changes, nothing will change, no matter what my advice is.

A real FTE burns bridges and forces change; a fake one does not.

The coldhearted fact is, the more responsibilities assumed, the stronger the *SCRIPTED* grip becomes. Responsibility can be the yoke of many things: car payments, student loans, credit cards, mortgages, alimony, children, and yes, even man's best friend, your dog Fluffy. I know this isn't popular, but I'm not here to balm chapped lips.

The Maricopa County Animal Control shelter in Phoenix is known as Slaughterhouse Central, routinely killing hundreds of animals every week because pet owners are morons. One of the most common reasons innocent dogs are surrendered and killed twenty-four hours later? We can't afford him. Duh, but I betcha can afford that iPhone 14, huh champ? Too many people go stupid blind when they see a cute snout, and suddenly they can't cognitively connect that dogs need feeding, training, grooming, walking, medicating, vaccinating, and toys. Nope, he's just so cute! And bam, thousands of sweet, adoptable pets end up at Animal Auschwitz, all because of rampant human stupidity.

My point is this: *Responsibility necessitates consumption.* Stack extemporaneous responsibility into life and consumption is mandated. And the *SCRIPT* loves consumption.

THREAT #4: FEAR

A real "fuck this" event fears nothing.

An epiphanic FTE understands that the world doesn't end when you lose your job. However, you'd never guess it by how many people remain in jobs they hate. Deep down, they are consumed by fear. Fear of the unknown, humiliation, failure, and gossiping friends. Fear of being left behind, driving a shitbox car and going without the latest. Fear of *Poltergeist* clowns. All unreasonable, overestimated, and fully incapacitating.

Whatever fear prevents commitment, ask yourself, "What's the worst that can happen?" And if it does, will it end your world? Is it life threatening? Will you go blind or lose a limb?

Underneath unreasonable fear is an unreasonable expectation of the consequences. Having to live with your parents for a few months isn't so bad. Working the fryer at Wendy's isn't a death warrant. Missing the latest episode of *The Walking Dead* is not the end of the world. You will survive.

AWAKENING THE DREAM

My dreams resurrected on a cold, blustery day, stranded on the shoulder of State Route 12. I can't explain what happened. Perhaps it was the suicidal thoughts or the trauma of hitting rock bottom.

Although I studied entrepreneurship for years, I didn't transform from *aspiring* to *being* until my "fuck this" event. Commitment swallowed interest. In my case, fear washed away. And mediocre comfort turned to pain. *I had enough of the nail.*

In the end, my FTE helped me see that I wasn't born a loser, but born a *chooser.* I was as I chose. That evening, I confessed every circumstance in my life—my job, my finances, my environment, my business failures—was simply threaded to my choices. From that day forward, I took responsibility. I started thinking about how I thought and how I chose.

Several months after my FTE, with no fear, I abandoned Chicago and moved across the country to Phoenix, Arizona. I traveled light: a mere $900, a rusty Buick, and a few personal belongings. I committed to entrepreneurial success and would do anything to make it happen.

And that limousine job would be the last job I ever had.

My last paycheck.

My last boss.

My last Monday through Friday.

In hindsight, awareness followed by a profound "fuck this" event marked an inauguration, the day my dreams rebirthed from a mathematical impossibility to a profound probability. (I detail my early entrepreneurial days in my first book, *The Millionaire Fastlane.*)

One of my haters recently accused me of "selling a dream." Gee, why are anonymous Internet geniuses living in attics so perceptive? As for "selling a dream," that's exactly what I'm doing.

You see, most people live their life while stalked by dark shadows, the rotting corpses of their dead dreams. Those shadows materialize early in life, usually right after your teachers, parents, or whoever told you, "That's not realistic." And then youthful dreams slowly decay into fairy-tales: winning the Powerball, getting discovered on *American Idol*, or winning some huge lawsuit because hot coffee spilled on your lap.

Want to know why everyone is so miserable?

The answer is simple: *they've given up.*

People who say, "He's selling a dream," don't have proxy to anything but their own mediocrity. It's like playing poker with transparent cards—the hand is dead by the flop, so why bother trying? Nope, just fold. Meanwhile, your life is big-blinded to the pot while everyone else plays for it.

Yes, mediocrity's vast cemetery of dead dreams loves company. And so do media companies, casinos, and state lottery coffers. What these fools can't see is that *pursuing the dream is the dream itself.* It's the process. The failures, trials, and tribulations. It's the self-growth, the self-awareness, and the self-discovery that occur during a dream pursuit. *To sell the dream is to awaken the dream—and once it's alive, you become alive.*

Some of the world's great entrepreneurs, inventors, and innovators live the *UNSCRIPTED* dream. A few plowing their passions into the world are Elon Musk, Lori Grenier, Bill Gates, Arnold Schwarzenegger, and Sylvester Stallone. A few others in history are Benjamin Franklin, Henry Ford, Sam Walton, and Ray Kroc. Heck, you could even say Jesus Christ was *UNSCRIPTED*. The common thread is these men broke the rules for their time. They didn't stick to the *SCRIPT* or cower to cultural norms and the Pharisees pushing them.

However, don't let the famous names and transcendent biographies scare you; you don't need to father a religion or be the richest man on the planet to *UNSCRIPT*. Once you have the formula, *UNSCRIPTION* can be anything minus the notoriety, and definitely minus the crucifixion. You won't need a start-up with $20 million in Series-A funding or an Instagram account with ten gazillion devout followers.

What you do need is better probabilities and a better system to fight the fight. While the *SCRIPTED* OS is the bear in battle, we have a secret weapon that can change our odds: The *UNSCRIPTED* Entrepreneurial Framework. Let's get to executing a change that changes results.

> ***An extraordinary life will require an extraordinary story. Whenever hardships, failures, and struggles are encountered, you are simply drafting the story.***

PART 4

THE ESCAPE...THE UNSCRIPTED ENTREPRENEURIAL FRAMEWORK

[3(B) ∩ (MP ∩ FE ∩ KE) ∩ 4(D)] / FTE

SOME ANGELS COME DRESSED IN BOARD-SHORTS AND FLIP-FLOPS.

PART 4: Author's Objective:

EXECUTION

Representing the bulk of the book, the objective is to give you the entrepreneurial blueprint for executing an *UNSCRIPTED* life, detailing both internal (mental) and external (actions) processes.

CHAPTER 15

THE UNSCRIPTED ENTREPRENEURIAL FRAMEWORK (TUNEF)

It is impossible to live without failing at something, unless you live so cautiously that you might as well not have lived at all, in which case you have failed by default.
~ J.K. Rowling, Author

WANT SUCCESS? STUDY FAILURE

In 2007, right before I sold my company for the second time, I started an entrepreneur forum focused on *real* entrepreneurship. And by *real* I mean businesses of innovation and creation—not "turnkey" businesses, such as selling network marketing crap or hawking Teespring shirts on Facebook.

For the next seven years, I dedicated my so-called retirement to breaking the scourge of mediocrity, do-nothingness, and entrepreneurial masturbation. During this time, I've seen thousands, perhaps millions, of wannabe entrepreneurs come and go. Most jubilantly proclaim independence from the nine-to-five only to disappear twenty-four hours later, surely back to their cubicle comforts, the hot video game, or some *TMZ* celebrity gossip.

Others stay for years and appear to walk the talk. Believers of their own delusions, they gibber about business, the newest motivational video or the latest IPO story.

But they never do anything.

They see, believe, and understand the theology, but *they don't live it.* Caught in a perpetual paralysis by analysis, these wanderers consume the forum like a drug, creating progress illusions, reading book after book, posting inspirational meme after meme, while accomplishing nothing.

Then there are the brave souls who act and document their failures, giving the community a great gift: we learn from their failings and accelerate our own learning curve. Because I interact weekly with thousands of entrepreneurs (and aspiring entrepreneurs) I have insight into their thinking and, more importantly, how they don't think. This is important with success because a survivor bias reigns supreme. Studying success isn't very helpful—*we should be studying failures.* Despite "paradigm shifts," most people still feel lost. Where do I start? What should I do? What do I learn? How do I find ideas? What this? What that?

So I challenged myself: If I could architect a master blueprint, something that would give entrepreneurs a distinct advantage for succeeding at life, liberty, and entrepreneurship, what would it be? After spending many years at my forum and in the *SCRIPTED* world, I identified five essential processes critical to *UNSCRIPTION* and creating an awe-inspiring life few dream of having. The *UNSCRIPTED* Entrepreneurial Framework, or (TUNEF), is the result.

THE UNSCRIPTED ENTREPRENEURIAL FRAMEWORK (TUNEF)

The *UNSCRIPTED* Entrepreneurial Framework, or (TUNEF) can be portrayed pictorially, mathematically, or chronologically. Whichever your preference, (TUNEF) is a five-phase progression of both thought and action, both uniting in a series of *macro-* and *micro-processes.*

Because entrepreneurship is a competitive sport, the framework provides an advantage over those who don't have it. The *UNSCRIPTED* framework is transparently impartial—it helps success, but it can also identify loci of failure. By paying attention for the last twenty-five years, I've reverse engineered hundreds, perhaps thousands, of entrepreneurial successes and failures. The framework underwrites all of them, including my own. If successful entrepreneurship had DNA, it would look like (TUNEF) under a microscope. And many of these successes aren't advertised in the trendy entrepreneur mags.

For example, there's Kevin Nguyen. Kevin owns a successful product-based eCommerce company. Some days he works three hours, some ten, some none. Despite his busy company, Kevin has globe trotted the world, from Antarctica to Iceland to Peru. Kevin's *UNSCRIPTED* abundance is travel. Six months out of the year, Kevin is on a plane to some exotic destination. You probably never heard about Kevin, but that doesn't change anything: He's perfectly *UNSCRIPTED*, despite being raised in an Asian family that demands *SCRIPT* allegiance from a STEM career. In 2013, Kevin bought his father a brand new Lexus. And now, Kevin's father is on board with his *UNSCRIPTED* lifestyle.

Then there's Steven VanCauwenbergh. Raised by a single mother, Steven's dream was simple: Escape the run-down and ragged one-bedroom apartment. The antiquated school system (which he struggled within) pressed him to learn a trade because he wasn't smart enough for college. Although Steven tried college, he dropped out to pursue entrepreneurship. For a few years, he stumbled around in several businesses before he came across the book *The Millionaire Fastlane*, which turned his life upside down. Focused on businesses with high entry barriers, Steven launched into action and acquired $5 million in rental properties and over 125 rental units. He sold two businesses, both for six-figure valuations. Now a multimillionaire, Steven has dived into more passionate pursuits, such as coaching, rehabbing, and authorship.

In other transformation, Dave Happe read *The Millionaire Fastlane* on the heels of a catastrophic business failure where his company was lost in a hostile takeover. For Dave, it clicked that if he could build a scalable business that wasn't lynched to his time, he could do whatever he wanted, including being location independent. Within a little over a year following the principles, Dave built a sustainable income where "time for money" was no longer required. In less than five years, Dave's security business exploded under an "unlimited income" dynamic. With a focus on proprietary products, by 2015 Dave and his family become location independent, financially free, and liberated from a *SCRIPTED* existence.

But again, these are just a few stories you'll never see plastered on the front page of some *SCRIPTED* news outlet. They're out there in shameless quantities.

There's Al Levi. Author of the *The 7-Power Contractor.* Al retired at 48 after systematizing his business so it could run on auto-pilot. Al explains the dream on his website, AppleseedBusiness.com/about:

> Today, I live most of the year in sunny Phoenix, overlooking a golf course. And when it gets too hot in Arizona, I head to my home in New York by the beautiful Atlantic Ocean. In short, my wife and I are living our dream. We kept our promise to each other – to retire from the rush of business before the age of 50, and then to help others do the same thing.

And then there are notable stories that might hit your news feed. Like Kurt Searvogel, the ultra-distance competitor who set a goal to bike every day of the year, a whopping 75,000 miles. As Kurt's story grabbed attention, a reoccurring question always appeared: How does he afford it and find the time? Kurt's response was from the *UNSCRIPTED* realm. He said:

> I am the owner of Applied Computer Solutions, Inc. Building a company into a very successful and profitable venture requires the ability to plan and execute as well as learning that recurring revenues are much more important than one-time sales. Owning the company also provides the needed income that is required to travel all over the USA to compete in ultracycling events.[29]

Make no mistake, famous or unknown, both groups share a personal anarchy: *They lead life; life is not leading them.*

THE UNSCRIPTED ENTREPRENEURIAL FRAMEWORK: DIGGING IN

According to renowned psychologist Abraham Maslow, self-actualization is a goal every human should aspire to. From Wikipedia, self-actualization is "Expressing one's creativity, quest for spiritual enlightenment, pursuit of knowledge, and the desire to give to society."[30] The *UNSCRIPTED* framework can help you discover your true purpose, giving you the freedom, the choice, and the money to do so, without the forbearance of *SCRIPTED* oppression. Frankly, this can be whatever you want. For me, it was writing. For you, it could be a life of politics, philanthropy, or continued entrepreneurship. The *UNSCRIPTED* Entrepreneurial Framework is defined via this 3D diagram:

THE UNSCRIPTED ENTREPRENEURIAL FRAMEWORK (TUNEF)

[3(B) ∩ (MP ∩ FE ∩ KE) ∩ 4(D)] / FTE

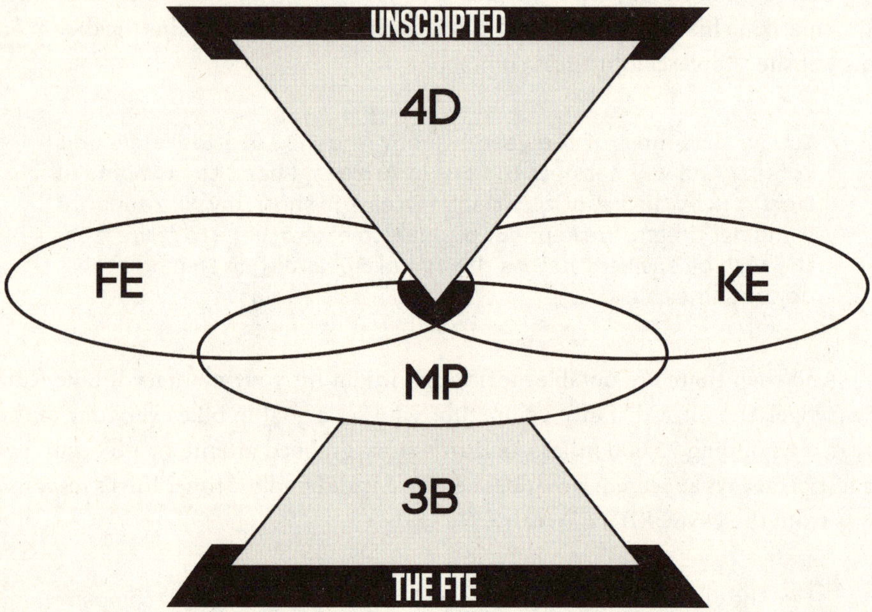

The base of the bottom triangle denotes your "fuck this" event (FTE) and launches the *UNSCRIPTED* process. Moving upward, each variable represents an *UNSCRIPTED* component. Atop your FTE, the upper triangle, 3(B)s, are beliefs, biases, and bullshit—the installation of a new mental architecture, which neutralizes the *SCRIPTED* OS. The three intersecting circles (the Venn diagram) represent entrepreneurship, containing three variable components: FE, MP, and KE. The top triangle, 4(D), represents the four *UNSCRIPTED* disciplines. The topmost part of the triangle constitutes the *UNSCRIPTED* afterlife—or self-actualization.

Defined by mathematics, the framework looks like this:

The UNSCRIPTED Framework = $[\,3(B) \cap (MP \cap FE \cap KE) \cap 4(D)\,] / FTE$

Or vocalized, "3(B) intersect (MP) intersect (FE) intersect (KE) intersect 4(D) divided by (FTE)." FTE is a Boolean value; it's either TRUE (1) or FALSE (0). Yeah, a fake (false) FTE creates a division by zero. Aside from giving mathematicians a conniption, it also invalidates the process. If you failed math, don't worry. This is as mathematical as we get. As for each variable, we will dive into each in the next chapters. For those who like things nice and orderly, (TUNEF) has a six-legged stair progression.

Result: ***UNSCRIPTION***
Step 6: 4(D)
Step 5: KE
Step 4: FE
Step 3: MP
Step 2: 3(B)
Step 1: FTE

WHERE LIFE CHANGES: THE ENTREPRENEURIAL G-SPOT

Regardless of the framework's presentational style, *UNSCRIPTION* occurs when all five shapes, the two triangles and the three circles, **intersect in the middle** and ascend toward self-actualized *UNSCRIPTION*. Hitting this five-point penta-intersection is figuratively the *entrepreneurial G-spot*—it's where life changes. It's where Sunday night no longer feels like Sunday night. It's where you wake up and have already made a day's wage. This is where you hit yourself over the head and ask, "Why the hell didn't I do this twenty years ago?"

I remember my *UNSCRIPTED* "G-spot" moment like it was yesterday. I just turned twenty-seven and it was one of the happiest days of my life. And get this: I lived poorly on a mattress in a tiny studio apartment. At the time, my business was growing. I created an in-demand web service and finally cracked a nut on finding customers. After walking to the bank and making a deposit, I walked outside. It was January and the weather on this sunny Arizona afternoon was stunning—warm with a gentle wind caressing the neighboring palms. Meanwhile 1,800 miles away in my hometown Chicago, it was just another dark day of snow, cold, and misery. I took a contented pause, thankful for my recent choice, and glanced at my bank receipt. It was over $8,000—more money than I'd ever known. Now I realize that $8K is not a lot of money; basically, it is bankrupt. However, at that moment in my life, it meant not having to get a job for at least another year. You see, *that $8,000 bought me one year of freedom*. Freedom to pursue my dream and what mattered to my heart and soul.

The truth is, the *UNSCRIPTED* dream begins NOT the day you retire or have millions in the bank, but the day you hit the entrepreneurial G-spot—the day when the *SCRIPT* retreats and you no longer exist, but live.

MICRO-PROCESS + MACRO-PROCESS = SUCCESS

Strip the *UNSCRIPTED* Entrepreneurial Framework naked and you'll find two processes fundamental to its execution: *micro-* and *macro-processes*. In general, a process is an action-series resulting in an outcome. For example, changing a blown tire is a process. Getting this book into your hands, another process.

The *micro-* and *macro-processes* scaffold the framework and grease the entrepreneurial G-spot, *UNSCRIPTED*'s birthplace.

The first subprocess is your *micro-process*. Your *micro-processes* are your thought patterns—your beliefs, biases, and your ability to self-reflect. It's how you think, feel, and interpret the world around you. For example, it's how you define money and *think* it's acquired. It's how you interpret luck and how you *think* it happens. It's what you *think* when you see a young kid driving a Ferrari. It's about how you look at your choices and their consequences, assuming you look at them at all.

Unfortunately, your brain and much of its *micro-processes* have been hardwired by the *SCRIPT*. Like an infection needing eradication, the *SCRIPT* has written your life rules, providing the mental architecture for autonomic behavior and knee-jerk thinking. As a result, we simply recycle old beliefs of parental or ancestral origin without giving thought to the whys behind them. Once wired together, what's left is a long list of lies engineering existence. Throw in a bunch of cognitive biases, proven psychological errors insulating the lies, and voilà—conventional living wrought by conventional wisdom.

The framework's second subprocess is a macro-process. *Macro-processes* are *repeated and modified actions*. The words "repeated" and "modified" are critical to results, changing the action from an event (a solitary action changing nothing) to a process (an action chain that changes everything). *Macro-processes* spin the wheel of cause-to-effect, effect-to-consequence, and consequence-to-change. Random, isolated actions are not macro-processes but impotent macro-events. The latter is ineffective at creating measurable change. *Effectiveness occurs only when macro-events become macro-processes.*

For example, want six-pack abs? Try working out at the gym once. Yeah, just once. As an action, one workout has ZERO effect on your appearance. It's a random macro-event. However, working out 290 times in the next year—the macro-process—will give you those abs. Unfortunately, when it comes to business strategy, many macro-events (and processes) are dynamic and change with time. What worked five years ago probably doesn't work today. When dealing with Internet time, we're talking six months.

Let me give you an example.

After my first book was released, a reader complained I left out an important detail: How did I grow from one hundred users a month to over 600,000? I omitted certain details because such details were no longer relevant as a macro-process. The macro-event was worthless. Seriously, does it help you knowing that I spent $4K a month at the LookSmart search engine? This search engine doesn't exist any longer. Heck, when I bought my company back after its first sale, "social media" wasn't a concept. Mark Zuckerberg was in high school fiddling with his Nintendo. The macro-process of scaling an Internet company is not the same as it was in 2003. Or in 2011. Or in 2015. Rules change. Playing fields evolve. This is why many "how-to" books are ineffective and largely a waste of time—the macro-processes mutate so fast that by the time they get into a book or an Internet marketer's latest scam program selling at $997, they're outdated and ineffective.

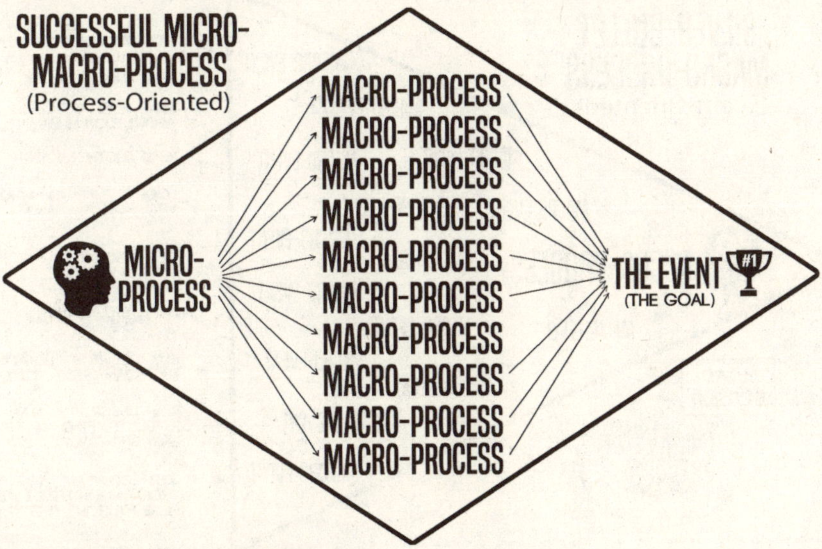

THE SILVER BULLET SYNDROME

One of the greatest travesties in self-improvement is this notion of the "silver bullet," a cherished macro-event—or "that one secret" that is error-proof, foolproof, and failure-proof. Scan the bad reviews for my books and you'll read a mélange of silver-bullet-syndrome responses.

- *MJ didn't give me the secret!*
- *MJ didn't tell me anything actionable!*
- *MJ didn't tell me exactly what to do, how, and where to do it!*
- *MJ didn't wipe my ass with scented wipes!*

Translation? I didn't deliver the king macro-event: *the silver bullet*. Specifically, these misguided souls are looking for one cherished macro-event delivering drive-thru success. The clear path and risk-free road. The color-by-numbers plan where the only thing needed is your box of crayons.

Such a macro-process does not exist, and it never will.

The reality is, most people like these fail, NOT because they lack the correct MACRO-processes but because they lack the correct MICRO-processes. A flawed micro-process materializes into the world as a flawed macro-process, hence making them macro-events—ineffective circle-jerking which doesn't build habits or change. This shot-gun splatter-like mentality then cascades into a system-wide failure barring the silver-bullet entrepreneur from goals and achievement.

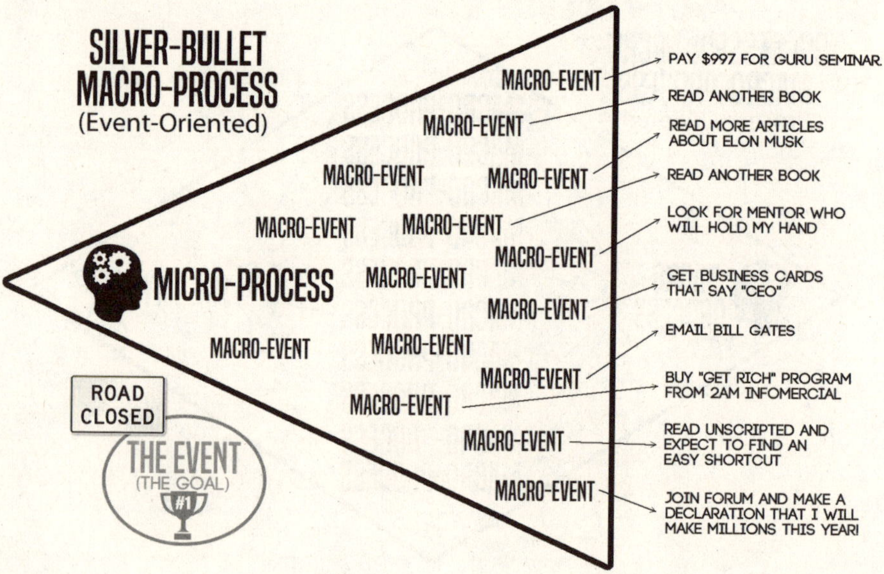

For example, engage the world thinking money is evil and all rich people have lied and cheated their way to wealth, and your actions will reflect such distortions, producing either inaction or no results at all. In other words, *your inside-self is defeating your outside-self.*

Rewritten micro-processes cause real change, so the macro-process can follow. Both are required, and (TUNEF) contains both. Additionally, I've made sure that all processes in this book are **transcendent**—their effectiveness today will equal their effectiveness ten years from now.

After your FTE, the next *UNSCRIPTED* step tackles your micro-processes—your 3(B)s: *beliefs*, *biases*, and *bullshit*. Change your head, change your results.

THE UNSCRIPTED ENTREPRENEURIAL FRAMEWORK

BELIEFS, BIASES, & BULLSHIT (3B)

[3(B) ∩ (MP ∩ FE ∩ KE) ∩ 4(D)] / FTE

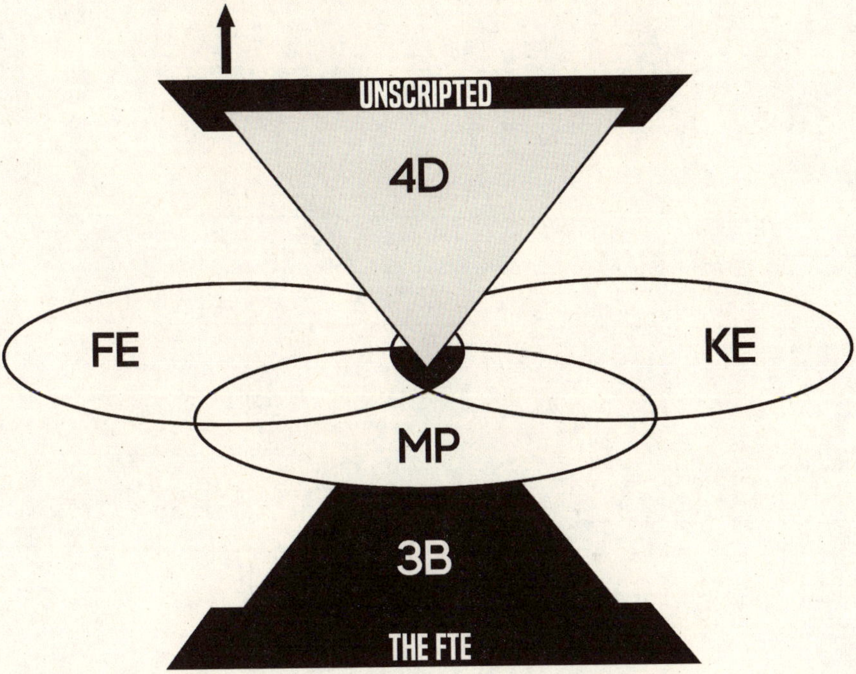

CHAPTER 16

OUR SELF-IMPOSED PRISON; BELIEFS, BIASES, AND BULLSHIT (3B)

Men are not prisoners of fate, but only prisoners of their own mind.
~ **Franklin Roosevelt, American President**

UNFUCKING WHAT'S BEEN FUCKING YOU

Despite almost forty years passing, I still remember my third-grade show-and-tell. Excited, I galloped to the front of the class. In my hands was a remote-controlled dune buggy with big tread tires and a cutesy flag poling its tailgate. I started my presentation by matter-of-factly stating my cool toy was a gift from Santa Claus.

Whoops.

Big mistake.

The classroom snorted laughter. In seconds, my suspicions were confirmed: Santa Claus wasn't real. And let's just say the rest of the third grade didn't go so well.

As you can see, grasping a wrong belief, a wayward bias, or a piece of bullshit can have consequences, even for an eight-year-old kid. Represented by the upper portion of the lower triangle within the *UNSCRIPTED* Entrepreneurial Framework, the 3(B)s are the mind maps driving—or derailing—your personal transformation. They are:

BELIEFS: What you think is true that necessarily isn't.

BIASES: Your mental shortcuts and default assumptions, either reaffirming or protecting your beliefs.

BULLSHIT: Your internalized narrative about why things are, or simply, the bullshit you sell yourself.

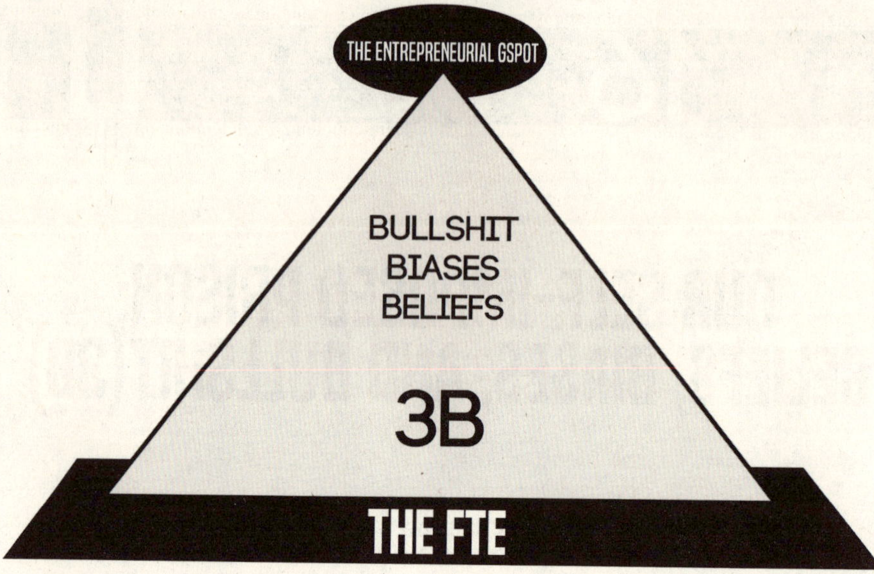

Many of us wander through life thinking we are architecting our will, living uniquely and brilliantly with purpose. But the truth is, we aren't. Behind the curtain, our brains are recycling impulsive and reflexive actions based on our preprogrammed 3(B)s. These beliefs, biases, and bullshit buoy the *SCRIPTED* OS telling us what to think, what to say, and what to do.

Life stuck in a rut? The 3(B)s are the shovels that dig. Trouble starting or finishing? Look to the ground—the 3(B)s are the trip wires. Until these rogue code blocks are reprogrammed, *UNSCRIPTED* pursuits are likened to road-tripping with four flat tires.

THE ENEMY WITHIN: YOUR BRAIN

I admit it. I'm a vitamin junkie. I think I've taken every fad fat-burner and muscle-builder out there. However, my madness is not about a shortcut; it's about leveraging the psychological power of my brain, otherwise known as the *placebo effect*. Ingesting the latest hot pill gives me the psychological edge of belief.

In my conversations with aspiring entrepreneurs, it's clear many dismiss their brainpower. Take for instance when I mentioned beliefs: I can guarantee many readers will skip this section. "Meh, not important—just tell me how to make money; give me exact steps."

The reality is, your brain is the battlefield for success, more so than any actions that come later. If your brain didn't skew results, why does the scientific method require placebos? *Your mind delivers a psychological impact—so impactful that it must be scientifically accounted.*

For example, try this experiment I learned in competitive sports. Stand up and look straight ahead. Extend your hand outward and point. Now swivel your torso to the left (or right) as far as you can go. Notice where your hand is pointing and landmark it. Now return to your normal standing position and close your eyes. Now *visualize* yourself swiveling back to the same position, except this time *see yourself* going farther. Visualize yourself swiveling with tremendous ease, limber and flexible. Do this for thirty-seconds. Now open your eyes and once again point forward and swivel. Voilà! You now should be able to swivel your body much farther than originally.

Your mind is understatedly powerful. In fact, I owe three orthopedic surgeries to this amazing power. By using visualization at the gym, I ably lifted staggering weight that guys twice my size couldn't lift. My brain's visualizations made these heavy lifts possible; however, after years of defying my small frame, my joints finally said, "No freaking more."

As you can see, belief's psychological impact doesn't correlate to truth or effective action. A falsely held belief is equally as powerful as one that is true. The difference, however, is what follows. A response imbued with a true belief is *actionable knowledge*. A response compelled by a false belief manifests as a mistake, an illusion, or an inaction. Sure I could believe and ultimately bench press 335, but my joints would eventually expose the truth. Exposing our beliefs as either truths or falsities clarifies whether our actions are based upon actionable knowledge or misperceived delusion.

Take for example the belief that your wife is trustworthy.

You might question this belief when, for the first time in years, your wife buys some sexy Victoria's Secret goodies. Suddenly you *suspect* she might be cheating, and the belief is questioned. This suspicion might not incite action, other than waiting to see if anything else fits your suspicions. Weeks, perhaps months, may pass.

Conversely, when you return home early from a business trip and catch her naked with Ricardo the pool man, you've moved from questionable belief, to actionable knowledge: She's cheating. Proof constitutes an immediate belief shift followed by action. Old belief: My wife is trustworthy. New belief: My wife cannot be trusted. Action: I want a divorce; I'm moving out; Ricardo, meet my fist.

Validated beliefs unveil truth, and truth is the best basis for decision-making. On the flip side, false beliefs do the opposite: they produce either inaction or errant action. In self-help circles, such lies are called "limiting beliefs." Under psychiatric diagnostic criteria, they aren't so kind—they're called "delusions."

For example, if you believe in Santa like I did, you might leave him cookies on Christmas Eve and hope your name isn't on his naughty list. Believe that broke blogger's advice that "do what you love" is the secret to success and you might fail twenty businesses. Believe that suicide is the doorway into an alien spacecraft tailing Comet Hale-Bopp and you might kill yourself like the thirty-nine believers of the Heaven's Gate cult did in 1997.

As you can see, delusional beliefs cause erroneous actions. But their consequences don't end there. Delusional beliefs also cause erroneous *inactions*. For example, if you believe "entrepreneurship is risky," you'll avoid starting a business. If you're a woman and believe "lifting weights makes you big," you'll avoid lifting weights. If you believe the Earth is flat, you'll avoid a Carnival cruise. Actually, no one should ever cruise Carnival, but that's another story. The point is, delusional beliefs cause both flawed action and inaction, spitting out one gigantic shitstorm of undesirable consequences. And sorry, because life isn't a book, turning the page isn't an option—you suffer the consequences.

Unfortunately, on your *UNSCRIPTED* quest, you'll battle many conspirators affirming your delusions and keeping your 3(B)s *SCRIPT* aligned. Until they're addressed, nothing changes. Simply put, *the road to "fuck you" starts with unfucking the things that are fucking you.*

Flawed premises yield flawed results.
Different results need different premises.

? ***If your brain was a separate person who spoke to you daily, would you label it a friend and an ally? Or a nay-saying enemy?***

CHAPTER 17

THE LIES WE BELIEVE: THE 8 BELIEF SCAMS

A man who wants to lead the orchestra
must turn his back to the crowd.
~ **Max Lucado, Clergyman and Author**

THREE MEN MAKE A TIGER

The Chinese proverb "three men make a tiger" refers to our ability to accept inaccurate, absurd, or irrelevant information as long as enough people repeat it. In effect, the crowd tells you how to think (and live), while critical thinking is shoved under the rug.

Reflect on your life's current circumstances and ask yourself, have "three men" put you here? Have "three men" smothered your life in debt? Have "three men" awarded you with an art history degree that can't get you a job? Have "three men" asked you to forsake five days of personal sovereignty for two? Have you surrendered to crowd-based conventions and now you're wondering, "Crap, is this all there is?"

Once again, the consensus fallacy underscores the "three men." When universal ideas are repeated and lived by the majority, they are rarely questioned. Has anyone really stopped and asked WHY we think and do what we do? Tradition? Because our teachers say so? Because Facebook made it a trending news story?

WHY are we indoctrinating our kids to follow the same path we've taken when that path has been a token failure?

WHY do people think trading time for money is the only way to make money?

WHY do parents force their kids into debt for the promise of jobs that might not exist?

WHY do couples rush to get married based on their age, not based on the quality of their relationship?

WHY do Republicans believe that unconstrained capitalism has no effect on the environment?

WHY do Democrats believe that success should be progressively penalized and that somehow it will translate into better-paying jobs? Why do they believe that government bureaucrats are virtuous and selfless, while the citizens they regulate are not?

WHY has your brain been co-opted by a political party, a church, a news outlet, a blog, a radio station, a Facebook group, or books translated by long-deceased conquerors?

You see, anytime you allow a homogeneous group to write your thoughts, you slowly poison free thought. For example, many of my readers have already boxed me into a category: MJ is one of these libertarian goons with a cache of guns! MJ is a corporatist! MJ this, MJ that! The truth is, if I disclosed my views on hot-button issues, such as religion, gay marriage, or environmentalism, your eyes would pop their sockets because no box fits me. Perhaps that makes me "independent"—but I call it someone who hasn't crowdsourced their thoughts to the likes of Jon Oliver and poorly written *Saturday Night Live* skits.

Behind our willingness to outsource thought sits our beliefs.

Beliefs are merely concepts, ideas, and thoughts that we regard as true. And no matter what your beliefs, there's an identical group who believes the same. 9/11 was a government conspiracy? You've got a group. Aliens living among us? You've got a group. While we are free to question and investigate our beliefs, few do. Instead, we seek to ratify them through a collective groupthink. And as a result, they escape critique and transcend, year after year, producing the same old results. Many times, these beliefs aren't our original thoughts but carbon-copy doctrine planted by seeders or co-opted from the crowds we identify with. In other cases, they are generational, passed from ancestry.

"Get a job, baby!"

That's my mom screaming up the stairs. She screeched at me weekly in a voice that could shatter windows and incapacitate an invading infantry. It was after college and I was still leeching off Mom while I struggled to find my entrepreneurial way. My mom was staunchly old-school and regularly hurled these "get a job" Hail Marys straight from the *SCRIPTED* play-book. For her, success was earned nine to five, Monday through Friday.

The point is, thank your parental seeder for some, if not all, of your crowdsourced beliefs. As children, we internalize the beliefs of those around us. If you come from a third-generation military family, you've probably adopted a military mindset. If your parents believe a particular religion, so do you. On my forum, countless young Asian adults complain about their demanding parents who unequivocally, without negotiation, insist they become an engineer or a doctor. The *SCRIPT* might as well be etched in stone.

Besides parental conditioning, crowdsourced beliefs also come from your usual gang of seeders: authority figures and communal associations, such as political parties and advocacy organizations. If your favorite actor endorses a particular politician or undertakes a noble crusade to save the dolphins, you will likely adopt a similar belief. If you're a Republican, it's blasphemy if Jim and Joe legally get married. If you're a Democrat, a proposed corporate tax cut feels like a pick-pocketing from Exxon Mobil.

And then there's the worst mind-controlling seeder for belief conscription: the media.

Through selective censorship and headlining the media tells you exactly what to think, when, where, and how much. That anti-gun state senator in California caught gunrunning for criminal gangs? Real story, but meh, not important—give it six-seconds. Miley Cyrus's tongue and her leotard jammed up her ass? Let's give it five minutes and the lede.

The media has morphed from respectable journalists into a pathetic tribe of useful idiots serving useless idiots, looking for the next hot headline—*SCRIPTED* goulash potted in propaganda, garnished in distraction, and flavored for obedience. Journalism isn't dead but "undead," where hyperrealistic red meat is grilled and then fed to an army of hungry zombies couched in their living rooms. As you can tell, turning this tide ain't gonna be easy.

The American media is mostly controlled by six large corporations whereas thirty years ago it was diversified among several dozen, thus, a handful of powerful executives control the media narrative for millions.

In the latter half of 2011, the media fermented the stench that was the Occupy Wall Street (OWS) movement. Founded by a Canadian anti-consumer and anti-corporate group, the movement's contentious issues were social and economic inequality caused by corruption, particularly corporatism, banking, and government. When I first heard of the movement, I was like, anti-Wall Street? Anti-consumption? These are *UNSCRIPTED* virtues; hell yeah, let me check it out!

Unfortunately, after looking deeper into their pet grievances, in my opinion it was nothing but a socialism orgy in a fecal-infested park, a pity party for the lazy, the unemployable, and the intellectually challenged. Of course, their issues weren't about economic inequality but about wealth redistribution and getting something for nothing. I earned a degree in medieval literature! Aren't I entitled to a $250,000 salary after graduation?

The sad thing about the Occupy movement is it had an opportunity to be special—a movement of *SCRIPT* awareness and rebellion. Instead, it's a gaggle of Marxist mouthpieces who failed economics and world history. And despite their ridiculous fairy-tale Christmas lists, the media erected them their very own bully pulpit cast in *SCRIPTED* gold.

Anyhow, OWS doesn't need more grease than I've given; however, one positive of the uprising is worth mentioning: They put "We are the 99 percent" into the national vernacular. Indeed you are. This cute little 99:1 ratio embodies an *UNSCRIPTED* truth: *Common 99 percent thinking won't get you uncommon 1 percent results.* Let the crowd do your thinking and you will indeed believe as the crowd and, unfortunately, find yourself with the results of the crowd. This systematic brainwashing is how mediocrity is born, lived, and then buried.

The uncomfortable truth is, our beliefs have been brushed and varnished for years by a brush we haven't owned. Like an antique chair that's been painted over and over, stripping the layers for a fresh coat isn't as easy as a book in one hand and a glass of Merlot in the other.

First, old beliefs must be questioned so inattentional blindness is eliminated. Once the seeds of distrust are planted, they can spawn virally, reprogramming old *SCRIPTED* ideas and thought processes, replacing them with new revelations and new ideas, hence generating new actions. And once the seeds root, your reticular activating system (RAS) will give you a helping hand.

Rewriting the *SCRIPTED* OS starts specifically by exposing, and then polarizing, its eight belief dichotomies. Specifically, when the world thinks WHITE, you're thinking BLACK. When the world is BUYING, you're SELLING. It's switching teams from the perennial loser, the 99 percent, to the perennial winner, the 1 percent. And yeah, its difficulty is likened to a lifelong Chicago Bears fan abruptly trashing his Ditka sweater and becoming a cheesehead Packer.

Like the *SCRIPTED* hyperrealities, the eight belief dichotomies are natively deceptive. In fact, I indict them as cold-blooded scams. Culturally engineered and universally foisted, the belief scams ritualize the *SCRIPTED* life paths (Slowlane/Sidewalk) producing 99 percent results aspired by none. Expose, then polarize, the belief dichotomies and suddenly your results can hobnob in the realm of the 1 percent.

CHAPTER 18

BELIEF #1

THE SHORTCUT SCAM: ORDINARY DOESN'T COMPEL EXTRAORDINARY

Little deeds are like little seeds, they grow to flowers or to weeds.
~ Daniel D. Palmer, Founder of Chiropractic

THE DICHOTOMY: EVENTS (99%) VS. PROCESS (1%)

During a sleepless night in 2015, I finally downloaded Words with Friends, the famous Scrabble-like game played by millions. Considering "words" are my current livelihood, I figured I'd give it a play. After suffering crushing loss after loss, something smelled rotten. My opponents seemed to be fluent in genetics, molecular biology, and PhD-level horticulture. Played against me were words like "amitoses," "auxins," and "zoea". After a quick search online, I found the stink's source: the game is filled with cheaters.

Turns out, there are multiple hacks giving *players,* and I use that term loosely, the best word to play given all options. After uncovering the scheme, I could only shake my head in disgust at my fellow humans.

I share this story because it typifies the laziness that plagues society, both mentally and physically. It typifies how the shortcut scam of the event/process belief dichotomy keeps mediocre lives mediocre while stifling accomplishment and personal growth. *The shortcut scam is the idea that extraordinary results can be achieved by uncovering a secret bypass or a miracle weapon, and such can skirt the real hard work that actually creates the extraordinary results.*

For example, most infomercials are predicated on the shortcut scam.

Busting out of your Calvins? Muffin top crying for mercy? No problem, here's a fat-suffocating girdle that can compress that huge gut of yours. Your friends will think you've lost twenty pounds overnight! Or better, why bother with corsets when there's the XL-960 Fat Shredder pill! Never mind the shitshow in the pantry headlined by a Costco-sized crate of Oreos. None of it is a match for XL-960 Fat Shredder! Hell, that stuff is endorsed by Dr. Shnoz!

And while we're on the subject, have you noticed that every year some diet guru is peddling some hot new "secret ingredient" that will magically reverse decades of nutritional neglect and make you a supermodel in just weeks? And then, once it's discovered it doesn't work and the fad dies, next year another super-ingredient appears. Coffee Bean! Garcinia Cambogia! Giraffe Urine!

The same game is played with success and financial independence. Just order my awesome new "Internet secrets" program for just three easy payments of $39.95, you'll be on your way to millions. But wait, there's more. Act now and you'll get a free website too! Once you fire up this templated plug-and-play website, the cash will roll in! But wait, there's more! Order today and you'll get one free month of secret access to our secret toll-free hotline with our secret coaching superstars. Oh, don't worry, these "coaches" aren't minimum-wage stiffs hired off the street. Nope, they're actual millionaires who have so much time on their hands that they're willing to sit in a call center eight hours a day fielding calls from the fools who believe it!

Oh, and my favorite shortcut scheme? It's pharmaceutical companies who aren't in the business of curing disease; they're in the business of obscuring symptoms. Heck, I've suffered through enough drug commercials that I'm thinking prescription drugs are the transformational secret from a sedentary existence into an action-packed life. Moderate to severe depression? Ask your doctor about *Axapraxacoris* and in no time you'll be mountain biking in Italy and zip-lining in Costa Rica! Side effects? Anal leakage, diarrhea, liver failure, heart palpitations, stroke, and sometimes death. Clearly the product works; guys who shit their pants and die horseback riding solve their depression.

Going back to my Word with Friends story, the implications of the shortcut scam are clear: My competitors weren't interested in improving game skills, vocabulary, or visual perceptions (the macro-process). Instead, the shortcut scam goaded them to install a cheat program so victory could be claimed without effort (the event), while simultaneously misrepresenting that they're brilliant.

Not surprising. As bees are to honey, so is the world's thirst for the shortcut. Look everywhere, Buzz Lightyear, the promise of shortcuts, shortcuts, shortcuts. That guru, the drug company, that financial planner, that plastic surgeon, the personal trainer—everyone claims to have the secret shortcut that will make you millions, snuff out that turkey neck, abolish that pregnancy weight, and make you an instant Casanova in bed. Just hand over your cash and the secret is yours.

We live in a microwave culture that demands fast results—not next week, not tomorrow, not after breakfast, but NOW. We want what we want, and we want it quick and easy.

The truth is, many folks reading this book are looking for a shortcut. And after they discover there is no shortcut perched on a silver platter, and instead hard work and late nights are required, they'll tweet to their seventeen followers that this book is crap. Boo hoo, MJ didn't give me the easy button!

EVENT IDEALISM: THE ROAD TO DISAPPOINTMENT

The shortcut scam's genesis comes from a culture that encourages and promotes *event idealism* while dismissing the *process-principle.* Event idealism is when your behavior is geared toward fabulous outcomes with a predisposition toward short-term gratification and quick results. It denies process, overlooking the necessity of daily rituals and habits and, instead, expects fantastic results effortlessly. Conversely, *the process-principle is an intelligent awareness that extraordinary results require an extraordinary effort consisting of daily habits, routines, and sacrifices.*

TLDR; To put it another way, the shortcut doesn't exist.

Everything in life can be analyzed by the event/process model. Its partnership is inseparable as cause and effect. Process slowly heats the cause while events boil the effects. For example, if you bake a soufflé, the recipe and the timed mixing of the ingredients are the process; the sight and smell of the finished product are the event. When Michael Phelps wins nine gold medals in the 2008 Olympics and consequently makes millions in endorsements afterwards, his triumphs are the **event**. Behind the wins was a grueling **process** that largely goes ignored: relentless, rigorous training and yearly sacrifices—the daily routines that make the event a possibility.

To the untrained brain set on an event idealism, processes that birth great events are largely dismissed and definitely not very interesting. Awakening at 4:00 a.m. and diving into an empty pool to swim laps? Meh. On the other hand, events grab headlines, herd eyeballs, and elicit talk around the watercooler. Gold medals? Endorsement deals worth millions? If only I could be so lucky to have such genetics! A twenty-eight-year-old entrepreneur who sold his company for $50 million is newsworthy; the fact that he drove a beat-up Civic and hadn't had a vacation in years is not.

The *UNSCRIPTED* understand that uncomfortable processes precede progress which causes the event. Without it, progress can't exist and the event never arrives. And whenever you try to circumvent that process, you become event-driven and vulnerable to shortcuts. And shortcuts cost you money.

Take for example diet pills. When you buy the latest diet fad pushed by the latest diet guru, cut the bullshit and admit what you're doing. You're trying to accelerate or buy fitness (the event) instead of suffering exercise and dietary change (the process).

When you finance a new Beemer for seventy-two months because you're cash short (the event), you're *buying* success instead of *earning* success (the process). Heck, if ya can't *be* rich now, perhaps you can *look* rich now? Two hours of nauseating negotiating, a signature on thirty pages of documents, and wham, success! Never mind your rocking new ride parked on your parents' driveway.

Another purveyor of an event modality is Hollywood, infecting young, impressionable minds with grandiose event-driven ilk. I could write a book on it, but for the sake of brevity, here's a few paragraphs.

A common plot device used by crappy screenwriters is *Deus Ex Machina*—or God from the Machine. This is where, seemingly from nowhere, an unsolvable problem or untenable situation is suddenly resolved by a weakly contrived and unexpected *event*. There's that word again implying quick and magical results.

When you're tied up and sentenced to death by Nazis, isn't it fortunate that the Ark of the Covenant spits fire and kills them all? Or how about Earth is getting annihilated by space aliens and they just happened to fail astrobiology, forgetting that bacterial decontamination is Space 101?

Oh, and there's the sappy "chick flicks." How many of them end with a spectacular wedding ceremony? *Hitch. Runaway Bride. The Wedding Singer.* The list is mountainous and I haven't even gotten into the new millennium. Anyhow, you know how the closing scene rolls: After a big epiphany that the two jilted lovers can't live without each other, a big wedding event is paraded; everyone smiles ear-to-ear while jubilantly dancing with a feel-good song strumming in the background. Bride and groom kiss at sunset. Onlookers cry and smile. Fade out with elevation. Story ends. The credits roll. Happily ever after. Or is it?

Hollywood marriage is the ultimate event idealism and molestation of the process-principle. In movies, marriage is always represented as a grand event. The expensive affair has spawned the term "bridezilla," which is code for a woman who believes a six-hour event shall be life's pinnacle, something headlining *TMZ* and stopping Earth from spinning. For the bridezilla who's seen the movies—*Pride and Prejudice*, and the 90,000 others—the wedding declares you and your partner have arrived, and happily ever after will be your gift. Just like Facebook, these movies present the sanitized version of marriage, the shared experience, the party—the event. Swept aside is the real process that must come afterwards: the compromise, the growing old together, and the hard work that marriage naturally requires of its partners—the process.

Of course, you don't see process. But what you do see are the credits rolling. Your mind fills the gaps and immediately resigns "happily ever after" as an event, not a process. Do nineteen-year-old bridezillas pissing their panties for a wedding know it's an hour-long event and a marriage is for life? A 50 percent divorce rate shouldn't shock anyone; without process, it's just two delusional people sharing expenses and suffocating under the shortcut scam.

The Hollywood-marriage plotline is one example of how the media subliminally frames us into event idealism and one that is destructive not only to marriage but to life. Events become the focus, and process becomes the proverbial redheaded stepchild. Event idealism is the secret to accomplishing nothing and failing at everything.

For example, another event-driven consequence evolving from shortcut thinking is what I call: "action-faking." Action-faking (as opposed to "action-taking") is when you take solitary and/or uncommitted action that is NOT a part of a bigger process. Instead, you're acting not to imbue real change but to "feel good" by momentarily fooling yourself about progress. Action-faking can be many things, from trivial busywork to data research to reading books—none of which coax progress. You might indeed act, maybe once or twice, but your actions aren't directly correlated to what moves the needle. Instead, we're tricking our brains into secreting a momentary dopamine high, fooling ourselves with progress illusions, when in truth, we're wasting time.

For the aspiring entrepreneur who wants to get rich, be his own boss, and blah blah blah, "action-faking" is ordering business cards from Vistaprint. Look at that, they say you're a CEO! Woo hoo, you're the head honcho of a zero-revenue, zero-customer, zero-asset company!

Action-faking event.

It's spending a fortune on office desks and equipment before you've landed your first customer. Wow, look at those mahogany desks! Imagine the deals going down there!

Action-faking event.

This type of entrepreneurial masturbation is jerking your meat, convincing yourself that you're "making progress" while the sad reality persists: you aren't any closer to finding the love of your life, finding a customer, or making a profit.

Do you lift? Ask anyone who works out regularly and they'll stinkface the affirmative: Januaries SUCK at the gym. Every January, gyms experience overcrowding as new faces storm in—event idealism "action-fakers"—New Year's Resolutioners who decide after X decades, this year is different! I'm getting in shape, losing weight, and changing! And bam, three weeks later, the gym is back to normal. Classic action-faking. In fact, anytime I hear someone say, "I'm on a diet," I want to throat-punch them and shout, "Action-faker!" The word "diet" implies temporary. It implies failure. It implies that whatever you're doing for three days or three weeks will NOT become habit or a part of your lifestyle. Diets die. Habits do not.

Real, permanent change does NOT come from event idealism or from shortcuts. It comes from a daily, regimented process woven into the fabric of your life, automatic and nearly instinctual.

EVENT-DRIVEN ENTREPRENEURSHIP: A FAILURE OF PROCESS

Unfortunately, wayward entrepreneurs with event modalities are the rule rather than the exception. Examine the poor reviews for this book, my last book, and any book relating to money or entrepreneurship. The common theme will be that the paint-by-numbers shortcut was not bibbed and spoon-fed into the entrepreneur's salivating mouth. And for those lost entrepreneurs, the search continues tirelessly, at least until their next job hunt.

For example, this is the type of frustration I feel when trying to open the eyes of event-idealized thinkers.

Wannabe Entrepreneur: I want those beautiful roses blooming across the river. Can you help me get them?

MJ: Sure, but learning to cross the river isn't easy or quick.

Wannabe Entrepreneur: Learning? Can't you just give me the roses?

MJ: Excuse me?

Wannabe Entrepreneur: You've already crossed the river; just give me your big boat; or better yet, just give me the roses.

MJ: Uhh…ever heard about learning to fish versus given a fish?

Wannabe Entrepreneur: Fishing? Rivers? I don't care about this stuff. My focus is on the roses. On Instagram people advertise their roses and I want them too, and I want them fast. What guru webinar should I join that will give me the exact steps?

MJ: *Sigh*. If you want the roses, you need to learn how to cross the river yourself. There aren't any shortcuts. I can give you the blueprint for crossing but you're going to need tools, hammers, wood, nails, and some other things, so you can build a system for crossing. It might take some time to find and learn these tools, but trust me, once you cross, the roses are incredible! It's worth the effort.

Wannabe Entrepreneur: This doesn't sound fun or easy, and it's not my passion. I want to do what I love. How about this ice cream cone I'm eating? I love it and I'm passionate about it. Will stuffing my face with it help me get the roses?

MJ: Huh? What does your ice cream have to do with the roses or the river that stops you from getting them?

Wannabe Entrepreneur: Mmmm…but I love this ice cream cone.

MJ: {furrows brow} Did you hear anything I just said?

Wannabe Entrepreneur: {looks up from his cone, face smothered in ice cream} So…can you give me your boat?

In this story, the roses are the event (success) and the raging river is the obstacle: sacrifices, struggles, and the failures (the process). The advice (the tools) given don't sound easy, fun, or quick, so the wannabe focuses on irrelevancies, namely, a continued search for the tasty event-driven shortcut (give me your boat, give me cash) underscored by love and passion. And finally, the ice cream cone is the action-fake—it feels good now; it doesn't help and is gone in minutes.

POLARIZER: THE PROCESS-PRINCIPLE

My first book took me three years to write. This one nearly three as well. In both cases, I had urges to quit. Multiple times. I'd write six chapters, read it, and end it in the shredder. I'd flail my hands in the air and whine like a baby because my perfectionist mind ruled: It sucks. Sometimes I'd pen my frustrations on my forum so everyone saw process is not easy. And each time the angst boiled, I set it aside and reaffirmed to myself that *if it was easy, it wouldn't be worth it.*

This is what happens when you vacate event idealism and adopt a process-principle. Frustration and angst, while felt, are squashed. Expectations adjusted from ease to challenge. Obstacles, expected and overcome. And most important… shit, while not quickly, gets done. Here are nine steps to help you moving toward the process side of the event/process dichotomy:

1. **Intelligent Awareness**
2. **Modify Expectations/Realign Difficulty**
3. **Identify and Visualize the Change Target**
4. **Apply Mathematics to the Goal**
5. **Segment Goal into Its Daily Action**
6. **Identify Threats to the Target**
7. **Identify the Right Battlefield**
8. **Attack Bad Habits with Inconvenience/Pain**
9. **Act until Echo**

STEP #1: INTELLIGENT AWARENESS TO NEUROLOGICAL DEFAULTS

Obviously, an "intelligent awareness" of event idealism isn't sweeping the nation. The diet and weight-loss industry is $60 billion strong.[31] The infomercial marketing business, $170 billion.[32] The automotive industry, ginormous, more than $1 trillion, accounting for a whopping 3.5 percent of the country's entire GNP (gross national product). Oh, and since you're reading this book, the self-improvement business, nearly $11 billion.[33]

The sad truth is your brain is not wired for process but for event-oriented shortcuts intended for efficiency. And it loves assumptions, basing everything on memories or past reference points. Without our brain's optimization features, we'd be no better than a goldfish swimming on instinct. But this mental efficiency has its exploitive drawbacks. For instance, magicians leverage our neural bias toward shortcuts and "fill in the blank" gap assumptions. Magic is all about attention and distraction, using our lazy brains and their cognitive shortcuts and algorithms against us. Unfortunately, that same neuroscience giving magicians power also gives the *SCRIPT* power through event-driven thinking, putting you on the perennial losing team. This neurological awareness is the first step toward a process modality.

For example, the best event/process model is our health because it reflects process preceding progression or regression. That beach babe with the guns of steel and flat stomach? Process, daily exercise and a disciplined diet entailing huge sacrifices. The visual result of a fit and healthy body is the event. Likewise, that fat dude I saw last week at the casino, who ate his way into a wheelchair and went back to the buffet six times, is morbidly obese via process: decades of sedentary living and poor dietary decisions. American fatness is a consequence of event idealism—an eating event feeds our addiction to feel good now, as opposed to the disciplined process of eating properly and feeling good later.

The next time you go grocery shopping, try *cart-creeping*—spying into other people's shopping carts. Pick any outlier—someone obese or someone fit. Match their food content in their carts with their body type. More than likely, they'll be a perfect match. This exercise gives you the ability to do the impossible: *you can witness a process before the process occurs.* By examining someone's food choices, you get a sneak peek into their eating habits for the next week. Spot a fit guy and he will have lean meats, vegetables, and raw, "close to nature" choices. The person who'd sink a small canoe will have highly processed and sugary foods: cookies, soda, chips, and whatever else "highs" their now. *Obesity is a dereliction of process, while fitness is a testament to it.* Health can't be shortcutted—bought, stolen, cheated, bribed, operated on—and it can't be injected. It must be earned. Indeed, we are walking advertisements for the event/process dichotomy.

STEP #2: MODIFY EXPECTATIONS AND REALIGN THE SOURCE OF DIFFICULTY

After awareness, the next step is realigning expectations: *extraordinary results demand extraordinary efforts.* That means give up the ghost and kill the shortcut search. Kill the idea that excellence can be accomplished with mediocre effort. The real difficulty is accepting there is no shortcut. Give up the assumptions about those who accomplish great things and that their results are automatically *Deus Ex Machina*, not process.

The fact is, people struggle with their goals because they refuse the process-principle. Jumping from one promised shortcut to another, their *difficulty is not related to process, but to the everlasting search for a shortcut that doesn't exist.*

I just can't lose any weight! Oh really? I've known you for two decades and you've never hit the gym or eaten properly. In other words, *you can't lose weight because you can't find the shortcut to lose weight.* No wonder it's so difficult! And the research proves America's thirst for shortcuts and process adversity. According to Marketdata Enterprises, roughly seventy-five million dieters admit being fickle and simply shift from fad to fad.[34]

Success is simpler than you think: ax the shortcut, honor the process-principle, and do the necessary work. Dump the diet pills, the fat girdle, and the fads; eat properly twenty meals out of twenty-one and get your ass to the gym, sprint, play tennis—for the love of God, do freaking something. And wham, you succeed.

STEP #3: IDENTIFY AND VISUALIZE THE CHANGE TARGET

What exactly do you want? Envision yourself time-shifting one year into the future at a New Year's Eve party. Envision yourself celebrating the year that was, the year that changed everything. Take a moment and reflect on the accomplishments you hope to celebrate. Did you win a fitness competition? Did you start a new business and double your income? Complete a full-length novel? Identify EXACTLY what you want to feel and see yourself there. *If you don't identify where you want to go, the road to get there stays hidden.*

STEP #4: APPLY MATHEMATICS TO THE GOAL

After envisioning how awesome your new year will be, attach a numerical figure to your goal. If "lose weight" is the goal, this would translate into "lose twenty-five pounds" or "get to 12 percent body fat." Likewise, if your goal is to "start a business," you would need to identify a numerical number, say sales, profits, or number of customers.

The mathematics of change are crucially important as ambiguous milestones cannot be measured and often are preludes for action-fakes. For instance, my gym once publicly posted the goals of some members. As I scoured over them, I'd guess two-thirds of them were subjective goals, such as "get healthy" or "feel better." If ambiguous statements delineate goals, you short-circuit the feedback loop because there is no measurement apparatus. You also bury the finish line.

STEP #5: IDENTIFY THE DAILY ACTION TARGET

After isolating the goal and quantifying it, break it down into its core "take-action" component, or what I call "the daily target." What daily routine will get you there? For example, if your objective is to write a novel, your daily target could be to write 500 words every day, or a minimum of two hours. If your objective is 12 percent body fat, your daily target would be to work out and/or eat no more than 2,000 calories. The important thing here is to isolate the macro-process that builds the habit. If your goal cannot be measured, use daily accounting. For example, if "get smarter" is a goal, the daily target could be to learn one new thing every day.

> ***Everything significant started insignificantly. Amazon started with one line of code; Harry Potter with one paragraph; McDonalds with one hamburger.***

STEP #6: IDENTIFY THREATS TO THE DAILY TARGET

What threatens your daily target? In order to hit your targets, identify what will stop you from achieving them. What impedes success and prevents real change? Success is more about what you need to STOP doing versus START doing. Are you spending five hours a day on Facebook playing the latest game? Are you jumping from one idea to the next with no focused action or plan? Does your ego require an expensive BMW—which then requires a sixty-hour-a-week, soul-sucking corporate job? The hardest part of the process-principle is repetition; *greatness is a lot of small things done daily.*

STEP #7: IDENTIFY THE PROPER BATTLEFIELDS

You can't build new habits without an intelligent awareness applied to the *proper battlefields*. Most people fight their wars on the wrong battlefield, resulting in loss after loss. If you only knew where to fight, you would have a fighting chance to create the change you want. If you want to lose fifty pounds, pinpoint where the battle is won and lost. Most would think the battle is fought in the kitchen. As you walk in, the battle begins:

- *OMG, don't eat that ice cream! Pick something else!*
- *Mmm, I'd love a cold Pepsi right about now...but I shouldn't.*
- *Those Cheetos are calling my name...but I should have the celery.*

Sorry, but you already lost before you entered the kitchen: *The battle isn't fought in the kitchen but at the grocery store.* The instant you put this crap in your shopping cart is the instant you lost the war. Likewise, if you're spending hours watching mindless reality television, the battle isn't on the couch with the remote control; it's on the telephone. Pick up the phone and cancel the freaking cable TV. Wage war on the wrong battlefield and you'll be armed with sticks and stones while regression fights with an AR-15.

STEP #8: ATTACK BAD HABITS WITH INCONVENIENCE AND/OR PAIN

Once battlegrounds are identified, you can attack your bad habits. How? By leveraging your natural human instinct to seek the path of least resistance. Put the shortcut scam in your corner by turning bad habits into a royal pain in the ass. Make them invasive. Inconvenient, and with no shortcuts.

In our refrigerator example, if you've won the war at the grocery store, you now have attached inconvenience to the bad habit. If you want ice cream, you've got to hop in your car, drive to the store, troll the grocery aisle, buy it, and drive home. Not super complicated, but certainly not super convenient. If you're trying to stop playing video games, pack up your Xbox console and sell it. Or throw it in the attic. Now if you want to play, you've got to climb a ceiling ladder and crawl through a dusty attic to unpack it, wire it up, and play.

STEP #9: ACT UNTIL ECHO

A process modality's final step transforms actions into habit. Whatever your goal, *act until echo.* Take disciplined action until a feedback loop kicks on. Vow to work until your first echo occurs and then—and only then—decide your next step. Do I continue? Adjust? Or stop?

Years ago, my college sweetheart left me for some big-shot ad executive who wore expensive suits and talked with a slithery tongue. Back then, I was lost and, let's just say, she deservedly needed to jump ship. Anyhow, to assuage my grief, I hit the gym for the first time in my life. The gym medicated my sorrows. While this distraction started as an action-fake, it later transformed into a process. By the time I was over the breakup, I experienced my first feedback echoes: I felt better and my gangly stick arms grew some apples. People commented on my subtle transformation, and the echo reinforced the activity from a temporary distraction into a process. Once your effort strikes echoes, it reaffirms your actions, becoming habit, sometimes addictive, and as automatic as brushing your teeth.

The point is, whatever the goal, work until you strike your first echo. And when that happens, notice how you feel. Once you get to that first echo, there's usually no going back. Even if it's marginal results, you empower yourself forward.

I recently heard a great analogy for this in Gary Keller's book, *The ONE Thing* (recommended read). The process-principle and its echoes can be visualized as a line of dominoes, where each sequential domino gets progressively larger. When you start, the very first domino knocked over is incredibly small. When it drops, nothing is felt or heard. However, its velocity is enough to knock over the next, slightly larger domino. That domino continues the progression, toppling the next larger one. As the dominoes get bigger and fall, suddenly you start hearing and feeling them drop. It's music to your ears, motivating you forward. The process continues until the last domino tumbles over, a gigantic domino symbolizing your goal—competing in a fitness competition, saving a million bucks, getting out of debt—and it started with a tiny, insignificant domino, which cascaded into incredible change velocity. And yet, the ascending dominoes perfectly illustrate why event-driven failures fail: They start at the biggest domino and are powerless to budge it. If they only saw that *it's the little things that cause the big things.*

CHAPTER 19

BELIEF #2

THE SPECIAL SCAM: "I'M NOT GOOD AT THAT"

To me, the function and duty of a quality human being is the sincere and honest development of one's potential.
~ **Bruce Lee, Martial Artist**

THE DICHOTOMY: FIXED (99%) VS. GROWTH (1%)

In 2004, at the age of twenty-seven, Josh Waitzkin won a world title in Tai Chi Chuan. He also went on to win thirteen national championships. Later, he'd become a championship coach, leading his team to several world titles. He's also a black belt in Brazilian jujitsu. If this is the first time you've heard about Mr. Waitzkin and his achievements, you might guess he was born with talent. Or that's he's been practicing martial arts ever since childhood.

In both cases, you'd be wrong.

Josh's accolades are indeed impressive. However, what's more impressive is that Josh's didn't start studying martial arts until he was twenty-one. And before that Mr. Waitzkin was, let's just say, more geek than athlete. He was the story behind the Hollywood movie *Finding Bobby Fischer*, as he was the only person to win consecutive chess championships: the National Primary, Elementary, Junior High, High School, US Cadet, and the US Closed Juniors.

Early in Josh's childhood, he was labeled "a prodigy," and one might argue he was. However, according to Josh, the greatest thing that ever happened to him was when he lost his first national chess championship. The defeat taught him about the psychological traps of definitive, fixed labels—such as "You are special" and "You are a prodigy"—and how they can create false impressions so that hard work suddenly becomes optional.

As he put it, "I had felt my mortality," and after the breakthrough, he would go on to dominate the scholastic chess scene for the next eight years.[35]

The point of this story demonstrates just how dangerous *the special scam* is, even to a world-class achiever. *The special scam is a double-edged belief that our innate talents are enough to accomplish our dreams—OR that our innate talents are immovable, fixed characteristics immune from improvement.* The special scam tells us hard work is optional because we're already awesome, or it's worthless because we can't change our skills. Either way, the special scam says, "I wasn't born with that kind of talent" or "I'm great; I don't need to improve." Both justify avoiding the grind of improvement.

Compliments of today's over-coddled and over-selfied culture salted by an anti-success and anti-competitive media, the special scam has granted us trophy kids: youngsters born rock stars, awarded trophies for no particular reason; participative prodigies worthy of a crown, a stage, and an audience. Sometimes trophy kids take the stage on *American Idol* as horrific singers, making for great laughs and ratings. Underneath these failed performances are delusional vocalists who have fallen for the special scam—they believed the counterfeit adulation showered upon them from prejudiced stakeholders: parents, siblings, and friends. And the next thing you know, Simon Cowell is grimacing and telling talentless crooners to pound sand.

Take Instagram, for instance. In my opinion, it's one gigantic shit-show of self-important narcissism. Some people have Instagram accounts with over 1,000 photos posted. The 1,000 photos are not what's impressively sad; it's that those photos are of themselves in various stages of flex, undress, partying, whatever. Narcissism is being damn kind; this is sickness. Clearly achievement's barometer nowadays is measured by how many likes and comments your margarita selfie receives. Me, me, me, as if anyone really cares.

The special scam also has created a vocal tribe of "Dunning-Krugers"—a psychological deficiency where incompetent people don't know they're incompetent because they can't distinguish between the two. Dunning-Krugers infest the internet, particularly in the comment sections wherever comments are allowed.

The other day, I read an article about celebrated entrepreneur Elon Musk, a businessman whose accomplishments put him in the 99.99 percentile. Unfortunately, I was in the mood for a little self-mutilation and mistakenly read the comments. A majority of them thought 99.99 just wasn't that impressive. Comment after comment criticized Musk, a virtual convention of armchair do-nothings who, unfortunately, have a platform to voice their stupid opinions founded on nothing but their ability to construct a sentence from their parents' basement.

Underneath the special scam lies the greatest destructive force to our dreams: a *fixed mindset. A fixed mindset is the belief that talent alone causes success and that your basic qualities of intelligence, athleticism, and even rhythm are fixed traits that cannot be changed or improved.* Ha, yes, rhythm!

In college, my dorm neighbor was a Puerto Rican kid who could hip-hop dance with the best of them. Anytime he showcased his moves, the dance floor parted like the Red Sea and it was an instant *Night at the Apollo*. Anyway, I started hanging out with my neighbor, going to clubs and dance raves. Slowly, I picked up his skills. He took notice and started guiding me. In a matter of months, I was dancing like him, parting my own Red Seas. If you're not impressed, you should be; I was a geeky, uncoordinated white kid from the suburbs. Soon we were dancing in Chicago's inner hoods and battling with the best of the best. Heck, every once in a while, we'd really live adventurously and pop into an Omega Psi Phi party. Anyhow, the demonstrative point of my hip-hop escapades is that *new skills can be acquired and mastered regardless of your current level of talent or intelligence.* And yet, had I suffered from a fixed mindset, I would have resigned to fixed statements of existence: "I can't dance and have no rhythm; I'm just a pasty white dude from the suburbs."

Fixed-mindset research has been well documented, studied, and proven.

Carol Dweck, PhD, is the leading researcher in the field of motivation at Stanford University and the pioneer behind the fixed-mindset discovery. Her book *Mindset: The New Psychology of Success* explores just how dangerous a fixed mindset is to personal growth, success, and even child development.

In one of her studies, Dweck and her colleagues gave fifth graders ten easy problems from a nonverbal IQ test. After completing the problems, the kids were given either of two types of praise: (1) fixed, intelligence praise, such as, "That's a really great score; you must be smart"; or (2) growth, effort praise, such as, "That's a really great score; you must have really worked hard."

Later in the experiment, the children were then given an opportunity to do another test of their choice, one described as easy, or one described as challenging. Their preference heavily swayed upon the type of praise they received prior. A whopping 67 percent of the intelligence-praised children opted for the easy test, while 92 percent of the effort-praised chose the challenging one.

Dweck goes on to explain how fixed-mindset praise can create an environment where students feel the need to prove intelligence while simultaneously avoiding risks or challenges. She explains, "As a result [of the fixed praise] they enter a fixed mindset, they play it safe in the future and limit the growth of their talent."[36]

Further in the experiment, the students were given an impossible test designed to incite failure. Once again, the fixed-mindset group performed statistically poorly against their effort-praised counterparts, becoming frustrated easily and giving up early. And lastly, each group was given one final test as easy as the first. These results proved costly as well to the fixed-mindset group: the average score dropped by 20 percent, while the average score of the effort-praised group increased by 30 percent, a staggering 50 percent difference.

Further testing also uncovered another unsettling outcome: Children who receive fixed praise view imperfections as shameful, so much so that the kids lied them away. Dweck admits, "What's so alarming is we took ordinary children and made them into liars, simply by telling them they were smart."[37]

These results were so profound it was tested six additional times, each yielding the same outcome. Furthermore, students praised with participation trophies and "you are special" affirmations don't do well later in education or in life. Their reaction toward challenge, equally disheartening. They readily admit cheating over studying. After failing, they simply look at someone else who did worse just to make themselves feel better. And in countless study after study, they flee from difficulty.[38]

Remember my brush with cheaters in the Words with Friends game? Take a look at the reviews for the cheating app allowing fixed-mindset types to flee from difficulty:

> I began using this app approximately one month ago and instantly became one of the top players in my lodge!

> All my friends seem to pretty much beat the pants off me. So having this app, or anything I can use to even up the odds, is something that really makes me happy.[39]

Yeah, these are actual reviews for the cheating application. Makes me wonder how much these players received fixed praise as children. Mommy said you're a genius. Teacher said you're special! And now that the real world exposed the lie, hearty challenges are not worth effort, and instead, cheating becomes cool. Notice the words used as well: "top players" and "even up the odds." Uh, no. You're not the top player and you didn't even up the odds—*you fucking cheated*.

People with fixed mindsets aren't spending time improving or developing their skills; instead, they're focused on proving, finding, or documenting their talent or intelligence. (Comments section, anyone?) And in many cases like my Words with Friends example, hiding their lack of it. Criticism, nonessential and rejected. Obstacles, avoided. In fact, when a fixed mindset is presented with an error, their brain activity is virtually dead, while the brains of those who thrive on challenge are on fire.[40] And the success of others? That's when you hear such blathering as "luck" or "he knew the right people."

The reality is, a fixed mindset is destroying our younger generation's ability to cope. Whatever they call it, "self-esteem building" builds nothing and instead cripples dreams, creating fragile buttercups who can't handle life's harsh realities. Such evidence took center stage after the 2016 presidential election of Donald Trump. After winning, thousands took the streets to whine, cry, and riot. Professors canceled exams. Nationwide, campuses offered students free counseling, therapy dogs, and Play-Doh.

Bruce Tulgan, the author of *Not Everyone Gets a Trophy* (recommended read) mentions the deficiencies of the millennial generation as seen by today's employers and recounts one employer's assessment who said: "It's very hard to give them negative feedback without crushing their egos…they walk in thinking they know more than they know."[41] Once they figure out that, nope, you're not special because you showed up—you're only special when you earn it—they're crushed.

POLARIZER: THE KAIZEN PRINCIPLE

I have a confession. I'm not interested in fame or the spotlight. I hate public speaking, interviews or whatever throws me on the public stage. I, by all definitions, am a hardcore introvert. And yet, despite my "hate" for these activities, I still do them. Why? Because I'm not very good at them. And to get better at them, I have to do them. And so it goes with a *growth mindset.*

While doing a gazillion podcasts won't turn me into an extrovert, they do help me improve. Extroversion and introversion have been proven to be genetically predisposed; however, how one reacts to the predisposition is where the coffee is perked. Had I been infected with a fixed mindset and the special scam, I wouldn't bother with interviews. Instead, I'd justify, "I'm an introvert and not good at those." Case closed.

However, how you approach your strengths and weaknesses comes down to your mindset. Do you accept your characteristics as facts, rigid constructs of existence, immovable and impervious to alteration? Or do you accept your weaknesses as malleable and open for improvement? Once you become aware that *neuroplasticity*—your brain's ability to form new neural connections—is possible, intelligence and skill no longer await just the victors of the genetic lottery.

We live in a spectacular time. The world's encyclopedic knowledge is accessible with a few simple keystrokes at Google. You can learn, discover, or find anything. For example, here's a comment by a former wage slave:

> After 5 years of college, I got a degree. Right out of the gate, I was at the top of my field, earning a solid mid 5-figure salary. There was no upward mobility. I did that for 3 years. With free info from the Internet and one $299 course, I learned everything I needed to know to make 3x that salary in a year and a half. In another 5 years, that meager college-degree salary will be so far in the rear view mirror that I won't even remember what life was like to make so little. The Internet has largely rendered college, and education in general, irrelevant. For those that want to learn anything, open your browser and get to it.[41a]

You see, you might not be the sharpest pencil in the box, but don't fret—you're surrounded by pencil sharpeners. *The world is already yours, but only if you're willing to go get it.*

> ***The web is rife with inexpensive learning institutions (Ex: Udemy, Code Academy, Lynda, Stanford Online) where new skills don't require cash; they require a growth mindset and a Kaizen commitment.***

A growth mindset is how Josh Waitzkin goes from a chess champion to a champion in martial arts. It's how I go from knowing nothing about programming to coding a web application. A growth mindset knows where challenge lies and accepts the Kaizen Principle (and the process-principle) as part of the build.

The Kaizen Principle is to endeavor to create tiny incremental improvements in your daily life with an aim for mastery over performance, while forsaking external comparisons, unless such comparisons inspire. The three key operands here are: 1) Tiny incremental improvements 2) mastery over performance and 3) external comparison.

First, the only concerning metric is YOU. Have you done something today, no matter how small, to improve whatever needs improving? Are you moving the needle or action-faking? *You are your only competition*, and the process-principle will drive that change.

Second, aim for mastery over performance: be the best at something YOU can be. It is 100 percent YOU-oriented and not centered on performance or competitive rankings. Mastery doesn't care about how you are judged by others. It's only about "getting better" (you) over "being better" (others).

And third, refrain from comparing yourself to others, especially rock stars in your field. If you're aiming to improve your fitness and finished your first month of training, it's probably not a good idea to compare your bikini body to some Instagram fitness model with three million followers. *Comparison is the path to perpetual misery.* There's always someone richer, faster, hotter, fitter, or whatever. And yeah, I also advise staying off Facebook so you're not comparing everyone's highlight reels to your daily rigor. That is unless it inspires you.

And lastly, don't believe your own press clippings. I get a ton of email thanking me: a life changed, a fortune being made, or a paradigm being smashed. It's flattering but an invitation to a fixed mindset. These raves could wallpaper my office, but ogling them implies, "I am successful" or "I've made it," and both suggest fixed permanence where I can sleep in, show up last, and leave first.

So, if Mom raves you're the best thing since sliced bread, don't believe it. If coach says you're the best quarterback he's trained since Drew Brees, thank him, smile, and ask, "How can I get better?" Through her breakthrough research, Carol Dweck has give us a defense to a fixed-mindset while promoting its antithesis: growth. Never praise talent or ability, either for yourself or for a child. Instead, praise the process-principle. Praise improvements, habits, growth, and efforts. Praise how far you've come, and one day, you'll praise your results.

CHAPTER 20

BELIEF #3

THE CONSUMPTION SCAM: HOW MUCH TIME DID THAT COST?

No society ever thrived because it had a large and growing class of parasites living off those who produce.
~ **Thomas Sowell, Economist**

THE DICHOTOMY: CONSUMER (99%) VS. PRODUCER (1%)

During a visit to the county landfill, I parked my truck in front of a junk heap and stared. As I meditated on the garbage piled as high as a demolished apartment building, it struck me that everything in this gigantic entangled mass was once new. State-of-the-art. An object of want. There were BBQ grills, bikes, toys, lawn furniture, stoves, picture frames, wine racks; it was a graveyard of past desires, a swollen scrap heap of residually accumulated consumption. Then I thought: Someone once opened their wallet, swiped a credit card, and bought this stuff. And now, here it lies as worthless junk, while its debt probably remains.

The consumerism hyperreality has consequences. Behind the debt and the landfill, those consequences are belied by *the consumer scam—a belief where consumerism is perceived exclusively interdependent of production*. That is, we rarely link our consumption to its equal or corresponding production necessity and the time it requires.

The consumer scam's cognitive disconnect starts as kids. As toddlers, we're programmed to attribute consumption with emotions, whether it's fun, happiness, or a particular status. Throughout the years, we badger our parents for toys and other playful things. Underneath these innocent desires an unfortunate neural connection builds: the idea that "stuff" can induce positive emotions without consequence. And because our parents pay the tab, such mental connections carry a destructive payload: *consumption and production are not correlated.*

In the classic film *A Christmas Story*, Ralphie is irrationally obsessed with a Red Ryder BB gun. For Ralphie, the gun represents many things: happiness, fulfillment, coming of age with responsibility, and even rejection of authority ("You'll shoot your eye out!"). Like Ralphie's lust for the BB gun, adults attach the same irrational zealousness to their wants. Buying this car will make me feel, "I've made it!" This purse gives me the feeling that I'm affluently refined and classy! While there's nothing wrong with aspiring to own a Porsche while adorned in Armani, what's ultimately lost in these wants is *production*. Specifically, what is the true cost of owning these things in terms of debt? Life rations? Will a cute four-bedroom suburban house with its thirty-year mortgage really take thirty years to pay off?

According to a study by Urban Institute, 35 percent of Americans are PAST DUE on some type of debt. More than one of three people not only owe money, but they are delinquent on what they owe. In fact, according to a survey conducted by CreditCards.com, more than 18 percent of those indebted expect to never pay it off.[42] Nope, they will carry it till death takes them underground.

Behind this American insanity lies the consumer scam—the notion that consumption is unabashedly unconditional with zero correlation to production. People live and work to consume today and think nothing of tomorrow.

In 2008, millions of homes sunk into foreclosure because buyers didn't give two-shits about buying a house they couldn't afford with money they didn't earn. Similarly, I see the consumer scam and its emotionally inflamed buyers commiserating on exotic car forums. Always worth a snicker, these folks max themselves financially by purchasing an expensive sports car and yet cannot afford routine maintenance, insurance, and gas. Uh, you didn't know a Lamborghini clutch is $12,000? Duh. But hey, at least everyone in traffic is fooled.

Oh, and the next time you feel inadequate driving your ten-year-old rust bucket while the sleek new Mustang speeds by, don't. Chances are that driver isn't as styling (or smart) as you think. *Nearly 85 percent of all cars on the road are financed.*[43] Yup, that Audi has a ridiculous car payment. Not only that, but the average loan now extends over sixty-five months—more than five years! Translation? People buy more car than they can afford. So the next time you're stuck in traffic surrounded by new cars, remember those numbers: 85 percent and 65 months. These aren't life's victors but victims of the consumer scam.

The *SCRIPTED* playbook is written in the language of consumerism and bound by alienating production. Grab a dollar and give it a stare. The difference between a lifetime of wage slavery or freedom is entangled in that little paper hyperreality and its relationship to its kissing cousin, consumption. The consumer scam is WHY the freeway is jammed with cars at 7:00 a.m. on a Monday morning. It is WHY people have no options. And it is WHY people are enslaved until death—at least until you stop being a consumer first, and a producer last.

The consumer scam's greatest impact is on the Sidewalk within the *SCRIPTED* OS. The distorted relationship between consumption and production is why some people, even the seemingly affluent, are one misstep from insolvency. Kanye West allegedly is $53 million in debt and is tweeting Mark Zuckerberg for handouts.

Rapper 50 Cent filed for bankruptcy. How are these rich celebrities going broke? The consumer scam, where consumption annihilates production. Big paychecks and huge business profits are no match for the consummate consumer; it wants every dime earned and, compliments of credit, more than every dime.

Think of it this way. *Debt, spending more than you earn, is consumption exceeding production.* It isn't money owed; it's a production deficit.

DEBT = PRODUCTION - CONSUMPTION

If you have a negative net worth of $500,000, you have effectively consumed $500,000 more value than produced. In lieu of the debt, you promise the debtor future production. This is why strapping yourself with six figures in college loans is dangerous. *Debt mandates the necessity of future work—even if you cannot find work.*

For example, Antoine Walker is an NBA basketball player who earned over $110 million during his ten-year career. And yet, even at that staggering production level, he couldn't outrun consumption. According to a story at Yahoo Finance, Antoine spent his millions on luxury estates for family members, exotic cars (Bentleys, Maybachs, BMWs), luxury gifts and vacations for his entourage, and even the best designer wardrobe money could buy. Geez, his consumption was so feckless he wouldn't wear the same designer suit twice. When the real-estate crash hit his investments, the party ended. With no safety net, Walker filed for bankruptcy in 2010. Over $110 million pissed away on *stuff*—the final tally was a negative $8 million in excess consumption.[44]

Sorry to say, but Mr. Walker earned like the 1 percent but spent like the 99 percent. He successfully produced in a skilled entertainment endeavor with fierce demand and yet had an insatiable thirst for consumption, one that consumed production itself. In the end, it cost him his NBA championship ring and, more importantly, his ability to live forever *UNSCRIPTED.*

Lottery winners and athletes who overspend and go broke is symptomatic to the underlying problem which is a SCRIPTED mindset anchored by CONSUMPTION.

The consumer scam bases its power on fluid spending. Ever notice that regardless of income, it's always barely enough to live? Earn an extra $500 next month, and it's blown: a new gadget, a few extra drinks, or whatever else fancies your soul. Spending what you earn, balancing the middle ground between producing and consuming (while saving nothing), is 99 percent thinking. A severe production imbalance is 1 percent thinking.

And then there are Sidewalkers who don't acknowledge production at all. For them, consumption and production is not balanced because production is hidden to them like it was in their childhood. Now as adults, these freeloaders produce nothing other than votes for power-hungry politicians. In their warped delusions, someone else should produce (work), covering their basic needs—food, shelter, drugs, cell phones, Internet, and health care—often arguing it's their "right" to such production, never once thinking a producer has to have their production confiscated (stolen) to enforce such "rights."

Which reminds me…a lot of people nowadays throw around the phrase "income inequality" as their pet political grievance, but know what I never hear about? "Production inequality," "work inequality," and "value inequality." Only in the American republic do we see hordes of voting-ready consumption warriors demanding unrequited access to consumption with zero production. What do these Trigglypuffing mouth-breathers give to the tax base? To the economy, society or jobs? Oh yeah—NOTHING, but a Twitterized delusion of self-importance.

Bottom line, by merely existing and breathing, we incur basic consumption needs. Rejecting this truth is rejecting adulthood. All adults must fight the war between production and consumption. Adults living as children aren't interested in this responsibility. They want their Red Ryder BB gun and they want it free, preferably wrapped with a cute little bow. Consumerism has no balanced middle; *you're either a consumer or a producer.* Or worse, you deny the paradigm altogether.

POLARIZER: PRODUCERISM

What consequences has the consumer scam and debt had on your life? Can you quit your job and pursue a dream? Has the daily grind negatively affected your health? Anytime you hear a "riches-to-rags" story like Antoine Walker, examine it from the consumer/producer dichotomy. Pay attention to how the consumption teeter can permanently disintegrate the production totter.

If I examined my life's freedoms, I owe it to one truth: I've rejected consumerism and hit the entrepreneurial G-spot by honoring production through *producerism.* Production steamrolls consumption. Disproportion over balance. And it's why I am debt-free. It's why I own my house free and clear. And it's why I own the most important thing of all: my time. I also enjoy substantial life luxuries because of producerism: owning any exotic car I want, dining at nice restaurants, getting good Cirque tickets, and flying first class. And yet my life is far from the scarcity suck-fest peddled in *Money* magazine.

Producerism respects the interlinked relationship between consumption and production. *If you want to live well, produce well.* The more production value you thrust into society, the bigger your house, the faster your car, and the juicier your steak. In other words, *stop looking to take and start looking to give.*

Like many *UNSCRIPTED* beliefs, producer reorientation requires a polarized shift. First, expect your entrepreneurial efforts to produce far beyond your consumption. In later chapters, I will show you how.

Second, a consumer-to-producer shift means behaving like one. That means:

- ✔ You lead the herd, not follow it.
- ✔ You pave new paths, not harden the already well-worn ones.
- ✔ You create and sell franchises, not buy them.
- ✔ You receive rents or royalties, not pay them.
- ✔ You lend, not borrow.
- ✔ You create and sell a brand; you're not buying the brand.
- ✔ You hire employees, not seek to be hired as one.
- ✔ You sell products on late-night infomercials; you're not buying them.
- ✔ You sell on Black Friday, not buying on Black Friday.

As a producer, everything turns upside down. Producers don't spend money on the latest hot trend; *they're inflaming and profiting from the latest hot trend.*

And finally, as a member of team producer, constantly put yourself in the shoes of a business owner. Watching an infomercial? Think about the process from idea to prototype to on the air. Did the commercial move you to buy? Did it irritate you? If you owned that product, what would you have done differently? The next time you buy something, pay attention to *why* you bought it. Was it the marketing copy creating an element of scarcity? The photos? The great reviews? Your interaction with customer service? Was the product delivered on a trial basis, showing value first, then you bought?

Producerism is being a lifelong student of production. Tune your RAS to see what everyone else cannot. And soon you will be doing what everyone else cannot.

> ***Effective producerism rarely evolves from trading your time for money, but instead manifests itself from investing your time into a scalable business system.***

> ***To consume richly—nice homes, luxury cars, world travel— you (and your business system) will need to equally produce as richly, if not more.***

CHAPTER 21

BELIEF #4

THE MONEY SCAM: I CAN GET RICH BY WANTING TO GET RICH

The value of a man should be seen in what he gives
and not in what he is able to receive.
~ **Albert Einstein, Physicist**

THE DICHOTOMY: MONEY (99%) VS. VALUE (1%)

Being broke sucks. I know, because I was for most of my early twenties. While my friends drove new cars and dressed new threads, I rolled in an old Buick Skylark while adorned in secondhand-thrift-shop fashion. Yeah, let's just say my dating life at the time was about as directionless as a politician's moral compass.

Anyhow, behind my lack of money definitely wasn't a lack of effort. I was motivated. Driven. And obsessed.

Unfortunately, I was obsessed about the wrong thing—and that thing was money. For me, it was everything. It symbolized freedom. Job liberation. Validation, self-worth, and social acceptance. And yet, despite my obsession, I had no clue what money represented, how it moved, why it existed, and how to get it.

Underneath my perpetual brokenness, *the money scam* was working—*a 99 percent thought line, where money is viewed as an elusive and mysterious concept, one that must be hunted, manipulated, cajoled, legislated, or pried away from someone else.* Money's pursuit is akin to a pig riding the proverbial donkey chasing a carrot on a stick—money is the carrot; the *SCRIPT* is the pig; the ass is you.

Whenever the money scam prevails, one becomes what I call a *money-chaser.* Money-chasers jump from one business idea to another, one job to another, one opportunity to another. Money-chasers view money tangibly like a sofa or a car, something that can be stalked like a tyrant aspiring for the emperor's throne.

As such, money-chasers are the "show-me-the-money" types who creep markets looking for quick cash, of course effortlessly and risk-free. These entrepreneurs step to the plate with one idea, strike out, and then quit. These couch-dreamers find hope in a late-night make-money infomercials featuring smiling millionaires camped on the beach with an open laptop because, after all, that's where all millionaires go once they hit it big. Others are found on "make-money-online" forums, asking generalities like:

- *What's a good business to start with fifteen dollars?*
- *How much money can I make selling black staplers on Amazon?*
- *How do I make $1 million dollars in the next six months?*
- *Can I make money trading the Forex market?*
- *What's an easy product to import from China?*

Inside these questions stinks the money scam. The lost entrepreneur sees money as prey, and they are the hunter. The money-chaser rummages behind every nook and cranny, searching for sunken treasure undiscovered by their 10,000 predecessors who just dived the same dive.

Remember, money is only a hyperreality. Just because you can see, touch, and smell it doesn't mean it's tangible, other than its paper form. The truth is, most of the world's money is represented *intangibly*: in pixelated numbers on a monitor, a number on a paper check or a bill, or a number represented by a ledger entry at a bank. If you have $5 million deposited at Bank of America, you cannot physically walk into the branch and withdraw it, at least not without substantial notice. In every six- or seven-figure transaction I've done, from selling houses to businesses, I never touched the money. A number simply moved from one party to another based on a mutually negotiated exchange.

So, before we remove the teeth from the money scam, here's a question: At its fundamental core, what is money to you? Something that buys stuff? A tool for power? A payment for work performed? While all of these things are uses of money, they don't define money itself.

Removing our cognitive hang-ups, what does money really represent?

If you've said production, you're wrong.

A medium to facilitate barter?

Nope, but getting closer.

Value?

Wrong again, but now you're getting hot.

Try this.

Assume you have something I want. Let's say it's an eighteenth-century gold statue, and I pay you $50,000 for it. In this exchange, we mutually agree and reach equilibrium: I value your statue at $50,000 and you value losing it at $50,000. The transaction mediator in this exchange is money. We agreed. No one was held at gunpoint and forced into the transaction. Money is not hunted, cajoled, or manipulated in the deal; it merely mediates and bridges the deal once equilibrium is reached.

Afterward and thanks to the money bridge, I get your statue and you get $50K; this stores the transaction value NOW so you can exchange it for something LATER. Let's say a week later you buy a new Cadillac for $50K. In essence, money bridged and stored our perceived value assessments between two vastly different items: I get a statue; you get a Cadillac or the "option" to buy a Cadillac.

However, here is where things get murky.

Let's say that during our sales negotiations, you represented the sculpture to be pure gold. After paying $50,000, I later discover the sculpture is not gold but bronze covered in cheap electroplate. I feel scammed. Why? Because you misrepresented value. *Perceived value did not translate into actual value.*

In response to this misrepresentation, I approach you (the seller) and ask for a $49,000 refund, since my *new* perceived value of the statue is only $1,000. You laugh and tell me to pound sand. I get in your grill and threaten you. You punch me in the noggin. I drop to the floor and the statue shatters to the ground in a hundred shards. As I pick up the pieces, frazzled by your unforeseen MMA skills, I notice a tiny black satchel among the debris—apparently molded within the statue was a satchel hidden for centuries. I open it and find what appears to be a huge crystal rock. Unfazed, I pocket the rock and leave bloody angry while cursing you a crook.

Next week, I have the crystal rock examined by a geologist. He tells me that it's a diamond and appraises it for $4 million. I call you and sneer a self-satisfied thank you. The punk gets punked.

Despite these swings in actual value, nothing changed with respect to the transaction because *money is just a transaction mediator where agreed perceived value is stored.*

Unfortunately, as demonstrated in our story, perceived value has a caveat: *actual value and its delivery sometimes don't match.* And that's an important distinction. Money's velocity is only predicated on *perceived* value, not *actual* value. When you sold me your gold statue, we agreed to $50,000 in perceived value. However, actual value fluctuated from $1,000 to $4 million.

If you're fired from a job which pays $50K per year, your employer has decided that your actual value is not matching the perceived value, your salary. While most world transactions amount to a fair exchange where perceived and actual value closely match, sometimes they do not.

So, imagine the lunacy of hunting something without knowing anything about your prey. It's like hunting stags by stapling Bambi photos to the trees. Most people are broke and remain broke because the money scam has made them perpetual chasers of something that cannot be chased—*it can only be attracted by offering perceived value.*

One of my favorite metaphors highlighting this disassociation is likened to a slippery cat scampering loose in the neighborhood. Money-chasers stalk the cat, hoping someday to catch it—around the bushes, up the tree, and in between the parked cars. That someday never comes. Meanwhile, the *UNSCRIPTED* ignore the cat and instead offer it something attractive. A cracked can of tuna later, and wham, that cat slinks in and leaps to your lap.

The money-chasing ideal is unfortunately (and disgustingly) common in the entrepreneurial subculture. Ask many aspiring entrepreneurs why they pursue entrepreneurship and you'll likely hear something about money, passive income, or world travel. I witness this several times per day.

At the end of my forum registration process, I ask: "Why are you joining our community?" The question comes with a warning: answers are evaluated, and fudged registrations are deleted. Despite the clear instructions, the most popular answer is simply "money." Other popular answers are "get rich or die trying," "want to own a Lambo!" "travel," and other inconsequential cringe-worthy shit. These responses expose money-chasing "dreampreneurs"—a class of wannabe entrepreneurs who somehow mistook starting a business with a ride on the Ferris wheel with a stick of cotton in one hand and a Slurpee in the other.

Lost in the money hunt is money's true nature. And it's something few talk about. *Money is stored perceived value* intangibly accounted, value that you have created, acquired, and communicated. In effect, *your net worth scoreboards how much perceived value you've created, communicated, and sold beyond your consumption of it.* Billionaires (or their heirs) have been privy to a massive value operation. And the actual paper? That's our universal agreement to transform the intangible number into the tangible. Throw in some fancy paper, ink, and dead presidents, and voilà, money!

Money doesn't have a brain but its possessors do. Therefore money responds indirectly to a value stimulus, but it also can hold biases and prejudices.

POLARIZER: THE VALUE-VOUCHER PRINCIPLE

Stop hunting money and start hunting value.

Money is not prey.

Instead, erase "money" from your vocabulary. Vow to never utter the word again. As a producer, start thinking of "money" as *value-vouchers—a store of perceived value produced, communicated, and delivered to the world.*

If your goal is ten million dollars, the new goal is ten million value-vouchers. And acquiring those ten million value-vouchers requires facing money's true nature. Be valuable. Wanted. Demanded.

Sadly, most live life polarized to money and wonder why they can't make any. The money scam's insanity is like focusing on a toaster to make toast—while ignoring the paramountcy of bread.

Picture it this way. Put two magnets together and how do they react? Either they *attract* or *repel*. The money scam and its money-chasers are polarized, where marketplace interactions are magnetically incongruent, creating repellent action. Ahh, the irony. Money's hot pursuit actually repels money. However, flip the magnet and forget about money and focus on value—and the magnets attract.

So how can you polarize the money scam and attract value-vouchers? First, understand how value-vouchers move. To HONORABLY attract value-vouchers, money bridges must be constructed with these four building blocks:

1. **Value (product/service creation)**
2. **Perceived value communicated to another party (marketing and messaging)**
3. **A mutual agreement, an equilibrium with that party (closing)**
4. **Actual value delivered (execution)**

Notice that word "honorably"?

I hope so, because *UNSCRIPTED* entrepreneurs aren't just focused on perceived value; we're focused on delivering **actual value**. Yes, there is a difference, and we'll get into that next. For now, possessing and executing on these four items is what attracts value-vouchers as well as a good night's sleep. Expecting money while spitting on value creation is like expecting jobs while spitting on business owners. Without value, you're sailing without a mast.

So, back to my forum and its registration process.

I recently ran an SQL query on the registration question, "Why are you joining?" Guess how many registrants mention "value"? Solving problems? Helping others? About fourteen of every thousand—and that's with many users who are students of my first book. Coincidentally, that's about 1 percent. The other 99 percent? They mention money or some other selfish motive. Getting rich. Fast cars and fast living. Freedom, travel, and other classic dreampreneur shit. Indeed, let the money scam be your axe in the money hunt and you won't get rich, but you will die trying.

CHAPTER 22

BELIEF #5

THE POVERTY SCAM: "I'M POOR BECAUSE YOU'RE RICH"

A life is not important except the impact it has on other lives.
~ **Jackie Robinson, Athlete**

THE DICHOTOMY: SELFISH (99%) VS. SELFLESS (1%)

I'm in Las Vegas at the Bacchanal Buffet in Caesars Palace, probably the best buffet in the world. Next to me is a man who must be tipping the scales at 400 bills. As I watch him waddle back and forth to the buffet, double-plated for the umpteenth time, I curse the man in my head: because this selfish ass can't stop stuffing his face, someone else on the planet is starving.

So…

What do you think of my heartless assertion?

Hopefully, you don't agree and think it's ridiculous. Hopefully, you know that obesity and overeating are not subject to binarism—a gluttonous human who can't put down the crab legs does not create one that is starved. To think otherwise is an absurdity that directly relates to our next belief scam, *the poverty scam.*

The poverty scam is the zero-sum belief that you are broke because someone else is rich. And of course, if you're rich, you're selfish. These associations are about as ridiculous as our big buffet man having a direct correlation to a child starving in Africa. Behind the poverty scam is a deviant belief that evolves from the money scam: when perceived value and actual value do not match, *the villain narrative* is born.

THE POVERTY SCAM'S VILLAIN NARRATIVE

As in our gold-statue transaction, whenever actual and perceived value do not match, the poverty scam sprouts wings. And left behind is the villain narrative.

The villain narrative is the belief that rich people (or corporations) are, by default, selfish, greedy, or untrustworthy. Inherent in the villain narrative is also the presumption that those who acquired wealth did so through subterfuge or fraud. Hence, you are poor because everything you buy is some type of theft.

With the villain narrative, money's relationship to value is erased and its mutualism stolen. Money no longer is a consensual agreement but a forced coercion. Gee, does that sound like taxation? Or being forced to buy health insurance? Listen to our intellectually gifted protesters over at Occupy Wall Street and you'll hear some variant of the villain narrative.

As demonstrated earlier, value-vouchers are moved by creating perceived value, not actual value. And unfortunately, the scammers know it. Behind every fraud, bad product, and dissatisfied customer, is an effective communication of perceived value that does not translate into actual value. When a diet pill promises six-pack abs in six weeks and it doesn't deliver, perceived value is sold, not actual value. You see, capitalist villains aren't dealing in actual value but perceived value because *they know perceived value makes money.*

For example, in the early twentieth century, Victor Lustig claimed to possess "money printing machines," which could create perfect copies of hundred-dollar bills every six hours. Despite the machine's slow output, Lustig's boxes commanded a tall price for the era, sometimes over $30,000. Herein lies the essence of perceived value and how all scams work. Lustig's boxes did indeed output hundred-dollar bills, but only two of them, and neither were copies, but merely placed there by Lustig to perpetuate the value illusion. After dispensing two real bills, blank paper came out. By the time the victim figured it out, Lustig was long gone, and $30,000 richer. The perceived value equilibrium was $30,000—the actual value was $200—and another villain was born.

Likewise, in the late twentieth century, it was common for unscrupulous stockbrokers to set up "boiler rooms" and sell worthless stock to unsuspecting investors. Many of these stockbrokers got rich because they could splendidly sell perceived value. These talented salespeople could sell horseshit to farmers, and many became rich, famous, even worshipped—and unfortunately, indicted.

Anyhow, I bring this up because the same phenomenon happens today, except it's not worthless stocks peddled, but worthless products sold via Internet marketing.

"BRO-Marketing" is a term I coined, which sums up the Internet marketing racket. Instead of boiler-room operations ("BRO") selling worthless stocks, we now have boiler rooms (or basements) selling worthless PDFs, marketing secrets, and whatever else can be packaged for $997 with a landing page, fake testimonials, and a countdown timer. BRO-marketing is huge—and it has corrupted entrepreneurship.

Many *entrepreneurs* are morally and ethically bribing their souls, persuading themselves that it's OK to sell worthless-shit products just because they make money. Using the usual tools of the trade—persuasive copy, click-bait headlines, trip wires, fake reviews, sales funnels, and the usual boiler-room mishmash—they believe their own apostasy, ignoring zero reorders, bad reviews, and terribly high refunds and chargebacks. You see, whenever you blow $2K for some generalized marketing advice you could find in a free white paper or ten-dollar book, you've been duped by a BRO-marketer selling perceived value.

In effect, scam artists, BRO-marketers, and other perceived-value hustlers still live by the money scam. And since they're focused on hunting money, they're willing to do ANYTHING for it—including deception, cheating, or worse, fraud. As a result, money-chasers graduate to *value-cheaters* who only play in perceived value's sandbox. Some are skilled at selling perceived value and, hence, Eskimos buy ice. Vegans buy steaks. And subsequently, the villain narrative wins another soldier leaving the *SCRIPTED* army thinking they're poor because these assholes get rich.

Here's another example that's very personal to me: In the summer of 2014, my forum was hitting record traffic, revenues and users. You'd think I was happy, right? Wrong. My forum was growing, but it was attracting the wrong entrepreneur: BRO-marketing value-cheaters who didn't care about actual value, only about perceived value. As these folks infiltrated my forum, the daily discussion morphed into stupid launch schemes, slick copywriting strategy, ethically challenged marketing, and marginally deceptive advertising. Product discussions that delivered actual value? Superior, selfless customer service? Meh, this didn't interest them.

In August of that same year, I exiled these individuals from my forum, prompting an exodus of like-minded thinkers. While my traffic suffered, my integrity didn't. For the *UNSCRIPTED, perceived value and actual value match*. And yes, marketing and copywriting are absolutely critical in the value chain. However, for capitalist villains, slick marketing steals wealth through value illusions, much like Mr. Lustig did decades ago.

THE VILLAIN NARRATIVE: HOLLYWOOD, POLITICS, AND CORPORATIONS

Ever notice the evil rich person is Hollywood's favorite archetype? The wealthy tycoon slots the villain role perfectly. Ballyhooed as some megalomaniac hell-bent on pillaging the common folk, this frequent personification happens as often as an Adam Sandler appearance in a pea-brained comedy no one watches.

In James Bond's *Diamonds Are Forever*, the megalomaniac wants to take over the world. In *Spiderman*, the eccentric millionaire skirmishes around town as the Green Goblin, causing chaos and destruction. In *It's a Wonderful Life*, warped, frustrated old man Potter wants to turn Bedford Falls into a mini Las Vegas. Other fictions portray successful businessmen willing to commit theft, fraud, and murder, all in exchange for profit and power. Movies and television are rife with corporate and capitalist villainy.

The Virginia-based Media Research Center documented this fact when they released a report detailing the results of researchers watching a whopping 863 sitcoms, dramas, and television movies broadcast over prime-time networks (ABC/

NBC/CBS/FOX). The researchers' findings? "Businesspeople tend to be portrayed as venal and unscrupulous," explains Tim Lamer, coauthor of *Businessmen Behaving Badly*. "They engage in criminal behavior. As a group, corporate types commit more murders on TV than any other occupational category—even career criminals."[45]

Aliens, Resident Evil, Avatar, and *Network* are all recent examples of seedy corporations or their henchmen doing evil deeds. In an article for *Politix*, movie critic Nell Minow agrees with the corporate villainization and those who run them. She explains, "The corporate bad guy in stories has been around as long as the corporation. One of the best-known characters in literature is Charles Dickens' Ebenezer Scrooge, a stingy moneylender without any vestige of kindness or compassion."[46] And yet, has it ever occurred to anyone that maybe the real persona behind an entrepreneur is not crusty Mr. Potter, but perhaps George Bailey?

The villain narrative, or class warfare, is also prevalent in politics and often determines who gets elected. Campaign demagogues know a winning candidate is the politician who successfully paints the villain narrative against his opponent, while minimizing it for himself. Democrats successfully used the villain narrative against Mitt Romney, portraying him as a ravenous capitalist working for the evil private-equity company Bain Capital. Comments from his wife about owning a horse and its expenditures sealed his defeat.

Political class warfare is a *SCRIPTED* tool for obedience. According to OpenSecrets.org, the average net worth of a congressman, Democrat or Republican, is about $10 million. Remove the Senate Democrats from the calculation and the average falls to about $7 million. If you believe that rich people are evil and you're broke because of them, look no further than Washington, DC. The political game being played is just another *SCRIPTED* trick: Engorge the peasantry that money is evil and those who have it, have acquired it nefariously. (But never mind us wholesome folks over here on Capitol Hill because we're working for you.) Don't be a chump; politicians and their media henchman are not your friends. Think they are and whip out the Wahl; you're about to be sheared.

Another villain-narrative confirmation comes from publicly traded companies operating as capitalist villains. Personally, I have no love for Monsanto, Comcast, McDonald's, and the other corporate monoliths who seemingly don't care about their customers. You see, once a corporation goes public, something dramatic eventually happens—it shifts priorities and causes the value equation to flip to a value-cheating villain. Customers are no longer the corporation's number-one stakeholder, *it shifts to stockholders*. And what do stockholders want? Rising share prices by way of profit.

Whoa, look at that—suddenly value creation and happy customers become casualties to the primary motive: money. That frothy, feel-good corporate mission statement on the wall? It morphs to bullshit window-dressing where it now says, "Our organizational mission is to appease shareholders, squeezing every dollar out of our customers so we can meet or beat Wall Street's consensus earning estimates."

This is the Wall Street reality, which translates into a well-deserved reputation of corporate greed. Tie in the politicians and the lobbyists, and it becomes crony capitalism. Furthering the perception, anytime a money-chaser cheats value and is exposed for fraud or poor business practices (people like Madoff, Rothstein, Pearlman, or corporate leadership like Koslowski, Ebbers, Lay), it makes headlines, ruffling feathers and tarring perceptions. Defrauded investors, cheated customers, and unsavory business practices herd eyeballs; entrepreneurs living with integrity do not.

While I don't deny corporate misdeeds and stakeholder abandonment, they aren't the prevailing majority for small business. For every negative story grabbing headlines and spotlighting the villain narrative, there's a buried bag of positive stories you'll never read about.

The masses confirm the villain narrative every time a business cheats value. This Green Tea Fat Burner doesn't work! This expensive real-estate seminar is just a big upsell into a more expensive seminar! That politician promised me free health care! Sorry, *you're poor because you keep buying shit you shouldn't buy—including fantasies that don't exist.*

In aggregate, these overt messages obscure the money hyperreality and darken its shadow to some murky apparition ready to smother its victims into poverty. Value, erased. Solutions, solved but forgotten. The end result is the poverty scam: "Income inequality! I'm poor because that dude's rich! Give me my poster board so I can protest!" Find yourself believing such dualistic nonsense ratified by the villain narrative and, sorry, enjoy your tent in Zuccotti Park while you "Feel the Bern."

The real truth eviscerated underneath the political campaign slogans, the subliminal plot narratives, and the bureaucratic henchmen seeking to destroy jobs, lives, and rain forests isn't so vile. Unfortunately, that truth doesn't sell movie tickets or cause protesters to take to the streets with homemade posters shouting about CEO pay.

That truth is this: Everything great in society has happened because money moved massively due to massive value creation and delivery—and yes, this created rich people. Without wealth, you'd be transported back to the dark ages, where you'd shit in an outhouse, burn candles for light, and use pigeons to send letters to your nana in Akron.

Money doesn't escape your wallet because there's a gun to your head (unless it's the gun of the government); you buy because you perceive value, enough of it that it compels you to say, "Yes, here's my cash; give me what you have."

POLARIZER: THE FIDUCIARY PRINCIPLE

Imagine a world where you needed to crap in a bucket, haul it outside to the woods, and dump it in a hole you had to dig the week earlier. Imagine a world where that same bucket is used later to catch rainwater so you have *clean* drinking water.

Wherever you are, right now, take a look around you.

I'm sitting at Starbucks. The aroma of ground coffee fills the air, while a holiday song spirits the background. Outside, the temperature hovers in the fifties, which by Arizona standards, might as well be absolute zero. Inside, as I type away at my six-year-old laptop while drinking my mocha latte, it's a balmy seventy-five. My iPhone, which rests nearby, shows it's 3:43 p.m., which means I have seventeen minutes left to finish this chapter before driving to the gym. Instead, I ignore my self-imposed deadline and pause from my writing.

As I look around me in total comfort and convenience, I am overwhelmed with gratitude and humility, not just to God, the universe, or whoever else is running the show, *but to rich people.*

GASP! What?

A careful reflection yields a humbling truth: Every single thing in your life was once invented and created by someone, or by someone executing on a corporate initiative. Yes, every comfort, convenience, and functionality you now enjoy was once someone's idea. Someone's work, dream, or passion. And now you benefit from that output. Just examine my snapshotted Starbucks moment, a mere blip in time:

- My old laptop, which still surprisingly works...Bill Gates and a boatload of millionaires at Microsoft
- My writing platform, Scrivener...Keith Burkholder
- My research at Google...Sergey Brin, Larry Page, and another crew of rich people
- My iPhone, which keeps me organized and scheduled...Steve Jobs and a slew of other rich people
- My Facebook newsfeed...Mark Zuckerberg and a lot of other rich people
- My yummy coffee and comfortable writing respite...Howard Schultz and the original Starbucks founders, Jerry Baldwin, Zev Siegl, and Gordon Bowker
- The electricity powering the coffee grinders, the lights, and the heat providing comfort...Thomas Edison, George Westinghouse, Nikola Tesla (although he died poor)
- My progressive glasses allowing me to see the great things surrounding me...Benjamin Franklin, followed by Owen Aves and Carl Zeiss
- My durable, comfortable jeans...Levi Strauss
- My upcoming workout at Lifetime Fitness...Bahram Akradi
- My fifteen-minute drive to my upcoming workout, which would have taken two hours by foot and twenty minutes by bike... George Selden (patent), the Ford family for making it mainstream
- My ears, inspirited by the holiday music orchestrating in the background...Josh Groban

Everywhere I go, I'm thankful these artists, inventors, and entrepreneurs have enriched my life with ease, comfort, security, personal growth, and even entertainment. *Every one of them deserves to be rich.*

So the next time you're on the throne with diarrhea and you can press a lever having that miserable stink miraculously disappear into nowheresville, be happy someone, somewhere, is rich because of that convenience. The next time you order pizza and your pizza's cardboard box isn't sagging into the cheese because of that cute little plastic tripod, be happy that Carmela Vitale invented the Pizza Saver, and be happy that Carmela is rich. The fact is, these people and their corporations have become fiduciaries to society's advancement—creating things making our lives easier and more enjoyable. And therein lies our polarizing principle that reverses the poverty scam: *the fiduciary principle—a resolution that as UNSCRIPTED entrepreneurs we will serve selflessly to serve the selfish.* A thorny challenge indeed. As humans, we are born selfish, and such selfishness is human nature. However, going against our human nature explains why so few succeed at providing value: *we're too preoccupied with what WE want; we can't see what OTHERS want.*

For example, there's an old folktale demonstrating just how selfishness blinds us to opportunity. It goes like this:

> There once lived an old man who had a wish. He prayed to God that before he died he would get the chance to see the difference between heaven and hell. One night an angel appeared before the old man's bed and granted his wish. The angel blindfolded the man and spoke: "First you shall see hell."
>
> The old man felt a momentary weightlessness and then the angel removed the blindfold. The old man found himself standing in a boundless dining hall filled with large, rounded tables, ornate with gold. Each table was piled high with the most delicious of foods: fruits, vegetables, breads, cheeses, meats, desserts—everything you can imagine was there and exquisitely prepared. The man salivated at the sight as the intoxicating aromas filled his nose.
>
> However, the old man noticed everyone seated at the dining tables was sickly with gaunt, morose faces seared with frustration. Each diner held a long spoon. These spoons must have been over three feet long. While the people cursed to hell could reach any tasty food they wanted, they could not get the food into their mouths because the spoons were too long. The hell-dwellers were in a constant state of torment, starved and desperate to taste what was just inches away. Sickened, the old man cried, "Please stop—take me to heaven!"

And so the man was blindfolded again. "Now you will see heaven," the angel said. After a familiar weightlessness, the blindfold was removed. The old man was confused. It was like he never left. He was once again in a great dining hall with the same round tables piled high with the same culinary lavishness. And just like hell, he saw these people also had long spoons preventing them from feeding themselves. However, as the old man looked closer, he noticed that the people in this dining hall were plumply vivacious and smiling; laughter and cheer filled the air. As he panned through the hall and processed the joyous sounds, the difference between heaven and hell finally struck him: The people in heaven were using those long spoons to feed each other.

Whenever our selfish blockheadedness is cast aside (even temporarily) and we focus on the selfishness of others, we become fiduciaries, and suddenly the value of long spoons is evident.

As a fiduciary, resolve to be a societal asset, advancing its ease and enjoyment. Resolve to be treated how you want to be treated. Put customers as kings in the stakeholder chain, being trustworthy and honorable to a standard that squashes the villain narrative. A fiduciary mindset is selfless, where an external exploration of needs and problems becomes clear.

The real truth is hit when the poverty scam is polarized (and the money scam): Great value precedes great wealth. *If you want to make millions, impact millions.* Become a worthwhile fiduciary to your fellow man and you will stop being worthless. Or we can suffer through another millennial idiot protesting corporatism, whereas afterward, he snapped an Instagram selfie wearing Nikes, hopped into the Prius his parents bought him, drove to Starbucks and bought a latte, and logged into his Facebook from his iPhone on a Comcast 5MB Internet connection, all while being smugly ignorant that everything in this entitled twit's life was delivered by capitalism.

How we manage our selfishness determines if we operate our business within the gray area of value-cheating or the sunny skies of value-providing.

Your relationship with money is defined by one of the three monetary identities: 1) money-chasing, 2) value-cheating, or 3) value-vouchering. Which is it?

CHAPTER 23

BELIEF #6

THE LUCK SCAM: YOU DON'T PLAY; YOU DON'T WIN

I believe in luck: how else can you explain
the success of those you dislike?
~ Jean Cocteau, Director

THE DICHOTOMY: LUCK (99%) VS. PROBABILITY (1%)

Luck. Behind the superstitious creed for losers, do-nothings, and dreamers is *the luck scam—the belief that life's outcomes, both positive and negative, are primarily dependent on fluke randomness.* If not randomness, a bipolar fairy dosed on Prozac oversees the luck of the universe, a mystic arbiter who at a moment's whim decides who receives fortune and who receives coal.

While I don't pay attention to my haters, every so often I stumble across their drivel. Cast from the Sidewalk, the common theme in their hallucinogenic opinions is luck. MJ got lucky! And you know what? *They are right.*

In fact, I've been experiencing this strange "luck" phenomenon for over twenty years.

For instance, I was lucky when *I chose* to study when in college as opposed to getting trashed every weekend like my peers. I was lucky when *I chose* not to get a corporate job after college and instead focused on entrepreneurship. I was lucky when *I chose* to start, and then fail, in the supplement business, the jewelry business, and the mortgage business. I was lucky when *I chose* to start, and then fail, in four network marketing schemes. I was lucky when *I chose* to stick to my entrepreneurial dreams despite three more business failures thereafter. I was lucky when *I chose* to swallow my ego and suffer jobs more appropriate for a high school dropout: delivering pizza, flowers, and newspapers, all while my buddies had cushy corporate jobs. I was lucky when *I chose* to work as a limousine chauffeur because, just maybe, I'd like to own a limo business someday. I was lucky when *I chose* to read books every day about emerging Internet technologies while camped out at airports, weddings, and drinking holes. I was lucky when *I chose* to do something after I spotted a need in the limo business. I was lucky when *I chose* to work on that business every day instead of partying or getting lost in *Seinfeld* reruns. I was lucky when *I chose* to win a negotiation for a great domain URL back when premium domains were being sold for six and seven figures. I got lucky when *I chose* to sell my company, in 2001, to a Silicon Valley start-up. I got lucky when *I chose* to repurchase my company at a fire-sale valuation during the dot-com implosion, reasoning that the financials outweighed the irrational fear smothering the markets. I got lucky when *I chose* to not only survive the dot-com crash but to thrive. I got lucky when *I chose* to explode profits while minimizing expenses and employee overhead, enjoying sixty-plus months of consecutive profitability, mostly seven figures per annum. I got lucky when *I chose* to save most of my earnings into safe, inflation-beating assets instead of investing it into risky assets touted by the mainstream. I was lucky when *I chose* to sell real estate right before the real-estate market crashed, despite everyone—including the National Association of Realtors—saying, "Now is the time to buy." I got lucky when *I chose* to sell my company (again), in 2007, to a private-equity company for a multimillion-dollar valuation. I got lucky when *I chose* to create a forum dedicated to entrepreneurship, one enjoying nearly one million page views per month because, you know, building a huge community is as simple as popping a pill—download the software and bam: traffic, users, and engagement.

I can go on and on for another five pages about selling millions of dollars in books, investment decisions, health choices, and more. But hopefully you noticed a trend in my rant, and it wasn't a lucky hot streak: *I got lucky when I chose, then acted*. And then continued to act.

If you believe you're unlucky, I have no doubt—you are. Instead of seeing action interacting with immeasurable probability, you see a cosmic genie levering a luck spigot. You are continuously unlucky if you do not *move probability* in your favor. In fact, luck's mysticism is another hyperreality, a shadow seen as real when statistical probability casts the shadow. The keyword in this oh-so-dismissed concept of moving probability? *You must move it*. You must choose, act, and repeat. Ahh, the process-principle peeks in. Again.

So, making sure we're on the same page, when I say "luck," I'm not referring to people born with a "bad hand." If you think that's you, I'm sorry; it probably isn't. A bad hand is being born in a third-world country without education, sanitation, or clean water. A bad hand is being born in a tyrannical land where you'd be thrown in a gulag for reading *UNSCRIPTED*. A bad hand is being born with a debilitating disease like cystic fibrosis or cerebral palsy. The sad fact is most people think they've been dealt a bad hand when they've been given one of the best hands in the world. If you popped out of Mom in America or another industrialized republic, congratulations; you have pocket kings.

If you're reading this book, you're relatively wealthy by world standards. You probably have multiple televisions, shoes, electronic devices as well as more than one shirt for the week. If you had the means to buy this book (thank you) or steal it (thief), both reflect a great hand. You have freedom to choose. You can see, read, and surf. And the ultimate tell: You're not starving or homeless because you can pursue self-actualization through a book. See, you're one lucky bastard, just like me.

TESTING YOUR LUCK

To diffuse the cloud that shadows luck, try this experiment. And be honest. Call a coin flip. Winner wins a smile and pat on the back. Ready?

((((((((((((FLIP))))))))))))

It's tails.

Did you call it correctly? If so, take a moment and think about your accurate prediction. Would you now label yourself as "lucky"? Or if you called it incorrectly, do you suddenly consider yourself unlucky? Probably neither because you know the probability: coin flips are fifty-fifty chances of losing or winning.

Now let's switch gears.

What if a correct coin flip call would win $10 million? Suddenly the outcome might be considered luck simply because the attached outcome is significant. And yet the flipping odds or the mathematics never change. What changes? *Your perception.* In its purity, this is the essence of probability. When life's chaos diffuses into outcomes, probability becomes clouded and superstitious explanations become likely.

Let's take it further.

What if you had TEN chances to correctly call one coin flip to win the ten million? Would you keep flipping? Or stop and reason, "Eh, I'm just not lucky." You see, moving probability is about trying. Hitting heads on one coin flip is 50 percent, but ten flips moves the probability to 99.4 percent. That means, just because no one shared or commented on the great blog article you wrote doesn't mean the game ends. Just because your invention didn't get funding or the 2Gs blown on Facebook ads sold nothing, doesn't mean dig your grave. *Keep freaking flipping!*

The luck scam cripples your personal power. Motivation becomes anemic. Believe in some mythic karmic force operating against your will and it will beat you into bullshit excuses. Seriously, why try if you're the unluckiest person alive? When that happens, probability is not moved, and yeah, you fail to be lucky.

University of Hertfordshire psychologist Richard Wiseman, author of *59 Seconds* (recommended read) and the founder of the "luck school," has studied luck for years. He says, "Unlucky people have almost no insight into the real causes of their good and bad luck, their thoughts and behavior are responsible for much of their fortune." Explaining further, he says, "Luck—bad or good—is just what you call the results of a human being consciously interacting with chance, and some people are better at interacting with chance than others."[47] So how do you move the probabilities? You change your statistical universe.

LIFE'S GUMBALL MACHINE

Here's how to change your luck.

First, picture a row of large gumball machines. Each machine has 1,000 gumballs of four assorted colors: white, orange, red, and gold, each varying in their colored consistency. A cursory examination of each gumball machine reveals mostly white and orange gumballs; while some machines have many reds and no golds, others have few reds and many golds.

These gumball machines represent a life path, and the colored gumballs represent the potential outcomes and consequences of that life path. When you choose a life path (or wander through life), you're assigned a machine and their corresponding variation of colored gumballs. To receive a gumball, a coin is deposited and the dial turned. This deposit and turn is *action*—the effort that spins the wheels of chance.

Once a coin is deposited, a gumball magically pops out. The gumball is a consequence, a reaction, or an echo of your effort. After doing this several times, you notice the gumballs spit out are mostly white, with a few oranges. A white gumball simply means nothing, like an ineffectual macro-event. Your effort yielded no results, consequences, or feedback. No harm done. However, the orange gumballs represent some type of feedback, either as a learning experience, a caution, a failure, or even a warning. The orange gumballs often have cryptic messages etched on them, giving you more clues for your next spin.

Most of my life has been filled with orange and white gumballs. An orange gumball told me it was time to sell real estate in 2006, sell my company in 2007, and write another book in 2015. And then, every once in a while, a red gumball pops out and messes everything up. Red is a catastrophic consequence, such as a bankruptcy, an accident, or even getting caught driving intoxicated.

As you continue depositing effort into the machine, eventually it happens. *A rare gold gumball pops out.* Congratulations, that's when you hit it big: the event from the process-principle! Success, fame, or fortune! And when it happens, life's

SCRIPTED couch warriors will accuse you of being giftedly lucky. Of course, none of them witnessed your prior mis-spins and failed efforts or your skilled decoding of orange balls. Once the starry-eyed see gold, it's just "luck"!

Our life circumstances and their consequences are like this four-colored gumball machine. Right now, you have a machine. Question is, what are its contents? Is it filled with too many reds? Is your chance at hitting a gold one in 1,000? Or perhaps it's zero?

A Sidewalker's machine has no golds, many whites and oranges, and frankly, too many reds. Treading the Slowlane? Similar outcome pool: Mostly whites, some oranges, many reds, and few golds. Stock-market crash? Red. Lost your job? Red. Laid off? Red. Health suffering because of too much work and too little pay? Red.

Within the *UNSCRIPTED* 3(B)s, *our objective is to change your gumball machine's contents.* A Slowlane or Sidewalk existence cranks for mostly everything but gold. If life's best-case scenario is a 2 percent pay raise, well, enjoy the celebration dinner at Red Lobster. The fact is, many people work harder than I do—the problem isn't their work ethic; it's their gumball machine. An *UNSCRIPTED* pursuit modifies this universe: reds disappear and golds sneak in.

POLARIZER: THE PROBABILITY PRINCIPLE

The probability-principle replaces luck by modifying behavior on five fronts. The first two behaviors acknowledge the causal effect of your gumball machine.

First, change your universe. Play games with better odds and returns without accepting more risk. Your career path, your lifestyle, and your behavioral routines determine your universe. And the best gumball machine available is the *UNSCRIPTED* Entrepreneurial Framework.

For example, take two brothers: Brother A and Brother B both work as plumbers for the same company. After work, Brother A watches television, plays video games, and drinks cheap beer. For hobbies, he goes on casino binges, often wagering a week's salary in the process.

Brother B doesn't have a television. Instead, he's an aspiring entrepreneur who dives into books, learns code, and sells his inventions on Amazon. He binges on webinars, trade shows, and *Shark Tank* on Hulu. Now picture each brother's gumball machine.

Brother A's machine contains mostly white, few oranges and reds, but absolutely no golds. Life's best-case scenario is tripping at the casino and being awarded an insurance payout. Brother B's machine has a different constituency. It also has some reds, many oranges and whites, but most important, it has some golds. Brother B has changed his probability universe while Brother A is dialing for white gumballs by doing nothing.

The second behavioral modification is *action* so probabilities are altered. You must deposit coins into the machine so probabilities are moved. Effort! Action!

Work! Crank, crank, crank! Depositing three coins and giving up because your spin yielded two whites and one orange? Sorry, that's not cutting it!

Imagine if you had a great talent for something and your default gumball machine was filled with 20 percent gold balls. Throw in a growth mindset and the gold balls increase to 25 percent. However, without effort deposited into the machine, the probabilities are never tested. If you knew your machine had twenty-five gold gumballs among 1,000, would you just stop at one crank? No, keep cranking! Fifty spins beats five. Untested probability means "good luck" avoids you.

The next three behavioral modifications are suggestions from Richard Wiseman, the experimental psychologist on luck. His experiments conclude our behavior can change luck if we mimic the traits associated with lucky people while eliminating the unlucky ones. These three traits are *intuition, routine, and positivity.*

In Wiseman's research, *intuition* is critical to luck. People who trust their gut and instincts are luckier than those who ignore them. Such *feelings* can serve as alarm bells while the unlucky person ignores their intuition and instead thinks about things too rationally. For example, here are two things in the past that seemed rational, but my gut screamed, NO!

- *Hey, my cousin made $100K last year flipping real estate with interest-only loans. I'm going to start doing it too!* (Uhh, isn't your cousin a bus driver?)
- *Hey this Vegas restaurant is a great investment. The famous Joe Blow invested; so did [name-drop and name-drop]. You should too!* (Seems like a lot of risk for the return?)

Another modification is *routine*, or specifically, breaking routine.

If life follows the beaten path, the path is beaten for a reason. A step outside your comfort zone modifies the gumball machine and alters probability. In a Telegraph.co.uk article, Wiseman explains that unlucky people tend to be creatures of routine, talking to the same types of people, traveling the same routes to work, while lucky people spread variety into their lives.[48]

Want to be lucky? Add variation, do something different, crank the spoke of the wheel!

The final modification is *positivity.*

Instead of seeing the glass half-empty, see it half-full. Be thankful you've won the geographic lottery, have access to clean water, a warm bed, and a hot shower. When tough times knock, spin it positive and imagine how it could have been worse.

In 2003, I bought a new Viper. A few weeks later, it was on fire and wrapped around a palm tree with me in the car. I walked away unharmed, which amounted to a life-or-death coin flip. And yet, not once since the accident did I reason "bad luck"—after all, I destroyed a $90,000 car in minutes and jacked up my insurance rates for the next seven years. It was good luck. I could have killed someone or myself. Bad luck? No way. *You choose the interpretation of your life events and then you choose how to act on that interpretation.*

You choose, like I chose. With such power, you can influence luck and modify the gumball machine you tow.

Change your universe.

Change your luck.

Change your life.

Unlike money, luck has no brain and holds no grudges or prejudices. It only reacts to the mathematical probabilities of an applied stimulus.

In your life today, what behaviors, actions, or inactions are crippling probabilities and muzzling your luck?

CHAPTER 24

BELIEF #7

THE FRUGALITY SCAM: LIVE POOR; DIE RICH

It is difficult to free fools from the chains they revere.
~ **Voltaire, Philosopher**

THE DICHOTOMY: DEFENSE (99%) VS. OFFENSE (1%)

Imagine playing baseball for fifty years and never batting. Imagine playing defense the entire game, chasing after hits from the real players who get to the plate. And now try imagining how stupid it would be to *think* you could win the game. Unfortunately, such a paradigm exists in the *SCRIPTED* world. It's the frugality scam of the defense/offense dichotomy.

When it comes to money management, most people live like Gollum in *The Lord of the Rings*. They cower in a shabby trailer, shrilling about "my precious" and how it must be guarded with dear life. Such is the existence of someone consumed by *the frugality scam—the belief that obsessive expense reduction, penny-pinching, and experiential deprivation will someday pay off in the opposite: rich life experiences, freedom, and abundance.* The frugality scam is like chopping off your head and bragging you'll never suffer migraines again.

For *M.O.D.E.L. Citizens* who've chosen a Slowlane path, the frugality scam is the lead horse. Grab any "early retirement" or "millionaire success" book and you'll suffer through a seasoned turd-pile of defensive strategy. Spend your entire Sunday clipping coupons. Work a second job. Buy a high-mileage used car, but surely not the car with so many miles it endangers your safety. Stop eating out, stop going to movies, stop going on expensive vacations, stop this, and stop that. That is, you *SCRIPTED* fool, stop living and start dying. Live poor so you can die rich.

Other gurus trademark defensive tactics into slick platitudes like "the latte factor," where your future millionaire empire is hitched to a six-buck Starbucks cappuccino. Heck, if these people thought picking your nose and flicking it into a snot pail would save ya two bucks, they'd recommend it while patting your shoulder with one hand as the other picks your pocket. Sorry, but saving pennies on coffee isn't going to make you rich; it just makes you another deprived fool deferring life for a flimsy promise that requires an immortality deal with the devil.

Of course, the frugality scam's problem is not frugality itself. The problem is, it is *defensive*, focused on expenses, or outflows. And to have outflows, one must first have inflows. Let me explain. If you put "liquid net worth" (LNW) into an equation, it would be:

LNW = TOTAL INCOME EARNED - TOTAL EXPENDITURES

If LNW is positive, congratulations, you've been a saver or a net producer. Negative? Sorry, you've been naughty at the mall or not very productive.

Within the *SCRIPTED* OS, wealth creation is mistakenly promised by massive, mind-numbing expense reduction. Seriously, let's call it what it is: You become an obsessive-compulsive cheap-ass, who covets every dime as if it were a weeping porcelain statuette of the Virgin Mary. Understandably, living in a 150 square foot "tiny-house" and stiffing the college kid waiting tables saves you money, but is it really a path to abundance and freedom? Or does your financial fantasy require the life expectancy of someone living in Okinawa, Japan?

The problem with a defensive strategy is expenditures are subtracted from net earned income. *If you don't have a sizable income, it doesn't matter how cheap you are!* You can't squeeze a dime from a nickel!

POLARIZER: CONTROLLABLE UNLIMITED LEVERAGE (CUL)

People get rich quick everyday.

Think about it. You can't be the youngest billionaire on the planet by getting rich slow. You can't become a teenage millionaire by perfectly timing an S&P 500 investment at age 12. Get rich quick might indeed exist, but don't mistake that for get rich easy. Years of disciplined, focused work channeled into the right business system can make it happen. Easy is not a part of the equation.

Behind the "get rich quick" stories you'll discover two critical items: 1) A strong offense underscored by *controllable unlimited leverage* (CUL) and 2) a detachment from intrinsic value (trading your time for money) in lieu of a business system.

First, controllable unlimited leverage means your entrepreneurial venture has leverage through scaling probability. This means your income has either a high ceiling, or none at all. You could be making $4,000 monthly and by next year, it could grow to $40,000 monthly. The controllable unlimited leverage principle is the income/production side of the net-worth equation where your income (or assets) explodes so violently that your consumption expenses are outmatched—so outmatched that they cannot compete.

For example, if you own a software service, you can conceivably grow your user base by 1,000 percent and, subsequently, your income can grow by the same metric; if you own a shoe store on the corner of Main and Elm, you cannot because scale is capped by a geographical region (we go deeper on this later). Comparing the two strategies is like the Dallas Cowboys suiting up to play football against Concord Middle School. One changes lives; the other pays bills.

Every so often, an entrepreneur posts a CUL "holy-shit" experience at my forum, reporting year-over-year income gains of 400–500 percent. Try getting that from a job.

The second element which makes "get rich quick" possible is clipping the strings of "time for money" or intrinsic value. Intrinsic value is the value of your time in a job endeavor. If you stock shelves at Target, your intrinsic value might be rated hourly at $12. If you're a doctor, it might be rated annually at $200,000. No matter which, income is capped and measuredly limited by the number of hours in a day, or years in a life. Creating massive wealth quickly requires this relationship to disintegrate.

Once the offense kicks into gear (and "get rich quick" graces a probability) saving money is not only easy, but it doesn't feel painful. For instance, my savings rate for the last fifteen years (net income less expenses) has been greater than 50 percent, sometimes as high as 70 percent. Save 10 percent of your paycheck? Funny. I can save big percentages of my income because my producerism is focused on ventures with controllable unlimited leverage. With an offensive mindset, I don't trade my time for money, I trade them into CUL ventures.

Assume this: Instead of earning $40,000 a year, you now earn $40,000 a month. At that income, can you keep consumption quarantined, or marginally linear? Or will you fall for the consumer scam and ramp up spending parallel to production? And more importantly, at $40,000 a month, could you now save 50 percent of what you earn? And be debt-free in a matter of weeks?

Earlier in the consumption/production dichotomy, I mentioned Antoine Walker and his $110 million career earnings. A spectacular offense, right? But ZERO defense. A great offense gave him championship enjoyment for years—fine living, luxury—but ultimately, a matador defense put him back in Shitsburg.

You see, once you're making five and six figures per month, as *UNSCRIPTED* entrepreneurs do, decades or centuries aren't needed to become a millionaire—but years, sometimes months. *An extraordinary life is won on offense; it is then preserved through defense.* With an offensive game plan (earning thousands per month instead of thousands per year) time is no longer a hindrance. Once you witness explosive income via *UNSCRIPTED* producerism, tossing nickels in a mason jar and waiting fifty years for stock-market miracles suddenly seems silly. In the race to win your freedom, an offensive stallion wins—not a defensive mule.

CHAPTER 25

BELIEF #8

THE COMPOUND-INTEREST SCAM: WALL-STREET AIN'T MAKIN YA RICH

The main purpose of the stock market is to
make fools of as many men as possible.
~ **Bernard Baruch, Businessman**

THE DICHOTOMY: WEALTH (99%) VS. INCOME (1%)

Nobody gambles in Las Vegas expecting to lose. Nope, you arrive at this opulent casino shimmering in imported crystal chandeliers and marble thinking you'll be the next big winner. You roll dice, hit some blackjacks, and plunk a few coins in the quarter slots. Your goal? To win the wealth that surrounds you. And yet, like the millions who gambled before you, it never clicks that *such grand palaces aren't built on winners, but on losers*. Sadly and unbeknown to the *SCRIPTED*, such duplicity also exists in the financial markets.

Thanks to the consensus myth perpetuated by a complicit government, an abetting media, and a cartel of financial conglomerates, the world's megacorporations forever enjoy a steady spigot of "wishful-money" much like the Vegas casino. In turn, the smart money, the few who own the casinos, then "slow cook" and manage the money, becoming fabulously wealthy in the process. While wishful-money victims take the gambled wait for the deferred promise of wealth, the *SCRIPTED* straitjacket cinches tighter. Meanwhile, bankers make bank.

Take for instance this story about Billy Banker and Iggy Investor.

Iggy, the consummate *SCRIPTED* Slowlaner, has fallen for temporal prostitution's BFF: *compound interest*. Iggy believes regular retail investments in stocks, mutual funds, and 401(k)s produce future wealth, provided Iggy patiently waits a few decades.

Fascinated by the market's wealth-curative powers, Iggy wins a tour of New York's financial district. Excited to witness how his money is managed, he meets his tour guide, Billy Banker, a successful hedge-fund manager.

The tour begins on the exchange floor with the opening bell and proceeds skyward to the penthouse offices. The elevator slides open, where Iggy enters a large atrium, overpowered by brash ivory and money-green marble floors. Atop a centerpiece, a lush floral arrangement of roses, orchids, and gladiolus scents the room—the last time Iggy saw so many flowers was at a funeral. Ahead, a large reception desk fashioned in similar-colored marble embosses the fund's official corporate insignia, a platinum sculpture probably sculpted by Picasso himself. Indeed, the ninety-eighth floor is presided over by the financial empire known as Dewey, Cheatem, and Howe.

The penthouse offices, each backlit by the imposing Manhattan skyline, home a variety of astutely manicured men, cuffed in tailored suits and diamond watches. Gregarious red-pinned leather chairs station large mahogany desks, exuding the type of power reserved for an emperor's throne room.

As the tour continues, Iggy peeks at the employee parking garage. It rivals an exotic car dealership featuring Mercedes, Maybachs, and McLarens. Others reveal that such trivialities are not needed and transact in caviar-stocked limousines and yachts docked at the marina.

By lunchtime, Iggy is amazed by the surrounding magnificence. He's enraptured that these bankers, stockbrokers, and hedge-fund managers are wildly successful managing money—his money. Billy Banker catches Iggy's enchantment and winks, "C'mon, we're not done yet."

After a short drive to Greenwich, Connecticut, Iggy is escorted into a guard-gated community featuring majestic brick estates with turreted architecture, grand porticoes, and brick-lined driveways winding through the pristine acreage.

"Here," Billy Banker explains, motioning to the stately mansions, "is where we live."

Iggy affirms, "Wow, finance is a great business to be in!" Billy Banker nods his head and corks a mercurial smile. Impressed his money appears in good hands, Iggy asks, "So Billy, if this is where you live, where do your customers live?"

Billy Banker signals his hand toward his BMW 7 Series and says, "Let me show you."

A short drive later, they are in Bridgeport, where Billy parks his Beemer on a street lined with narrow two- and three-story row houses. Iggy steps outside the car and absorbs the neighborhood.

The stench of diesel fuel steams the summer air. The potholed street is lined with broken cement sidewalks that have lost their battle with the years. Hugging the curb, a tireless Civic sits stilted on cinder blocks, its back window shattered in half, beaming like a perilous guillotine ready to behead an unsupervised child. Unlike the community they just visited where the skies were painted green with the flowering treetops from mature oaks, the sky here is littered with an entangled mass of electrical cables and telephone wires, feeding each house like breathing tubes to a comatose patient.

Iggy courts a momentary thought of Oz and Kansas. Unlike the distinguished residences he just saw, the homes here are panicked in unique distress. Some have white picket fences, which are no longer white and no longer picketed. Other homeowners have outlined their properties with chain-link fences, which mostly lie nonfunctional and slumped over in disrepair. Box fans smother open windows; their curtain comrades dance unceremoniously, a coerced acknowledgment to the artificially induced breeze. The houses themselves stand incongruently organized, gangly and marred by rotting wood and flecking paint, each standing curbside like a chorus line of aging centurions proud to have withstood the turbulent decades.

Billy Banker pans his Rolex-wrapped hand outward and showcases the distressed avenue like a grand prize on *The Price is Right*.

"This, my friend, is where our customers live."

WALL STREET WON'T MAKE YOU RICH

News flash! Compound interest is a scam. The stock market isn't going to make you rich. And neither will that ETF, that mutual fund, or that 401(k). That is, unless you plan on managing that ETF, that mutual fund, or that 401(k).

The truth is, the good folks on Wall Street aren't in the business of making you rich; they're in the business of making themselves rich. And now that the government has backstopped their failures (but not yours), be assured, the compound-interest scam will remain one of most whitewashed belief scams in existence.

The compound-interest scam is this serendipitous orthodoxy that the stock market will someday make you, the common man, uncommonly rich. Shoveled down your throat in gag-worthy quantities and upheld by the frugality scam, this financial ideology cries for regimented saving, investing, and of course, patience, hopefully followed by a long life expectancy.

Again, peek inside any personal finance book. Within minutes, I guarantee you'll read the same old tired dance, a preachy sermon which sounds like this: Invest X dollars into the stock market every month for X decades, and abracadabra, just like magic, you'll have X millions by your sixty-fifth birthday! Such magical outcomes are then backed by magical charts, which undoubtedly show your financial empire magically ascending into the stratosphere. Such utopian claims are then paired with what I call the *Utopian Graph*—a financial chart illustrating how much money compounds after fifty years if you just stop drinking coffee and, instead, religiously invest those savings with Billy Banker.

"Start investing early and often," the articles say. "Compound interest is the most powerful force in the universe," echo the financial acolytes. #SlowClap. #RollEyes.

Anytime the Utopian Graph rears its face—be warned—you're about to be laundered in the compound-interest scam.

The same narrative powering Las Vegas powers the compound-interest scam: *a survivor bias.* When someone wins, you'll hear about it. Big winners grab headlines.

When a coworker wins in Vegas, you'll hear about it in a Facebook status. And while he won $263, thousands of others lost hundreds, thousands, and yes, even millions.

Those losers? They say nothing. Crickets. They don't appear in headlines, and they don't make the statistics. But these statistics do peek insight into the survivor bias's size and who goes home a quiet loser: The Wynn Casino cost $2.7 billion to build. Bellagio: $1.6 billion. Singapore's Sentosa: just under $5 billion.

Similarly, when Iggy Investor wins at Wall Street, we're guaranteed to hear about it—on Yahoo's front page, in best-selling "Millionaire" books, or in some financial magazine whose ad revenues are funded by the money megafirms. Every day someone, somewhere, trumpets these frugalicious stories. The subversion method, always the same: plaster the photo of a young couple and their kids standing in front of a cute house, arms crossed, ceremoniously smiling with a shit-eating grin, and then tag with click-bait...

- *Millionaires in the making: Joe and Cindy have amassed a half-million-dollar nest egg while dumpster diving for expired meat behind Trader Joes!*
- *Twenty-nine-year-old millionaire reveals how he built his wealth never earning more than $80K a year!*

And then you're hit with the shtick. They're possessed by the frugality scam—ridiculously obsessive about money, coupons, and thrift but squanderous with time. Defensive Gollums. They're the ones asking the Safeway cashier to do a thirty-five-cent price check on the bananas, stealing seven minutes of your life you'll never get back.

Or worse, some "survivor" articles are hoaxes.

In October of 2014, Yahoo Finance featured an article about a twenty-seven-year-old millionaire (named Anton), which trumpeted the compound-interest scam. After reading the story and the cursory numbers, I immediately thought something smelled fishy. I know income and investment returns, but his numbers simply didn't add up. I posted my skepticism on my forum. A week later, my suspicions were confirmed: the story was fake and "Anton" acquired most of his wealth through inheritance, not via market investments.

Thanks to the survivor bias, you aren't getting the real story. What you don't read are the financial failures. You don't hear about Ted, who lost half his savings in 2008's market crash. You don't hear about Martha, who lost her pension because of fiduciary mismanagement. You don't hear about Harold, who trusted the compound-interest ruse for thirty-two years and died young at fifty-two, never enjoying the fruits of his thrifty savings—a casualty to dying rich in cash but poor in experience.

You see, the survivor bias keeps successes spotlighted and failures buried. It showcases the few who win and ignores the rest. Statistics of non-survivors? Good luck finding them. And if such statistics were sought, who would fund it? The government? Vanguard? JP Morgan Chase? Nope. Truth doesn't keep *SCRIPTED* slaves enslaved.

And then we have compound interest's prejudicial parties, people who sell more fairy tales than Disney. Turns out, these fiscal hypocrites aren't rich because of compound interest, but are rich from teaching it. Through best-selling books featuring survivors, syndicated radio shows, and incentivized financial products, the financial gurus make millions propagating the scam.

In 2015, Tony Robbins released the book *Money: Master the Game*. Before I could buy the book, my inbox blew up with emails from those venting that his new book was another compound-interest conspirator. Tony seemingly morphed from an awesome motivational guy to just another Wall Street shill. Anyone with a scant of intelligence knows Mr. Robbins amassed a fortune selling books and high-priced seminars, not mutual funds. Could it be that the book is really a "trip wire"? A tool stumbling starry-eyed idolaters into a back-end sales funnel, which makes millions on management fees, referrals, seminars, or whatever else carries a big price tag? The duplicity cost Tony a fan, but I doubt he's worried. As for the book, readers told me to avoid it, hence sparing me the pain of gouging out my eyes with an ice pick.

And finally, the compound-interest belief is missing the most important things of all: youth and abundance. In all of recorded history, *not one person* has gone from zero to $50 million in ten years because they invested in the S&P 500. Did you ever hear the story about the thirty-year-old billionaire who got rich clipping coupons and investing in mutual funds? Ha, nope, neither have I. However, there are plenty of Wall Street millionaires/billionaires under thirty, as well as entrepreneurs. An eighteen-year-old multimillionaire entrepreneur exists—the eighteen-year-old coupon-clipping, miserly stock-market multimillionaire does not. Oh wait, or does it?

In December of 2014, *The New Yorker* magazine published an article featuring eighteen-year-old Mohammed Islam, who claimed making $72 million trading stocks, ETFs, and oil-futures. According to Islam, he earned this staggering return while trading on his lunch break. After reading, I concluded, once again, bullshit. I called it out (again) on my forum. My reasoning? Mathematically impossible. Sure enough, twenty-four hours later the story was exposed as a hoax. Islam made it up. Turns out, he was another easily impressed young man fascinated with the Wall Street hyperculture—ya know, the place where sordid characters like Gordon Gekko and Jordan Belfort are hero-worshiped by money-hungry sycophants.

In short, a few outliers find fortune in Las Vegas; however, most do not. Instead, gaudier slaughterhouses rise into the sky, feeding their hustlers steady drips of cash while the sheep they impress get slaughtered. The compound-interest scam is temporal prostitution's pimp—a gambled trade where your young-years are sacrificed on the pedestal of patient mediocrity while hoping to get paid old-years later. Brilliant, eh?

THE TRUTH TRIFECTA: KILLING COMPOUND INTEREST WITH ITS OWN BLOOD

Behind compound interest and its Utopian Graphs are mathematical truths driving exponential growth. For example, if you grew one hundred dollars at 10 percent interest compounded annually for fifty years, you'd end up with over $11,000. If you saved one hundred dollars monthly at the same rate for fifty years, you'd end up with more than a $1.4 million. Cue Darth Vader because that's impressive, most impressive. And these compound-interest calculations are not conjecture but mathematical absolutes as much as one plus one equals two. Indeed, compound interest is powerful, as the emperor has foreseen.

Unfortunately, *mathematical absolutes and human reality aren't the same thing.*

Compound interest's ineffectiveness is like trying to survive a sinking Titanic. You know the boat will sink in 2 hours and without a lifeboat, you will die. And yet the compound interest cheerleaders have brainwashed you into believing another story: They say a lifeboat will save you if you just patiently wait 8 hours for it to arrive. On our sinking death boat, we simply don't have 8 hours.

Nonetheless, I do agree that compound interest is a powerful concept. Seriously, if my five-year finance degree taught me anything, it was that. However, you know what else is powerful? And not so forgiving? The fiscal **TRI**cycle.

- ✔ (T)IME.
- ✔ (R)EALITY.
- ✔ (I)NFLATION.

Wheeled by (**T**)ime, (**R**)eality, and (**I**)nflation, the fiscal TRIcycle debunks compound interest, and it's why it won't make you rich. Mathematically speaking, compound interest is like the fastest man on the planet, say Usain Bolt. He's powerful when unencumbered, like simple compound-interest calculations. However, saddle him on a tricycle, the three-wheeler of time, reality, and inflation, and suddenly he's impotent and slow-moving. It's like putting Jeff Gordon in a school bus and expecting 800-horsepower performance. Utopian Graphs with grand promises cannot be trusted because they're unencumbered analyses based in a hindsighted vacuum void of mortal time, reality, or inflation. Here's how the fiscal TRIcycle castrates compound interest as a reliable wealth creator.

TRUTH #1: TIME

Dead millionaires tell no tales.

They also don't go on luxury cruises down the Rhine, make love with their hot wives, or relax on the Riviera, Cognac in hand. Time cannot be stopped, avoided, or beaten. It's the ultimate human reaper, and it's why time is the first ax in compound interest's castration.

First, "buy and hold" has no exit. No one ever talks about selling because it's buy and die. The common denominator in all Utopian Chart extrapolations is time, and a heaping load of it. Not months or years but decades, amounting to more than 83 percent of your life, starting at age eighteen. Your typical Utopian Graph shows a nominal investment grown over fifty years, usually starting when you're eighteen years old. Not sure about you, but I didn't save shit when I was eighteen. Instead, I spent everything and piled on debt.

The truth is, most people don't start saving until their thirties. (This also falls in line with "reality," but that's next.) According to a BankRate.com survey, 27 percent of Americans have ZERO savings, while 76 percent of Americans live paycheck to paycheck with enough savings to last only six months.[49] Six months? The average American can't save a multi-monthed emergency fund, let alone a multi-yeared retirement stretch. That means mimicking the ubiquitous Utopian Graph is impossible because too much time has already passed. The S&P 500 won't grow $1,000 into $2 million in twenty years. And while the compound-interest blowhards advocate starting at any age, portfolios give zero shits. They are apathetic to your life expectancy, your circumstances, and your health. Like the honey badger, the markets don't care.

A dead millionaire is still, well, dead.

For example, I ripped this from the web, showing how blinded people can be when it comes to the compound-interest scam. The article headlined:

> Warren Buffett Tells You How to Turn $40 Into $10 Million.

The body stated:

> A few years ago, Berkshire Hathaway CEO and Chairman Warren Buffett spoke about one of his favorite companies, Coca Cola, and how after dividends, stock splits, and patient reinvestment, someone who bought just $40 worth of the company's stock when it went public in 1919, would now have more than $5 million. Yet in April 2012, when the board of directors proposed a stock split of the beloved soft-drink manufacturer, the figure was updated and the company noted that the original $40 would now be worth $9.8 million.[50]

So, who is this magical *someone* who magically invested forty dollars in 1919 and is rolling in cash today? *Turns out it's nobody.*

If you were sixteen years old in 1919 (born, 1903) and somehow got your hands on forty dollars, which then was about a thousand bucks, you'd now be 113 years old. In other words, you'd be a dead multimillionaire. And yet you're supposed to believe this unicorn exists, someone who survived polio, the Spanish flu, both world wars, the Chosin Valley, Hamburger Hill, the Carter administration, the FDA food pyramid, and cancer.

You can't make this shit up, and yet people salivate at the charts like a butcher's dog.

Folks, this ghost thesis isn't a compound-interest study but an example of how most people fail to think critically about time and money. Resign yourself to compound interest for wealth and you've resigned yourself to "hope and time" for freedom: hope I'm alive after X decades; hope my money is worth something after X decades; and hope the markets yield X percent after X decades. Sorry, hope based on variable returns, variable market instruments, and variable life expectancy is a bad plan. And a band of Billy Bankers are hoping hope is your plan.

Think of it this way. Every year, you are advised to snip off body parts: a finger, a toe, a spleen, a kidney, or an earlobe. Your body parts are then "invested" with Cryogenics Asset Management, LLC, who cryogenically freeze your parts for later sale. The government, the media, and your trusted advisors say, "After five decades, your body parts will be worth millions, and you can retire and travel the world!" Then after following diligently for half a century, you discover that (A) the cryogenic freezing process failed, (B) your body parts weren't worth the promised millions, or worse, (C) your body is so ravaged with missing parts and other ailments that you're either dead or your millions cannot be enjoyed. Starting over, reversing course, or switching gears is now impossible. Too much time has passed. *When wealth now is traded for a promise of wealth later, you're snipping body parts.*

TRUTH #2: REALITY

Another trick upholding compound interest is a denial of reality.

Behind the Utopian Graphs and their perceived wealth powers is a magical interest rate, or a growth rate, that no one can mimic, at least in practical real-world application. Specifically, there's an interest-rate illusion, which is always upheld "matter-of-factly"—an arbitrary number implying stress- and risk-free investing. A typical Utopian Graph pegs their growth rates as 8, 10, and sometimes even 12 percent and then assigns that growth to some risky asset class cherry-picked from hindsight.

- *A $10,000 investment in gold ten years ago would now be worth $X!*
- *If you invested in the S&P 500 right after the 2008 crash, $10,000 would now be worth $X!*
- *If you invested in 100 shares of Apple Corporation back in 1999, it would now be worth $X!*

Again, these returns are based on hindsight and aren't risk-free. For every Apple, there's an Enron. For every commodity boom, there's a commodity crash. Bubbles come and go, bankers get bailed out, and you're left holding the bag. Chasing a growth rate is a fool's game, and the last time a 12 percent yield was offered by a financial firm, it was run by a guy now jailed at the Butner Federal Correctional Facility. The risks associated with 10 percent growth rates are more suited for Hollywood stuntmen, not Mildred and Walter living in Sun City.

Second, arbitrary compound-interest calculations planted within the nexus of the financial markets are another deceptive shadow. Simple math solving compound-interest calculations is real—a hypothetical interest rate is plugged in with a time frame, and bam, you get a large number befit to an agenda. Unfortunately, the obscured truth is different.

In the financial markets, *an interest rate (or a growth rate) must be attributed to a financial instrument*, such as a stock, bond, or an asset class. Interest (or growth) rates cannot exist without a corresponding instrument or asset class attached. This creates the rate! And each instrument carries risk, which means you could lose some, or all, of your money.

What should the Utopian Graphs really be based upon?

The risk-free growth rate. After all, when you arbitrarily plug a number into a formula and magically see your thousands turn into millions, you aren't taking a risk. It's simple, risk-free mathematics.

So what's the risk-free rate? Its number is pegged by the three-month US Treasury bill rate, which I'd argue isn't risk-free, but that's another book. Anyway, as of October 2015, guess the rate…

It's a staggering .03 percent.

That's three-hundredths of a percent. That means, plugged into our Utopian Chart, one hundred dollars grows to $101.51 after fifty years. Enjoy the buck! On monthly one-hundred-dollar investments, it grows to more than $60,000, which adjusted for inflation is barely $8,000 in today's money. That is what's expected taking the "risk-free" approach.

Interested in taking on more risk? Well, that's what Billy Banker is hoping!

There are catastrophic consequences when trying to make the Utopian Charts work based on simple plug-in growth rates: Yield chasing. Unacceptable risks. Greed. All cloud your judgment. When your Wells Fargo savings barely pays .02 percent, it's easy to feel frustrated. And suddenly liars, cheats, and scoundrels have your ear. Underneath any financial scam is a victim chasing a growth rate promoted by a Utopian Chart and an opportunist offering it.

For example, there's David Fleet. Through a variety of newsletters and advertisements placed in church publications, Fleet advised potential investors using a message similar to my own: the stock market is risky. Instead, he recommended an investment in his real-estate business, offering investors a guaranteed 10 percent annual return. He raised over $17 million, mostly from elderly investors, and then in the ultimate irony, lost it all in the stock market. In December 2014, the SEC charged Fleet with multiple counts of securities fraud, proving again two things:

(1) the market is no place to create wealth, just like a strip club is no place to find your future virgin wife; and (2) for every yield-chasing fool, there's a yield-offering con man. And in this case, it wasn't outrageous, like 20 percent per year, but a mere 10 percent!

In another example, F-Squared Investments, an investment firm headquartered near Boston, exposes more reality checks pertaining to Utopian Charts. This firm claimed to own a sophisticated computer model that could time market entries and exits. Investors bought the tale, investing more than $28 billion. F-Squared claimed returns of more than 198 percent since 2001. In December 2014, the SEC found otherwise and levied the returns were entirely made up, a fabrication hatched by its company's CEO. As usual, investors took a haircut.

No Utopian Charts were updated.

And these are just recent examples.

The financial world is rife with tales of defrauded investors, all chasing yield and the charted illusion of wealth. The most egregious example of wealth destruction via the stock market was the 2008 market crash, which incidentally almost crashed the entire financial system. Now does that sound like a "safe" place for your life savings? As the market swallowed portfolios and early retirement aspirations died, reality took over. And that reality?

Fear.

Most sold, and suddenly Utopian Charts became dystopia. And to date, many have not reentered the markets. According to a University of Michigan analysis conducted on Federal Reserve reports, market participation was at a dismal 16 percent in 2013, compared to 30 percent in 2001.[51]

As I write this, the markets are at record highs. And despite the market fervor, the middle class is not better off. The sudden stock-market growth should've elevated America's heartland into prosperity, and yet such prosperity is curiously absent. Compared to the late-nineties market exuberance during the Internet boom, we're not seeing the wealth effect with the market recovery because people are fearful. And suspicious. They've learned that compound math on a napkin and compound math complicated by a financial instrument is like the difference between gambling with Monopoly money and gambling with your firstborn. Utopian Charts never account for FEAR.

These two scam scenarios exemplify when the reality of human emotion, fear and greed, poison simple compound-interest equations that buoy Utopian Charts. Investors chase. They get greedy. And they get screwed. Meanwhile, Billy Banker makes bank.

On the whole, compound-interest calculations based on simple math don't require resilience, they don't face fear, they don't time markets, and they don't need to manage risk. Compound-interest calculations based on reality? Actual financial instruments that can go from hero to zero in a matter of days? That requires nerves of steel, a risk appetite, and also a heaping pile of hard-earned money. The financial world is filled with market prognosticators who promise mythical returns foretold by mythical charts. Tune in to CNBC on any day and one expert predicts skyrocketing markets while another predicts doom and gloom. One recommends, "Buy gold!" and the other admonishes, "Sell gold!" The point is *no one fucking knows*. But know what they do know? Your guesses, whether right or wrong, will make them millions.

TRUTH #3: INFLATION

Compound interest has an evil twin, one who doesn't seek attention or grab glory from the front pages of financial blogs. It lies hidden for years, silently ravaging portfolios like termites in an old barn. The third and final compound-interest castrator also has the same power of its sibling: *compound inflation*.

Every Utopian Chart ignores plausible growth rates, plausible fear, and plausible inflation. The reality of your money-printing government? One dollar today will be worth much less tomorrow. And with our government's continued debt appetite, your dollars might end up worthless.

Back within our original compound-interest calculation of $100 monthly investments, $1.5 million in "fifty years later" money might only buy you a new Chevy. It might only be a down payment on a double-wide in a mobile home park. It might be today's equivalent of $50,000, which simply isn't much to live on, at least not abundantly or freely.

The Utopian Chart propagandists want you blind to inflation. They want your focus on the end result: X millions after fifty years with today's thinking. Today's thinking projects those millions with today's health, today's buying power, and today's circumstances. OMG, I'll have $7 million if I follow this simple one-hundred-dollar plan? I'll be able to travel the world and buy a mansion in the suburbs with a Lamborghini parked in the driveway!

The inflationary truth is more sobering. One hundred years ago, a quarter bought many things: several loaves of bread, a can of coffee, or a pound of sirloin steak. A quarter in my childhood got me a pack of gum and ten minutes on Pac-Man. Today it buys nothing. From 1913 to 1940, total inflation was a nonfactor at 43.8 percent, or an annual average of 1.6 percent. However, from 1940 to 2013, it was more than 2,000 percent.[52] That means the ubiquitous Utopian Chart would need to grow 2,000 percent just to break even!

Despite the media's contention that inflation is under control, American families aren't finding it so. From February 2000 to April 2014, the cost of living has skyrocketed. Utilities, up 81 percent. Auto insurance, up 69 percent. Medical supplies and drugs, up 60 percent. Food to fill the refrigerator, up 43 percent. Gas to fill the car, up 70 percent. Meanwhile, wages and salaries have not followed.[53] According to Pew Research, the average wage peaked more than forty years ago when about $4 an hour had the same purchasing power as $22 dollars today.[54]

The Utopian Charts cannot be trusted because trust is not in the calculation. Can you trust the government to be a good steward of taxpayer money? Can you trust fiscal policy makers to keep inflation from exploding? Can you trust a growing economy for five decades? Answer these questions honestly and you'll realize inflation is a gamble and your bet is placed with people who historically have not been prudent. For me, I'm unwilling to make a multi-decade-long gamble reliant on ivory-tower economists, financial megacorporations, and a lying government who can't stop lying as they print money. Compound inflation is as powerful as compound interest.

CONSIDER THE SOURCE

If the devil funded a study reporting that 91 percent of hell's inhabitants were happy, would you believe it? Such duplicity is common in pharmaceuticals and agriculture. When the public needs assurance that the latest drug, chemical sweetener, or frankenfood is safe, the conglomerate funds research studies to support their agenda. When such conclusions come from the mouths of corporate giants like Monsanto or Pfizer, many people are skeptical, including myself. Interestingly, drug and agricultural studies from biased interests face critical scrutiny, even from the *SCRIPTED* populous. However, the financial world gets a mulligan.

Never a week passes where the world is spared from seeing another insufferable Utopian Chart shoveled out by the mainstream media, another pseudo proclamation that wealth's secret rests in Wall Street's grimy hands. For example, my last sufferance came from Business Insider. The juicy headline?

- *Every 25-Year-Old Needs to See This Chart…*

Of course, it was a Utopian Chart arguing the stale compound-interest mimetic. My headlined rebuttal would be a bit different. It'd read:

- *Every 25-Year-Old Needs to <u>WAKE THE HELL UP AND</u> See <u>WHO IS PROMOTING</u> This Chart*

The creator of such a fine mathematical analysis?

None other than JP Morgan Asset Management.

Instead of believing the narrative, start questioning WHO wants you to believe the narrative. Consider the source. Instead of sanctifying this crap as if Moses ambled down from Mount Sinai and delivered the missive himself, ask who benefits from your belief. Where are the millionaires?

Investor.gov is an arm of the Securities and Exchange Commission, the government's regulatory body for financial securities. On Investor.gov, I found a variety of resources, including a compound-interest calculator. Odd, the calculator had no field for inflation. In fact, Investor.gov had no such calculators—inflation, cost of living, or otherwise. There was also no mention of the current $20 trillion federal deficit.

Other compound-interest sponsors are the finance websites and magazines who are collusive in perpetrating the scam. Financial companies pay kings' ransoms to promote a variety of banks, brokerages, and fund companies. Such advertising is then buttressed by survivor articles.

> *See how Charlie Cheapskate became a millionaire while driving a taxi six days a week!*

And then you're hit with the shtick. He's a scarcity whack job smitten by the frugality scam, sewing his own clothes, refusing to dine out with friends, and pedaling a bike to the store. Simply put, his life sucks ass. It's like money possesses these people, transforming them into religious fanatics who don't worship God, but nickels and dimes. Like dangling Marionettes, these poor saps are limited by wherever their money strings lead— or I should say, don't lead.

Another peeving example came from *Forbes*, a magazine I genuinely like. In 2013, Forbes sponsored a video aptly entitled, "How to Get Rich." The video pushed the "wealth fantasy," featuring your usual run-of-the-mill financial chauvinists, like Jack Bogle and Meredith Whitney, each championing the financial markets, compound interest, and your typical hodgepodge of *SCRIPTED* doctrine. After watching the video, I could only chuckle at the unspoken hypocrisy.

So I did a little research into *Forbes* cover models. I was curious how many Forbes millionaires and billionaires actually followed this advice as recommended in the video.

Look for yourself. Try and find ONE *Forbes* cover model whose fortune was created because they diligently invested with Wall Street like we retail investors, a.k.a. Iggy Investor, are instructed to do. Go ahead. I'll wait.

Welcome back. What did you find?

Let me guess—nothing.

Subtract the entrepreneurs, the inheritors, the sports and entertainment titans, the corporate insiders, and those that serve the financial industry over investing in it, and you'll find exactly what I found: *the stock market isn't making investors wealthy; it's making its servants wealthy.*

As expected and cleverly ignored, not one Forbes cover model got rich following the "wealth fantasy," but an overflowing basket of them got rich perpetrating the advice. In other words, *if you want to get on the cover of Forbes, don't take advice from Forbes.*

In September 2012, the SEC charged radio personality Ray Lucia for allegedly spreading misleading information about his pet investment scheme, the "Buckets of Money." To obtain clients who would be charged advisory fees for their services,

Lucia claimed to yield-chasing attendees that his strategy was empirically backtested, even during bear markets.

The SEC felt differently. According to the charge, the SEC claimed Lucia used a lower 3 percent inflation rate for his backtesting methodology, even though historical inflation was much higher. Furthermore, the SEC claimed that Lucia's "backtesting" failed to account for the negative effect his advisory fees would have plundered from the strategy, a strategy in which funds weren't even allocated by the strategy he purported.[55] LOL. And yeah, no Utopian Charts were updated.

Again, this shouldn't shock you. The greatest game in town is not investing in the markets but managing the money of those who do. Perhaps Mr. Lucia will be the next big smile gracing *Forbes*' cover.

What? Who? I'm sorry, I hear a heckler in the cheap seats.

What about Warren Buffett? Carl Icahn? Bill Ackman?

They got rich from the stock market, right?

Sorry, despite what you've heard from good old Warren, he's NOT a traditional stock investor like you or me but an activist investor. I know, I know—when Warren Buffett speaks, the lemmings' ears bleed gold. However, instead of falling to your knees and convulsing in an orgasmic tizzy, I'd recommend putting on your research cap and examining what Warren says and what Warren does—are they always equal?

Anyhow, if you aren't familiar with activists, these are moneyed investors who purchase huge blocks of stock with the intent of influencing corporate strategy. Yes, Buffett doesn't buy stock and "hope" it goes up. Instead, activists take large positions where they can move markets, acquire voting rights, and appoint board members. *They exert control and influence corporate policy*, a key element separating YOU, Iggy Investor, from Buffett the activist.

Bottom line, people like Warren Buffett and those pushing the compound-interest agenda aren't using Warren Buffett's conventional investment wisdom; they're the ones profiting from it. While the *SCRIPTED* peasantry buys the funds, the compound-interest apostles run the funds. And the ultimate fact: There are no experts in the financial markets. One expert says Dow 30,000; another says Dow 10,000—both clueless, both equally likely to be correct, and both hoping you'll buy into their circus. A market direction cannot be predicted, but you know what can? Juicy management fees from *M.O.D.E.L. Citizens.*

POLARIZER: THE CAPITAL-PRINCIPLE

You probably think I hate Wall Street. Or that I don't own any stocks, mutual funds, or financial instruments. Both would be incorrect. In fact, my approach to Wall Street is identical to my approach to Vegas. Just because I know Vegas produces more losers than winners doesn't mean I don't go.

You see, instead of looking at Wall Street or Vegas for *what they can be*, I look at them for *what they are*. When I hit the Vegas Strip, I'm not looking to get rich or to defy the odds. Instead, I'm looking to be entertained. I bet in ten, maybe twenty-five-dollar increments, effectively transforming a gamble into entertainment.

Likewise, when it comes to Wall Street, I take the same approach. I'm not using the markets for how they're marketed—to create wealth—but instead I use them for what they are: *the buying and selling of capital in exchange for income (interest) or equity (appreciation)*. According to Investopedia, the formal definition of a capital market is that it "channels savings and investment between suppliers of capital such as retail investors and institutional investors, and users of capital like businesses, government and individuals."[56] Note, the definition says nothing about getting rich.

> ***Failure is normally temporary and can be remedied by trying again. A compound-interest failure is permanent because its attempt spans decades. Trying again is impossible.***

In Chapter 47, I will go into significant detail regarding the capital-principle, but for the purpose of this belief dichotomy, it's this: The capital markets are to be used for income, capital deployment, liquidity, and asset speculation. *And when you have a lot of money to deploy, suddenly compound interest reverses its tide; it becomes an effective tool for creating 100 percent reoccurring passive income.*

For example, a lot of my net worth is invested in bonds: municipal (tax-free), corporate, emerging-markets, and closed-end funds. Other investments are in dividend stocks, like Southern Company, Holly Energy, and a nice allocation of REITs. See? I don't hate Wall Street because Wall Street allows my money to work for me 24/7. The net effect is I let compound interest pay me monthly, 99 percent hands-off residuals payments, *but only once compound interest becomes an effective growth multiplier.*

For example, take a paltry 3.5 percent return, which is offered on a municipal bond. The effective return, because it's exempt from taxes, is nearly 7 percent. Take a look at the difference in monthly, passive returns.

- $1,000 investment = $2.91 month
- $4 million investment = $11,666.66 month

More than $10,000 per month, tax-free, doing absolutely nothing, and with a tiny interest rate. Imagine the joy. Imagine the freedom. Imagine. And yet, I don't need to imagine, because this is my reality. You can activate compound interest's praised power only if you can earn and save millions fast, not when you use it to turn nickels into dimes as the compound-interest scam implores. Explode wealth by leveraging producerism through the *UNSCRIPTED* framework—*then compound interest can pay you residually for the rest of your life.*

Another aspect of the capital-principle is as a tool to beat inflation. If you're looking to devalue money through time, stick it in a bank or under the mattress. Money does in fact sleep, but only when it's not properly deployed. I use the capital markets to deploy cash so it outpaces inflation. Sometimes that is foreign currencies, short-term bonds, or yes, even a mutual fund or two.

Asset speculation is another component of the capital-principle. This is akin to gambling, like in Vegas, and please, don't bother arguing it isn't. You can look at technical analysis charts all day, analyze income and cash-flow statements, smoke tea leaves, and pray to the holy Cramer, but no one knows if Company X will be the big winner, or the big loser. We can make educated guesses, but that's all they are: guesses. That said, I engage in asset speculation regularly by investing in companies I understand and like, and with money I can afford to lose. Sometimes things go well; sometimes they don't. Sounds like Vegas, eh?

And the best and final use for the capital markets? Liquidity. When an entrepreneur sells his company in an IPO, it's like winning the Super Bowl. Either indirectly or directly, the capital markets transfer liquidity from the selling owners (the founders and early seed capitalists) to the public (investors and speculators).

In the end, Wall Street is not a place for growing wealth but a place for asset speculation, earning income, and deploying capital. Yes, save early and often. However, don't think you can sail to the promised land on a compound-interest wave—it's ineffective for creating wealth unless millions are amassed FIRST; then it's powerful, perhaps as powerful as Lustig's money-printing machine.

? ***If your wealth strategy is compound interest, what uncontrollable variables are lagging and endangering your retirement? Market returns? Savings rate? Job stability? The economy? Life expectancy? Inflation?***

CHAPTER 26

THE BIASES: YOUR BRAIN'S DELUSIONS

Fortunately for serious minds, a bias recognized is a bias sterilized.
~ **Benjamin Haydon, Artist**

AUTHENTIC YOU VS. YOUR BRAIN

In the *Seinfeld* sitcom, Newman is Jerry's mortal enemy. In our *UNSCRIPTED* fight, our Newman isn't an external adversary—it's our brains.

Every one of us fights an inner battle between our soulful desires and our brain's reflexive impetuses. In one corner, there's an *authentic you*—striving for success and happiness. In the other corner is your impetuous brain—an emotional, obstinate machine that hates change and loves *SCRIPTED* protagonists: predictability, shortcuts, and security.

If the "AUTHENTIC YOU vs. YOUR BRAIN" battle were a football game, your brain would be favored by four touchdowns. Recognize the war and you can win. Others have no idea it exists. And if you aren't aware of it, guess what? You're losing.

Your brain's offense in this battle is its biases: *SCRIPTED*, self-defeating cognitive obstructions defended and reinforced through autonomous thinking patterns, allowing snap judgments and worldly inferences, often in an illogical fashion. Other obstructions mislead, pickpocketing time and effort through misinformation. All together, these biases keep you mired into either inaction or wrongful action.

Exposing these obstructions (and their misinformation) starts with being less human and more Vulcan—a conscious shift from the emotional to the logical. Move from hearing your brain to watching it, as if it were a detached entity unto itself. In other words, *start thinking about how you think*.

As you pursue *UNSCRIPTED* using (TUNEF), there are seven primary brain battles you'll face. They are:

Change Adversity
Antithetical Apathy
Podium Popping
Momentum Paralysis
Righteousness
Semmelwashing
Survivor Spotlighting

CHANGE ADVERSITY: WHY REFUSING CHANGE IS REFUSING EXCELLENCE

Your brain's quarterback in the (Authentic You vs. Your Brain) war is *change adversity. Change adversity is your brain's predilection for comfort and status quo despite being surrounded by change.* Behind change adversity is what's called a status quo bias—our brain's preference for predictability over instability. With change adversity as our brain's frontline defense, change adversity's threats are double-edged.

The first threat thwarts behavioral change. By default, we prefer our actions to be routine and familiar. Whatever your situation, it marks the baseline where change is felt negatively as discomfort, pain, or loss.

In business, change adversity is felt whenever a major website is redesigned. Change a website's user interface (UI) and watch feathers ruffle. Anytime Facebook changes their UI, a lynch mob marches in Menlo Park. Major website overhauls always spark resistance and friction, regardless of improvements. This is change adversity speaking.

Additionally, change adversity writes the script in today's politically correct culture of mediocrity. Take for example the "fat acceptance" movement, where people want obesity's health hazards whitewashed. Recommend that people stop Big-Gulping huge vats of unrefined sugar and—look out—you'll be labeled a "fat-shamer." Underneath the PC BS is denial—a denial of truth and reality so the pain of changing to a better diet can be avoided. In this case, change adversity protects us from loss—loss of our Cokes, our Papa John's, and our Ben and Jerry's.

Change adversity mesmerizes us into behavior normalization: *an errant conviction that great change can happen without a great behavior change.* As the old saying goes, "The definition of insanity is to do the same things repeatedly and expect different results." In the end, life does not change because we won't change. It's like trying to roast marshmallows without a fire.

For example, I've been lifting for twenty-five years. However, I admit I suffer stagnate periods where my regular effort doesn't yield results. Within these moments, I step outside my brain and admit *regular* has happened; it's time to change—diet, regime, something—and change it in a big way. The greatest physical improvement happened when I replaced my afternoon workout with a fasted 4:00 a.m. workout. As a night owl, this was a huge change, and huge results I received. I saw my abs—as a middle-aged dude, let me tell ya, that's huge!

Change must precede change. Would you believe this is the big secret for success? Obvious, eh? Well, not really. Because change is an uncomfortable choice, people try anything to get change without change. Everyone wants positive results, and yet, no one wants to change their choices. Instead, we would rather plod through the same routines with the same skills and the same behavior, hoping NOT to get the same results. The diet industry preys on change adversity: "I lost thirty-five pounds and didn't stop eating my Twinkies!" Sure you did.

Behind any great story is a great change story led by a choice, which recirculates back to the process-principle. Don't like the job or lackluster results? Then choose change, and act until echo.

The second threat of change adversity is how we react to it, or choose not to see it at all. This is the difference between making or missing a fortune, or going bankrupt. *Opportunity is served on the silver platter of change and change is ALWAYS happening.* Change precedes fortune. I made a fortune because I recognized and took advantage of a shift in search behavior. Others make fortunes in how people use technology, from ordering a car (Uber) to ordering a movie (Netflix). Mobile gaming, self-publishing, solar power and hundreds of other industries are changing, and hence, creating fortunes. If you miss one change—don't worry—another is coming.

On the flipside, RadioShack, the small electronics store often bookending strip malls, went bankrupt in 2015, and it's a classic example of an organization resisting change. Even the name is synonymous with stuck on stuck—they might as well been named "Typewriter Emporium". Radio is a mid-century technology, and when RadioShack refused to rebrand and change their operations, they sealed their fate. Remember Blockbuster Video? They refused change while Netflix saw the future for on-demand movies. By the time Blockbuster realized it was drowning by a change tsunami, it was too late.

Do you see other companies on the verge of extinction because they are too slow or refuse to change? In my opinion, Major League Baseball is a dying sport because it refuses to adapt to an attention-impaired culture accustomed to a media diet of instant and controlled gratification.

In the end, change marks the black ink of billionaires and the red ink of ruin. When change adversity is stamped out, we can be on the winning side of change by changing ourselves. *Change keeps you poor or makes you rich.* You decide which.

RIGHTEOUSNESS: WHY YOU'D RATHER BE RIGHT THAN RICH

Askhole.

That's the name for someone who asks for advice and doesn't take it. Instead, they'd rather argue the advice or ignore it altogether. Askholes are quite common on my forum, and it has nothing to do with stubbornness but with their righteousness. *Righteousness is not about being fair or just but about our urgency to see and hear only things that support our biases, while discounting, ignoring, or arguing the rest.*

For example, if you're a left-wing Marxist who thinks Mao and Chavez were the greatest leaders since the invention of electricity, you probably get your news from

MSNBC. Likewise, if you think former President Obama was born in Kenya and prays five times a day for Salat, you're probably tuned in to the Fox News Channel. Both statements are ridiculous, but I guarantee you probably loved one of them and hated the other. The point is, you will fortify and quarantine your beliefs from adverse incursion—it's simply easier nodding your head in agreement rather than spending mental energy examining conflicting or challenging thought patterns.

Worse, it has been psychologically proven that our convictions actually get stronger when presented with conflicting evidence. This is why political arguments on Facebook are pointless, regardless of how many charts, graphs, and data you present. Political derision is so polarized nowadays that facts don't matter—you could have video evidence of a partisan politician slaughtering puppies and murdering grandmas; voters wouldn't care. Nope, that's my guy.

Anyhow, righteousness works hand in hand with change adversity.

Your immediate need to be right (confirming your biases) often trumps your will to win a victory in the future. Those askholes on my forum? They're more interested in being right, right now, than being wrong but profitable and successful later.

I experienced this inconsistent behavior in money management recently. Several months ago, I tried selling an overpriced bond investment I predicted was due for a correction. Selling would lock in profits. I placed a limit sell order and then left for the day. Unfortunately, I forgot about my order until several days later where I shockingly discovered that the order never traded and I still owned the shares. During that time, the share price significantly declined, costing me thousands. Think I was upset? The truth is I wasn't. In fact, I was indifferent, maybe even a little bit happy. Why? *Because I was right.* And we love being right.

The point is, our brain seeks confirmation that we're right, often without considering if we really are. And the idea of confirming our rightness feels awfully good. You see, *you'd rather be right than rich.*

Another danger of righteousness is it shields you from red flags. Instead of righteousness preventing fortune, it could prevent happiness. For example, there's a young man on my forum who, by all accounts, won his dream job. He designs video games for one of the largest video-game developers in North America. It's a high-paying, highly sought job and whenever there's a similar job opening, resumes pile up and lines form around buildings. Anyhow, he believed wholeheartedly he had his dream job. After he won the position over hundreds of other candidates, his brain celebrated, affirming "this is your dream job," and righteousness took over.

At first he was excited, but it later faded. As the job dragged on, he ignored his soulful whispers clouded by his confirmation bias. He wasn't happy. His hobby was art, and he no longer had time or passion for it. He was working long hours and exhausted by the weekend. His relationships suffered. And yet, his righteousness kept him at that job for years, convincing him over and over "this is your dream job."

Whenever he cashed his fat paycheck, he'd smile for a few hours and reason, "I earned this." Whenever he got a pay raise for a loyal year, he'd pat himself on the back and reason, "I'm good at what I do." And whenever he heard there were thousands of college grads clamoring to have his job but none were available, he'd reason, "I'm lucky to have my job because thousands of others want it."

Meanwhile, his soul spoke differently: this isn't my dream job but a death wish. And his gagged heart would not be heard until he exposed his righteousness for the liar it was, showering him with righteous urges and confirmations that, "Yes, this is my dream job."

And the final blow from your righteousness comes as reinforcement for *SCRIPTED* thought.

Take for example the typical claptrap that rich people are selfish and greedy, their corporations are evil, and whatever else incites impulsive thinkers to soil their panties and tweet their fingers raw. If you own such notions, your brain will actively seek to confirm its rightfulness. Anytime a story of corporate malfeasance makes headlines, you're on Reddit, upvoting the post. Look, Comcast treats their customers like shit! OMG, Verizon charged a ninety-two-year-old grandma $15K for data she didn't use! Likewise, anytime you read about a rich person who is suspected of (or caught in) nefarious activities, you're blowing up your social media accounts: George Soros is taking over the world! The Koch Brothers are behind it!

Look, I get it. This shit happens. There are greedy people managing and owning corporations. Just as there are greedy rich people, there are greedy poor people. Rich people don't have a monopoly on greed or evilness—*the human species does.* The problem is *whatever you want to see is what you will see.*

Your reticular activating system and its confirmation biases (the psychological henchman that drives righteousness) will do the rest, delivering such evilness to your perceptual stage, while the reality remains backstage and hidden. Not only does your RAS confirm what it wants to see, but it overestimates its frequency and discards the rest. *Your perception is not the reality.*

ANTITHETICAL APATHY: THOSE SUFFOCATING SHOULDN'T HATE AIR

If financial freedom and autonomy are your goals, your beliefs must align with those goals. If they don't, you'll either (A) lie to yourself, or (B) sabotage your effort, causing tension and stress. Both make goals unobtainable.

In our example above regarding rich people, let's assume you righteously believe wealthy folks are evil and greedy. And yet, you also want to be wealthy. See the problem? Do you aspire to be greedy? Or evil? Of course not. But then how can wealth be a goal? The implication firing the subconscious strife is clear: To become wealthy, you must compromise something. Do you choose rich but evil? Or poor yet kind?

Two diametrically opposed beliefs are at war. This mental battle, *antithetical apathy, happens when two contradicting values or beliefs tangle in our consciousness.* The internal polarization causes apathy, stress, sabotage, or even intellectual dishonesty.

As such, the belief might cause you to abandon goals: "I don't want to turn into an evil capitalist dick!" It might cause unwarranted expectations: "Do I really want to compromise my morality to succeed in business?" Or the belief might justify unethical actions: "Everyone uses deceptive marketing, so I'll use it too."

People who "fear success" usually have antithetical apathy; one part of them wants success while another part believes success has a compromising price tag crossing moral or ethical boundaries.

Similarly, the most common use of antithetical apathy is a dishonest excuse for change adversity.

In 2012, Maria Kang, "the fit mom," Facebooked a buff picture of herself in skimpy exercise gear with the question, "What's Your Excuse?" As expected, an Internet firestorm ensued. Millions were offended, whining about being "fat-shamed." Others rebutted with terse antithetical apathy crutches, such as "My children are too important" and "Spend some time with your kids." The psychological pandering in these rebuttals is dissonance: *to be healthy, you have to sacrifice your children or your motherhood.* The implied deduction is even worse: any mother who is incredibly fit is a bad mom. Can you see why it's easy to have an excuse and maintain the status quo?

In the end, Ms. Kang was not advocating that moms need to be fitness models who live at the gym; she was advocating being healthy. For the offended, this message bounced, and it's easy to see why. When your brain is exposed to hidden truths that want to remain hidden, offense is taken and plausibly denied using antithetical apathy and polarized "binary" logic—*I won't abandon my kids to live at a gym.* And as another offended reader stated, "I'm not about to give up ice cream and cake," which exposes your real agenda: Feeding your sugar cravings is more important than your health. Yup, now I understand your anger; it's not about protecting your kids but about protecting your Häagen-Dazs. And if you're not healthy, how much quality time will you really be spending with your kids?

Nowadays, everyone is offended because everyone's brain is running wild.

If someone tells you, "I'm offended," it usually means you've exposed a truth they want to keep denied. As Charles Bukowski once stated, "Censorship is the tool of those who have the need to hide actualities from themselves…." Rest assured, my writing will offend some folks. And you know why they're offended? *Because they know I'm talking about them*—and they hate being called on their bullshit.

In the end, hating air while suffocating is foolish. Confront your antithetical crutches—or drop them altogether. Yeah, you can be moral and ethical and still be rich. You can be a fit, healthy mom and still love your children and spend time with them. Stop letting your brain run roughshod and instead think about how you think.

SEMMELWASHING: UNCONVENTIONAL COMPELS CONVENTIONAL REACTIONS

In 1847, Dr. Ignaz Semmelweis made a legendary discovery in the field of medicine and obstetrics. He unconventionally proposed that washing your hands with a chlorinated lime solution would drastically reduce child-born fever, a common illness of the day. Think his peers showered him with rewards and accolades?

Unfortunately not.

Because Dr. Semmelweis's discovery conflicted with conventional medical knowledge, the mainstream medical community blasted his claim, rejecting it as bunk and hooey. While some dismissed the discovery (and the data) based on scientific reasoning, others spurned it because it was unconscionable to presume that an upper-class gentleman, a physician, would have untidy and unclean hands.

Despite ridicule from his peers, Dr. Semmelweis stood convicted to his discovery for years. By opposing the consensus, eventually his colleagues branded him a whack job and banished him from practice. In 1865, Dr. Semmelweis was committed to an insane asylum where he'd die just weeks later, purportedly at the hands of asylum guards. While his committal circumstances were never verified (perhaps having your life's work disparaged?), his death went relatively unnoticed, if not celebrated by those who contemptibly viewed his discovery.

Several decades later, Louis Pasteur's medical breakthroughs in germ theory exonerated Dr. Semmelweis and proved his main hypothesis. Dr. Semmelweis's defiance toward convention marched him toward death, labeled as a pariah, but time now marks him as a legend. And like many legends, he has a university named on his behalf.[57]

This renaissance story demonstrates the next bias you'll face on your *UNSCRIPTED* path: Semmelwashing. However, Semmelwashing doesn't come from your mind; it comes from the hive mind of the mainstream. It's what happens when unconventional crashes into conventional. When traditional paradigms are opposed or questioned, not only is the message attacked but so is the messenger. A Semmelwashing is the friction we face when other people discover we aren't following the conventional *SCRIPTED* brainwash.

For them, you'll likely come across as unwashed, a rubber band needing a "snap back" to reality, namely their reality. For example, prepare for a Semmelwashing after telling your parents you'd rather skip college so you can remain debt-free. Prepare for a Semmelwashing after Facebooking that you've quit your job to pursue something impressively fulfilling instead of remaining depressively employed. Prepare for a Semmelwashing when your trendy friends can't understand why you're driving a decade-old Camry while they drive new cars. Anytime you defy convention and stamp a path where few tread, expect oppositional floggings from ordinary people with a reeducation on what convention demands.

Unfortunately, like many pitfalls of the brain, Semmelwashing has no defense other than awareness and expectation. When you deviate from *SCRIPTED* paths, expect clashing, especially from those closest to you. Expect to be questioned and maybe labeled "crazy" or "eccentric." For example, this book and I are prime candidates for a Semmelwashing. OMG, did he just say compound interest is a scam? Is he advocating not going to college? The truth is anyone who's sold their soul to convention or earns their paycheck selling it won't shelf this book on the mantel. I expect these ideas to be skewered and burned at the stake by misquotes, misinterpretation, and whatever else can marginalize me or the message. Semmelwashing confirms your message's threat by those who have chosen to die by it. Stand resolute and your reward is not the pursuit of happiness, but happiness in your pursuits.

PODIUM POPPING: WHY SOMEONE ELSE'S PEN CAN'T WRITE YOUR STORY

The "leaping syndrome" is coming. Years from now, thousands of people will mistakenly kill themselves "leaping for success." How? Well, as the story goes, leapers jump from the roof of the city's tallest building. Seconds later, thunk. And instead of success, they find death.

If you're wondering what possibly compels rational people to commit irrational acts (without influence from narcotics or a zombie apocalypse), you'll have to trace the leaping syndrome back to its origins. Several years before the epidemic, Lonny Leaper climbs to the rooftop of his city's tallest building. A failed author, father, and husband, Lonny has given up on life. His rooftop mission is suicide. As he stands at the ledge contemplating, a crowd gathers on the ground. Onlookers stare, some plead, others record via their smartphone.

And then it happens: Lonny jumps. The spectators scream and scatter as if the foot of Godzilla approached.

Thud.

When the spectators hesitantly peek at the crash site, they see the unexpected.

Instead of a grisly bloodbath, they see Lonny sitting upright on his butt, alive and gripping his head in shock.

Miraculously, Lonny survives the forty-story fall. The crowd is mystified. His jump, recorded by several bystanders, hits the Internet and goes viral. His incredible fall is viewed over 500 million times. Lonny becomes an instant celebrity, rivaling Grumpy Cat and suddenly, his two failed novels go from obscurity to number one and number two on *The New York Times* best-seller list.

As it turns out, Lonny is actually a talented writer. For the years that follow, he goes on to write five more best sellers and rivals the success of JK Rowling, becoming part of the billionaire authors club.

Unfortunately, the leaping epidemic grows wings after Lonny does a rare interview, his first in years, with one of the nation's top business websites. The billionaire is asked, "Lonny, what one piece of advice can you share with those struggling to succeed?"

Without expression, Lonny confesses, "Well, that's easy…jump off a building." The rest is history…

Of course, the "leaping syndrome" is just hyperbole. However, it demonstrates the first psychological trap that arms our brains for complacency and plagues self-development: *podium popping. Podium popping is the ineffective application of various success strategies cherry-picked from individuals who have a broadcast podium.* Much like an addict pops pills, a podium popper will "pop" random bits of advice from famous personas spotlighted in the mainstream.

For example, millions of folks hero-worship Warren Buffett and roll out the red carpet for whatever musings dribble from his mouth. Warren Buffett says do this! Do that! Seriously, if I have to suffer another article about Warren Buffett, I'm going to pull out what remaining hair I have left. Just to give you an idea how ridiculous it is, I recently read an article about Warren Buffett's diet. According to the article, he "eats like a six-year-old" and consumes five cans of Coke a day.[58] Great. Now we have a bunch of people who believe the secret to becoming a billionaire octogenarian is eating 200 grams of highly refined sugar every day. Well done, Warren. Next, we'll hear about how Warren shits every day at 3:00 p.m., which of course will be copied by his devoted followers, as if mimicking his toilet habits will help usher his success.

In our leaping-syndrome example, thousands of people hear that Billionaire Lonny succeeded because he jumped off a building, so they start doing it—ignoring the randomness of the event as well as the other fourteen million factors that attributed to the outcome.

Behind the podium-popping epidemic, you'll find another psychological sandpit—*the narrative fallacy*, popularized by Nassim Nicholas Taleb's best-selling book, *The Black Swan*. As we go through life, our brain connects seemingly random and meaningless pieces of data and transcribes them into narrative form. That structured story is then used to justify or predict cause and effect. The narrative fallacy attempts to make sense of unpredictable and hugely variable events, when in reality, there is very little, if any, causation. Specifically, it oversimplifies life processes that are anything but simple.

Podium popping grabs its narrative structure by grabbing random advice from random articles about random people and drawing the conclusions "That's why they're successful!" and "If I do what they do, I'll succeed just like them!" The narrative fallacy and its aftermath of podium poppers is probably the most ubiquitous form of bias. Hit your favorite entrepreneur website and it's all about feeding the poppers their pills…

- *The 14 Productivity Hacks of Elon Musk!*
- *9 Life Tips from Steve Jobs*
- *12 Super-Secrets of the Super-Rich!*

While the above stories might have interesting and useful information, you're getting only a minor, fragmented story behind the success. How much? I'd say about 1 percent of it. And yet, because of the narrative fallacy, you will misattribute it to much more—30, 50, 70 percent—and the next thing you know, you're jumping off a rooftop.

I witness the narrative fallacy and receive "pill requests" practically every day at my inbox. Email after email, someone messages me asking for critical, life-altering advice, as if I know the right answer:

- *Do I quit my job and start a business?*
- *Should I quit the military after five years?*
- *Do I drop out of college?*
- *My wife is the ultimate Slowlaner; do I divorce her?*
- *Do I wipe my ass with my left or right hand?*

Let me get this straight...you want me, a stranger on the other side of the planet, to decide one of your most important life decisions based on a paragraph written in forty-five seconds? It's ridiculous, and yet it happens daily.

Podium popping's consequence is that it makes you think you can retread someone's story into your own. It makes you think that because "X worked for him; X will work for me." The first issue with this thought line is it disrespects time and circumstance.

For example, the specific steps I used to start a company twenty years ago are absolutely irrelevant today. Social media didn't exist. Neither did the phrase "two-sided marketplace." I had to drag my butt down to the public library and find paying customers by scouring the nationwide Yellow Pages. Do Yellow Pages even exist anymore? Likewise, the strategies and tactics I used to start my business forum in 2007 would also be vastly different today. Publishing a book in 2010 versus 2016? Again, different. The point I'm making is this: You and I are in the same boat. If I wanted to start and succeed with a new project, I would not be as advantaged as you think. *New successes blaze new roads; they don't trail old ones.*

Another problem with podium popping and the God-like worship of success tidbits is it presumes people are homogeneous, when in fact, we're all unique based on countless variables: genetics, personalities, education, upbringing, experience, management style, leadership style, financial resources, network associates, and culture are just a few qualities that make cherry-picked strategy practically worthless.

I have tremendous respect for Steve Jobs's entrepreneurial accomplishments, and yet by many accounts, the guy was a first-class douchebag: parking his Mercedes in handicapped spots, humiliating employees, and throwing tantrums when he didn't get his way.[59] Shall we presume any of these negative traits accounted for

Jobs's iconic success? And if so, shall we now aspire for douchebaggery, considering it might be responsible for a legendary company like Apple? I hope not.

We're all perfectly imperfect. Including our heroes. While doing X, Y, and Z might have worked for Jobs, it might not work for YOU. Every one of us needs to stop hero-worshiping mortal beings and be our own heroes. Be a hero to your wife, to your family, and to your children. Stop trying to write your story with someone else's pen and, instead, start using your own.

SURVIVAL SPOTLIGHTING: FAILURES KEEP THEIR MOUTHS CLOSED

Billionaire Lonny Leaper says the secret to success is jumping off a building. He's a living testament to that advice. And unfortunately, he's also a living testament to the next psychological trap you'll encounter on your journey: *survival spotlighting.*

Survival spotlighting, which is similar to podium popping, is when you focus on the survivors of some process because they're showcased, while overlooking those who are not, usually due to lack of visibility, and hence, you come to an inaccurate conclusion.

After Lonny dispenses his landmark advice, "Jump off a building," thousands of people jump off buildings and die as a consequence. And since we can't hear from those who have leaped and died, the media reports them as suicides, and life goes on. However, if the dead could talk, they'd expose the truth: this is the worst advice ever voiced; success was my intent—not suicide.

This is how survival spotlighting works—a survivor of some process is rolled out to a stage and dispenses glorious survivor advice. What don't you hear about? Everyone else that follows the same advice and has failed at it, is failing, or will fail. A lottery has millions of invisible losers, and yet, one winner rises to the podium and is photographed and congratulated. When your buddy wins in Vegas, he's bragging on Facebook; losses are sequestered and replaced with pictures of the Bellagio fountain instead.

Behind survival spotlighting is the logic error, *the survivor bias.* And like the life-or-death consequences of the leaper syndrome, the survivor bias's discovery also has its origins in life-or-death circumstance.

During World War II, Abraham Wald and his colleagues were commissioned by the government to study long-range bombers, a notoriously high-risk job for pilots of the day. Their sole task? Figure out how to keep more bombers and their pilots in the sky.

The research started with simple observation. After a bomber returned from enemy territory, it was examined for damage. Data were graphed for each surviving plane. After a while, a pattern emerged. The common damage clusters always occurred in the tail-gunner area, the middle underbody, and the wings. Riddled with shrapnel and bullet holes, Wald's colleagues concluded that these were the most vulnerable parts of the plane and should be reinforced with extra armor. Conversely, the front and rear undersides of the planes hosted little or no damage and, they reasoned, shouldn't be modified. Wald, a mathematician by trade, interrupted the groupthink and theorized the opposite. Can you see why?

Wald argued that the damage clusters exhibited strength—not weakness—revealing exactly where the bombers could be hit and still survive the flight home. He added further that the most vulnerable areas of the plane were where there was no damage—those areas needed reinforcement because planes exhibiting those damage clusters were blown out of the sky, not surviving the flight home.[60] The Navy listened and reinforced the correct parts of the plane, more pilots survived, we won the war, and yes, the survivor bias was born.[61]

Fast-forward seven decades and the survivor bias has not only survived but thrived.

Take for example the compound-interest scam described in Chapter 25. It's predicated on survival spotlighting. Millions play the Wall Street casino for wealth, and few live to enjoy it. Those who do are spotlighted and hero-worshipped on the front page of Yahoo Finance. Behind the miraculous tale, you find a Lonny Leaper: a lifetime employee who hasn't suffered a job crunch or unexpected layoff for forty years; a man who never dealt with a health crisis or an ugly divorce; a man who had foresight to "sell" in 1999 and 2008, and "buy" in 2002 and 2010; a man who hasn't vacationed or dined-out in decades. Yes, just a caged, experience starved existence barred by a job, a shack, and an obsessive relationship with money and a retirement date that may never come. In other words, you hear about a man whose epitaph shall read, "Here lies Bob: a man who lived poor but died rich."

Here's another tale proving compound interest's survivor bias: I recently read a story fronting Business Insider, which told the miraculous tale of a thirty-year-old millionaire who was currently succeeding the Slowlane via a deprivation-and-saving strategy. This article also mentioned my *Fastlane* strategy, implying that it was BS because this poor guy was succeeding a Slowlane. This man also mentioned that his astonishing story was featured in *The New York Times*, on Business Insider, and in various other media outlets.

Duh, ya think?

These results are so rare, so miraculous, so "outlier" that they're newsworthy and belong in the pages of an international newspaper. However, you know what stories aren't featured in *The New York Times*?

Multimillionaire entrepreneurs who retire forty years early and live lavishly, not because of Wall Street, experiential starvation or mind-numbing frugality, but because they provided massive value. Hmm, maybe I should nickname myself "Money MJ" or "Dollar DeMarco"?

But these stories never make the front page of some financial website because *they simply are not unusual*. Notably, a penny-pinching millionaire is newsworthy—an affluent entrepreneur living large is not—and such might incite the masses.

Behind the extraordinary survival stories are the walking wounded: the people who have been living Wall Street's fairy tale and are treading failure. That's

Walter and Helen in Sun City, who lost half their retirement portfolio in the 2008 crash. Financial advisors told them, "Be patient—the markets will bounce back." Unfortunately, Walter and Helen don't have the luxury of patience; their story didn't make it into *Kiplinger's* but instead made *Sun City Independent's* back-page obituaries; they died early, "waiting" for the markets to bounce back. So much for that European cruise they wanted to take.

Then there's your average middle-class, middle-aged worker who's been saving diligently, but not enough, because the stinking job market hasn't given a competitive salary opportunity. Or the capital markets aren't yielding 10 percent as promised by Utopian Charts. For him, compound interest is a mortal impossibility unless he lives to 130 years old or starts making $500,000 a year. He'll never retire and will work until death. Where's his story?

In fact, where are all the baby-boomer millionaires and billionaires? If compound interest was so effective, those nearing retirement should be set for life! And yet, they're not.

According to Teresa Ghilarducci, a professor of economics at The New School for Social Research, 75 percent of Americans approaching retirement age in 2010 had less than $30,000 in their retirement accounts.[62] Seventy-five freaking percent! This begs the question: If 75 percent can barely scrape up and invest 30Gs, how much do the other 25 percent have? Think they're all millionaires?

Of course not!

The median saved in this outlier group is a mere $55K; the average amount is barely $110K. Smell the smoking gun yet?[63] This data disrobes the emperor: Survivors of compound interest and its ridiculous demands on savings and frugality are probably less than 1 percent. And yet the sky continues to rain leapers.

MOMENTUM PARALYSIS: WHY YOU CAN'T MOVE DESPITE MOVEMENT

Ever hear the phrase "throwing good money after bad"? How about "only dead fish go with the flow"? These statements best describe the next *UNSCRIPTED* battle fought, *momentum paralysis*. Momentum paralysis is not about immobility but being unable to depart from your current course of action. It is our tendency to allow momentum, or flow, to carry us through life rather than making proactive decisions, which are decidedly better for our future, even when those decisions have painful or uncomfortable attachments.

For example, several years ago, I read *Fifty Shades of Grey*, which probably ranks as one of the biggest mistakes of my life. Anyway, as an author, I was curious about the book. Seriously. With all the hype and hoopla, throwing women in a tizzy and banking millions, the book warranted an investigation. Several chapters into the book, I concluded a sulfuric acid bath would have been more pleasurable. Paragraph after paragraph, I found myself mimicking the Jackie Chan Internet meme, WTF. How many more times do I need to hear about Christian's gray eyes? His tousled hair? And her juvenile reaction to it? And yet, despite the *Fifty Shades of Literary Torture* I was suffering, guess what? I finished the damn book.

As you can see, momentum paralysis keeps you attached to the same poor decision when the right decision is to stop, reverse course, or let it go. Behind our reversing inability is a fear of loss. In my *Fifty Shades* example, I continued reading because I didn't want to feel I wasted two hours of my time. So I wasted three more thinking it would get better. I also continued reading because of FOMO—I didn't want to miss out. Was there literary genius lurking later in the book? A shocking plot curve curing its ills and explaining its Louvre-worthy reverence? Unfortunately, redemption never came—just more tousled hair and piercing gray eyes.

Momentum paralysis is why people lose fortunes in the stock market.

When you pay one hundred dollars for some hot stock shares, say eToys.com, and then it drops to eighty dollars, oh no, you can't be wrong, can you!? So you buy more at eighty dollars. Then it goes to fifty dollars and, yet again, you buy more. And then you repeat this insanity all the way to zero. Behind your rationale was not stubbornness but righteousness and your desire not to miss the great gains that surely will be forthcoming.

Are you in a soul-destroying relationship that needs to end? Momentum paralysis will keep you in it until you address the paralysis and the illogical excuses that keep you there.

- *I'm great friends with his sister.*
- *I love his child.*
- *OMG, the thought of being single and dating again scares me.*

Whatever the rationale, it compels unchanging and continuing displeasing momentum. And the longer it goes on, the harder the momentum is to break. And then the excuse becomes, "But we've been together for twelve years!"

The cognitive machinations behind momentum paralysis is a *sunk-cost fallacy.* Sunk costs are time or money investments that cannot be recovered. These costs, and the perceived pain of acknowledging their loss, are what keep you doing shit you shouldn't be doing.

For example, let's say you tragically followed the advice, "Do what you love," and opened a restaurant in your city's historic district. After six years and multiple business repositions and marketing initiatives, it's clear: Your eatery is barely profitable, earning your time a net of six dollars per hour on a seven-day, eighty-four-hour workweek. But yeah, you're "doing what you love," right? So is it time to quit and do something else?

Logically, yes. But momentum paralysis says no. It says, "Hang on," and then unabashedly reminds you of the sunk costs: Remember that long fight with city hall to get this location? Remember how hard it was hiring Chef Chavez, one of the city's best chefs? Remember winning the Daily Gazette's "Best New Restaurant" title six years ago? All of these memories, the sunk costs, keep you grinding a grind that should no longer be grinded.

In Chapter 40, we explore the business side of this quitting decision, but on the mind's side, *momentum paralysis keeps you chained to your past while wasting away your future.* This is important, especially for new entrepreneurs, because multiple failures precedes success. If momentum paralysis causes your first entrepreneurial failure to stew for ten years, you're going to run out of life.

Momentum paralysis and sunk costs are also why aspiring entrepreneurs stay aspiring. On my forum, there are several medical doctors who are tired of medicine and its domination by insurance companies and government regulation. By day, they manage emergency rooms. By night, they're building businesses. In my chats with these professionals, I can see their greatest challenge won't be business struggles but letting go of sunk costs associated with medicine.

Our past decisions have deeply etched emotional attachments. And the greater those emotional attachments are—years of schooling, training, residency—the harder abandonment becomes, hence not choosing what's best for the future but instead desiring to not see your past investment wasted.

In the end, momentum paralysis is an illogical reaction to loss aversion. Again, thinking how you think gives you the logic to diffuse emotions stoking the fires. If you had to walk twenty miles to see your favorite musician, and during your walk's thirteenth mile discovered the concert was next week, would you walk the next seven miles? Or would you logically admit the mistake and turn around? Of course you would, but inertial paralysis keeps us walking toward an empty venue. What empty outcomes are you walking toward?

CHAPTER 27

BULLSHIT FROM BULLSHITTERS: CRUTCHES, CLICHÉS, AND CULTS

The most common lie is that which one lies to himself;
lying to others is relatively an exception.
~ **Friedrich Nietzsche, Philosopher**

THE THREE ORDERS OF BULLSHIT

Spend any time at the gym and you're probably familiar with the guy who skips leg day. The "skip-leg-day" guy is the waist-up muscular dude who has toothpicks for legs. Of course, these guys don't skip their leg workouts periodically; they skip them entirely. Instead, their gym focus is tight-shirt aesthetics: arms, chest, shoulders—visible assets attracting the ladies' eyes. Confront "skip-leg-day" dude about why he doesn't press or squat and he'll say some bullshit like this:

- *I have bad knees.*
- *Both my ankles are shot.*

How do I know? LOL. Because I was once that bullshitter. And yeah, those were my excuses. Thanks to basketball injuries and a motorcycle accident, both excuses had slivers of truth. However, both were straw-man excuses: superficial justifications I grasped while avoiding squat rack pain. This story exemplifies the next B among the 3(B)s: *bullshit*.

Bullshit 1.0 is *crutches*: the stinking pile of excuses and manufactured fairy tales we tell ourselves. These scapegoats justify do-nothingness. Other times, they explain away failures or circumstances. And as long as we clutch these convenient fantasies, change adversity and righteousness bribe us into buying our victimhood.

Bullshit 2.0 is *clichés*: a bunch of meaningless mantras and proverbs revered as gospel; pithy slogans, sweet and soothing, reassuring, and unfortunately, invitations for more do-nothingness.

And Bullshit 3.0 is *cults* and their leaders: gurus and slithery figureheads who will fill your head with whatever you want it filled with.

BULLSHIT 1.0—CRUTCHES: YOUR CEREBRAL DOGMA

The bullshit dwelling in our heads is what I call *cerebral dogma*—a mental menagerie of crutches and specious vignettes that insulate our egos and protect us from doing what's uncomfortable. As you can see in my crusade against the squat rack, cerebral dogma is an equal opportunity employer.

However, behind the cerebral dogma neuroscientists found a much larger story woven. An internal story of self, identity, and reason. An internal story upon which we cling, a mental framework that guides us, protects us, and helps us organize and map a chaotic world—*your narrative bias.*

Whereas the narrative fallacy storyboards random data and events for other people, your narrative bias storyboards yours. Your narrative bias parts your identity and glues the construction of self. It's how you make sense of the world, even if that sense is based on a lie. The negative or inaccurate part of your narrative bias is your cerebral dogma, the thought snippets skewing truth, clouding reality, and routinely excusing action. And like other *SCRIPTED* fibbery, your cerebral dogma acts like a protective mother, insulating egos from the harsh realities of harsh truths.

See that young guy driving an expensive supercar? Your cerebral dogma argues, "Meh, spoiled trust-fund brat" or "Lucky". This explains away your failures and spares your ego a confrontation with lurking truths. Many times that narrative is a momentous lie constructed from a filament of truth. Yes, my ankles are about as reliable as a '72 Pinto. But no, they wouldn't *really* prevent me from pressing a rack.

Other times, your cerebral dogma exposes itself as a self-defeating soundtrack, an inner monologue constantly reminding you about your weaknesses, your dire circumstances, and your failings. For example, commit to *UNSCRIPT* and expect your cerebral dogma to fire up the Rolodex of excuses…

- *You don't have any money.*
- *You don't have the right skills.*
- *You are too old.*
- *You are too young.*
- *You live in the wrong neighborhood.*
- *You are too ugly.*
- *You have a family to support.*
- *You don't have the right degree.*
- *You don't know the right people.*
- *You know it's too hard.*

- *You know your job keeps you too busy.*
- *Excuse 93, 94, 95...*

In other instances, cerebral dogma honors our self-immolated sacred cows—short, succinct statements regarded as solid obstructions when they're anything but. Things like:

- *Oh, I hate living in Chicago, but we can't move—my family is here.*
- *We vacation every year—finances can't stop our family tradition.*
- *The best jobs are in Silicon Valley—good tech jobs aren't elsewhere.*

And because your sacred cows are regarded as fact, you're excused from the dinner table. Inaction, mediocrity, failure—there's a good reason for all of it! Legs? Hell no, my ankles are shot!

Like a crutch, cerebral dogma props up your ego and your biases: righteousness, antithetical apathy, change adversity, and the rest. Like a little devil perched on your shoulder, your narrative dogma advocates for the status quo. Until we start surveilling our thoughts, our brain risks remaining feral and unfit to command the troops.

BULLSHIT 2.0—SCRIPTSPEAK AND FRANKENPHRASES

Beware of juicy mantras and clever platitudes shoring up mediocrity. Bullshit 2.0 is the syrupy *SCRIPT*Speak everyone loves to repeat but no one interrogates. And NO to critique means YES to bullshit. Many of these dictums shine your glass house while seeding its lawn with do-nothingness. Yes, more change adversity and antithetical apathy. Anytime you accept *SCRIPT*Speak as an incontrovertible statement, you risk allowing that cliché to distort the process-principle, hence distorting results. Here are some popular ones not limited to business:

- *Fat makes you fat.*
  These SuperSnacker Cookies are fat-free, so I just ate ten! I'm sure my metabolic syndrome won't be impacted by all the sugar I just ate!
- *It takes money to make money.*
  I'm broke and will always be broke. No sense fighting a battle that can't be won.
- *Good things come to those who wait.*
  I'm just gonna sit here and twiddle my thumbs while waiting for "good things." Maybe when it finds me, it will have a $100,000 check.
- *Better safe than sorry.*
  I know I'll eventually find a zero risk opportunity some where. Until then, I'll play it safe.

- *Eighty percent of success is just showing up.*
  Once I graduate and get my degree in gender studies, employers will hire me because I'm a good person with a good degree. I'm confident I'll make at least $250K/year.

- *It's not what you know but who.*
  Success is knowing the right people, so why bother improving my skills? I'm just going to email Jeff Bezos and see if he is willing to mentor me. I'm sure he'll welcome me into his inner circle.

- *Money doesn't buy happiness.*
  I can be happy being broke (aside from the money fights with my wife); besides, there's no way I'm going to turn into one of those rich pricks!

Let's talk about my favorite BS *SCRIPT*Speak: "Money doesn't buy happiness." Whenever someone shoves this turd in your face, get ready for some real laughs. I've been broke and rich, and let me tell you, the comparison is like canned Spam to five-star steakhouse Kobe. No matter what study or academic research concludes, there's no truth to "money doesn't buy happiness" because the studies never account for *how* the money is used. Is it used to consume? Or is it used to maximize freedom within our free-range cage?

Take for instance this old folktale floating around the web. It's an idealistic sap story implying that money doesn't buy happiness. It goes like this...

> An American businessman stood at the pier of a small coastal Mexican village when a small boat with just one fisherman docked. Inside the small boat were several large yellowfin tuna. The American complimented the Mexican on the quality of his fish.
>
> "How long did it take to catch them?" the American asked.
>
> "Only a bit," the Mexican replied.
>
> "Why don't you stay out longer and catch more fish?" the American then asked.
>
> "I have enough to support my family's immediate needs," the Mexican said.
>
> "But," the American then asked, "what do you do with the rest of your time?"
>
> The Mexican fisherman said, "I sleep late, play with my children, take a siesta with my wife, take evening strolls to the village, where I sip wine and play guitar with my amigos. I have a full and busy life, señor."

The American scoffed, "I have a Harvard MBA, and I could help you. You should spend more time fishing, and with the proceeds, you buy a bigger boat, and with the proceeds from the bigger boat, you could buy several boats. Eventually you would have a fleet of fishing boats. Instead of selling your catch to a middleman, you could sell directly to the consumers, eventually opening your own cannery. You would control everything. You would need to leave your small village and move to the big city to manage your expanding enterprise."

The Mexican fisherman asked, "But señor, how long will this take?"

To which the American replied, "Ten to fifteen years."

"But what then, señor?"

The American laughed and said, "Well, that's the best part. When the time is right, you would sell your company and become very rich; you would make millions."

"Millions, señor? Then what?"

The American said slowly, "Then you would retire, move to a small coastal fishing village, where you would sleep late, play with your kids, take a siesta with your wife, take evenings strolls to the village, where you could sip wine and play guitar with your amigos…"

The reasonable moral to the story is "Money doesn't buy happiness." Except you didn't hear the rest of the story…the one that isn't shared. Here it is:

Soon after the American left, things changed. The government, desperate for tax dollars, levied a series of boating, gaming, and license fees: To continue fishing, the Mexican must pay $400 for a fishing license, a $200 environmental fee, a $350 game endorsement, and $1,800 in mooring fees. If he doesn't pay ASAP, the Mexican will be barred from fishing.

Unfortunately, after paying all the fees, the Mexican has little money left to insure and license his boat. Unable to legally operate at his favorite coastal town, the Mexican fisherman drives three hours south to another town, where the quality of the fish is poor. The long drive takes its toll on the Mexican's car, where it ultimately breaks down. In order to fix his car, he needs $200 for a water pump and $400 for a radiator. This is after he pays $600 to get his car towed back to his village. But this story is about to get worse. When the Mexican fails to pay

> the mooring fees to the harbor master, he loses his boat. The Mexican fisherman who spent most of his days in a state of unpreparedness and merriment—strumming around with his friends, sipping wine—is now unable to support his family. His wife divorces him. The Mexican now sings a different tune with his amigos ... something along the lines of "Money can buy happiness."

Which one of these stories sounds more realistic? In both stories, the Mexican has the same goal: freedom with his friends and family. That's worthy. Unfortunately, when money is removed from a real-world existence, idealism turns into a nightmare—a repeated reality found in every civilized country worldwide: bills, fees, taxes, life overhead, and money problems.

The problem isn't the Mexican's goal—freedom; the problem is he was lazy and disrespected money's role. He didn't save, prepare, or produce in excess of consumption. *Money buys happiness when you let it buy your freedom.*

WHEN FRANKENSTEIN TALKS, HE SPEAKS FRANKENPHRASES

Entrepreneurship is also rife with clichés and "mantras du-jour," which I call "frankenphrases." Frankenphrases, synonymous with the famous zombie Frankenstein, turn aspiring entrepreneurs into parroting windbags. Frankenphrases are buzzy buzzwords that enter the business vernacular, from "fail fast" or "agile" to "lean" to "start-up" to even my own ideology: *Fastlane.*

The problem with frankenphrases is they can become obstacles to effective process. Now I'm not suggesting that these phrases are without merit; the issue is when entrepreneurs parrot these phrases and don't know what they mean. I see this happen at my forum, which isn't immune to either cerebral dogma or frankenphrases.

"Is this Fastlane?" has been asked on my forum about ten gazillion times in the last seven years. *Fastlane*? Do you even know what that means? Have you read the 300-plus-page book? Do you know the five commandments? No. No. And no. But hey, it sounds like it can make me rich fast, right?

Here's another scenario repeated just about every week. Let me give you the CliffsNotes: I just spent ten dollars at Facebook to funnel traffic to a landing page I spent ninety seconds creating to advertise a product I found after ten minutes of searching at Alibiba. I have a zero conversion rate, a 100 percent bounce rate, and average visitor time of 3 seconds...should I "fail fast" and try something else?

And then there's my favorite: the word "start-up," which apparently is now ubiquitous for everything not involving a job. Let me get this straight: You send exploding glitter in the mail? Start-up. Lemonade stand? Start-up. Installed WordPress and bought a $29 dollar theme? Wow, you've got yourself a "start-up." Unfortunately, calling your venture a "start-up" puts you no closer to your first customer, your first dollar of revenue, or your first conversion any more than driving through Bel Air and calling yourself "The Fresh Prince."

The point of my rant is to stop with the damn frankenphrases. Stop asking if something is "Fastlane" or a "start-up" or "lean," and start asking what needs to be done to win your first customer.

BULLSHIT 3.0—CULTS: BEWARE OF GURUS BEARING GIFTS

Whatever you want to believe, there's a guru cult out there helping you believe it. And most of it is bullshit.

Want to believe in shortcuts? There's a shortcut-and-loopholes guru who will tell you all the secret special "hacks" to accomplish anything while bypassing the difficult steps.

Want to get rich sitting at the Wall Street craps table for fifty years? There's a legion of gurus who, for a commission, are willing to steer you into the right hedge fund, the right mutual fund, or the right ETF.

Want to believe "do what you love" is the secret to life? There are gurus for that too, people who claim to "do what they love" while selling "do what you love." Interesting.

And my favorite—if you want to learn how to perfect masterful sales funnels so you can upsell a bunch of worthless PDFs, secret reports, and antiquated marketing strategies to the same fools over and over, there's a pack of gurus for that as well.

In my first book, I affectionately called myself an "anti-guru," and while that cantankerous position might label me a "hater," I'm not hating; I'm cautioning. My issue with most gurus is something I addressed in my first book: *the paradox of practice.*

The paradox of practice is the art of selling a strategy that the author doesn't really use or that isn't responsible for making him rich. It's not practicing what you preach. It's selling real-estate books but you don't own any real estate. It's selling entrepreneurship but you never built anything profitable. It's selling fitness but you're flabby. It's selling a get-rich book but, well, you're not rich.

A member of my forum once complained in a thread, "All guru books are a road to nowhere." Of course I interjected and responded, "I disagree." *All guru books are a road into their sales funnel.* Earlier I mentioned Tony Robbins and how he lost my fandom. His latest book was rife with duplicity and practice paradoxes. When did Mr. Robbins morph from motivational speaker to a compound-interest shill? Is that why he's achieved the 1 percent among the 1 percent? Does the switcheroo have something to do with a back-end sales funnel and potentially herding readers into "recommended" firms where his involvement and monetary association could be suspiciously questioned? Obviously, Tony and I won't be doing any podcasts soon.

Anyhow, when it comes to gurus, and even public figures, ask yourself, is this person genuine and speaking from the heart? Or speaking from the cash register? Is he famously wealthy from his advice where what he says equals what he does? The only true test to guru believability is this: *authenticity.*

Authenticity is congruence. Truth over lies. Practicing what you preach. Authenticity is writing a book to change lives, not trip-wiring your unsuspecting reader into big-ticket seminars, commissioned financial products, or coaching programs. Authenticity is not a hidden agenda. Authenticity is speaking the truth and not caring about whom you might offend and how it impacts your book sales.

I've been critical of Warren Buffett, and that's not to impugn his mega-success. My challenge is authenticity. In my opinion, he portrays himself as a retail stock picker, as if he buys stock like you and I while slurping his fifth Coke of the day. The truth behind his fortune isn't buy-and-hold investing but value enhancement through entrepreneurship and corporate influence. In reality, Warren's billionaire status has little to do with buying stocks like Iggy Investor and everything to do with business building and shareholder activism. Warren is the ultimate producer who can move markets with the mere mention of new equity investment. And when the *SCRIPTED* stock picker walks into the casino and invests in this system, it keeps that system churning with new money, and hopefully, bigger share prices.

So the next time you're lapdogging the next salacious piece of advice from your saluted hero, ask yourself, is it authentic?

Is it truespeak from the heart or doublespeak from the wallet?

As you know, I don't recommend network marketing or patronize their bots. I lose thousands of dollars in book sales because of this authenticity. And blasting the mainstream's sacred cow, compound interest? Yeah, that's not going to endear me to the financial world, and it certainly won't sell this book either. That's the price of authenticity. So before you kneel before Zod and salute the next guru walking the plank of sanctimony, consider this: *the best gurus aren't gurus at all.*

Shark Tanker Kevin O'Leary, known for his vitriolic outspokenness, isn't interested in protecting your feelings when he posits your crappy invention sucks. When he spouts off, "You're insane," because you think $10,000 in revenue equates to a $10 million valuation, he's not aiming for political correctness. He's authentic. And *authenticity is the only true test of gurudom*, whether the individual knows it or not.

When Kevin O'Leary gives advice, I know I'm not being greased for a sales funnel or a back-end agenda. When Peter Thiel speaks or writes a book, I listen because I hear authenticity—I know he isn't at the Hilton Garden Inn hosting $10,000 seminars for "silver-bullet" entrepreneurs who are urged to "act now, grab your credit card, and run to the back of the room."

BURYING BULLSHIT: THREE BULLDOZERS

TECHNIQUE #1: SOCRATIC QUESTIONING

Burying bullshit requires hard questioning. If you want to weaken the *SCRIPTED* OS, call yourself out. The key to having an effective "callout" is *Socratic questioning.* Socratic questioning is a disciplined inquiry into *trains of thought*. By looking into the depths of these trains, biases, assumptions, and possible blocks of progress are uncovered.

Take this example: You see a young man driving a supercar and automatically label him a trust-fund brat. Socratic questioning looks like this:

- *Why did you conclude the driver is a trust-fund brat?*
  Because he's young, and young guys can't afford stuff like that.
- *Do you have evidence supporting this conclusion?"*
  No, but one guy I know drives a BMW 3-Series which he got for his birthday.
- *Is this direct evidence in this circumstance? A fact?*
  No, I guess not.
- *If your thought was proven false and the young man was actually self-made, how would that make you feel?*
  Then I'd guess I'd feel inadequate, even jealous.
- *Why do you think you feel that way?*
  Probably because I haven't done much with my life and I still live at home with my parents.
- *Why would you feel like that? Is it justified?*
  Pretty much, I play a lot of video games and haven't found a good job. The last time I read a book was *To Kill a Mockingbird* in high school.
- *What's the effect of thinking or believing your assumption?*
  I guess it gives me a good reason to keep doing what I'm doing and feel OK with it.
- *What could change if you no longer held this assumption?"*
  That anything is possible, even for me. Well, assuming I work hard and get some luck too.
- *Ahhh luck...let's talk about that...*

Socratic questioning drills into mental roadblocks. It probes assumptions and demands evidence. When you dig deep into underlying positions and are honest about your thoughts, you'll find (once again) that your brain is protecting your narrative bias, which protects your ego or a status quo. How would eliminating the belief, or reversing it, set a different course? Changing your head means throwing on your Perry Mason hat, whipping out the Marlboros, and putting your brain in the interrogation chair.

TECHNIQUE #2: THE CANCER COROLLARY

C-A-N-C-E-R.

Cancer. Quite possibly the most powerful word in the English language.

From a doctor, it's the most devastating thing you'll hear. From a loved one, it marks the starting line of the most harrowing emotional journey one can face. And I pray you're spared from both scenarios. However, if cancer ever had a shred of positivity to it, here it is: It's called the *cancer corollary. The cancer corollary is a hypothetical syllogism that exposes cerebral bullshit and eradicates it.* Used willfully, it kills paper crutches and dartboarded excuses. Anytime your cerebral dogma mouths off and argues you're too young, too old, too poor, too this, and too that, the cancer corollary breaks the pattern.

I apologize for the suggestion, but it works like this: Hypothetically assume you've been diagnosed with cancer and your mortality has been redefined from decades to months. Also assume a cancer cure exists. The cure, formulated by one individual named Joe Blow, is just $5,000. And you aim to buy it.

Now consider this. Before opening your wallet and giving your cash to Joe Blow, will you consider (or ask about) any of Joe Blow's personal characteristics or motives before buying?

For example, what if you learned that Joe was just nineteen years old? Would you still want the cure? How about eighty-three years old? What if Joe was the ugliest guy on the planet, with a broomstick for a leg and breath so bad that he could offend a skunk? Still want the cure? What if Joe failed gym class in high school, didn't have a college degree, and hated every moment while creating his cure? Still interested in saving your life? What if you learned that Joe was a gay atheist who had fifteen bucks in his checking account, owned a gun, was a member of Greenpeace, and voted Republican? Still want to buy the cure?

As you can see, *when someone has what you desperately want or need, their backstory becomes irrelevant.* And this is relevant because it proves that race, education, divorce, marriage, ugliness, this, that, all are self-funded delusions. The fact is when you have what others want, no one cares about your circumstances, your whys, your motives, your degree, your history, your anything! Money's velocity is driven by one simple question: *do you have something I want, and if so, what will it cost me?*

Politics are the only thing that can poison consumer buying decisions turning buyers into boycotters. The more urgent the need/want, the stronger the defense.

TECHNIQUE #3: IDENTITY CATACLYSMS

My mother smoked cigarettes most of her youth. She tried quitting for years and couldn't shake the habit. Then one day she saw a television PSA that showed the blackened, charred lungs of a chronic smoker. At the time, she was pregnant with me and the sight of the cauterized lung mortified her. Was this what I was doing to my lungs? And what about my unborn child? Instantly, everything changed and her identity shifted. In that moment, she went from a "smoker trying to quit" to a "nonsmoker." Mom never touched a cigarette again, and as she recalls, it was an easy quit.

You see, when your identity shifts from what you WANT TO BE to WHAT YOU ARE, your actions will fight to maintain the identity. If someone offers me a cigarette, I don't ponder the question; the answer is an instinctive and immediate "NO THANKS" because my identity is "I am a nonsmoker." The truth is, most books (including this one) are ineffective change agents because readers rely on willpower to drive action. Willpower and motivation have been proven ineffective as depleting resources. They rarely work at creating habits, the agents of permanent change.

Real change comes from *identity* and *self*—not from interim motivations jump-started by books or YouTube binging. Basically, you have to **BE** what you want to become **FIRST** so the actions can follow. *Don't TALK about it; BE about it.* **BE. ACT** on being. Then **HAVE**.

For example, if you're in the "aspiring entrepreneur" category, it's most likely because your identity is not consecrated as an entrepreneur, but instead something like "I'm an Intel employee, and I would love to quit my job someday and start a business." You're not a nonsmoker who's experienced a shift cataclysm; you're simply a smoker *trying* to quit and, unfortunately, will probably be for life.

When you identify as an entrepreneur, you will do whatever it takes to quit your job and succeed as one because your identity seeks congruence. Identified as an "employee looking to quit," and **your identity is congruent with the status quo**—you won't do what's necessary, and instead, actions become convenient and trivial.

My identity shifted when I saw a Lamborghini as a teenager. From that day my identity was 100 percent entrepreneur, keeping me tracked forward even though my actions weren't always entrepreneurial. Debt and five years of corporate grooming at college can do that. To keep the boats floated and the dream alive, I worked menial jobs better suited for a high-school dropout, not a dual-degreed college grad who tossed his cap with honors. It took me over ten years before my identity as an entrepreneur (BE, followed by ACT) matched my results (HAVE). That's the power of identity.

How you see yourself makes or breaks the foundation you work with—the sturdy ground of THIS IS ME or the motionless treadmill of THIS MIGHT BE ME.

So how do you change your identity?

First, identify what you want to be and label yourself as such. Unfortunately, this isn't easy unless it's attached to an emotional episode, *a shift cataclysm*, which also can double as your "fuck this" event. For me, it was a white Lamborghini—for my mom, a scarred lung; for you, perhaps it's the boss taking credit for your work. Whatever it is, allow your emotions to do the shifting.

Second, reinforce and ratify your identity by taking regular action, no matter how small. If your new identity is someone who's decisively decided to be healthy after a stroke, a small action might be "no thanks" to happy-hour pizza.

Unfortunately, unlike my mom's identity shift causing her to go cold turkey with immediate 100 percent compliance, such isn't likely. Instead, aim for the daily action and improvement found within the process-principle. James Clear, author of *Transform Your Habits* (recommended read) says "prove your identity" daily. This happens with small wins and minor improvements.

If your new identity is "I am an author," write a few paragraphs a day. Build on your prior effort, where the net effect is an upswing. As I mentioned in the process-principle, once feedback echoes pour in, congratulations. That's when things get easier, habits dig in, and others take notice. A 1 percent daily evidentiary shift for one year will transform you into a new person, to the point you wouldn't recognize your current self.

> **?** ***I am an author, entrepreneur, and an investor. How do you currently identify yourself? Unemployed college grad? Car salesman? And does it serve your goals?***

ENTREPRENEURSHIP LIVES OR DIES IN YOUR HEAD

Life, liberty, and the pursuit of entrepreneurship live and die in your head—reversing beliefs, unbinding biases, and confronting bullshit. An autopiloted brain, which isn't trained to think how it thinks, will find their *UNSCRIPTED* effort likened to an hour at the casino—short and not sweet. Entrepreneurship is a tough but rewarding sport. But *it must be lived, not tried*. Master the 3(B)s and congratulations; shift your tassel and graduate into the heart of the *UNSCRIPTED* Entrepreneurial Framework, the first circle (MP) where happiness is unearthed…

Meaning and purpose.

THE UNSCRIPTED ENTREPRENEURIAL FRAMEWORK

MEANING-AND-PURPOSE (MP)

$$[\ 3(B) \cap (MP \cap FE \cap KE) \cap 4(D)\ ] \ / \ FTE$$

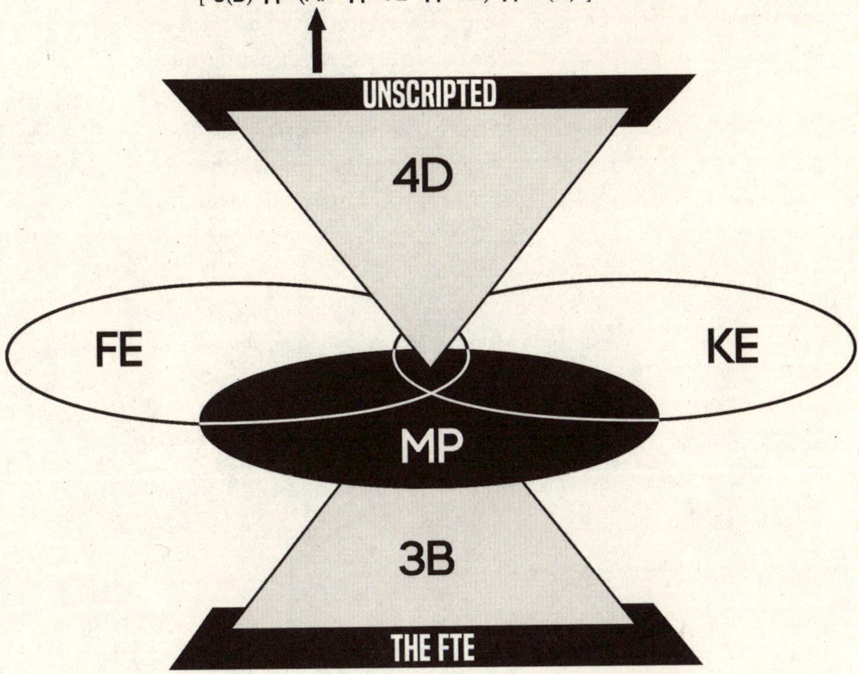

CHAPTER 28

MEANING-AND-PURPOSE: THE UNSTOPPABLE WILL TO WIN

There is one quality which one must possess to win, and that is definiteness of purpose, the knowledge of what one wants, and a burning desire to possess it.
–Napoleon Hill, Writer

THE MOTIVATION CYCLE: HOW TO ACCOMPLISH GREAT THINGS

Great results require a great commitment. Commitment fires the process-principle where habits become lifestyle and lifestyle becomes winning results.

When everyone sleeps, the ballerina is at the studio practicing. When everyone orders pizza, the fitness competitor orders salad. When everyone parties like it's 1999, the inventor locks himself in his basement and grinds his idea.

So where does this kind of commitment come from?

Not from willpower or motivational videos.

If commitment had a spark plug, it would be *meaning-and-purpose—the core reasons WHY you act and continue to act, even through hardship, criticism, failure, and seemingly impossible odds.*

Like a Kevlar vest, meaning-and-purpose is an "I don't give a crap" attitude toward the YouTube comment trolls who called your latest video stupid. It yanks you to the stage to speak when you're scared shitless. It's your latest business venture despite the nonbelievers in your family who say you're nuts, often citing your nine earlier failures.

Meaning-and-purpose is the fuel that powers *the motivation cycle*—the heat that churns your soul, torpedoing you forward when others crawl back to bed.

As we ascend into the *UNSCRIPTED* framework, your meaning-and-purpose and its motivation cycle are the catalyst to act, persist, and win. While rewritten 3Bs inspire starting, your meaning-and-purpose and its motivation cycle inspire finishing.

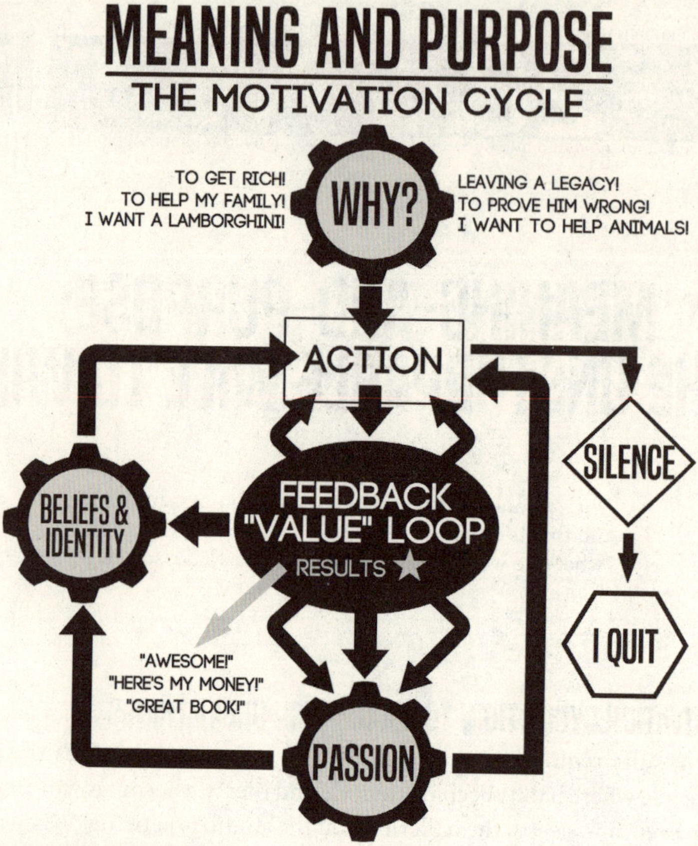

THE WHY: YOUR CORE DRIVER

One can never underestimate the power of a moment. For me, it was a seemingly insignificant conversation. My memory, however, would prove otherwise. I stood in the fraternity hallway talking to three of my brothers. It was just days from graduation, and my friends and I were discussing their post-graduation jobs. When I disclosed my future employment, which was nil, I confessed: I didn't job interview because I'm an entrepreneur. (Notice my identity!) One of my fraternity brothers snickered and with smug impunity said, "Yeah, I'm sure that's going to work out for you." He then crowed about getting hired at some entry-level accounting job from a "big-three" firm, braggadociously predicting that within a few years, he'd be earning a six-figure paycheck. I, with equal smugness, retorted, "That's awesome; maybe someday I'll hire you."

This conversation lasted minutes. And yet, for some inexplicable reason, it seared my mind. It was something I'd remember and think about often. It fired me up, pissed me off, and deepened my convictions. While I never saw this frat guy again, his belittling comment served me for years and ignited one of my many whys—the specific motivations behind passionate action.

Aside from my pompous frat brother, here was my list of WHYs:

- ✔ I hated suits, and the thought of wearing one was unbearable.
- ✔ I wanted to own a Lamborghini.
- ✔ I wanted to ease the burden for my single mother.
- ✔ I wanted to retire early and write a book about retiring early. (LOL)
- ✔ I didn't want "money problems" to potentially damage a marriage.

Whatever your WHYs, they must be strong enough to incite action that borders on the obsessive. What "whys" will compel you to work on a Saturday night while your bros are partying? What "whys" will compel you to drive the 160,000-mile Honda when your wingman drives a new Camaro? And are these "whys" hot enough to steam water when things go cold? Fiery WHYs overpower expiring willpower and fizzling passion. Lukewarm WHYs translate into neither meaning nor purpose, but action-faking. Without solid WHYs, effort sinks in the first storm.

For example, the most common storm new entrepreneurs face is called the *desert of desertion*. The desert of desertion is the duration from idea to your first sale. It is the absence of the feedback loop in the motivation-cycle (and within the process-principle) and it could go on for months, perhaps years. In one instance, an entrepreneur at my forum designed his own luxury brand of sunglasses. From idea to creation to first sale was nearly two years. This two years of high activity and zero feedback is the arid desert. Without reinforcement, quitting becomes easy. Too easy. Life gets in the way: your job, the kids, or the lure of the next hot opportunity.

Without outside confirmations, it's easy to rationalize greener pastures: "Eh, this isn't going to work" or "No one is going to buy this" or "There has to be something easier."

Meaning-and-purpose is the camel you want in this desert—not willpower.

Another storm meaning-and-purpose overcomes is pain and ridicule.

Several years ago, a young man posted a forum proclamation that he would be a millionaire by twenty-five. Unfortunately, his lengthy declaration lacked substance, and the forum denizens ridiculed him. However, as the years passed and the failure crystallized, I noticed something: Despite public ridicule, this entrepreneur was persistent, highly visible, trying different things, and overall, saturating the world with his effort. Suddenly, he didn't seem like an average drive-by looking to get rich. When I reread his original post (now a few years old), something slipped my eye on the first skim: *He said his purpose was to free his mother from poverty.* Instantly, I became a believer. Even though he failed, and might fail again, eventually he'll strike gold. The mountaintop shall be his because he's backpacked a great WHY buttressed by meaning-and-purpose—a weapon capable of slaying forum skeptics and "you're crazy" doomsayers.

As you can see, I have a love/hate relationship with my forum. For over eight years, I've observed entrepreneurs (and failed entrepreneurs) from the bleachers. I love that I can occasionally take the field and make a difference. And I hate that no matter how much I try, there's always an entrepreneurial stampede thinking that extraordinary results can be wrangled with an ordinary effort. The world has no shortage of people seeking lounge-chair, remote-control success—they want all that life has to offer—just as long as it comes in comfortable harmony. This young man striving to save his mother from poverty? He's a force-packing Jedi Knight among a legion of soulless stormtroopers.

Unfortunately, entrepreneurship, along with life and liberty, is a tale of periodic pain now or perpetual regret later. Namely, how bad do you want it? How much are you willing to give up for it?

Everyone wants the perfect wife, but few want to work toward becoming the perfect husband. Everyone wants the *Muscle & Fitness* cover body, but few want to workout daily followed by "no thanks" to break-room pizza. Everyone wants the big bank account and the passive-income business, but few want the risk, the long hours, or the unpredictable income. Without sufficient WHYs, you're no better than everyone, and "everyone" is not an echelon for aspiration. *To be someone, you can't be driven like everyone.*

In fact, it's not uncommon for elderly retirees, lifelong employees who finally retire, to die shortly thereafter. Without their job and a sense of contribution, they lose their meaning-and-purpose. Without a purpose obsessively cored as identity, you won't survive. When sifting through life's jungle, you want a sharpened scythe to break through the weeds—meaning-and-purpose are its grinding stone.

Don't confuse a WHY with a DESIRE. DESIRES are often superficial and transient, whereas WHYS are firm and transcendent through time.

CHAPTER 29

BEWARE! THE WONDER TWINS OF EPICALLY BAD LIFE ADVICE

There is only one passion, the passion for happiness.
~ Denis Diderot, French Philosopher

FOOL'S GOLD: "DO WHAT YOU LOVE" AND "FOLLOW YOUR PASSION"

In 2005, Steve Jobs gave a legendary commencement speech at Stanford University. He echoed over and over, "Love what you do." The now-famous statement has morphed into its syrupy cousin, "Do what you love." And every time I hear it, I lose another millimeter off my molars.

Jobs's universally accepted maxim exemplifies just how impervious a misinterpreted sound bite can become when eulogized literally—unite *podium popping* and *survival spotlighting* and, wham, you get horrific life advice incontrovertibly ordained. And suddenly, hordes of people are jumping off buildings.

But wait, there's more.

"Do what you love" also has a twin: the pithy proverb "Follow your passion."

Again, another perilous dose of direction, usually dispensed by unknown bloggers with unknown track records who unknowingly don't know the theology is hogwash.

Put 'em together and what you get is *The Wonder Twins of Epically Bad Life Advice.*

This cattle call of the self-development world has spawned a worshiping army of "passionites," where "do what you love" and "follow your passion" supplant demand, business models, and economics. Both need to be stricken from your vocabulary, and the sooner done, the sooner you can *UNSCRIPT*. Here's why:

Again, both phrases bastardize *survival spotlighting* and *podium popping.*

Think about it.

Everyone is passionate about one thing or another. The problem is *no one interviews passionate failures.* Failed passionites have no stage, no audience, no one salivating at their greatness. The bankrupt passionite who's followed his passion for twenty years and didn't get featured in *Inc. Magazine* isn't dispensing advice.

Think of it this way. Are *American Idol* winners passionate about singing? Of course they are. Does it make sense to sing auditions when you're dispassionate about it? Therefore, the 190,000 people who also auditioned and went home crying failures were also passionate. Will you ever hear from them? Nope.

Second, consider the cancer corollary as it pertains to Steve Jobs's "love what you do." Do you remember why you bought an Apple product? Did you consider Steve Jobs's personal motives or internal narratives when you forked over cash? Was Steve Jobs's "love what you do" a factor in your decision process? Is anyone waiting in line for eighteen hours at the Apple store thinking about Steve Jobs? Or Tim Cook?

Of course not. You spend money on these great products because, well, they're great products. Within your purchasing decision, you identified perceived value, and after purchasing, perceived value transformed into actual value. Bam. Satisfied customer. The founder's selfish sentiments had no place in your decision tree.

Let me put it another way. You're at a fancy restaurant and order steak, medium rare. The steak hits your table and it tastes like grilled leather and isn't fit for a vulture. You complain to the server and refuse to pay. The server retrieves the owner, who's also the chef. When the owner/chef arrives at your table, you explain that your meal tastes like baked cardboard and refuse payment. He replies, "I'm sorry, sir, but I love to cook. And since I love cooking, you must also love what I do."

Bottom line, no one cares about the motives driving you. *No one gives a shit that you love what you do!* No one cares that you want to "be your own boss," "get rich," or any other selfishly conceived motive.

Remember the cancer corollary, where value trumps all: If you have something that hasn't been commodified and you effectively communicate its value to me, you get my money. If you hated formulating a cancer cure—doesn't matter—you still get my money. Passion, love, and everything else are irrelevant.

Third, the moment you straddle the wonder twins as your life compass, the fiduciary principle is violated and selfishness becomes your navigator. This disposition aligns with *SCRIPTED* thinking, the same herd mentality that causes consumers to trample into a Walmart at 2:00 a.m. on Black Friday. Whenever you're partnered with selfishness, it makes you blind to opportunity because you're too focused on what you want (and don't want) versus what other people want.

For instance, I had an acquaintance some years ago who was hooked by the wonder twins. I cautioned him, but the promise of glory was too alluring. At the age of thirty-six, without an income, he quit his job as a sales representative. And with help from *The Bank of Enabling Parents*, he took a stab at "doing what he loved."

His idea? Let's start a blog, as if the other eleven million blogs weren't enough. Worse, his business model was apparently writing about himself incessantly: me, me, and more me. You see—I'm special, I'm unique, and I'm following my passion! I should be raking in the Google AdSense revenue in a few months! For over a year, I watched this poor guy write about shit no one cared about. I cleaned out my garage; don't the shelves look bad-ass? I just read this book that says, "do what you love," you gotta read it! Here's a funny story when I was nine years old! In the end, his only fans (customers?) cheering from the gallery were his enabling family. For me, the train wreck got old and I stopped paying attention. And his thirty-one Twitter followers probably did too.

Once again, the point needs to be driven home: *no one fucking cares.*

Your parents said you were special. Maybe, but in the eyes of the market, it's a fantastic lie. The market is one selfish rat, and if you insist on being selfish yourself, you don't have a prayer. *When passion doesn't solve people's problems, passion doesn't pay bills.* And those are points number four and five.

Does a market even exist for what you love? Do other people need what you love, and if so, are you exceptional at it while communicating a unique value proposition? If you aren't, be prepared to prostitute your love in the name of paying bills.

Markets flooded with "do what you lovers" are extremely crowded and rip-your-hair-out competitive. Does the Internet really need 190,000 weight-loss blogs? Yes, I get it—you lost weight; you're passionate about the accomplishment; now you want to spread the gospel. But so are 400,000 other people, and unless you're doing something different, you remain unremarkable.

Saturated markets mean mediocrity and average products, and wonderland "do what you lovers" cannot survive unless they're an outlier. Excess supply suppresses price, and suddenly, your love is commodified where "best price takes all."

I can attribute my early business failures to these two mantras. I followed my interests and passions while ignoring market needs and marketable value propositions. From vitamins to automotive audio, everything I tried never offered or communicated unique value to the marketplace. Need, nonexistent. *Passion didn't pay the bills because passion didn't hit a market need.*

If only my blogger buddy asked first, "Does blogging about myself for 300 days straight solve anyone's problem or, at the minimum, create outstanding entertainment?" No and no.

On my forum, one member figured it out the hard way. He said:

> Oh, you like to snowboard, so you're going to build a snowboard business? Your passion is NOT a reason to go into business. I lost eight months and made ZERO sales attempting to "follow my passion" when I knew nothing about how to add value in this particular market.[64]

Practically every week, a corrupted "do what you love" drone storms into my forum and asks such telltale questions: "Should I start a fitness blog?" "Do I start a car social network?" When I probe further, "What value are you offering" or "What are you doing different that hasn't been beaten to death elsewhere?" the answer is always the same: *nothing.* For the lost, "do what you love" and "follow your passion" are suddenly a business model impervious to market economics.

Take for example personal training—a career rife with "do what you love" and "follow your passion" go-getters. The fitness person thinks, "Hey, I love fitness, so I'll be a personal trainer!" Great, except you are an ant on an anthill. Thousands more think identically, and as a result, the aggregate trainer pool could fill fifty coliseums. Thousands are eager to undercut your livable wage. And once that happens, guess what? Your love withers into hate.

Another injurious effect stemming from the dynamic duo of bad advice is *opportunity compression.* Opportunity compression limits your exposure to new opportunities in alternative industries that are ripe for new value offerings. For example, if you're passionate only about sewing and scuba diving, you will compress your available opportunities to those industries only. If those industries represent only .00002 percent of GDP, you limit yourself to that small pool of opportunity. Don't microscope yourself into a puddle when you should be surveying the ocean.

The snowboard entrepreneur quoted above who had zero sales following his passion? He went on to start a successful company in the pet industry, owned it for a few years, sold it, and—last I checked—was on a three-month vacation in Thailand. And get this: he didn't have a dog nor was he passionate about the industry. Myself? I camped in the limousine industry for over a decade, and yet I had no passion for that particular space other than the process of adding value to it.

The fourth reason why "love" and "passion" shouldn't be your bread-maker is called the *overjustification effect.* The overjustification effect is a psychologically studied phenomenon lending credibility to the idea that "do what you love" and "follow your passion" are destructive career advice. Namely, once you get paid extrinsic rewards for something you once did freely due to sheer intrinsic motives, your interest in that activity suffers. According to Wikipedia via *Psychology: The Science of Behavior*, the overjustification effect occurs…

> …when an expected external incentive such as money or prizes decreases a person's intrinsic motivation to perform a task. The overall effect of offering a reward for a previously unrewarded activity is a shift to extrinsic motivation and the undermining of pre-existing intrinsic motivation. Once rewards are no longer offered, interest in the activity is lost; prior intrinsic motivation does not return, and extrinsic rewards must be continuously offered as motivation to sustain the activity.[65]

So, if you're doing something freely because you're passionate about it, suddenly getting paid for it might poison that passion. I see failed passionites report this frequently, including my own experience. I started chauffeuring because I loved to drive. By the time I finished that job, I hated driving. Fast-forward twenty years and guess what? I still hate driving.

"Do what you love" can kill your love.

The same story was repeated on my forum, except from a user who, like me, was passionate about six-figure sports cars. "Do what you love" killed his love. He wrote:

> From the earliest I remember, I was car obsessed. I ate, slept, and drank cars. Naturally, I was desperate to learn and passed my driving test at seventeen. Two weeks after, I passed my race license. I loved it; in the first twelve months of driving, I covered 25,000 miles for no reason other than I enjoyed it.
>
> After passing my race test, I got my instructor's card and became a self-employed racing driver at the age of eighteen. I worked for two local companies that did driving experiences with customers. I was paid to drive Ferraris and Lamborghinis on a racetrack. Yes, I was paid to drive exotic cars most people dream of sitting in, let alone owning. And I was paid well for it.
>
> In the first three years of being licensed, I owned fourteen different cars, sometimes three cars at the same time. All of my earnings went to my cars, and I loved life. I could work at whatever racetrack I wanted. Sounding more like a success story, right?
>
> I worked in that industry for four years, and by the time it was over, I HATED driving. The one thing that defined me—my love of cars—was absolutely killed by that job. Everyone who got in a car with me said I had the best job in the world, and for a while, I agreed with them. But after 30,000 laps on the same track, I can tell you I want nothing more to do with them.
>
> Don't "do what you love," because even if you are lucky to make a living doing it, you won't love it for very long. You should love the value you create. The process is hard, but it's justified by your love of the value that is created through it.[66]

"Do what you love" can kill your love.

One of my few hyperrealistic vices (or loves) is watching NFL football. During a game, my friend quipped that he'd love to be an NFL referee as they work one day a week and make bank—six figures and more. I argued that for the crazed football fan, it's a horrible idea. As a referee, you would systematically destroy your love for the game, where games would become unwatchable. Instead of absorbing a game as entertainment, you'd be forced to observe the game as segregated units of action for the purpose of catching penalties. You'd never watch the game in the same way.

The final reason why "do what you love" and "follow your passion" are crummy advice is perhaps the most potent and destructive: they're Trojan horses into a fixed mindset, a justification to avoid pain and discomfort, and hence, inhibit growth. Let me explain.

In Chapter 18, I confessed that I'm an introvert. That means if you're a random stranger and email me a coffee offer, I'll decline. It's not that I don't like you; it's just that I'd rather dive into a good book surrounded by solitude. Introversion also means that I have no desire (or passion) to be famous. I hate public speaking, interviewing or doing podcasts. Nonetheless, I do them because they align with my meaning-and-purpose. To spread the *UNSCRIPTED* message, I have to get out there, speak, and spread the good word. If I grasped the mentality of "do what you love" or "follow your passion," I'd never do these things because I hate them. Public speaking? OMG, I hate that! I don't love it, nor do I have passion for it! I'll pass!

And this highlights the ultimate irony: *the secret to success isn't "do what you love" but "do what you hate."* How much pain and anxiety you'll endure tells me how much success you're willing to achieve. You see, passion doesn't move me to do podcasts or live radio interviews. And passion certainly doesn't put me on stage in front of an audience for two hours—*meaning-and-purpose gets me there.*

In the end, the wonder twins maliciously give you good cause to decline anything that looks like work, seems discomforting, and isn't aligned with passion. Simply put, *you'll never grow into the person you need to become because you're too busy avoiding transformative pain.* And in the world of passionites, it's perfectly justifiable because, after all, Steve Jobs says, "Love what you do."

THE FEEDBACK LOOP: THE KEY TO PASSION (AND GREAT RESULTS)

So… was Steve Jobs's advice, "Love what you do," wrong? Should we ignore the billionaire's advice and instead listen to millionaire advice from me? Isn't that a significant demotion? Well, if the ante is one billionaire against me, I'll raise you two billionaires: Mark Cuban and Marc Andreessen. Both recently echoed a similar opinion about our infamous wonder twins. In a series of tweets, Andreessen posited:

> <u>TWEET #1:</u> "Do what you love" / "follow your passion" is dangerous and destructive career advice. [67]

Andreessen then tweeted a few more times about the survivor bias and how "do what you love" failures have no platform. And then he dropped this golden nugget:

> TWEET #5: Better career advice may be "do what contributes" -- focus on the beneficial value created for other people vs just one's own ego.[68]

A similar sentiment was echoed by another billionaire, Mark Cuban, on his blog, BlogMaverick.com. He stated:

> What a bunch of BS. "Follow Your Passion" is easily the worst advice you could ever give or get.[69]

So, in the battle of billionaire advice (and my insignificant millionaire self), who's right? They all are. Whenever I hear Jobs's Stanford speech, I know exactly what he was talking about, and it wasn't the literal interpretation. He wasn't giving us the golden key unlocking the secret into pain-free success. He instead gave us insight into the joy and love one receives *when the world values your value.* Notably, when the world kicks on your feedback loop and says "This is awesome" or "I like this; here's my cash," you too will love what you do. Let's look back at the motivation cycle.

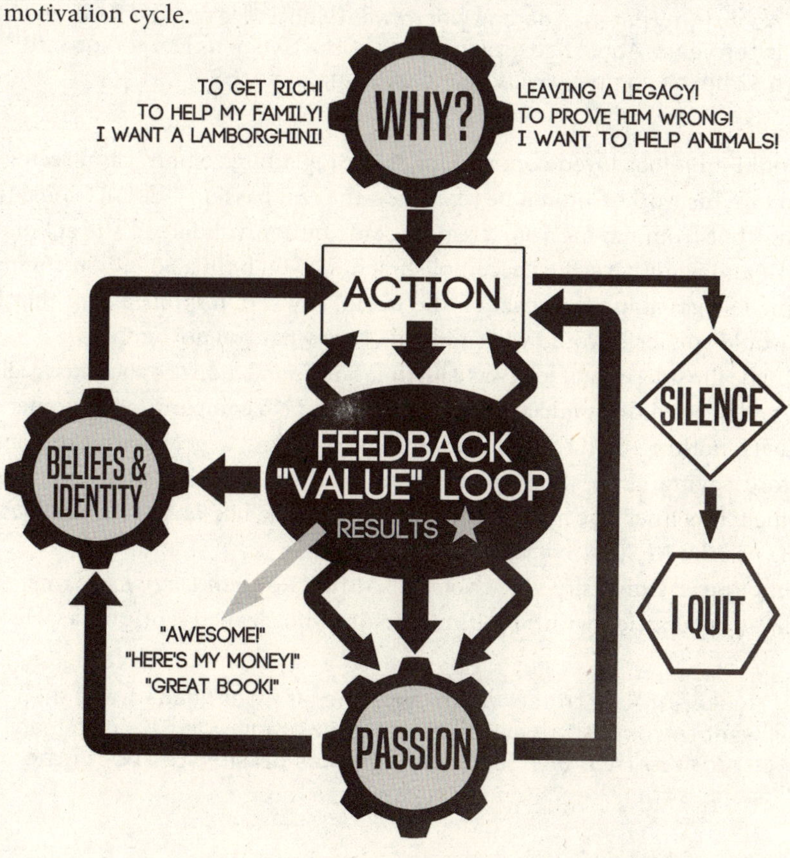

Followed by strong WHYs compelling ACTION, your FEEDBACK LOOP does the heavy lifting, driving passion and, hence, results. Whenever there is silence, or an absent feedback loop, the cycle sputters out into quitting.

Ever notice that when you start a new project, you're incredibly passionate? If you survive the desert of desertion and launch a product that isn't well received, expect passion to fizzle. *Every blogger starts their blog with passion.* However, after one or two posts and encountering market silence—no one has read, shared, or commented on their legendary prose—the passion fades. *When no one values our value, passion quits us.*

This explains why a gazillion blogs are abandoned after two or three articles. Think those people would quit if their first blog post had a million views, 500 comments, and 12,000 shares? *The feedback loop drives passion, which drives action, which drives results.* See, it's easy to love what you do when others do too. Think I'd write another business book if my first book sold just forty-one copies?

Passion flows when effort is rewarded.

Likewise, Jobs said this during his speech:

> I was lucky; I found what I loved to do early in life. Woz and I started Apple in my parents' garage when I was twenty. We worked hard, and in ten years, Apple had grown from just the two of us in a garage into a $2 billion company with over 4,000 employees. [70]

Could it be Jobs loved contributing, building a huge empire, and seeing the world love his work? Could it be real love—the real passion—doesn't come from "doing" but from having your creative contribution validated? The act of self-growth and worldly verified accomplishment? If you built a $2 billion company, you made a gargantuan impact on the world. If you're responsible for that feat, how would you feel? Would you suddenly "love what you do"?

On the flip side, what if Jobs was a lifetime failure and didn't connect his feedback loop, and hence didn't build a $2 billion company? No company, no customers, no products, nothing. Still think Jobs would be speaking to graduating students at Stanford, saying, "Love what you do"? You see, the mechanism underneath Jobs's statement is neither love nor passion for specific work, but *having love and passion for the positive RESULTS of your work.*

In a Prager University video voiced by Mike Rowe of *Dirty Jobs* fame, Mike recalls a conversation with a multimillionaire who cleaned septic tanks. He said:

> I looked around to see where everyone else was headed, and then I went the opposite way. Then I got good at my work. Then I began to prosper. Then one day, I realized I was passionate about other people's crap.[71]

Ever notice when a sports team is winning, everyone is smiling and having fun? And yet when that same team is losing, they're sulking and looking like they're attending a funeral? Winning inspires passion; losing does not.

Here's another example I recently read: In 2011, Leonard Kim started a WordPress blog after leaving his job. He wrote three posts. And no one read it. And then he quit.

Later, he gave Quora a try, figuring, "Why not?" In his first month, he received a similar result, 102 views. Nothing spectacular. However, Kim's *luck* would change. One day someone who was inspired by his writing promoted it to over 1,000 people. And those people loved his work, compelling more views and kick-starting Kim's feedback loop. This inspired Kim to write more. In his next month, his writing received 3,000 views. The next, 61,000—followed by 162,000 views. After eighteen months, Leonard is now over eight million views on his writing, including this fan in Arizona.[72]

What changed since those first three blog posts that no one read?

A positive feedback loop.

Similarly, did you know that Chipotle's founder Steve Ells originally had no interest in starting a Mexican fast-food restaurant? He started Chipotle hoping it would fund his passion, a fine-dining restaurant.

However, the market had a different idea.

As customers loved his fast-food concept and profits soared, his feedback loop fired positively. Suddenly "follow your passion" became irrelevant. In a *Huffington Post* interview, Ells said:

> I remember feeling a little guilty every time I opened a Chipotle. I felt guilty because I wasn't following my true passion. But that eventually went away. And I realized that this is my calling.[73]

Ahh, and that's the amazing power of a positive feedback loop—suddenly "do what you love" and "follow your passion" are exposed as the frauds they are.

In *The Millionaire Fastlane*, I mentioned passion was the motivation behind results. Unfortunately, this too was misinterpreted into "follow your passion." Ugh. My intent was that a solid meaning-and-purpose, a why, drives action into doing whatever it takes. For instance, the example I used was about a man who recounted his impoverished childhood, where things were so bad that his family used melted snow for toilet water. These moments created a transcendent WHY for him—"I'm not going to live like this for the rest of my life!" A powerful WHY underneath meaning-and-purpose produces many things: stubbornness, focus, discipline, persistence, and yeah, even passion.

My current purpose—spreading the *UNSCRIPTED* gospel—compels action. That action translates into hard work, which sometimes isn't fun or passionate. Nonetheless, work's positive results spawn more passion. When I wake up and discover I already earned $1500, I feel passion. When my inbox has several "you've changed my life!" emails, I feel passion. When my book wholesaler orders 300 books, I feel passion. And yet, I don't feel passion having to spend thirty minutes processing orders. I don't feel passion when I'm preparing for an interview or staging myself to speak, but I feel it after.

So, if all this gibberish about passion, meaning, and purpose is making your head spin, let's clean it up. Within (TUNEF), your beliefs shape your identity and pierce into your meaning-and-purpose, or your whys. That purpose drives you into action, which in itself can be extremely difficult and discomforting. Both pain and passion accompany this journey. Once you feel the positive results of your effort—feedback, sales, success stories, stray dogs saved, etc.—more passion is generated, which advances the entire motivation cycle. I'm not passionate about dog poop, but I could own a multinational company that cleans it up if it aligns with my purpose in making the world a better-smelling place.

Passion is self-replicating and greases the entire system. Your positive impact generates passion. Don't be passionate about what needs to be done; be passionate about what you WILL BECOME.

Be passionate about your vision as it compels doing whatever it takes. Passion focused on specific activities does not. In the end, *passion isn't something you follow; it's something that ebbs and flows within you.*

Daily UNSCRIPTED pursuits are challenging and fraught with discomfort—expect passion to abandon you during the grind but return once the feedback loop fires.

Core drivers for action and fundamental life shifts are 1) IDENTITY 2) MEANING/PURPOSE (why) and 3) PASSION via the feedback loop.

CHAPTER 30

IGNITE YOUR PURPOSE, INVIGORATE YOUR SOUL

Man cannot live without some knowledge of the purpose of life. If he can find no purpose in life, he creates one in the inevitability of death.
~ **Chester Himes, Writer**

FINDING YOUR PURPOSE

If you're unsure of your meaning-and-purpose, sorry, you don't have one. If you're crying because your favorite hockey team lost the Stanley Cup or because NBC canceled your favorite television show, guess what?

No meaning. No purpose.

On the contrary, if there's something obsessive in your life keeping you awake at night, congratulations, young Skywalker—the Force is strong with you. And therein lies the chasm between interests or commitment; shallow desires don't compel sacrifice, whereas a committed purpose sacrifices everything. It borders obsession.

Again, consider the cancer corollary.

If you were diagnosed with cancer and your mortality came into focus, would you struggle to find meaning-and-purpose? Would hyperrealistic distractions finally get the demotion they deserve? And what about passion? Would survival and kicking cancer's ass suddenly have the power to generate passion? You see, meaning-and-purpose sit in the driver's seat; passion rides shotgun. It inspires you to do what others won't, from breaking comfort zones to obsessing about process and progress. In fact, meaning-and-purpose are so powerful it can be dangerous.

If you're willing to do whatever it takes, your "whatever" might regress into the unethical or even criminal activity. For example, in F. Scott Fitzgerald's classic *The Great Gatsby*, Jay Gatsby is a rags-to-riches socialite whose WHY for becoming famously wealthy was to win the attentions and affections of a past love. Except his fortune was nefariously obtained—a ravenous purpose sank him into the abyss, where he found a young death.

The common thread among the famous as well as the infamous is a dominant meaning-and-purpose. And likewise, the common thread amongst the *SCRIPTED* sheeple is they have no meaning. Instead, hyperreality babysits—this is why we have a society addicted to *Game of Thrones* and whoever wins some stupid singing contest. With meaning, this shit cannot compete. Social media showboating is no longer entertaining. Sporting events—fleeting entertainment not worthy of tears or a sibling smackdown. Pop culture: who's dating whom, who got fat, who's styling a new bikini—a pointless insult and trivialization of your purpose. Once you own that reality is steeled by meaning-and-purpose, hyperrealistic distractions are, well, distracting.

So how do you find your meaning if you're unsure of yours?

Surprisingly, it can be virtually anything. The things that fire you up might make me yawn. A powerful meaning could be something as insignificant as the sight of a Lamborghini or a pompous friend mouthing-off. It could be the fear of having to sardine yourself into a commuter train. Or it could be an uninvolved parent who curses, "You'll never amount to anything." Many times, your "fuck this" event (FTE) is enough to clarify purpose.

If you're still coming up empty, try this: Imagine winning a billion dollars. After winning the fortune, *what specifically would you do*? I'm not talking about "travel the world" or "buy a fleet of exotic cars"—I'm talking about **AFTER** you've done all that. **AFTER** you've bought everything and seen everything—what would be next? Writing? Philanthropy? Making movies? Whatever it is, it's a clue into what gives your life meaning or purpose.

Still, if none of this clarifies your purpose, there's not much you can do to find it other than instigating life. Recluses won't find purpose living out their days in a sacred bubble. Partake in commerce, start working out, volunteer, go on a mission. Do freaking something. Like a "fuck this" event, many times a committed meaning is uncovered in tragedy, hardship, or momentous life events. From having your first child and wanting to be the best parent you can be, to being pink-slipped after fifteen years of loyalty are just a few examples of how events can instigate purpose.

Unfortunately, if you Google "finding your purpose," you'll find your usual hodgepodge of selfish flagellation, mostly dry humping the wonder twins. Namely, every teenage boy wants to get paid to play video games, and little girls have Cinderella dreams while riding ponies. Not meaning. Not purpose.

THE VALUE CHALLENGE: PERHAPS YOUR PURPOSE IS THIS SIMPLE?

If you haven't pinned your purpose, try this experiment. I call it *the value challenge*: Start by simply smiling at a complete stranger—and not just any forced smile. Smile as if that person was the first person you saw after being stranded on an island for years. Do this as many times as needed until you get a return smile.

Then observe how you feel. Pretty cool, eh?

Congratulations, you just added value in someone's life.

Continue the value challenge by helping one person in the next thirty days. Add value to just one life, and do so by virtue of your own creation, ingenuity, and hard work. Also, you must do this by learning a new skill, or something unfamiliar to you. DO NOT STOP UNTIL ACCOMPLISHED.

Your value challenge could be as simple as buying an old dresser down at the Goodwill, refinishing it and then reselling it on Craigslist. Or you could write a short story and sell it on Amazon for ninety-nine cents. Whatever you do, the key is to create value for someone else AND do it by a new process (or skill) that you must learn on the fly.

Again, like the spirited smiling, pay attention to how you feel the moment you accomplish the value challenge. You should feel good, maybe even a rush of excitement. This same feeling happens in entrepreneurship once your feedback loop transforms into a *value loop*. I call the experience "entrepreneurial heroine." And once you feel it, there's no going back. Countless forum users have reported this "high," and it's what happens when your creative sweat creates value for someone else. The value loop confirms with your first sale, your first customer, or your first "your product rocks!" testimonial.

Now imagine if you didn't provide value to just one person, but thousands...

The point is, creating value loops and getting paid handsomely to help people is indescribably rewarding. It's like watching your firstborn win Wimbledon. Perhaps buried deep behind our "whys," we all have the same generic meaning-and-purpose—*to simply solve each other's problems and make the world a better place.*

THE HAPPINESS SECRET (WHILE DOING WHAT YOU HATE)

But MJ, I can't be happy doing something that I don't enjoy! I want to race cars, sell legal weed, and become a famous Hollywood actor! I'm passionate about this stuff and I want to go for it! Hail, do what you love!

If you're in the campy camp that believes you can't be happy owning something completely unrelated to the gravity of your life, I understand. If you can reconcile your specific passions and loves with a legitimate market need or demand, by all means, go for it. I certainly hope the next Michael Jordan finds his way to the basketball court. Better to try than not try at all.

My polemic against the wonder twins wasn't monism or a condemnation against trying, but a rejection of these proverbs as universal and the one true path to happiness. It simply isn't true.

In fact, want to know what really holds the key to your happiness? It's the reason why you're reading this book. Money? Business success? Respect? Nope, none of the above. The great happiness secret is *autonomy*. Freedom. The ability to feel in control of your life, to stockpile options, mobility, and whatever else you self-determine and endorse. Remember my *UNSCRIPTED* moment outside the

Bank of America when I realized I didn't need a job for at least a year? It was one of the happiest moments in my life because it gave me autonomy.

You see, anyone who tells you that money can't buy happiness isn't spending it correctly. Money buys autonomy, or it buys a down payment on debt and anti-autonomy. I shit you not. Autonomy is so influential it could cause you to love life poor and hate it rich.

In 2014, I came across a headline that read, "Billionaire Who's Proof that Money Can't Buy Happiness."[74] Before I clicked the link bait, I speculated on how a billionaire could feel this way. After a few seconds, my guess was that the billionaire lost autonomy, or control of something—like a nasty divorce, lawsuits, or children with interminable troubles. Turns out two of my three guesses were correct. Psychologists say parents can never be happier than their least happy child.[75]

In *The Millionaire Fastlane*, I defined wealth (and interchangeably "happiness") as having three contributing factors called the 3 Fs: freedom, family, and fitness. These 3 Fs and their happiness correlation aren't speculative. Scientists agree and evidence supports it. For example, according to Roko Belic, director of the documentary *Happy*, autonomy, or intentional behavior and choice, accounts for a whopping 40 percent of our happiness quotient, followed by circumstances at 10 percent and genetics at 50 percent.[76] Based on this, you can manipulate your happiness baseline by 50 percent through winning choices and improving your circumstances.

In another instance, a report by *The Journal of Personality and Social Psychology* cited "autonomy" as the number-one contributor of happiness.[77] Not respect, not a jaw-dropping bod, and not 60,000 Instagram followers—autonomy. Of course, when you're pounding your car's dashboard because traffic's backed up, you have no autonomy. When your job feels like a mandatory prison sentence, autonomy is locked away and paroled for the two-week vacation. For the *SCRIPTED*, autonomy isn't the elephant in the room; it's the elephant stuffed in the garage, waiting for the weekend.

According to data from the US Census Bureau and the Centers for Disease Control, New York City was ranked as the number-one city where Americans are unhappiest.[78] Yes, the home of Broadway, Central Park, and Times Square isn't stroking happiness. Could autonomy be behind this metropolitan misery? Considering perpetual gridlock and an insane cost of living requiring a constant cash drip of life rations, I think so.

In other research, the psychological self-determination theory (SDT) is another theory that supports autonomy as well as connectedness as a critical factor in happiness. Studied by researchers Richard Ryan and Edward Deci from Rochester University, SDT posits that best forms of motivation and engagement, including persistence and creativity, come from our experience of autonomy, competence, and relatedness. Specifically, Deci and Ryan postulated that these needs, when satisfied, enhance self-motivation and mental health (well-being), and when thwarted, do the opposite.[79] Basically, intrinsic improvement and growth (competence), freedom (autonomy), and family (relatedness) are core constituents of happiness.

And there's more.

Research also shows autonomy has a significant impact on health and morale. In one study, Yale psychologist Judith Rodin encouraged nursing-home patients to exercise more control over their choices, from environment to facility policies, and as a result, 93 percent became more alert, active, and happier. Some lived longer.[80]

Another researcher, Angus Campbell, author of *The Sense of Well-Being in America* (recommended read) concurs with autonomy's significance and perhaps knew before all of us. Commenting on a University of Michigan study, he stated:

> Having a strong sense of controlling one's life is a more dependable predictor of positive feelings of well-being than any of the objective conditions of life we have considered.[81]

Much of this research also explains why certain jobs are incredibly fulfilling and why everyone doesn't need to be an entrepreneur. If your job fulfills meaning-and-purpose while also providing some autonomy, connectedness, and a feeling of competence, you've struck gold. According to CareerBliss.com, the top three happiest jobs are school principal, executive chef, followed by a loan officer.[82] Each job has its unique elements of connectedness and autonomy, while surely providing each a heightened sense of competency.

So, perhaps the secret to well-being isn't the wonder twins or a new Harley but simply self-growth and autonomy while sharing connectedness with others. And if you can't find the job that hits the sweet spot, what better way to monetize those needs than entrepreneurship? Maybe you can be joyfully fulfilled inventing a better mousetrap without being in love with them—and you just don't know it.

> ? ***If you are unhappy, what role has autonomy played? What choices have you made (or not made) that have eroded your ability to live autonomously?***

CHOOSE LIFE BY CHOOSING CONTROL

The word "Chicago" disturbs me. Mention it and my face will contort into a painful scowl as if I just ate a spoonful of wasabi. It's not that Chicago's a bad city; it just represents a twenty-five year long chapter of my life I'd rather tear out. During those early years in my life, I was miserable. Suicidal, jump off the Hancock building, to be exact. No matter how much I tried, I couldn't find motivation or happiness. And despite a strong meaning-and-purpose, something was still suffocating it.

That something was sunshine, which I craved more than success itself. But more importantly, it was suffocating because I held an external *locus of control.*

Your locus of control, first postulated by psychologist Henry Rotter, refers to how empowered (or disempowered) you feel to control the events of situations around you. If you have an internal locus, you unequivocally believe that you have the power to change and control your life, despite surrounding circumstances. In effect, *life is a game and you are its player.*

Similar to a growth mindset, you understand choices are a powerful human endowment, capable of manipulating outcomes—and you're not about to waste it. On the other hand, if you harbor an external locus of control, you marginalize choice and instead play "cards": the race card, the victim card, the seasonal-depression card, or whatever other forty-nine cards are left in the deck. This aligns with a fixed mindset where you become victimized by weather forecasts, your crooked front teeth, your bad neighborhood, your public education, or whatever excuse-du-jour feeds the moment—all reasonable scapegoats for life's sucky circumstances.

With an external locus of control, life happens TO you; YOU do not happen to life. The man is keeping you down. Personal responsibility, suffocated by entitlement. Whatever's going on in your life, it's always someone else's fault. "Blame," not "choice," is the operative word. Yes, your business went bankrupt because of Obama, not because your website was last updated in 1998. Or maybe your business did a face-plant because of Google's algorithm change, not because your product and the business model selling it sucks. And if you're broke and couched in front of a TV? It's because of those evil corporate oligarchs: big oil, big pharma, and heck, even big Jim, who's your bookie.

While an internal locus is proactive, an external locus is apathetic and reactive, like driftwood with a soul, a hapless casualty of life's undercurrents. In my case, the narrative I sold myself was seasonal depression. Chicago's lack of sunshine put me in bed and into a Doritos bag. While my seasonal depression was real, *what wasn't real was my perception that I couldn't do anything about it.*

A choice existed, one I couldn't see.

So the weather card was my trump card for years. I remember seeing photos of people who lived in sunny locales and lamenting how lucky those folks were, never once considering that I could move there myself. My cerebral dogma argued, "I can't control the bad weather," and it stood that way for years.

Then one day things changed. My sailor-mouthed girlfriend soured on my whining. After the fiftieth consecutive day of no sunshine and, hence, the fiftieth consecutive day of me sulking, she charged, "If you're so fucking miserable, why don't you move?" And at that moment, it hit me. *I did have a choice.* I could murder the sacred cow and alter my reality. And for the next few weeks, I accepted the idea as a possibility and immediately was inspirited with positivity. Then just a few weeks later, my blizzard-infused "fuck this" event sealed the deal. It was no longer, "I could move"; it was, "I will move." And a few months later, I did.

The point of this story is twofold. First, a meaning-and-purpose without an internal locus is a fairy tale. You might as well play the lottery. You have to believe that your purpose is possible by simply choosing. If you feel "out of control," it's just another self-induced hyperreality. You are free to pursue a unique path. No one has a gun to your head, forcing you to work at that call center. No one has forever condemned you to live in Podunk Anytown, USA. There is no law mandating that you can't party on Monday and work on a Friday night. No one has stamped "ignorant" on your forehead where acquiring knowledge is forbidden. Basically, all the things you think you can't control are webs you have woven, silken imprisonments caged by excuses.

On my forum, a common struggle comes from people who report they are miserable living in their city. There's no opportunity here! The weather sucks! Blah, blah. I know how they feel. And yet, when it's suggested they move, the excuses pile on. This is my home! My family is here! I love the Chelsea soccer club!

You see, you either want it or don't. You either do it or continue dreaming about it. You either choose to act or choose to complain. Don't be the dog sleeping on the nail—if you feel nailed to the floorboard, pick up a damn hammer and look for a new home.

The second reason why an internal locus of control is important is because it correlates with happiness. Specifically, autonomy. Anytime you feel in control, *whether it's an illusion or not*, you feel better about your circumstances. If you see a choice exists, you will experience a greater well-being. And this is why entrepreneurship is so compelling, because you control your destiny, not the boss, the corporation, or Wall Street. YOU.

So how do you swing the pendulum to an internal locus over an external? Again, everything starts by thinking how you think. And I say that as a student of the game, not as a master. I struggle with the same things you do.

If you're dwelling in unhappy circumstances, what specific choices put you there? Or what choices have you not made? What hidden options have been ignored and discounted due to sacred straw-men excuses? Who is writing the script of your life? Society? Your parents? Some stupid television show? In the end, everything is a choice, including how you perceive the circumstance.

Your power rests in choosing, not just action, but in thought. It enlivens meaning-and-purpose, invigorates autonomy, and gives you the tools to change your world. And YOU are what comes first. Everyone wants change, but no one wants to change themselves. Before championing an honorable cause, champion for yourself. This is your life to lead. Lead yours, and you can lead others.

Denying the control in your life denies your free-range freedom and blunts autonomy and happiness. You can always control what you do and how you think.

THE UNSCRIPTED ENTREPRENEURIAL FRAMEWORK

FASTLANE ENTREPRENEURSHIP (FE)

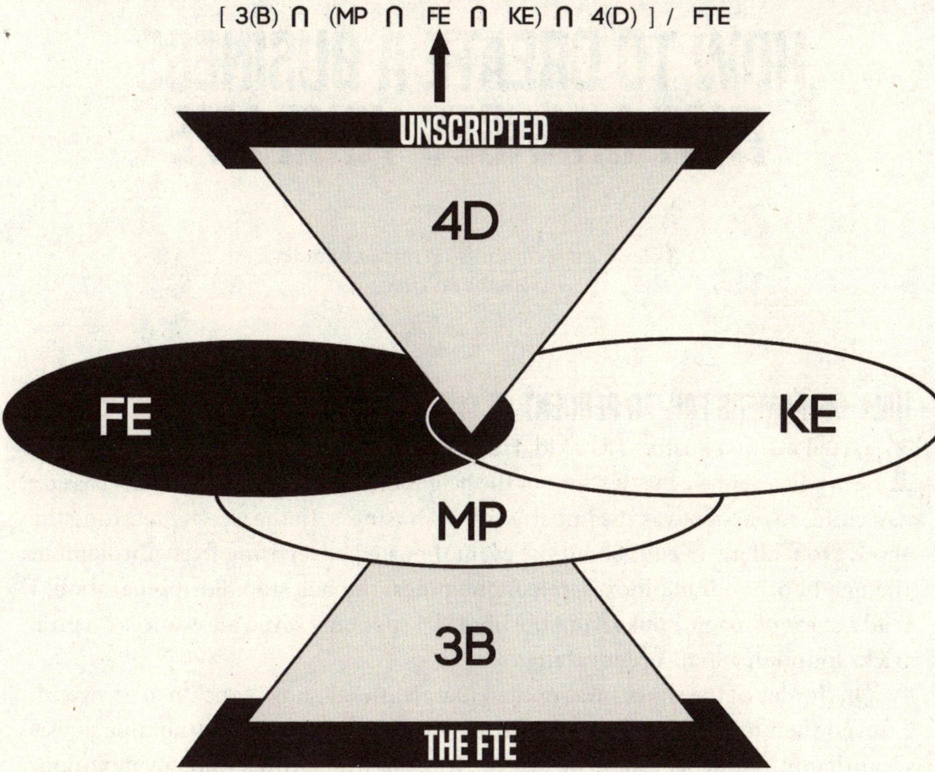

CHAPTER 31

HOW TO CREATE A BUSINESS THAT CHANGES YOUR LIFE

A clever man commits no minor blunders.
~ **Goethe, Writer**

HALL-OF-FAMERS FAIL 70 PERCENT OF THE TIME

I started my first business as a kid. However, it wasn't the typical lemonade stand but a paid event—a magic show for the neighborhood kids. Magic was my passion as a child, so passion was the impetus for my business. In the weeks preceding the show, I told all my friends about the event. I posted advertising flyers throughout the neighborhood: mailboxes, telephone poles, the bus stop. For preparation, I read a stack of magic books from the library. I spent my saved allowances on prop tricks found in a mail-order catalog.

On the day of the show, I was excited to unleash my showmanship to the world.

And then reality hit: As the time trickled past the event's starting time, it was clear that my audience would be just five kids, of which three were my next-door neighbors. Even my siblings were no-shows. Lacking an audience, let's just say that my garage-magician venture didn't make the local papers.

Afterward, I licked my wounds. The ticket sales didn't cover my costs, let alone the time I spent preparing for the show. It was my first failure, and in my eyes, a very public one.

In college, I put on another failed event.

Again, passion and interests led the way.

This time, because I was deeply involved in hip-hop culture, my fraternity brother and I thought it would be a great idea to sponsor a dance party at the basketball gymnasium. We paid a respected DJ from Chicago to spin the rave. In preparation, we posted flyers all over campus, hyped the event within our fraternity, and even placed a small ad in the student newspaper. On the day of the dance, the sting of my failed magic show repeated.

I opened the gym doors. Optimistically, I envisioned an anxious crowd lined up. Instead, I opened the doors to an empty plastic bag fluttering by. Vehicle traffic was light, pedestrians absent. While the thumping bass pounded the gym, I waited. And waited.

A few of my fraternity brothers showed up, not because they wanted to, but because our frat's social chairman obligated them to. Once they met their duty of a few moments, most of them quickly left, embarrassed at the travesty. Others sprinkled in only to leave once they learned the rave was an empty, cavernous basketball court speckled with the dumbfounded. Some asked for refunds.

Then our paid DJ arrived. We met in the locker room where he cheeked an anticipative grin as thunderous bass rattled the steel lockers. My heart sunk as I pointed out the tunnel onto the basketball court. As he lugged his record crate ahead of me and cleared the bleachers, he suddenly stopped short, like a pantomimed face-plant into an invisible wall. His smile instantly melted into a stinkface, as if he just smelled the most rancid flatulence, post bean burrito. He swiveled his head at me, eyes wide as limes. WTF is this?

I didn't know what to say. I muttered, "More people should be coming soon, don't worry." He nodded and ambled over to the DJ booth and mixed some records. After thirty minutes, it was clear: no one was coming.

My friend and I, hoping to cover up our colossal failure, told the DJ he could leave. Hurriedly, we locked the gym doors and refunded the few paying victims that remained. My friend posted a sign with "Dance Canceled" and quickly hung it on the gym doors. Within moments, we packed everything up and GotTFO. I never moved so quickly.

Another money-losing failure. And a laughable one that's retold anytime alcohol is involved.

Still, my failures continued after college. Several more, in fact. A supplement business, a jewelry business, a direct-marketing gig, a mortgage consultancy, several others—I could detail them here, but I think you get the picture: I've failed a bunch.

Every year, thousands of people start businesses and take stabs at "being the boss." From cutesy corner coffee shops to cheesy eBooks on how to get fit in two weeks, there's no shortage of people who roll the entrepreneurial dice. And every year, thousands of businesses like these crap out as disastrous failures. They say (not sure who "they" are) that 90 percent of new businesses fail within the first five years. Whatever the percentage, it doesn't matter. *You will contribute to the statistic at some point.*

The question is, will your updated resume be the death certificate of your entrepreneurial dreams? Or will you continue swinging?

You see, entrepreneurship is a lot like baseball. You take a lot of ugly swings: foul balls and strikeouts. A hall-of-fame baseball player bats .300, which means he only hits 30 percent of the time. You can fail 70 percent of the time and still be considered a legend. Heck, hit one home run at the right time and you can live legendary for life, even if you're a career 100 hitter.

The failure statistic simply means that entrepreneurs, in general, bat 100, or fail 90 percent of the time. Failure is a part of the game, just as whiffing is at baseball.

Think about it.

What if Steve Jobs quit pursuing his visionary ideas for computing after his Macintosh fluke? Or what if Walt Disney quit after Laugh-o-Gram, one of his many early failures?

So how can you improve your odds at connecting hits? Well, you take steroids. Except the entrepreneur's equivalent of steroids isn't illegal or cheating. Entrepreneurship's unfair advantage—the "FE" in the *UNSCRIPTED* framework—is *Fastlane Entrepreneurship.*

ENTREPRENEURIAL STEROIDS: FASTLANE ENTREPRENEURSHIP

Not to contradict myself with respect to the shortcut scam, but entrepreneurship has a secret sauce. However, this secret sauce is not a shortcut or a frankenphrase but a general foundation for starting a business and grabbing an unfair advantage. As pictured, the next phase within the *UNSCRIPTED* Model is "FE" or *Fastlane* Entrepreneurship, represented below.

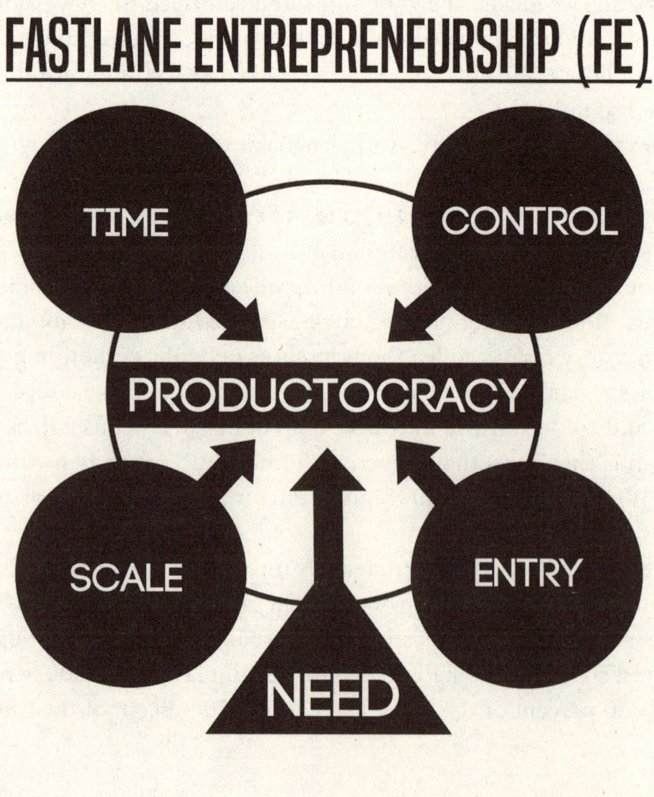

Represented by the left circle and unionized with a strong meaning and purpose coupled with rewritten beliefs, *Fastlane* Entrepreneurship is encompassed within one governing principle—*a productocracy*—followed by five core Commandments, frequently referred to as CENTS.

Overall, the structure has six ingredients. Include them in your entrepreneurial process and that dismal 90 percent failure statistic improves. In baseball terms, instead of hitting .100, you could start hitting .300. From the perspective of our gumball machine and luck, the *Fastlane* concept changes the consistency of the machine, swapping out some of its orange and red gumballs with golds.

Let's change your odds.

CHAPTER 32

THE PRODUCTOCRACY: HOW TO PRINT MONEY (AND SLEEP WELL)

Build a better mousetrap and the world will beat a path to your door.
~ **Ralph Waldo Emerson, Poet**

ADVERTISING IS FOR LOSERS (J/K!)

Sprinkled throughout the Phoenix area is a quaint little pizza chain called Oregano's Pizza Bistro. Each location is branded identically in an odd combination of Western rustic and midcentury retro. Hit the bar and you won't find HDTVs airing sports, but instead old black-and-white films of yesteryear. Instead of LeBron draining jumpers, you'll get Fred Astaire tap dancing or Jimmy Stewart galloping through Bedford Falls. And the Chicago deep-dish pizza? A diet-destroying, roll-your-eyes-in-the-back-of-your-head, delicious taste explosion. Yum yum.

Unfortunately, any Oregano's visit must be planned with girded expectations. Hit any location near dinner time and expect a crammed, tortuous wait. I hope you're patient or not very hungry.

Anyhow, the interesting thing about Oregano's?

I've never seen or heard them advertise.

Nope, not once.

I've never heard a radio commercial, seen a newspaper ad or been mailed a "20% OFF" coupon from the mailbox SuperSaver. The point is they don't flood the market with advertising because they don't need to advertise. They possess entrepreneurship's Holy Grail: a *productocracy.*

Whereas a meritocracy pulls power to the skilled, *a productocracy pulls money to the value creators, businesses who grow organically through peer recommendations and repeat customers, compelled by a distinguished product/service not readily offered elsewhere.*

FASTLANE ENTREPRENEURSHIP (FE)

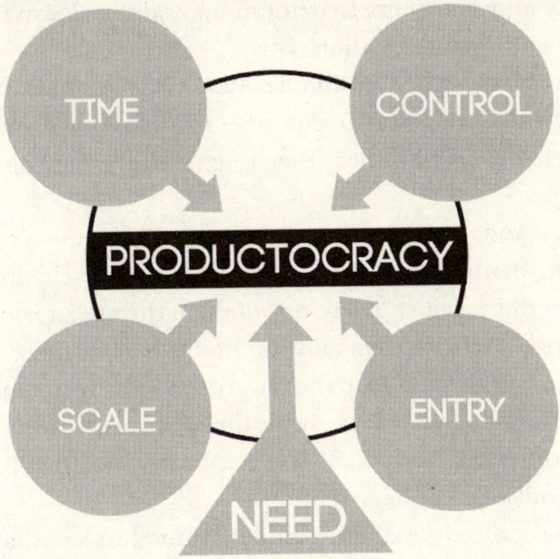

The short-and-sweet definition? Your product contagiously sells itself. Take for example the cancer corollary, a pure productocracy. If you owned the cure for cancer, how long until you made a fortune? Once a small group is cured, your product's growth would snowball by raves and recommendations. News organizations would stampede your office with billions in free publicity. The need to advertise would be like pissing in the Pacific Ocean to remedy a low tide.

Ultimately, a productocracy is what separates average, survive-the-month, zero-growth businesses who are ad dependent from ones who grow exponentially through an expansion loop, or network effects.

In my pizza example, the Oregano's product and concept is so good that satisfied customers fuel the expansion loop, repeating visits and recommending the restaurant. One satisfied customer creates more satisfied customers, accelerating growth. *One plus one equals three.* A productocracy is like a raging inferno, whereas advertising is the gas, an optional accelerant, not a necessity.

A productocracy is also the key to attracting value-vouchers, as discussed in the money/value dichotomy. With a productocracy, all excuses and drama become meaningless. No one cares that you failed four prior businesses. No one cares that your teeth are jacked or your dad didn't love you enough to watch your T-ball game. A productocracy is so impervious to externalities it can overcome a crappy location.

For example, there's a busy street corner near my gym that *looks* like a nice restaurant location, or so it seems. For years, this cursed corner killed so many restaurants it'd make Jason Voorhees's hockey mask smirk a grin. None of the upstart restaurants offered anything different. Average food, average ambiance, average experience. New restaurants would close down just months later.

And then Oregano's moved in. Not only has it survived, it's thrived. Curse? Bad retail location? Four prior restaurant failures at this same location? Immunity. A productocracy allows owners to print money, and it doesn't care that Coco's couldn't survive at the same location..

A productocracy is also behind another West Coast restaurant sensation, In-N-Out Burger. Anytime a new store opens, lines form for miles. Again, I can't recall ever hearing them advertise either. They might, and if they do, it simply stokes the fires.

So, think about your own city. How many restaurants are in your town that are always crowded no matter what time you go? And ask yourself, do they advertise or mail coupons? Or did you just "get wind" of them through a friend or the media?

Of course, a productocracy isn't just limited to restaurants.

Any product or service can reap the rewards of a productocracy. My first book sold hundreds of thousands of copies. By the time you read this book, it will probably be approaching the million mark. So did I bribe my indie publishing success by throwing thousands of ad dollars at it?

Nope. My total promotional ad spend amounted to less than $3,000—all of which was spent in the first two months of release. Moreover, I couldn't advertise on Facebook as they ruled that the book was a "get-rich-quick" scam. Additionally, my first edition's cover was a horrible orange-and-green goober that screamed "cheesy!" So let's just say, my self-publishing venture started like a swim with cement blocks chained to my ankles—I went to market with a two-buck cover and a roadblocked ad strategy, and the title stunk of greasy infomercial guru. Wow.

And yet it still sold. All because of a productocracy. Readers loved it and told friends, coworkers, and family. My reader emails often start the same: "My friend recommended your book…" For example, here's just one of many; however, this one unveils the power of a productocracy:

> Dear MJ, I'm twenty-nine years old, from Santiago Chile. I have a degree in software engineering. I had been always interested in self-development, business, and entrepreneur books. A couple of months ago, I was looking for something to read and I came across an article about the book *Money: Master the Game* by Tony Robbins. I was not convinced, but surely that would be my next book to read… until I read a comment in that article from a user named Chris.
>
> Chris said: "Before even thinking of purchasing this book, have a look at *The Millionaire Fastlane* by MJ DeMarco. This is the only honest business book I've read that spells it out clean and clear. No bull, just plain honesty. If you want to be wealthy, this is where you start. It's how I became financially free, and I'm thirty…not seventy.

Bada-Bing, Cha-Ching. Just like that, another sale.

And this is just one random recommendation from one random stranger made on one random blog about another author's book. How many others read the comment and did the same? And how many more similar comments are scattered throughout the web? A lot. And every one of them sells for me perpetually independent from my time, day after day, hour after hour.

THE PUSH (BUY MY SHIT) VS. THE PULL (YOU WANT MY SHIT)

Every podcast and interview I've ever done happened because I was asked. I didn't solicit myself in a cold email, begging to be interviewed. Likewise, I won translation licenses in the same manner: Publishers contacted me, asking to be a part of my book's success. My book did the selling, not me.

Behind this phenomenon is a *push-pull polarity*—the genome that determines if your company is one that grows spectacularly, a productocracy, or one that struggles to survive. Companies held hostage by advertising chain themselves to a *push*. Companies that grow like weeds and enrich their founders, boast the *pull*.

Not long ago, whoever spent the most on advertising would win the sales. If the toilet leaked, you searched "plumbers" in the *Yellow Pages* and phoned the one with the biggest ad. If you ate a new snack cracker, you either saw it advertised on television or it was slotted favorably in the grocery store, where its colorful labeling caught your eye. Both required wheelbarrows of cash. To sell large volumes of product, corporations had to buy large volumes of advertising. Advertising *pushes* its product to the masses, *pushing* sales.

Conversely, the pull in the push-pull polarity is a productocracy where products or services have gravity. Customers come to you. Each time the product/service is used, its gravity strengthens. The essence of a pull is word of mouth, social proof, and satisfied users.

A great pulling example is Tesla Motors. In an earnings conference call, Elon Musk implied that his advertising expense (in 2015) would be none. And yet Tesla has sold billions' worth in cars. How does that happen? The pull of a productocracy.

If clients are recommending and sharing your products on social media, congratulations, your product is pulling. Which side of the fence your company sits on is determined by one thing only: *the market's reaction to your product.*

When my book was first released, I don't remember its first sale or how many sold over the first few months. I didn't care because that wasn't important. What was important was spotting *gravitons*, or instances validating a productocracy's pull.

I do, however, remember the first email from a stranger who said the book was life-changing. Then the book was recommended on Twitter by a stranger. Then I saw the same thing on Facebook, and it repeated. These gravitons symbolize a productocracy and its pulling DNA. It also meant I could commit to my book and endeavor for worldwide scale. Without pull's gravitons, I'd be left with just an unappealing push. And that would make me no different from the other 900,000 books self-published that year.

No thanks.

Unfortunately, most companies operate from a push modality and rely on multimillion-dollar ad budgets to maintain sales or marginal growth. Many of these companies start as productocracies, but over time their operations disintegrate into pushes, usually due to stakeholder demotions (more on that later).

Think about it.

When was the last time someone recommended a McDonald's hamburger to you? Or a nice cold drink of Budweiser? Funny, eh? The truth is, I am suspicious of any company who advertises heavily because it suggests a product that can't pull.

For example, I avoid both Geico and Progressive Insurance like a stranger on the Vegas Strip snapping porn cards in my grill. Both companies advertise as often as a Chihuahua barks, so anytime I see "Flo" or the gecko, I'm reminded to shut off the television. Despite the advertising, I've never been recommended either.

The same suspicions flow locally.

Ever get one of those thick envelopes filled with coupons mailed to you? The one stuffed with advertisements from nearby home remodelers, pizza joints, and carpet cleaners? Again, the businesses that advertise every week are foisting the red flag of product mediocrity. I simply don't trust them, and I'd rather go online and post a query to the neighborhood Facebook group.

> ***The evidence of heavy advertising signifies an increased probability that a productocracy—an incredible "tell your friend" company—is not evident.***

To test my theory, I conducted an unscientific study. By memory, I wrote down every company who heavily advertises on the radio. Since I listen to a lot of sports talk radio, this was easy. Whenever a company advertises so much that I can't stop humming their commercial's musical jingle, they become top-of-mind—but not favorably. So within a few minutes, I came up with five companies. I removed their identifying names (but kept the industry). Here they are:

1. **AAA Flooring**
2. **BBB Air Conditioning & Repair**
3. **CCC Roofing**
4. **DDD Pest Elimination**
5. **FFF and Sons (HVAC)**

So after compiling these companies, I logged onto Yelp and examined their user reviews. Mind you, I didn't do any research into this; I simply wrote down my "top-of-mind" companies who advertised heavily. Here are the results:

AAA Flooring	77 reviews, Rated 1 star out of 5.
BBB Air Conditioning & Repair	22 reviews, Rated 2.5 stars out of 5.
CCC Roofing	18 reviews, Rated 2 stars out of 5.
DDD Pest Elimination	21 reviews, Rated 2 stars out of 5
FFF and Sons (HVAC)	149 reviews, Rated 2.5 stars out of 5.

The average Yelp rating for these advertising behemoths? A pathetic two stars.

And if you included many of the Yelp "not recommended" reviews, it would be in the ONE-STAR range. Conclusion? None of these companies is running a productocracy. Read their reviews and some of their customers go as far as saying they're running scams. *They need advertising to survive.* Newer, oblivious customers need to replace the dissatisfied ones—*the push is the business.* And if advertising is needed to drive sales, sorry, you've got a product problem.

The truth is, many companies aren't facing the reality of today's consumers: Few make buying decisions based on advertising. Instead, buying decisions are made through social media, personal recommendations, and peer reviews. Websites like Yelp, Angie's List, and TripAdvisor give consumers a voice where they can tell others about their favorite and least favorite companies. Before I buy anything, I find it first on Amazon to examine its reviews. Advertising might get me looking, but reviews compel me to buy.

The same buying behavior also happens within your community. For instance, I belong to a Facebook group where residents of my community, Fountain Hills, share local news and events. And yet, usually half the posts are recommendation inquiries. Looking at it now, here's what I found in the most recent ten posts:

- *Does anyone have any recommendations for places to stay and things to do in Bisbee, AZ?*
- *Need a recommendation for getting the A/C fixed on my truck.*
- *Big shout out to Craig over at West Appliance Repair for fixing my washer; he was in and out real quick!*
- *Check out the Flower Child, a new restaurant over in Scottsdale that finally has organic, GMO-free food, including grass-fed beef!*
- *Can anyone recommend a decent nail tech in town?*

Think about the last five things you bought outside normal groceries. Here are mine and what compelled me to buy:

- Quest Protein Bars (recommended by a fitness friend)
- Sonos Wireless Stereo (recommended by the web through thousands of positive reviews)
- Bulletproof Coffee (recommended by multiple friends)
- Norwegian Smoked Salmon (free sample, Costco)
- Myoplex Supplement (recommended by a doctor friend)

As you can see, none of these purchases happened because the company plastered a banner ad in my face. None of them sent me a slick ad mailer or interrupted my dinner with a telemarketing call. The product sold itself by being recommendable. And in the case of a free sample, tasty enough to buy. You see, companies grow geometrically, and sometimes exponentially, based on what our neighbors and peers say, not what advertising says.

Quite possibly the best demonstration of a productocracy's propensity to explode an enterprise comes from any illegal operation—say, a drug dealer. These ventures, albeit highly risky for their proprietors, are also highly profitable, often making their perpetrators fabulously wealthy. Have you ever wondered why? It's because they pull.

Any illegal profession is implicitly a productocracy because of either a skewed value equation or an economic imbalance. The product is scarcely available or deceptively represented as remarkably superior. So if you're dealing drugs, you have an economic advantage because your product is both scarce and hugely addictive. Users create more users, each very likely to repeat.

A productocracy would also be the pull mechanism behind Bernard Madoff's $30 billion Ponzi scheme. For years, he offered above-market returns to investors. Instead of earning 5 percent in standard funds, they could get a remarkable 10–15 percent from Madoff. When those investors saw those returns on paper, and sometimes in reality, they started telling friends. And those friends told their friends, and the next thing you know, the scam is attracting billions. *A scammer's primary weapon for explosive growth is a fake productocracy!*

Remember, *perceived value* is the only requirement of a money exchange, not *actual value*.

Unfortunately, too many entrepreneurs aren't interested in creating businesses that pull. Instead, they operate from a "push" axis, where solving problems or creating value is not a priority—money-chasing and/or value-cheating is.

These pushers, BRO-marketers on training wheels, aren't filling needs or making something easier; they're simply looking for a "plug-and-play" product—something that can make money through slick marketing and advertising. On my forum, "push entrepreneurs" reveal their push mentality by asking such questions as:

- *I'd like to write an eBook; what topics make the most money?*
- *I'd like to start selling on Amazon; what's a good product?*
- *What companies drop-ship, so I can start my eCommerce empire?*

A productocracy is an afterthought. Products that put smiles on customers and solve problems, a non-sequitur. Instead, the product is a mere spoke in the wheel, as nearly inconsequential as picking the color of your toilet paper. Value creation, and executional improvement are nowhere to be found. Instead, pushers and BRO-marketers sell mediocre products, or surrogates, just so money can be made. A productocracy is then supplanted by slick copywriting and marketing.

The Internet marketing subculture is rife with push marketers who lipstick pigs, repackaging stale and ineffective information into coaching programs, PDFs, and whatever else carries a hefty price tag. Behind the slick copy, the grand promises, and the cheesy bonuses, what you don't see are the poor metrics: 0 reorders, 25 percent refunds, and 10 percent chargebacks. As they say, all hat and no cattle. This isn't a business; it's a racket.

When your product sucks and no one reorders, or most customers leave bad reviews, advertising is the only card you can play in the deck. And when the advertising stops, so do the sales, and so does the company. In this case, there is no fire, just the spark of marketing to push a substandard product into the hands of the deceived. *Instead of selling actual value, push entrepreneurs are selling perceived value.*

At this point, you might think I hate advertising, sales, or marketing. Or that it's unnecessary.

It's neither.

In fact, sales, advertising, marketing, and copywriting are probably the most critical life skills you can have.

My advertising rants aren't to spurn its organizational imperatives but to demonstrate its relationship to the pull of a productocracy. In a product-centered organization, *advertising doesn't float the boat; it steams the boat.*

So if you already have a business, how long would you survive if you stopped advertising? If the answer is weeks or months, you've got a product problem. And with a product problem, ultimately, you will have a business problem.

> ***Perceived value hustlers are interested in having the best marketing, the best copy, and the best sales funnels—not the best product.***

ENGINEERING A PRODUCTOCRACY: IF IT MAKES CENTS, IT MAKES SENSE

As a newbie entrepreneur, whether you live in Menlo Park or in Podunk Park, your number-one goal shouldn't be sales, but a confirmation of a productocracy. A productocracy is entrepreneurship's grease fire: exploding growth, filling wallets, and keeping spouses happy.

Within the *UNSCRIPTED* Entrepreneurial Framework, a *Fastlane* productocracy intersects with the right beliefs and a strong purpose. Engineering your productocracy isn't as simple as a great product or doing something different from the market. While these help, a productocracy goes beyond your product.

A productocracy has five core Commandments called CENTS. They are:

- The Commandment of Control
- The Commandment of Entry
- The Commandment of Need
- The Commandment of Time
- The Commandment of Scale

Consider the CENTS framework the scaffolding for a productocracy and an *UNSCRIPTED* yellow brick road. In other words, if your business eventually makes CENTS, it makes SENSE.

CHAPTER 33

THE COMMANDMENT OF CONTROL: OWN WHAT YOU BUILD

Entrepreneurial profit is the expression of the value of what the entrepreneur contributes to production.
~ **Joseph Schumpeter, Economist**

SHARKS EAT; GUPPIES GET EATEN

It's the day of your birth. Before descending into earthly form, God throws a twist in your incarnation. Instead of living as a human, you will live as a fish in the Pacific Ocean. God gives you a choice: live as a shark or a guppy. Which do you pick?

Let me guess.

The shark.

And let me guess why.

You don't want to end up the shark's dinner.

Give one hundred people the same choice, and you'll hear a similar opinion: I want to be the king, the master of my domain! You'd be insane to pick prey over hunter, right?

Not so in the business world.

Most business neophytes skin themselves as guppies.

You see, whenever you co-opt your business to the uncontrollable and untenable whims of any entity, you tell God, "I want to be the guppy!" Shark status, relinquished. You become the cog, not the wheel. The end result is, instead of painting your own big picture, you become a swab of paint in someone else's.

Enter the Commandment of Control.

FASTLANE ENTREPRENEURSHIP (FE)

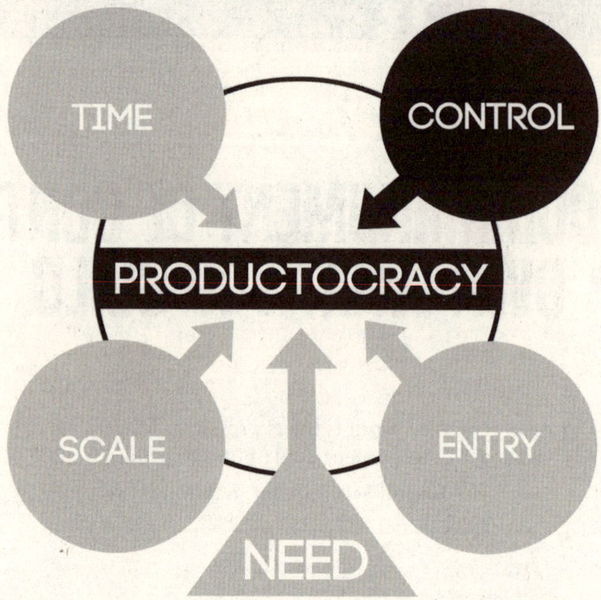

To ensure you're on the top side of the food chain, *the Commandment of Control requires that your entire operation, from product development, to marketing, to distribution, to other operational components, be within your sphere of influence, or diversified from influence.* It's owning what you build, effectively giving you black-swan insurance. It's immunity against catastrophic events that can derail your gig overnight. In effect, the Commandment of Control is risk mitigation allowing you to sleep well as a shark.

Behind the Commandment of Control is a simple question, which reveals your food-chain positioning: *is there one person or entity that can instantly kill your business with one decision?* Are you fishing in a pond controlled by someone else? And what happens to your business when that pond is taken away?

The Commandment of Control (and a productocracy) begs that this answer be NO. If it isn't, you're at the mercy of the sharks, and your pecking order on the food chain is demoted to prey.

Take for example network marketing. If you're not familiar with network marketing (or MLM), you might be familiar with its telltale pattern: Some long-lost friend you haven't heard from since Chumbawamba wants you to go to some ambiguous meeting at some ambiguous hotel so you can hear from some ambiguous speaker. And then you're told how you can make millions selling some overpriced product if you just sell it to your friends and family, and they sell it to theirs, and so forth. If you ever get fooled into a meeting, take a look around. The room is full of guppies. The sharks? They own the company or are chilling in the founders' circle.

Unfortunately, most people need to learn the hard way. And yeah, I was once "most people." Sometimes being told "the fire is hot" isn't sufficient—you need to get burnt. My burn came during my young twenties, and it marked the last time it would happen. I had brief success with one company until my top distributor quit. Her reason? The company discontinued a product favorite. Two events over which I had no control.

Hear that water being sucked out of the pond?

Instantly overnight, my income was slashed in half. Within months, it dwindled to nothing more than an entree at Applebee's, of course assuming I bought a shit-ton of product and stashed it away into a basement closet. But hey, if I just meet my $500 sales quota by buying this garbage myself, I'll qualify for that cool super $100 downline bonus! And I'll get a fancy gemstone title (Emerald/Diamond) that means absolutely nothing in the real world!

Anyhow, such events characterize the black swans risked when swimming as guppies. In the network marketing space, Solavei, Vemma, and WakeUpNow are just a few that recently have imploded, leaving millions of distributors (guppies) wriggling for dead in an empty pond.

In WakeUpNow's case, a letter from the current management blamed the former CEO for taking advantage of his position. Specifically, they stated the former CEO "made decisions that put the company on an irreparable negative trajectory; and sadly, he went to great lengths to keep many of these decisions secret from the rest of the management team and board of directors." Furthermore, they mentioned that the CEO's "deceptive actions had put the company in a position from which it could not recover. In the end, his decision for a privileged few outweighed the incredible heart and dedication of the many."[83]

Please. Spare me the political, cover-your-ass drivel.

Now imagine if your business relied on this company. Imagine giving this company your heart and soul for years, and that your family depended on them. And now, in a matter of days, gone. All because of ONE man and his ONE decision. Feel the burn? Hopefully, with the Commandment of Control in your corner, you won't.

In my case, my prior four failed network-marketing forays (fortunately congested into a brief moment of insanity during my youth) paved the way to enlightenment: The only people getting rich with this horseshit were the owners/founders of the company. From there, I committed to swim as a shark and to stop schooling with the guppies.

Unfortunately, most entrepreneurs don't escape Commandment-of-Control tragedies with just a bruised ego and a tiny income drop—years of work can unravel in hours. My forum is rife with such horror stories. For example, imagine having your company instantaneously shut down—and the only person standing between its failure or resurrection is a minimum-wage employee halfway around the world, who can't write clear English. Here's the post:

> It's written right there in the book. Black and white. CENTS. For anyone who's got a business that isn't in control, then be worried—very worried—and rectify immediately. I've just had 60 percent of my monthly business wiped out with one email. That one email simply states: "Your Amazon selling privileges have been removed," followed by a reason why that makes no sense.
>
> Here's what happens next. I submit an appeal and a plan of action as to why this issue won't happen again. Well, that's absolutely fantastic considering they haven't told me what the issue is. Just a pointer to a list of guideline links. So I've spent all morning writing my appeal, and I get one chance to save 60% of my business from collapsing in one miserable morning. Oh and guess what, the nice guys over at Amazon are going to keep the $15,000 of my money they are currently receiving interest on for 90 days.[84]

In this case, the entrepreneur depends on the Amazon ecosystem to the extremity that it IS his business. Without Amazon, there is no business.

Of course, we see this type of host/symbiont relationship in other business instances. And yet, here's another ripped from my forum pages.

> A few weeks back, my friend launched his brand new venture. He teamed up with a rock-star developer to build a product that would fill the gap when Google removed RSS alerts. My alarm bells went off; he was building a service atop of Google's platform, where he had no control! He was also violating their terms of service.
>
> After two months of intense work by him and his co-founder (done after their nine-to-five jobs), they built a lovely product. The design was flawless; 500 people had signed up for the launch. The launch date approached, and an email blast was sent out a day before, notifying users.
>
> Then on launch day, I got an email saying the product had been shut down—shut down because Google had just reimplemented alerts for RSS on their launch day. It's a shame he didn't read MJ's book, which I suggested months earlier. Instead, he read another launch book instead.[85]

These two stories are a forum normality.

Those who haven't read my book learn the hard way—those who refuse to heed the advice end up in stories like these:

- ✔ Control Violation #1: You manufacture and sell widgets to Walmart. Walmart is your only customer. When Walmart stops selling your product, your sales go from $600,000 a month to $0.

- ✔ Control Violation #2: You run an online eCommerce store leveraging the Amazon affiliate program. You've done quite well. Suddenly, Amazon decides to terminate all affiliates doing business in your state, due to a disagreement with your state's government. Suddenly, your store is empty, as will be your bank account.

- ✔ Control Violation #3: You're an affiliate marketer who sells XYZ's product, moving thousands of dollars in sales monthly. XYZ suddenly files for bankruptcy or disappears. You and thousands of other affiliates are left hanging out to dry.

- ✔ Control Violation #4: You're a network marketer and your company's founder is indicted for fraud. The FCC shuts down the business. Your downline that took years to build is gone overnight.

- ✔ Control Violation #5: You buy a burgeoning, relatively unknown franchise from a franchisor who likes to push the envelope with its advertising. The franchisor is interviewed on national television and makes some inexcusable, racist comments. The entire spectacle is a foot-in-the-mouth, social media shitshow. Suddenly, your business is regarded negatively. By the time the dust settles and memories fade, you've gone out of business.

- ✔ Control Violation #6: You run an online store selling a highly commoditized product that relies solely on SEO (search engine optimization). Most of your traffic and sales come from Google searches. Google's new "Panda update" changes their algorithm and penalizes your website for nefarious SEO and backlinking tactics. Suddenly, 10,000 hits per day are reduced to 100. Your product's margin is so thin that you cannot afford to advertise. You go from living large to not living at all.

Amazon is a perfect (as well as dangerous) illustration of how entrepreneurs "hitchhike" themselves into one-way trips with another business. *Hitchhiking is when your business is symbiotically codependent with another vehicle owned and driven by someone else.* And that "someone" cannot be trusted or controlled. Yeah, you're at the mercy of a corporate stranger and his driving, his decisions, and his motives.

In the case of Amazon, thousands of entrepreneurs have jumped into their bed, gambling that the bed won't be overturned. In fact, you could argue that my books violate control because they are primarily sold on Amazon. This is somewhat true. If Amazon removed my books from their website, my sales would definitely suffer. However, I would not be out of business, and I'd still be able to sell thousands. Why? Because diversification from influence is also a tenet of the Control Commandment. In my case, Amazon is just ONE of many channels I use to sell my books. Diversification from influence means your product pulls from multiple channels; not just Amazon, but other channels including your website. Leveraging one channel as your business model is a risky walk of the tight-rope.

However, more importantly, diversification from influence means that your business's core asset is immune from influence. In my case, my real assets that I can control are my personal brand, my reader list, and my platform. I spent nearly a decade building a forum that spreads my message and is within my control—a terms-of-service change at Facebook, LinkedIn, or Barnes and Noble cannot change the legacy structures I've created, although each of these venues is a critical element in the business strategy.

The CONTROL Commandment is not about absolutism but about risk mitigation and probability. You can violate CONTROL, defy the odds, and still succeed.

Think of it this way.

If Amazon refused to sell JK Rowling's latest *Potter* novel, do you think her sales would go from millions to hundreds? Of course not. She is fully diversified from influence because she controls her brand and her platform with the power of a productocracy: readers are fans, fans are disciples, and disciples are loyal to you, not the channel through which they buy your work.

Which brings us to the final element of control…

Your brand.

If you're taking risks and spending precious time to build a business, for the love of God, make sure your investment goes toward your brand and not someone else's.

If you're selling Avon, Herbalife, Amway, or some other branded product not invented by you, you are violating control.

UNSCRIPTED is my trademarked brand, and you might even say *Fastlane*—either way, when these terms are used in an entrepreneurial perspective, people know that they reference something I own: the *UNSCRIPTED* philosophy.

THE "BLACK SLIP"—ENTREPRENEURSHIP'S PINK SLIP

If you ever had a job, you know an infamous "pink slip" is synonymous with getting laid off. No job, no income. Unfortunately, many entrepreneurs play similarly when violating control—except these gambling entrepreneurs don't get pink-slipped; they get black-slipped.

In April 2013, the online poker world suffered what's called "Black Friday." It was a day when the federal authorities indicted three of the largest online poker websites: PokerStars, Absolute Poker, and Full Tilt Poker. Authorities charged the websites with numerous offenses, including money laundering and violation of several gambling acts. Instantly, those sites ceased to operate and thousands of "entrepreneurs" making stacks of cash were out of business. According to *The Wall Street Journal*, players at Full Tilt were out more than $300 million.[86] These player/entrepreneurs didn't get a pink slip but a black slip—the ruinous black swan, which takes you from king to pawn in a matter of moments.

UNSCRIPTED empires are built on solid ground, not thin ice. If you think of your *UNSCRIPTED* journey as the construction of a building, the Commandment of Control represents the land you build upon. Do you own it? Or is it leased or rented from someone else? Can someone misrepresent or ruin it? Change its terms of use? Not renew its terms?

You could have been the best online poker player in the world and it wouldn't have changed the eventual outcome—you do not own the house in which you play. At the end of the day, owning your own land, or being able to influence it, ensures that your business has longevity, mitigates catastrophic risk, and insures your work.

It also sets the stage for astronomical returns.

For example, every billionaire on the planet has become one through a method of control. One common method is to build a company and take it public. Controlling shareholders SELL their shares into a capital market where they become fabulously wealthy; folks like you and me are the BUYERS.

Take for example a company like Facebook, Airbnb, Alibaba, and Uber. None of these companies really owns anything, but instead, *they control things*. Facebook makes no content but controls it. Airbnb owns no real estate; Uber owns no cars; Alibaba owns no inventory—they all control it. As you can see, control does not always equate to ownership.

In another example, billionaire investor Carl Icahn is an activist investor. He doesn't buy shares of stock and "hope" they appreciate, like the *SCRIPTED* populous. The cornerstone to the Icahn investment philosophy is CONTROL. In a letter to investors, he explains:

> [W]hile the typical Graham & Dodd value investor purchases undervalued securities and waits for results, we often become actively involved in the companies we target. That activity may involve a broad range of approaches, from influencing the management of a target to take steps to improve shareholder value, to acquiring a controlling interest or outright ownership of the target company in order to implement changes that we believe are required to improve its business, and then operating and expanding that business. This activism has brought about very strong returns over the years.[87]

In order to influence your outcomes and mitigate risk within an *UNSCRIPTED* pursuit, you need control. It makes the difference between an "OK" return and an explosive, "holy shit" return.

In Icahn's case, his investment fund, Icahn Enterprises L.P. (IEP), has returned 1,674 percent since January 1, 2000, versus the S&P 500's 82 percent return. If you're going to ignore the compound-interest scam and its capital-principle outlined in Chapter 25, please do so by investing in an activist fund where control is a part of the investment philosophy.

In the end, decide if you want to lead or follow. Direct or be directed.

If it's the former over the latter, congrats, you have the DNA to do great things. I mean, seriously, why do you want to be an entrepreneur? So someone can tell you what to do, what to sell, and how to sell it? Do you want to risk getting "black-slipped" for some unknown reason?

When you violate the control, you essentially gag entrepreneurship with the mask of employment—someone in a gilded tower can fire you with one decision. That's not entrepreneurship, that's guppyism.

Tell God you want to be a shark.

CHAPTER 34

THE COMMANDMENT OF ENTRY: DIFFICULTY IS THE OPPORTUNITY!

If you wait for opportunities to occur, you will be one of the crowd.
~ **Edward de Bono, Psychologist**

EASIFICATION: EASY MEANS YOU AIN'T SOLVING JACK

Imagine you live in a bizzaro city with a bizzaro government. In this city, the government loves restaurants. To incentivize their creation, the city government will fully subsidize any restaurant proposal. To take advantage of their generous offer, you stroll into city hall, fill out a form, and wham, here's your blank check for your eatery. With the blank check comes an entire "start-up manual" on how to get your restaurant up and running.

Unfortunately, this government policy has not come without consequence. As you can guess, the city is jam-packed with restaurants. You can't walk ten feet without seeing a restaurant. Every commercial building has one. Every corner. Heck, even some residential homes are running restaurants out of backyard garages.

So let me ask you…

Is starting a restaurant in this city a good choice? A gold mine of opportunity?

Of course the answer is a big fat NO. Hopefully you see the obvious mistake (and foolishness) of starting a restaurant in a city smothered by restaurants. And yet, how is this foolishness any different from starting, say, the forty-millionth blog? Or joining a network marketing company that has saturated a particular geographic region? *The difference is simply visibility.*

When Main Street has fifty restaurants and forty-nine of them are empty, you can see strong supply and weak demand. You can see fierce competition and limited opportunity. Unfortunately, in the real world, we don't benefit from such visibility—unless you know the Commandment of Entry.

FASTLANE ENTREPRENEURSHIP (FE)

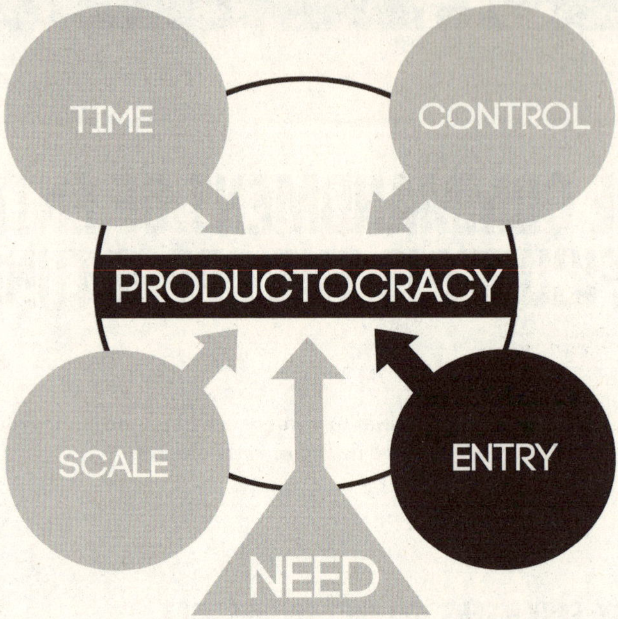

The Commandment of Entry identifies poor opportunities and crowded markets that should be avoided. The Entry Commandment also gives insight into where real opportunities hide. By definition, *the Commandment of Entry states: As entry barriers to any business or start-up process weaken or become "easified," so does the strength or the potential of the opportunity.* Simply put, the easier the opportunity, the worse it is. Conversely, the harder something is to solve, the greater the opportunity.

In our restaurant example, "easification" occurred when the government made it super easy and super cheap to open a restaurant. Suddenly, restaurants are everywhere because entry barriers—namely money, risk, and even experience—were removed from the creation effort. Anytime getting in business is as simple as filling out an online form or doing something so simple that a bum on a street corner can do it, the red flag of "easification" is flown. When that flutters in the wind, so flutters the potency of the opportunity signaling an entry violation.

Easification exposes entry violations and, hence, exposes weak opportunities overrun with competition and depressed margins. In effect, easification appeals to entrepreneurs afflicted by the shortcut scam. If business longevity (and profitability) is your goal, as it should be, your entry barriers represent the strength of current, and future, competition. Entry barriers represent the difficulty level in starting your enterprise.

For example, if you want to be the entrepreneur who creates the next generation of smartphones to compete with the iPhone, the entry barriers—capital, experience, technical know-how—are gargantuan. Even seasoned entrepreneurs are excluded from trying because the entry barriers are so strong. On the flip side, starting a blog takes two hours. A T-shirt business, using any one of the "print-on-demand" screen printers, takes minutes. While these ventures might rack up experience points, they probably won't rack up millions. Here are just a few "business ventures" that stink of easification:

- Blogging/forums
- Self-publishing/writing
- T-shirt businesses
- Network marketing
- Affiliate marketing
- Selling on Amazon based on some Amazon guru course

A recent example of easification comes from the publishing industry. Years ago, if you wanted to publish a book, you'd have to convince a gatekeeper at a publishing house who blockaded bad writing from entering the space. If you didn't get the publisher's attention, you didn't get published, and the world wasn't exposed to your work. Today, compliments of Amazon, the Internet, and eBooks, anyone can write a book and throw it up on the web. Suddenly legendary authors like Stephen King are swimming with hacks who spent thirty minutes writing 3,000 words of horrific literature.

After several successful indie authors made front-page news with stories of six-figure incomes, easification's lure was sweetened with tales of big money.

Hear that thunder in the distance? That's the stampede of money-chasing value-cheaters, storming into town, looking for easy money. And unfortunately, even my forum has contributed to such nonsense. In the self-publishing category, there are several great authors who are doing well (some sold millions!), but there are also the money-chasers who have no interest in quality writing or the authorship experience—they just want to make money. They've turned the entire process into a churn-and-burn: launch fifty books into the Amazon ecosystem and hope they sell. Now imagine when you have 100,000 starry-eyed entrepreneur/author/money-chasers doing the same thing.

The consequence? Declining margins and profitability. Ten years ago, the average eBook was priced at $9.99. Now it's $1.99. And it's why most ninety-nine-cent books are utter crap.

THE OPPORTUNITY OF DIFFICULTY: THERE IS NO FUCKING LIST

Failed entrepreneurs fail for many reasons. One is they don't understand entrepreneurship—what it is and what it is not. Entrepreneurship isn't about nomadding in Thailand on a beach with an open laptop while drinking an umbrella drink. It's not about flashy cars and fistfuls of cash posted on Instagram, passive income, or a *Forbes* cover story. *Entrepreneurship is about problem-solving, creating convenience, satisfying desires, and becoming valuable.*

You see, when you say, "I want to be an entrepreneur," what you're really saying is, "I want to be a lifetime problem-solver." Those solved problems then translate into value for those who need their problem solved.

On the other hand, an easified entrepreneur who's drunk the shortcut Kool-Aid wanders aimlessly: They love entrepreneurship's benefits, but they don't love solving problems. Instead, they're looking for plug-and-play, paint-by-numbers solutions, ironically created by the real entrepreneurs. Simply sign up here and you have a business! Complete this form and you'll get our FREE quick-start guide! Just follow this one step, and wham, you're now a CEO! The duplicity of an easified entrepreneur is like trying to speed skate but refusing to take the ice.

Easified entrepreneurs say shit like, "I have this great idea...but it's too hard!"

If you're an entrepreneur scoping for ideas, *the best ideas are the hard ones because the difficulty represents the opportunity.* When difficulty doesn't exist and the Commandment of Entry looms, another red flag is hoisted: you aren't solving any problems.

Think about that.

If you do something that takes minutes to accomplish or solve, was there really a problem? Or are you merely stacking yourself atop a mountain of already existing solutions? If you're starting a Mexican restaurant in a city full of Mexican restaurants, you aren't satisfying dire cravings.

The unfortunate reality of "it's too hard" as a roadblock is great ideas are overlooked. If your idea requires advanced programming and you don't know how to do it, you move on to the next idea. If your invention requires electrical engineering and plastic mold injection and you don't know where to find these people, darn, next idea. And then the circle jerk of idea-hopping ensues, a never-ending scavenger hunt for the next great idea, the one simplistically executed or invented, the one that exactly fits your skillset and knowledge base, and the one that, unfortunately, solves nothing.

Again, the difficulty is the opportunity. *The magnitude of the problem solved is the magnitude of the money you can make.*

There is no fucking list.

There is no fucking list giving you the exact steps. There is no fucking list telling you what to do, how to do it, and where to do it. There is no fucking list that tells you who the best Chinese manufacturers are and which products are the most profitable to import.

Speaking of importing, several times a week, I read about people who want to arbitrarily sell stuff on Amazon and head straight over to Alibaba, looking for that magical product that will put them into seven figures a year while lounging on a beach in Bali. Except, guess what? Everyone else on Alibaba is looking for the same thing. Crowds, simplicity, and easy access doesn't translate into opportunity because the opportunity has already been raped by the mob.

There is no fucking list and once you discover there isn't one, be happy about it.

Take for instance my millionaire friend who owns a successful business. He sells a ton of stuff on Amazon. Recently he examined a "Selling Millions on Amazon" eCourse put on by a guru. The price of this course was thousands of dollars. After reviewing the course material, you know what his opinion was? *Do the opposite.* Take whatever the easified crowds and guru coaching courses are doing, and go the other direction. Why? Because simplicity and the money-chasing crowds tailgating this shit never make a sustainable income. Remember that carrot?

In this Amazon coaching course, they include a ranking chart on potential product strengths in terms of market, demand, and shipping viability. Products that my friend would avoid like the plague were ranked highly desirable. Namely, easy to sell, easy to import, and easy to ship.

His product? It was ranked poorly. The crowd was told to avoid his product. It's freaking hilarious. And this guy lives a millionaire dream: travels half the year, owns his house clear, drives dream cars, and lives a life 99 percent of the world would love to have. You see, selling his product is difficult (and boring), which limits competitors; the products *they* recommended were easy. And while such ease might be profitable for a few weeks, they won't be profitable long enough to change your life. The churn and burn of "easy" attracts stampedes of easified entrepreneurs. And the only guy ultimately making bank is the BRO-marketing guru selling the coaching program.

Similarly, there also aren't any free handouts or mentors willing to sell out their golden goose.

I am looking for someone with experience in the pet industry who could shed some light on what products have a high profit margin.

This was an actual query at my forum. It seems pretty innocent, but once you think about it, it's ridiculous. And let me mention that in another thread, this man claimed business success was merely "copy and paste the most profitable businesses you can find." So ask yourself, if you owned a business selling high-margin pet products and were making a fortune, would you threaten your own family's livelihood and your freedom to give this forum stranger your coveted "list"? Sure, let me give you the name and number of the manufacturer I used to make $3 million last year. And since we're at it, here's the keys to my McLaren and my debit card, pin #3030.

In the end, easification flags are liabilities while difficulties are assets. Difficulty reflects the depth of the problem and the value magnitude. But more importantly, difficult entry barriers represents a natural moat which keeps easified entrepreneurs OUT of your space.

ENTRIFICATION: THE PROCESS RULES

The Commandment of Entry is underwritten by the process-principle: Starting a business, or entry, isn't an event, but a process reflecting the execution time needed to solve the problem. Much of this time is composed of a learning curve. Entrification is building a moat erected from difficulty, keeping easified entrepreneurs out of your castle.

For example, on April 16, 2011, entrepreneur Sal Paola had what seemed like a great idea. He posted this on my forum:

> I am starting this thread for anyone who wishes to follow my Fastlane journey. It will hopefully be useful for anyone following the path of inventing and manufacturing. They will be able to learn from everything I do and my mistakes I make along the way. I'm new to this. I know I have a lot to learn and will learn a lot.
>
> My plan is to start with one of my ideas that is needed in my current profession but still isn't available after all these years. I always wondered why this product isn't out yet and always wished it was. My workers and others in my industry often question this too. It is something that I believe everyone in my industry would want, and it wouldn't be a life-or-death decision to buy it, since it is inexpensive. At the very least, they would want to try it out, and if they did, I know they would want more.[88]

On April 7, 2012, almost a full year from idea conception, Sal completed his first prototypes. During that year, he endured the arid desert of zero sales but carried forward with a lot of action. He never lost the vision of his idea. There was no list. No easy path. No book. He dealt with design, sourcing, implementation, provisional patents, overseas manufacturing, importing, and more. He learned each step of the way, made some mistakes, but finally got the product he envisioned to reality.

On July 3, nearly three months later, fifteen months from idea inception, he got his first sale. In 2013, Sal started securing deals with national hardware and painting chains. Home Depot was also considering putting his product on the shelves. On April 4, 2014, nearly three years after the idea's birth, Sal and his partners appeared on national television's *Shark Tank*. His product, a paintbrush cover that helps painters save brushes, time, and money, was an instant hit with the sharks. They even fought over it. He sealed a deal with product passionista Lori Greiner.

Fast-forward to today and the product is sold internationally in the world's top hardware stores. Just the other day, as I spotted his product showcased in the Home Depot aisle, I snapped a photo, proud that I had a front-row seat during its execution. Notwithstanding the financial success this company will have on Sal's life, but the experience and contacts he will make in the process are immeasurable.

Another story born within my forum pages is the story of a Canadian entrepreneur, Vick. Vick didn't like the available selection of sunglasses and set out to create his own. It took him months, from idea to design, manufacturing, and import, to finally have a product for sale. And more importantly, before committing to a large inventory expense, he first confirmed demand by taking preorders. His target market loved the product. Two years after Vick committed to his vision, he ditched the *SCRIPT* quitting his job. A few months later, he wrote this:

> I have to admit, life is good. We barely work now. Income keeps pouring in. I'm free to do whatever I want. Hit the gym every day. Go running. Play games. Spend time with the wife and kid. Drive the R8.[89]

Again, there were no lists. No guidebooks. No "turn-key" distributor kits giving easy access to these opportunities. The process, from idea to creation to sale, was a marathon of exploration and learning—not a sprint. The process-principle determines if your product stands a chance at standing out. It's insight into the gravity of the problem you're solving. It also forecasts the strength of entry barriers once the market validates your product.

NEUTRALIZING ENTRY: EXECUTIONAL EXCELLENCE

If you haven't noticed, the Commandment of Entry is the Commandment of Control's cousin. Whatever lacks control usually lacks entry. In many cases, easy entry is a part of a shark's business model—for example, if you make your living on eBay, Etsy, or Amazon.

Take for instance book publishing.

Virtually anyone with a computer can throw a book onto Amazon—crappy cover, zero editing, and wham-bam-thank-you-ma'am, you're an author. The price of easy entry isn't just the crowd you have to compete against; it's also accepting control risk as you're subordinated to a shark or a corporate overseer.

Nonetheless, just because there is easy entry and weak control doesn't mean you can't succeed at it. Many self-published, indie authors are killing it on Amazon. Even I do. In affiliate marketing, some seasoned marketers are rolling in piles of cash selling other companies' products. And yeah, there is even a handful of network marketing guys who make bank. Underneath these successes is the only thing that can overcome the Commandment of Entry: *executional excellence.*

If you insist on violating entry, know that *two* Es *(executional excellence) conquer one* E *(entry).* Executional excellence is simply being better than everyone else. It means you've put 10,000 hours into your craft while everyone else has put in one hundred and quit. Your excellence rises like cream, where you stand out and can't be ignored.

Unfortunately, executional excellence is NOT congruent with the mindset of someone seeking easy entry. When entry is an event, usually the effort is as well. Look at blogging. It takes a few hours to start a blog, sometimes minutes. How many dead blogs have one or two posts? Millions.

Likewise, Amazon is littered with "one-book" stag authors who were lured by easy entry and the prospects of easy money. Unfortunately, when they didn't find the results of their effort (their one book) as simple as the entry, they quit, returning to their exhaustive search for the easy business that will make them the easy money with the easy effort.

You see, once again, we're back to the process-principle. Executional excellence is all about the process, the daily rituals and sacrifices, and the commitment. *It is your process that matters, not the goals.*

Anyone can trade the financial markets, but how many people are good enough at it to actually start a hedge fund doing it? How many young boys in little league baseball would love to play professionally? I'd guess most would love to play in the majors. And yet, only a tiny percentage will ever make it. Aside from injuries, executional excellence is the definitive lynchpin behind the rise to the top. Some players will be at the diamond taking batting practice seven days a week, six hours a day, while others will be playing video games, doing homework, or diversifying into other sports because they're fun.

You see, *the process-principle also holds that if you're not going to sacrifice to get into the game, you're going to need to sacrifice to win the game.* If there's a book inside you, by all means, write it. If you want to sit at home and day-trade the stock market, go ahead and do it. However, expect the expected: Any venture crowded with opportunists and easified entrepreneurs will require executional excellence for victory. And that means, prepare to do what others will not.

? ***How many opportunities or ideas have you passed on because "It's too difficult!" only later to see someone else solve the problem and make millions?***

CHAPTER 35

THE COMMANDMENT OF NEED: HOW TO ENGINEER OPPORTUNITY IN ANY INDUSTRY

There isn't anything in the world that can't be made better.
~ Jack Valenti, Businessman

IMPERFECT WORLD EQUALS PERFECT OPPORTUNITY

- *How do I find a great business idea capable of a productocracy?*
- *How do I find needs or create value?*
- *I can't think of any good ideas!*

Everyday I read something like the above. If you're a terrible idea person, what you're really saying is that you make convincing excuses. Remember, entrepreneurs are problem-solvers. Whenever you say, "I can't find ideas," what you're really saying is, *the world is perfect and it needs nothing.*

Only in a Utopian world are there no problems, needs, or wants. Everyone is happy. Content and roasting marshmallows over the campfire. Whining about not seeing ideas is admitting to world perfection. Or is the more likely answer? That there aren't any *easy* problems, needs, or wants to be filled?

People who don't see opportunity can't see it because they don't want to see what they need to see: unknown variables, new skills, hard work, trial and error, risk, and failure. Instead, they look for something that doesn't exist: the clear path, the step-by-step blueprint, complete with a millionaire mentor, a VC-funded bank account, and a fail-safe job waiting as a safety net. No wonder most people are idea-empty. As Thomas Edison famously said, "Opportunity is missed by most people because it is dressed in overalls and looks like work."

FASTLANE ENTREPRENEURSHIP (FE)

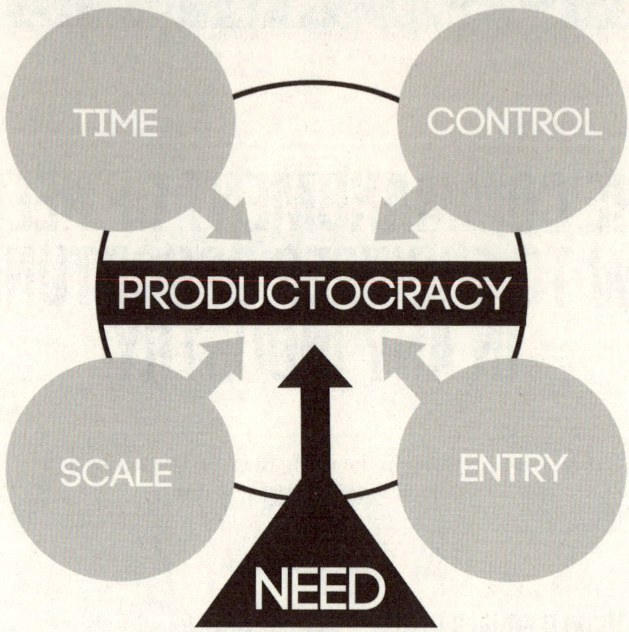

The Commandment of Need is our most important CENTS Commandment for a productocracy because it defines our opportunity. If CENTS were a table, the Commandment of Need would be the tabletop; the other four commandments the legs. *The Commandment of Need states that if you own a controlled and entry-barred enterprise that provides relative value, satisfying needs or wants, you will win growth, profits, and possibly, passive income for life.* You'd think that such a simple idea—needs and wants—was Captain Obvious. Entrepreneurship 101, right? Not exactly—more like advanced business strategy.

For instance, it's common for youngsters to declare such dreams as, "I want to be a billionaire when I grow up!" Or, "I'm going to be rich!" What don't you hear? "I want to provide massive value when I grow up! I want to produce for society!" And yet these are the things that lead to wealth. Wanting to be "rich" but disrespecting value is like trying to solve the quadratic equation without *a, b,* or *c*.

Even worse, I never heard about value, needs, or wants in any of my college business courses. Nope, instead we discussed marketing tactics like AIDA, the 4 Ps, and other textbook strategies designed to move merchandise. Product viability or needfulness was never discussed, let alone on the curriculum! I also belonged to an entrepreneur club where needs or wants were never emphasized as a success metric. In fact, a young entrepreneur at my forum confirmed something similar. He said:

> I recently had another meeting with my school's entrepreneur club. The topic was the essential steps for a start-up. I purposely kept my mouth shut so I could observe what other people thought. To my surprise, no one said to find a solution to a problem. Examples included: find partners, find something to make money, make sure you have enough capital, and marketing. I was shocked that no one said to create a product or service that somebody actually needs.[90]

After encountering thousands of young entrepreneurs over the years, I've discovered that the obvious wasn't so obvious. For instance, it seems every youngster under twenty-five who works out wants to start a fitness blog. Here's how it happens: An eighteen-year-old bubbling with postpubescent testosterone hits the gym for the first time in his life. Six months and ten pounds of muscle later, he suddenly wants to start a fitness blog. A similar story is repeated when the overweight dude suddenly starts exercising and cans crap carbs from his diet. OMG, I lost fifty pounds; I'm going to start a blog on weight loss!

Obviously, these would-be entrepreneurs are passionate about their story, as they should. Regrettably, it never crosses their mind to ask: does the world need another average blog backed by an average story dispensing average advice? Such examples exemplify (again) why "follow your passion" or "do what you love" is indifferent to market needs and not a business-building foundation. The market is a spoiled brat, narrow-minded and singular in its purpose. It doesn't care that you shrunk six dress sizes or can bench press 315. Its laser-like focus is centered on one fundamental truth: What value are you to me? What can I get from you that I can't get elsewhere, or am not getting well enough? Why do I need you or your business?

ENGINEERING VALUE (AND NEED)

Look up the word "value" in the dictionary; it reads *relative worth, utility, or importance*. The key phrase here is "relative worth" or "relative value." The Commandment of Need's central thesis is *relative value*, and it's the keystone to becoming needed.

The richest people in the world are rich not because they create, control, or manage just value, but value *relative* to what already exists. Specifically, your blog full of fitness tips might indeed be valuable, but it isn't *relatively* valuable—it is too ubiquitous when submerged into the global marketplace.

The importance of relativity could be seen in our fictitious city overburdened with restaurants: If you open a pizza bistro and there's already twenty-five other pizza places nearby, have you provided relative value? Your pizza might be darn good, but relative value doesn't exist because more than likely, a few other pizza joints are also darn good. Sand could be worthless or priceless depending on its relativity in the marketplace: Offered in the Sahara, it's useless. In a valley preparing for a flood? Worthy.

Value is always relative based on market economics. And yet, why do so many entrepreneurs insist on ignoring the market, and instead, selfishly think they can tame the market to their personal fantasies?

So let me ask you: If I challenged you to create a company and within thirty days that company had to achieve at least $10 million in sales, could you do it? I know I could. And I wouldn't need thirty days. Think about it again because yes, it's a trick question.

You see, my confidence in the challenge has nothing to do with my LinkedIn connections or business savvy. Hopefully you noticed that the challenge centered on $10 million in sales, not profit. To win, I'd offer a no-brainer value skew that would flood my website with orders. What's the no-brainer value proposition? *I'd sell hundred-dollar bills for fifty dollars.*

As soon as word spread that this deal wasn't a scam, sales would explode. Customers would order, over and over. And therein lies the secret to becoming needful (although not necessarily profitable) through the power of relative worth: *skewing value.*

PRODUCTOCRACY'S PULL: THE VALUE SKEW AND THE VALUE COMPETITION

In February 2016, at the annual *Fastlane* Summit, I spoke in front of 150 entrepreneurs and opened with this offer: I held up a fifty-dollar bill and offered it for sale at a steal of a price: just one dollar. Half the room raised their hands, indicating they wanted to buy the bill; the other half sat confused and silent. So I raised my voice and repeated the offer: "What's wrong with you people? Who wants to buy this fifty-dollar bill for one buck!?" Immediately a man in the tenth row jumped up from his seat and ran to the front flailing a dollar in my face.

Sold!

I took his dollar and he got my fifty. Look at that: I just created $1 in sales!

Then I made the offer again.

Except this time, I took out my entire wad of cash in my wallet, a pile of money that amounted to over $1,000.

Everyone's hand raised and several people jumped up.

"Hold up!" I said.

"You can buy my handful of cash for the same price: one dollar. Except now...I have one condition..."

The audience anxiously waited to hear the condition.

"Before buying my cash for a buck," I said, "you ALSO need to streak naked through the casino."

Suddenly everyone's hands went down. There were no buyers.

So what changed? *The value competition.*

Behind this offer is something rarely discussed in entrepreneurial circle jerks. Anytime someone gives you money, that person has said, "Congratulations, you've won the value competition." You see, everything you buy is subject to a value competition: a weighted evaluation with respect to your preferences. This evaluation ultimately determines who wins your money and who does not.

In our original offer, the value competition was straightforward: "Gee, for one dollar in foregone buying power, I receive fifty dollars in return for a net buying power increase of forty-nine dollars." The value competition is a no-brainer.

Unfortunately, in real marketplace exchanges, the value competition isn't so clearly defined. When I added the "condition" of a streak through the casino, suddenly the value competition got complicated. When potential buyers thought about possible consequences—getting embarrassed, potentially arrested, YouTubed, and whatever else they deemed a part of the value competition—hands sank like anchors. The net gain in net buying power didn't justify the other potentialities.

The value competition games your head anytime you consider buying something. It determines when Brand X is bought over Brand Y. Within this weighting game, you analyze multiple buying attributes for each offer and determine where the value skew exists. *The value skew identifies the winner in the value competition.*

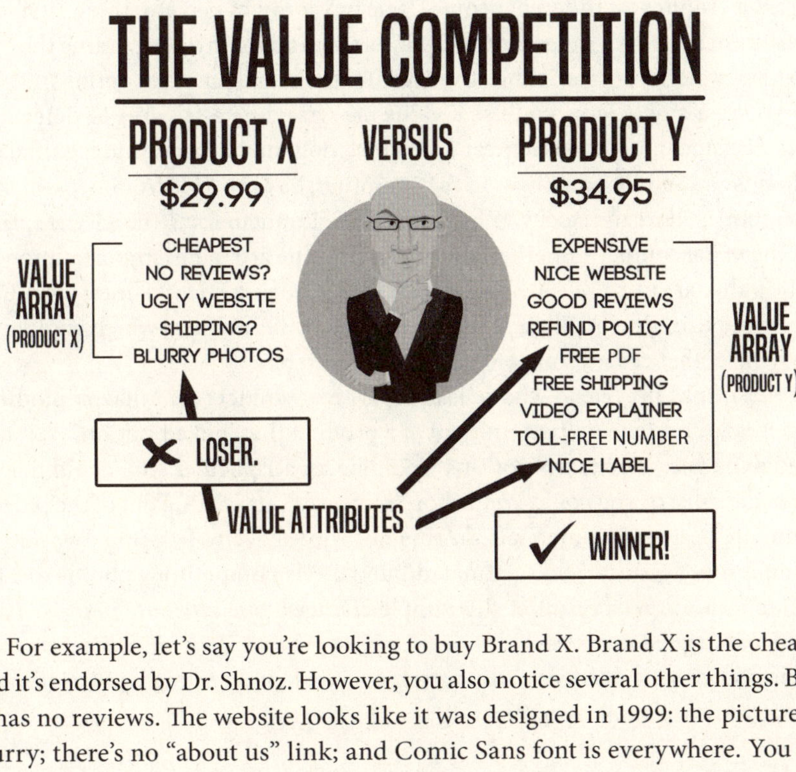

For example, let's say you're looking to buy Brand X. Brand X is the cheapest, and it's endorsed by Dr. Shnoz. However, you also notice several other things. Brand X has no reviews. The website looks like it was designed in 1999: the pictures are blurry; there's no "about us" link; and Comic Sans font is everywhere. You can't find a refund policy, a telephone number, or how much shipping costs. All these things are noted in your head.

Brand Y, however, is 22 percent more expensive and isn't endorsed by a celebrity. However, Brand Y has a professional website with clear photos, an "about us" page with an intriguing story, a clear refund policy, a toll-free number, and an impressive collection of positive reviews. Brand Y also has free shipping.

In your value competition of Brand X versus Brand Y, you make a weighted determination on attribute importance and make a decision. You might be swayed by Brand X's cheap price, whereas others might be dismayed by Brand X's poor public appearance. The point is: *this competition strikes everyone differently.*

HOW MONEY MOVES: THE VALUE ARRAY AND THEIR ATTRIBUTES

Underneath the value competition and a winning value skew is a collection of *value attributes, the value array*, which inherently characterizes all market offers. Just as you have attributes—height, weight, hair and eye color—each marketplace offer also possesses identical traits. These attributes and their corresponding value arrays are different for everyone.

In my streaking offer, an aspiring porn star might have accepted the deal because nakedness was discounted (or didn't exist) as a value attribute. Identical offers have different attributes for different people—one buyer might perceive three attributes while another twenty. Altogether, the value array and its attributes frame the offer to the consumer, who then subjectively evaluates it against other options.

If you're a single lady, you use a value array and its attributes to determine dating decisions: Justin has a great job, a nice dog, no baggage, and is tall, dark, and handsome, while Trent lives with his mother, has two kids from two different women, and is short and stocky. Which man do you want to date? The answer springs from the value competition, the value array, and the attributes important to you.

The value array and its attributes are the measuring stick delineating YES, I want to buy this, or NO, I'll look elsewhere. You NEVER know which attribute is the lynchpin that causes someone to buy or not to buy.

For example, my friend who sells competitive products on Amazon modified his photos to simulate motion. Instead of a product that looked stationary, it now looked dynamic. An example of this would be an air purifier: you could display the purifier as is, or you could Photoshop "air waves" emanating out of the purifier to simulate action. Infomercials do this notoriously as well, using a variety of techniques: bells, dings, and animated bursts. His competitor's photos did not simulate motion. As a result of this simple change—*one attribute improved and skewed*—he tripled his sales.

Here is just a sample list of value attributes that could frame your offer in the mind of your potential customer.

Your Price	Professionalism
Price Ambiguity	Compelling Story (About Us)
Ease of Ordering	Label/Packaging Design
Website Design	Affiliations or Associations
Cleanliness	Customer Service
Guarantee	Crisp, Clean Photos
Refund Policy	Public Reviews
Included/Excluded Ingredient	Celebrity Endorsements
Ambiance	Comfort
Product Features	Security
Payment Options	Shipping Speed or Cost
User Interface	Bribed Reviews
Employee Photos	Website Recently Updated

Skewing value and winning sales boil down to the value array. And if you don't have a business yet, the value array can be used to exploit potentially potent business opportunities.

The value skew pulls the Commandment of Need's cart. Skew value clearly and overwhelmingly, and that cart fills with cash. *The value skew is the force behind the pull of a productocracy.* Companies that do not skew value do not satisfy the Commandment of Need, and they do not survive.

In fact, not only is the value skew responsible for growing great companies, but it's also the dynamic behind any scam. Greed is a duet staged on irresistible value skews. If someone offers such a warped "too good to be true" value proposition, more than likely it's a fraud underway. When Jimmy thought he could meet a stranger in the Publix parking lot and buy a new fifty-dollar iPhone advertised on Craigslist, greed (the scammer skewing value) met greed (Jimmy the consumer, looking to get a screaming deal). A warped value skew—usually predicated on price, big returns, or incredible savings—is the "pull" behind all scams and their meteoric growth. Fortunately for us, we can succeed without misrepresenting value. We can own the skew by exposing and reverse engineering any product through its value array.

SKEW VALUE, KILL THE COMPETITION

Remember my fake "money company," where I sold one-hundred-dollar bills for fifty bucks? Let's assume the transaction process involves snail mailing a fifty-dollar check to a post office box. Two weeks later, you receive a hundred-dollar check in return. Here the value array consists of three dominant attributes:

1. **Monetary value**
2. **Convenience**
3. **Risk**

Fifty dollars spent, delivered fifty dollars more in clearly defined monetary value. Of course, value attributes aren't usually obvious but involve quick subjective interpretations. In this case, convenience and risk are also attributes. First, the order process is not convenient because one has to write a check to an anonymous post office box, which seems doubly dubious, peppering the transaction with risk. Once the communicated and perceived value (Buy $100 for $50!) turns into delivered value, sales will grow as word spreads. If communicated value isn't delivered—hence, you over-promise—word also spreads, except in this case, sales do not grow.

So let's assume that the deal is legit. Now let's assume that a new competing "money company" surfaces. They too are selling hundred-dollar bills for fifty bucks. Except this new company doesn't require you to snail mail a check to some post office box: they offer immediate, online processing; you PayPal them fifty dollars, and wham, ten minutes later, your PayPal account is credited with a hundred dollars. Both companies are selling the same product with the exact same monetary value. But which company will grow faster and steeper?

Obviously, the new company will outsell and outgrow the old company. They've dissected the value array and skewed value on *two additional transactional attributes*—faster processing and risk mitigation—while providing the exact same product.

Whenever a company grows exponentially, look no further than the value array and its attributes. How many of them have been skewed favorably? Exponential growth goes beyond just a cheap price; it occurs when multiple attributes have been skewed.

Take Uber, for example. They've disrupted the ground-transportation industry, specifically on-demand taxi service. Since my background is in ground transportation, I'm familiar with the industry's value array. When I first used Uber, it became pretty clear why the company has blown up to become its own verb—a.k.a., grab me a Kleenex and let's Uber it home. Every value attribute was skewed: not just one or two, but all of them. Here's the array and just a few of its primary value attributes:

Speed	Cost Ambiguity
Reliability	Comfort / Cleanliness
Accountability	Choice
Payment Ease	Cost

Compared against Uber, can you see why the taxi business is in trouble?

- ✔ Speed: Cab arrival is unknown. With Uber, you know when it will arrive.
- ✔ Cost ambiguity: You never know how much a cab costs. With Uber, you do.
- ✔ Reliability: After ordering a cab, dispatch always seems to say "ten minutes" and yet, ten minutes really means one hour.
- ✔ Comfort/cleanliness: I never know what gunk, gum, or jizz I'll find sitting in a cab or stuck to the door handle. With Uber, I see the car and know it will probably be clean.
- ✔ Accountability: Cab drivers aren't accountable to their riders. If an Uber driver doesn't perform, they receive a bad review and, hence, endanger their ability to do future rides.
- ✔ Choice: With a cab, you never know who will show up. With Uber, you have a choice.
- ✔ Payment ease: With a cab, you have to fumble with cash or give the driver your credit card. With Uber, all rides go through your pre-registered credit card.
- ✔ Cost: The Uber ride is usually cheaper than a cab; plus, you get all the benefits described above.

When a business goes from zero to billions in just a few years, you're witnessing a productocracy powered by a value skew, which goes beyond a good price. Multiple attributes get primped and groomed.

On the contrary, companies die when there is no value skew.

Think about the last time you made a buying decision and decided against a particular company. Ultimately, a value attribute (or a collection of them) prompted you to keep your wallet closed. For example, here is a list of attributes that have caused me NOT TO BUY:

- The product label looked like it was designed using MS Paint.
- There was no story behind the company.
- The company advertised like a BRO-marketer.
- The reviews were bribed. (*I got this product at a discount in exchange for an honest review.*)
- The product had an unwanted ingredient: Aspartame, Red 40, etc.
- The product was packaged in plastic.
- The service required a credit card before trying.
- The user interface was clunky.

In each case, the value skew wasn't strong enough to compel buying. Instead, another company received my money.

ENGINEERING VALUE SKEW

To dominate markets and win sales, engineer a value skew. It starts by identifying the value array and its attributes. Here's how:

First, examine both your product and its industry with the goal to identify every value attribute, no matter how seemingly insignificant. Remember, you don't know what's important to your customer, so brainstorming every one is the best practice.

The first attribute group is its primary attributes: your product itself, deconstructed down to its core components. Is there any one component or ingredient that you can improve?

For example, consider a knife. Seems like a simple product, right? Not exactly. It has many primary attributes within its deconstruction: the spine, the bolster, the handle, the tip, the thumb rise, the handle scale, the front quillion, the grind, the edge, the heel, the tang, and the rivets.[91] Each component represents an opportunity to skew value. Our rivets are titanium! Our tip edge is solid gold!

If you sell food or a personal product, every ingredient is a value-skewing opportunity. My friend started his personal-grooming company based on this method; he read common ingredient complaints he discovered on a men's forum.

The second attribute group is its secondary attributes, which consist of the product's marketing and delivery to the customer. This would be your website's design, order processing, photos, company story, customer service, shipping, refund policy, telephone (or lack thereof), sales copy, reviews, social media posts—*anything that could make or break a sale is an attribute.*

HOW SKEWING VALUE ATTRIBUTES ENLARGES YOUR MARKET

I rarely go to the movies. I hate fighting with strangers over dirty and uncomfortable seats, the crowded aisles, and overall, the entire experience. However, recently my local theater made a big change. They widened the aisles and replaced the dirty seats with spacious automatic recliners. On top of this, they started offering online seat reservations. Each of these improvements skewed value—better convenience, comfort, and ordering—and it turned me from a once-a-year moviegoer into one who went several times per month.

You see, your job is to identify *every* value attribute in the global pool, with the explicit intent to uncover skewing opportunities. The more attributes skewed without disrupting other skews (say price), the more sales you will win.

For instance, I used to drink a pre-workout supplement called Pre Jym. Over the years, I must have given the company hundreds, if not thousands, of dollars. However, in late 2015, I stopped taking the product, despite my chronic use. Why? The product uses Sucralose and is artificially colored with Red 40. These are two big NO-NO attributes in my value array. I stopped buying and money ceased to flow.

However, if the owner of Pre Jym was reading this book, he'd see an opportunity to skew value. The natural replacement for the artificial coloring "Red 40" is beet juice. Replacing Red 40 with beet juice would have no impact on the product in terms of effectiveness or cost. This change, by itself, skews value and compels new buyers to buy. Why? Because NO ONE on planet Earth would cry, "They removed the Red 40 and now I'm not buying!" And now the product could claim, "No Artificial Colors"—a benefit skew that might attract a new pool of buyers.

Likewise, if stevia or some other natural alternative replaced Sucralose, the folks at Pre Jym would win my money back. And again, another pool of potential buyers sensitive to artificial ingredients would enlarge the market size.

Wherever you can skew value within a product's pool of attributes, you stand out and cast a bigger market tent. The bigger the skew, the more attractive your company becomes to the consumer. Unfortunately, most business owners aren't aware of this powerful relationship. Instead they fall for one of six value myths and, ultimately, fail the Commandment of Need.

> ***A skewed value attribute expands markets without alienating others. For example, when your business endorses a political ideology, you both expand (those for) and alienate markets (those against.)***

VALUE SKEW: THE 6 MISAPPROPRIATIONS MYTHS

1. THE MARKET MYTH

The first is *the market myth*. This is where the business owner ignores the market and doesn't see relative value as a success metric. This is that poor guy who "does what he loves" and opens a coffee shop across the street from Starbucks, offering nothing unique or better. This is the finance dude who writes the millionth book on the topic of compound interest, 401(k)s, and mind-fucking frugality, and how it's going to make you rich by the time you're ninety years old. In most cases, none of this shit is needed. The market, the most important variable in the game, is dismissed. The entrepreneur selfishly pursues what *he wants* and not what *the market wants*. These failures are the worst of the flock because they never have a chance.

2. THE ISOLATION MYTH

The second misstep is the most common: *the isolation myth*. In terms of the dating game, it's isolating one attribute (attractiveness) while ignoring the rest (her jealous personality, her 82 IQ, and her self-absorbed 3,000 selfies on Instagram). Meanwhile, the gal who rocks Mensa, has the Jennifer Aniston personality, and watches the Blackhawks game with you while drinking beer is dismissed because she's not a ten, but an eight and a half. In business, the isolation myth is the figurative equivalent of going to a gunfight with one bullet in the barrel, evaluating value and opportunity contingent on one sliding variable: *price*.

If I offer the lowest price, I will get the sale! When business is isolated by one value attribute, price, it becomes commodified. Think gas stations. A ream of paper, flash drives, and commercial air travel. As consumers, we usually buy these items based on the best price because the outcomes remain uniformly predictable. An economy fare on Southwest Airlines and United Airlines both get you to Denver in identical discomfort—so cheapest price takes all. Loyalty? Bribed by a few bucks.

In a commoditized industry, your customer is indifferent to your existence, like an Olympic pool misses a stolen cup of water. I'd guess that half the crap on Alibaba (and then sold on Amazon) is commodified goods, patiently waiting for another wannabe entrepreneur to join the flooded ranks of commodity pushers, selling the same stuff and hoping to win the "Cheapest Price of the Day" award. Operating in a commoditized climate is a race to the bottom as margins deteriorate with each player deciding, "How small of a profit am I willing to accept to survive?"

As Peter Drucker said, "In a commodity market, you can only be as good as your dumbest competitor." Here's an impending commoditization (and money-chasing) tale foretold on my forum:

> I used to sell a "me-too" product. When comparing its competition, there were small things different about it, but I wasn't truly providing any value. A few questions nagged at me: Why do I exist in the marketplace? If I didn't exist, what would happen?
>
> For me, it was simple: Customers would buy another similar product from someone just like me and be just as satisfied. Did I provide anything significant that others in the niche did not? The answer was no. I was chasing money, and in the end, it wasn't worth it.
>
> I started selling a new line of products three months ago, and I have already eclipsed all of my previous best sales marks: best day, best week, and best month. And that's why I can confidently say my previous money-chasing was not worth it. In three months, I got to a place my previous business never got. It's not easy and won't happen overnight, but it's worth it. My resolution: provide more value.[92]

In the example above, the entrepreneur switched to a product predicated on the Commandment of Need and relative value. As an entrepreneur, you must always ask, why do you exist in the marketplace? What value are you skewing? And who will yearn for your company should you close up shop? Or would your sudden market absence be met with eerie silence?

When dreampreneurs ask mindless questions like, "What's a good product to sell on Amazon?" they're commoditizing their effort with a commoditized product. And seriously, if Widget XYZ was easily imported and sold on eBay, do you honestly think you'd be the only one selling it? Nope, you're immersed in the mob.

3. THE BLOCKBUSTER MYTH

The third misstep of the value skew is *the blockbuster myth*. This is where you errantly isolate the value metric based solely on your ability to craft a unique product never before seen. "I gotta find something no one else is doing!" In other words, you patiently wait for lightning to strike, that one legendary idea that no one among seven billion people on planet Earth have ever thought of doing.

Behind the myth of the blockbuster idea is the rationale that if you're the first to market, competition won't exist. And if competition doesn't exist, you can dictate the value skew, margins, and skate your way to millions. Unfortunately, being first to market is not pocket aces, or even a decent middle pair. Just ask the good folks who started Friendster, Netscape, Palm, TiVo, and Betamax.

As a result of the blockbuster myth, you never do anything because lightning never strikes. I just don't have any good ideas, so therefore, I'll do nothing.

The next two value myths closely correspond to the blockbuster myth and, ironically, usually postdate it. The first is the crowded-room myth.

4. THE CROWDED-ROOM MYTH

The crowded-room myth reasons that your idea is no good because someone is already doing it. The market is too crowded and there isn't room for you. The crowded room myth usually starts with a blockbuster idea that is thought to be new and novel but, turns out, isn't. A preliminary search on the idea uncovers several companies already executing the idea, and hence, the entrepreneur reasons, "Oh well, someone is doing it."

Most ideas usually fall into this category, which is why skewing value is so important—*it's how you get into the room*. Think about it. Alta Vista existed before Google. Budweiser before Sam Adams. Friendster before Myspace before Facebook. The crowded-room appears crowded because we don't typically think from a value skewing perspective.

If there are one hundred total players in the market and each possesses fifty units of market share, you only need to take one unit of share from each to get to the top. You would end up with fifty units, and the others would have forty-nine. If there is value to skew, there is always room.

5. THE EMPTY-ROOM MYTH

The other value misappropriation sits opposite the crowded room: *the empty-room myth*. The empty-room myth is the antithesis to "somebody is doing it" and instead uncovers *no one is doing it*.

Once the entrepreneur discovers the room is empty, the idea is devalued based on the rationale, "Oh, there isn't a market for it" or "There mustn't be any money in this industry." The empty-room myth is how blockbuster ideas get dismissed. In fact, put both the crowded- and empty-room myths together, and you get the ultimate entrepreneurial circle jerk of do-nothingness. Think about it. It doesn't matter what the idea is; it will always be dismissed with one of the myths. If someone IS doing it, darn, crowded room. If someone IS NOT doing it, dang it, empty room. The myths cement justifiable inaction. In essence, no idea is worthy.

6. THE USE MYTH

Did you hear about the atheist who sold thousands of dollars in Bibles? Toast the champagne glass—true story. How about John Sylvan, the founder of Keurig K-Cups? He recently reported that he doesn't use them.[93]

Me? I spent ten years in the limo business. Know how many times I've rented a limousine? Once. My friend owns a hunting business. Know how many times he went hunting? Never. Another friend? He owns a pet business, and yet he owns no pets. You see, it states nowhere in the entrepreneurial rule book that you have to be an avid user of your product in its industry. Yes, you must believe in your product and its superiority. You must be a fan of its value to the world, but you yourself? *The use myth* holds that only other people need to find it valuable; you do not.

> ***Opportunities hold no prejudices. Solved problems and filled needs don't care if you love an industry or use the product. Women can sell products for men and vice-versa.***

FINDING "FASTLANE" IDEAS (13 WAYS)

Finding *Fastlane* ideas and creating value comes from one of two sources:

1. **Innovation: You blaze your own path and do something never done before.**
2. **Improvement: You tread an existing path and do something being done already, but do it better by skewing value attributes.**

For the beginning entrepreneur not named Elon Musk, innovation is the least likely to succeed but the likeliest pursuit. Innovation entails anything new: an invention, a board game, a fashion accessory—any product or service never offered before. On the other hand, improvement is taking something that already exists and doing it better or differently. *Improvement is where most new business opportunities reside.*

When I started my company in the aggregation and lead-generation business, I deployed a combination of both. At first, I thought my idea was a blockbuster idea until I learned other companies did something similar. However, instead of foisting the crowded-room myth, I moved ahead and simply opted to IMPROVE what the other companies were doing, and not doing.

Then I added INNOVATION. I was the first company in the space (and quite possibly in any space) to abolish the pay-per-listing model and adopt a pay-per-lead model. Keep in mind, this was the nineties, when animated gifs and database functionality were considered technologically advanced. As a result, my company attracted paying advertisers by the truckload and grew practically every month—for the next ten years.

If you're in "I need an idea" mode, the focus shouldn't be either innovation or improvement but whatever the market tells you. Don't fight the tape. The market is a fluid, dynamic body of information. It speaks often. When it does, listen. Determine if YOU can fill its needs. Most of the market's demands can be met with little to no capital.

#1: LANGUAGE

So how do you hear the market, its demands, and its problems?

It's as simple as learning its language.

The market speaks a language of negativity and selfishness. And there's plenty of that, eh? Remember, the market is a spoiled brat, and it wants what it wants. Any complaining, whining, and dissent is a potential opportunity.

Here are opportunity's code words:

- *I hate...*
- *This sucks...*
- *I'm tired...*
- *I wish...*
- *How frustrating...*
- *I don't like...*
- *Why do I have to...?*
- *Why is this...[dangerous, unhealthy, hard, etc.]?*

This bickering should sound familiar because it's everywhere. Search Twitter, Facebook, or Topsy for these key phrases and you'll find a treasure trove of potential ideas. Anytime I run this search, I find several potential opportunities within seconds. On Instagram, I see fitness people complaining about people stealing their machine during supersets. On Twitter, one person complained that they hated packing, obviously for an upcoming move. Another person wished that drive-in theaters were as popular as they once were. Another wisher wished baby monitors had detailed data analytics. I found four potential ideas in thirty-five seconds. What could you find if you were really serious and spent an hour looking?

My friend takes this a step further. He searches Amazon for products that sell well but have poor reviews. He then dives into the complaints and determines if he can solve those complaints at the manufacturing level. If so, he develops his own products.

Complaints and pains are also opportunities. Seriously, just an hour ago I cleaned a goopy pan of dried-up bacon grease and muttered, "I hate this…." Pay attention to what you hate, no matter how nuanced or stupid it might sound. What do you wish was easier? More convenient? Less painful?

#2: INCONVENIENCE

Anything inconvenient is an opportunity. The inconvenience can be the product itself or the process surrounding the product. For example, in our "money company," one sales process involved snail mail while the other processed orders online. The same product delivered conveniently beats it delivered inconveniently.

The other option is taking inconvenience and making it convenient. Theranos, the controversial (and questionable) blood-testing company, is a notable attempt at making blood tests convenient. In the past, blood tests usually involved a doctor and an appointment. Whenever inconvenience is solved through a better process or a newer technology, or by improving the gadget, you skew value.

#3: SIMPLIFICATION AND/OR EASIFICATION

Anything complicated which needs simplification is an opportunity. For example, when I published my first book, ePub creation was extremely difficult. I knew this complication was an opportunity.

In fact, one would say that the oil and gas industry is the biggest industry on the planet. I'd argue it isn't; the industry of easy is the biggest. People love easy. Remember the shortcut scam? It fuels a multitude of industries: pharmaceuticals, supplements, sundries, self-development, entrepreneurship, and more.

Easy is also an easy sell. Turn-key business opportunities, network marketing, and anything "sign up and you're in business" sell simple. Instead of fighting the hard work that a real business demands (product creation, distribution, operations, etc.) someone does it for you.

#4: WANTS

The most ambiguous type of need is a want. A want is something desired but not necessarily needed. Utility and functionality are secondary. My past ownership history of Lamborghinis, Corvettes, and Vipers are all wants; I didn't need them. I spent money on these cars to symbolize ego, achievement, and an exhilarating experience. Similarly, the latest iPhone, the newest video game, and a pair of Louboutins are all wants—anything that constitutes a desire or an urge. Most wants fall into the vanity, entertainment, and fashion fields, where utility is secondary. Want opportunities are plentiful because demand can be influenced by marketing.

#5: SERVICE GAPS

Crappy customer service is an opportunity.

No one wants to be treated like shit, and yet this is standard from the average corporation. Step in, provide the exact same product or service, but treat your customers like gold, and you skew value. Exceptional customer service is one of the value skews that helped me outgrow my competition. Even today, I use this technique. My forum grows every year because I am there every single day, contributing and interacting with my readers. Good luck getting that kind of attention from any author who has sold millions of anything.

#6: GEOGRAPHICAL ARBITRAGE (CHANGING THE POND)

Geographical arbitrage, or changing the pond, is taking something common in your area and repositioning it to an area where there is an inadequate supply. On his show, Jay Leno once lampooned the ridiculous things sold on eBay. One of those things was a tumbleweed. A Utah man thought the idea was interesting since tumbleweeds were common in his area. So he created his own website and started selling them. His first perplexing thought was why would anyone buy one? Especially since they rolled around free in the Utah desert? His opinion was irrelevant, and the market answered: People bought them—so much so that he and his wife quit their jobs. And now his operation is a full-fledged business including a warehouse.[94]

Another example could be found in the Pacific Northwest. What goodness could you find strolling through the forest? How about pine cones? Did you know they're sold on the Internet? If you live in the Pacific Northwest, you could too—and your inventory would be entirely free.

Geographic arbitrage can also involve anything sourced in your area and presented globally for sale via any online marketplace: eBay, Amazon, or Etsy. For example, a rare, limited-edition book might not be particularly valuable in Topeka, Kansas, but it might hold significant value in Boston, Massachusetts. Likewise, a 1985 Chicago Bears Super Bowl ring purchased at an estate sale in Sun City, Arizona, would be worth more presented for sale in Chicago.

Of course geographical arbitrage usually isn't sustainable, but it demonstrates how relative value can be manipulated by the presentation economy. Geographical arbitrage is also a powerful bootstrapping method if you need both experience and capital. *Any value-adding experience is good experience.*

#7: CROWDFEEDING ENTRY VIOLATIONS

Feed the crowd and you shall never starve. "Crowdfeeding" emerges from the Commandment of Entry. Wherever entry is violated, opportunity arises. Why? Because the unlocked doors to an enterprise are always crowded, and crowds need to be fed, housed, and served. When the gold rush is in full bore, sell shovels.

For example, consider our hypothetical town overrun with government-subsidized restaurants. In our fictional town, assume Jimmy is an aspiring entrepreneur. Jimmy has read *UNSCRIPTED* and knows a restaurant business is a bad idea, despite the subsidized cost. However, Jimmy astutely embraces empiricism and notices something interesting. Bill, Bob, and Belinda are the richest people in the town, and none of them owns restaurants. Bill owns the real estate where the restaurants operate. Bob imports spices, fruits, and vegetables. And Belinda, who is the town's empress entrepreneur, tops them all: she owns a restaurant supply company, supplying everything a restaurant needs other than the food itself. The best opportunities rarely come from joining the crowd, but serving it.

When I started self-publishing, I was overcome with opportunity overload—opportunities to serve aspiring authors and publishers were everywhere. The pattern translates to all industries and past trends and continues into the future. For example, here's a historical chart of trends and the opportunities they presented:

BANDWAGON TREND	CROWDFED OPPORTUNITY
Websites (1997–2001)	Web developers, website hosting, advertising
Blogging (2004–2010)	Blog platforms, WordPress, templates, plugins
eCommerce (2008–2011)	Shopify, BigCommerce
Apps (2010–2013)	Affiliations or Associations
Social Media (2009–2014)	Ad serving, data analytics, metrics
Self-Publishing (2010–2015)	Editing services, cover services, books
Podcasting (2013–2016)	Podcasting courses, tools, books
Amazon (2014–201?)	Amazon courses, management tools

Today's most prolific companies have risen from crowdfed opportunities. Google, Rackspace, and GoDaddy are just a few that launched the modern Internet age.

A good story about crowdfeeding comes from a forum friend who fell ass-backwards into his business. Like many before him, he began self-publishing, hoping to grab a piece of the gold rush. After suffering marginal success (being kind), he sought to improve his book covers. When he looked to test different covers with various audiences, he couldn't find a solution. And then it hit him. OMG, is this the *need* MJ always talks about? It was. And so he built a website addressing the problem. Within a matter of weeks, his cover-rating service blew up—without advertising. The crowd demanded exactly what he needed. Obviously, he stopped writing to pursue the venture, which screamed for grease. And compliments of massive traffic and a positive feedback loop, he suddenly now *loves* his service more so than writing.

#8: VALUE ARBITRAGE

Value arbitrage (VI), the direct, straightforward approach to value creation, is another path to needfulness. With value arbitrage, 1+1+1+1 does not equal four but five. The incremental missing unit is your profit. The value arbitrageur is banking on the axiom, the sum of the parts does not equal the whole.

The mechanism behind value arbitrage is simply adding value. For example, when a home investor purchases and remodels a fixer-upper—adding new carpets, kitchen cabinets, paint, fresh landscaping—the value-added parts will exceed the sum.

Similarly, I have a friend who buys poorly marketed and designed websites. Once he acquires the websites, he retools and redesigns them and grows the bottom line. Once the bottom line picks up, he resells them at a tidy profit.

Of course, VI can be anything where value is added incrementally. Any thrift store, particularly ones in affluent neighborhoods, is a treasure-packed opportunity for anyone willing to work and use their brain. That old, ratty dresser with peeling paint and a broken leg? Fix the leg, strip the paint, refinish, and suddenly a ten-dollar dresser is worth ninety dollars. The same thing can be said for used cars. Some people on my forum use automobile bootstrapping for extra cash. Old, dirty cars are refurbished and resold for hundreds in profit.

#9: REPURPOSING

As I cleaned my garage, I came across a pile of scrap lumber and unused carpet. Although I had no use for this stuff, it pained me to throw it away. The average person sees junk; I see potential value. When you combine wood and carpet, you have the makings of an expensive cat condo. The last one I bought cost me a few C-notes. These spare materials were probably enough for four cat trees. The worthless pile of junk wasn't worthless.

While this story's lesson isn't about making fortunes in feline condos, it's seeing repurposing opportunities. If I was young and broke, I would have spent a few days and repurposed these raw materials into something valuable. So instead of trashing it, I listed it on Craigslist for FREE and gave it away.

Repurposing is taking various raw materials and reusing them for some other purpose not easily recognized. For example, did you know old, unwanted denim jeans have an industrial purpose? The Blue-to-Green (BtG) Initiative has collected over 200 tons of unwanted denim and turned it into environmentally friendly housing insulation. Instead of fiberglass keeping your house warm, it could be old Levis![95] In a similar vein, Lucrecia Lovera, an entrepreneur in Berlin, Germany, turns old VHS tapes into purses and sells them on her website, retape.de.[96]

You never know when or where repurposing ideas might appear. Aside from drinking copious amounts of vodka, long road trips cause my mind to creatively wander. While driving Interstate 10 on a ride home from a California summer, I spotted two repurposing opportunities. The roads were littered with "gators"—the truckers' word for shredded tire treads. Every few feet, a tire tread or other road debris—some incredibly hazardous—littered the road. I thought, of course, this is a problem. And problems are opportunities. According to National Highway Traffic Safety Administration Traffic Safety Facts, over 25,000 accidents are caused by road debris, including over 800 fatalities.[97] I wondered, why isn't anyone cleaning this up? Could the federal government or the State of California hire someone to keep our highways clean, while reducing costly accidents? While these government entities are virtually broke, both spend like drunken sailors with real Lustig machines.

However, the road debris idea soon gave way to another vision. As I sped along the interstate (of course obeying the speed limit), while hundreds of road gators flew by, I actually saw money. Just weeks earlier, I decorated my backyard with rubber landscape mulch and spent a fortune doing so. Guess what the mulch was made of? Repurposed, old shredded tires.

And at fifty cents a pound, those shredded tires littering the highway are dirty cash drifting in the wind.

One entrepreneur who sees the problem and overcomes its challenges will have a great little business with an incredible value proposition: reclaim, recycle, and repurpose. Hey, maybe both opportunities could be combined.

#10: MARKETING ARBITRAGE

If I ever sold my forum, the new owner would get a steal of a deal. From a marketing standpoint, my forum is not optimized to make money. Instead, I use my forum as a platform to spread my message. My number-one mission isn't to squeeze out every dollar from my users but to simply educate, non-intrusively.

Despite thousands of visitors and users, I rarely email updates, newsletters, or anything interruptive. I don't optimize, split-test, or trial-run advertisers. In marketing speak, I've left thousands of dollars on the table. If I sold my forum, the opportunity for marketing arbitrage exists.

Marketing arbitrage is simply taking an underexposed or under-leveraged asset and using it more effectively. For example, marketing arbitrage was a tool in the toolbox for my friend who bought and sold websites. For him, he'd examine the advertising channels (if any existed) and determine if it was the most effective audience channel. If it wasn't, marketing arbitrage occurred when advertising was retargeted to the appropriate channel. For example, here's a story posted at the forum:

> I read a story about a small physical products business, which made a few hundred dollars per month and later was sold for $5,000 to someone else. This new owner changed the website, added extra products, got better photography, better packaging, better fulfillment, changed prices, and was up to $50,000–$100,000 per month in revenue within six months.[98]

There are thousands of products out there that have the potential for profit but aren't marketed properly. Would you believe apartments fall into this realm? Jon Wheatley bought a Vegas condo for the sole purpose of renting it out on Airbnb. While his reported $13,000-a-year business profit won't make him a fortune overnight, Mr. Wheatley is a great arbitrage example as well as a great example for building an *UNSCRIPTED* future. He estimates he will have his condo paid off in just under four years.[99]

In another example, a clever marketer took a little-known household gadget and humorously advertised it to the masses. The Handjob! (INeedAHandJob.com) is a rubber disc that helps people unscrew those tight stubborn jar lids. I've owned one of these for years and always thought it was the most ingenious thing ever—but it was never marketed and presented to the public. The folks at Handjob! renamed it in a double entendre, repackaged and remarketed it via viral video, and wham bam, a scalable asset was created.

The truth is, the world is full of shitty marketers, bad salesmen, and poor communicators. You can create the greatest product on the planet and no one will know about it with poor marketing. If you can't persuade or motivate someone to buy and try, you'll fail. And that's when a marketing arbitrageur spots opportunity, swooping in and washing that dirty dog into a Westminster show winner.

#11: OVERCAPITALISM

Make no mistake, I'm a capitalist. However, don't confuse "capitalism" with "taking advantage of whomever I can" and destroying the environment in the process. As *UNSCRIPTED* entrepreneurs, we're fiduciaries first and capitalists second. Put your customers' best interests in front of your own. Deliver the value you promise. Make the world a better place, and money shall follow.

Unfortunately, thanks to modern media and its *M.O.D.E.L Citizen* push for politically mandated victimology, "capitalism" has become a naughty word. After all, rich capitalists get rich because they carry Glocks and force people at gunpoint to buy their stuff. It's as if the "money is evil" crowd would rather shop at an empty store than give credit to producers. Capitalism is the best economic system on the planet, and GDP numbers and advancements in technology, medicine, and social mobility have proven it.

Yet, it has many flaws.

Outside lobbyists, crony capitalists, and politicians for hire, *overcapitalism* is one of those flaws—and it's a great opportunity for you and me.

Overcapitalism is when any business organization abandons its original value-creating mission and instead prioritizes profit—so much so that it's disgustingly obvious. Yeah, ignore that honeyed mission statement on the wall, the one preaching honesty, integrity, and quality, because it's all bullshit.

Overcapitalism isn't fiduciary, and its best analogy is a wet towel.

The towel represents the product and its intrinsic value, while the water soaked within the towel represents the potential profit that could be "squeezed" out of it. Instead of focusing on the towel and how to improve it, the profit-centered corporation focuses on the "squeeze"—a systematic and measured extraction of money from its customers through cost cutting, reduced product quality, and increased prices without increased value.

Think food, cable, insurance, and electric companies. When a corporation performs its "squeeze," it usually appears in the mail as an apologetic letter that begins, "Dear valued customer…." Or your sixteen-ounce box of cereal is suddenly thirteen ounces, but it's still the same price. Now, if you're thinking, hell, that's every corporation on the planet! Well, not exactly, but yeah, it is a meaty percentage.

Take for example the agriculture and food business, an industry rife with overcapitalism. Through its use of GMOs, artificial sweeteners/colors, fillers, super-sugars, and various other questionable ingredients, the industry has slowly turned our pudgy bodies into sugar-addicted zombies fed an unrecognizable frankenfood filled with God knows what. Does the name Monsanto give you a warm, fuzzy feeling in your heart? How about that granola bar labeled *healthy,* the one with an ingredient list as long as *War and Peace?*

Some of my favorite natural-food companies have arisen and grown because of overcapitalism. For example, I pay a fortune for free-range eggs hatched from humanely raised chickens. Regular, mass-produced eggs are overcapitalism executed by cry-your-eyes-out inhumanity. And don't get me started on the "cage-free" scam. Stuffing one hundred chickens in one hundred square feet might qualify for your pithy "cage-free" designation, but it doesn't fool me. If you enjoy eggs for breakfast, I dare you to visually compare a free-range egg to a mass-produced one. The happy eggs are clear and silky; the overcapitalized egg is milky and gooey. Anyhow, the point is, opportunity and demand exist because others don't have eyes on what's best for you; they have eyes on your wallet.

The billion-dollar organic- and natural-food business is a direct consequence of the corporate squeeze. Consumers are fed up with garbage ingredients and have demanded healthy, natural alternatives. Of course, overcapitalism isn't found in just food and agriculture; it's anywhere entrenched corporations have lost sight of their purpose. Overcapitalism's downward spiral spins the minute a corporation's primary customer and stakeholder is demoted from the king of the castle to the servant mopping the floors.

#12: STAKEHOLDER DEMOTIONS

The perilous road to overcapitalism and its opportunities begins with stakeholder demotions. *A stakeholder is any person or group who holds a beneficial interest in another entity.* If you own an Apple computer, you're Apple's stakeholder. Likewise, if you're an Apple stockholder or employee, you're also a stakeholder. All businesses have multiple stakeholders, and the order in which they're prioritized determines if overcapitalism, new opportunities, and new competitors can grow.

For example, you, my reader, are my king stakeholder. I wrote this book for you, first and foremost. My primary stakeholder isn't appeasing some publisher, kowtowing to the financial industry, or even placating my selfish desire for a new Lamborghini—you are my stakeholder chain's top dog. As an *UNSCRIPTED* entrepreneur upholding the fiduciary mindset, your primary stakeholder at all times should be your customer. And in most cases for young, growth companies, this is true.

Unfortunately, this isn't true for mature companies.

Public companies are the worst. When an organization changes its primary stakeholder from you, the customer, to another entity—investors, venture capitalists, shareholders—opportunities arise because customers are no longer the priority. And overcapitalism becomes a risk. Think about the early days when eBay and Facebook were small and growing. People loved them. How about now, with millions of shares spread out among thousands of investors?

You can't serve two masters at once. You're either a servant to your customer or you're squeezing the towel and appeasing investors, shareholders, or Wall Street analysts. Capitalism's unfortunate consequence is that Wall Street expects perpetually improved margins and earnings per share (EPS), which requires strangling the life out of the towel, alienating once-happy customers.

Public companies have a difficult tightrope to walk: being a servant to customers while still appeasing financial stakeholders with profitability. Some companies walk the line the best they can—for example, Costco and Apple. However, once new stakeholders are added, things typically change, and not for the better.

For example, I know a friend who makes a modest living on Etsy, the popular marketplace for arts and crafts, similar to eBay. In 2015, Etsy went public. Rut-roh. I told my friend she should be prepared—and so should the thousands of others who rely on Etsy to put roofs over their heads and food in their mouths. My pessimistic caution is simply history repeating: Once a servant company becomes public, they no longer cater to customers first; they cater to profit, return on investment, shareholder value, and anything ensuring every last drop of cash is extracted from the towel. Namely, expect fees to increase while value stagnates or lessens.

But all is not lost. *Any company who serves shareholders first is vulnerable to you*—the entrepreneur who elevates his customer onto the marble pedestal. And in the global marketplace, that means any publicly traded or heavily funded company exhibiting stakeholder demotion is ripe to have market share stolen by a smaller, nimble company.

This amounts to thousands of opportunities and under-served needs. If you enter a $100 billion industry and take one one-hundredth of 1 percent (.0001), you just built yourself a nice little $1 million company. Hopefully, you now see ho ridiculous it is for an entrepreneur to say, "There are no good ideas." Any such person, I'd argue, is no entrepreneur.

> ***Stakeholder demotion usually begins once a company receives outside funding as customer satisfaction becomes secondary to investor satisfaction (ROI).***

#13: IMPROVEMENT (AND REMOVEMENT)

Few know that Thomas Edison didn't invent the light bulb—he merely improved it by using a carbonized bamboo filament which increased its illumination duration, ultimately making the light bulb commercially viable. And so it goes with the theme of most needs: Something is simply improved or changed.

Improvement is the muscle behind the Commandment of Need like iron to a workout. Improve something, effectively communicate it, and you will be needed.

Look, this isn't rocket science.

E.L. James took Prince Charming and gave him a helicopter, a billion dollars, and a sex room full of sadistic playthings, and wham, *Fifty Shades of Grey.* The *Cinderella* "rich guy sweeping you off your feet" archetype isn't exactly a novelty—but add a BDSM fetish, whips, and a trapeze hanging from the ceiling and suddenly the media wets its panties.

Sara Blakely, required to wear pantyhose in the hot Floridian sun for her sales position, modified hosiery by removing the stocking toes and improved both its comfort and functionality. Several years later, she's the world's newest billionaire. When Drew Houston couldn't find any reasonable storage solutions that seamlessly integrated with his files, he founded Dropbox.[100]

These worldly modifications don't take a PhD in chemistry or a rich uncle; they take persistence, vision, and the cinch to the pinch—a product that people want.

Improvement's counterpart is removement. Removement is when your product removes or subtracts something, becoming differentiated. It is addition by subtraction, whereas the subtraction is the removal of something while the addition happens within your value skew.

For instance, I've been working out for years and taking nutritional supplements to support my fitness. Unfortunately, in the fitness world lies the greatest hypocrisy of health: Most supplements are loaded with artificial colors and flavors—Sucralose, Aspartame, Red 40, Cancer 80, or whatever else sweetens the offer. Up until recently, it has been virtually impossible to find fitness supplements that were both naturally sweetened/colored and didn't taste like a bag of chalk.

Removement solves this challenge by eliminating the artificial ingredients. In urn, the value skew is improved. Fitness buffs who don't trust chemical shitstorms w have a product to trust.

Opportunities to remove features, ingredients, and hassles are opportunities to gain competitive advantages. Removement can occur in any industry but is most common in food processing. For example, if you owned the only product on the market that was Paleo focused or gluten-free, you would skew value and create a nice little market differentiation for yourself.

As consumer preferences change over time, removement opportunities appear if you just listen to them. From "GMO-free" ingredients in foods to "paraben-free" in skin conditioners to "animal-free testing" in cosmetics—consumers demand LESS just as much as they demand MORE.

WHY YOUR BEST BET AT FINDING A NEED MIGHT BE THE WORST

Your best bet at uncovering a great idea and paving your *UNSCRIPTED* path comes from the worst thing an entrepreneur wants to do: *get a damn job.*

You see, the biggest roadblock to finding legitimate ideas isn't your insensitivity to the concepts of needs/wants but a lack of experience—both in life and at the workplace. The fact is, most new businesses spawn from the founder's domain experience. *Domain experience is any activity or industry you are intimately familiar with.*

For example, if you spent the last five years working at a mattress store as a manager, you would have serious domain experience in the business of bedding. If you're on the water every single weekend, fishing or sailing, you have domain experience in those realms. Likewise, I ran a limousine company for several years, which gave me intimate knowledge about the nuances and inner workings of the industry. That domain experience led me to a great opportunity that spanned a decade. Similarly, I now own a publishing company and run a heavily trafficked forum. Both experiences have given me the aptitude to again spot a cornucopia of potential ideas in those fields.

A common theme in many successful entrepreneurial backstories is a need discovered while working a job: an employee suffers a problem or an unfilled need and decides to solve it. These successes always start the same: "I was working over at ACME Company and I noticed that there was a NEED/PROBLEM for XYZ and decided to solve it."

Unfortunately, many aspiring entrepreneurs remain aspiring for one simple fact: They refuse to acquire domain experience—namely, job experience. And in doing so, they isolate themselves from opportunity. If you're not getting out of the house and encountering life, you won't encounter life's problems. Opportunity doesn't ring doorbells and it certainly doesn't wait for "someday."

SOLUTION SELLING: SKIPPING DOMAIN EXPERIENCE

Don't have time for domain experience? Then ask the people who do. Every so often, a drive-by user posts this generic question at my forum: "What do you guys need help with most in your business?"

The question is perturbing because my forum entrepreneurs know what's happening. The questioner is circumventing domain experience and probing for problems, looking for opportunities. This practice, asking an audience about their problems, is called *solution selling.*

Solution selling is particularly popular in many entrepreneurial academies. It involves cold-calling professionals in a particular industry and explicitly asking them about their problems, for example, asking fifty dentists, "In your practice, what problems or frustrations do you experience most?" From there, a solution is evaluated to fix the expressed problem. Or you could attend any industry's trade convention and keep your eyes and ears peeled for the language of opportunity.

While solution selling shortcuts into industry needs, it plays second fiddle to real domain experience. During my ten-year stint operating an Internet company, I always knew which new competitors had domain experience and which did not—the ones without insider experience struggled.

Getting a job and being responsible is never failure. When you identify as an entrepreneur, a job is simply a means to an end, a part of your unfolding story.

If experience and money were no concern, what needs and wants would you pursue? And is experience and money really an obstacle, or just one of the 3Bs?

CHAPTER 36

THE COMMANDMENT OF TIME: EARN MORE THAN MONEY, EARN TIME

Don't stay in bed, unless you can make money in bed.
~ **George Burns, Comedian**

SO YOU WANT PASSIVE INCOME? SO DO 7 BILLION OTHER PEOPLE

The fourth CENTS Commandment is the Commandment of Time, and it is the conduit to abolishing the causal relationship between your time and income. Temporal prostitution is dethroned, and income no longer requires life rations.

FASTLANE ENTREPRENEURSHIP (FE)

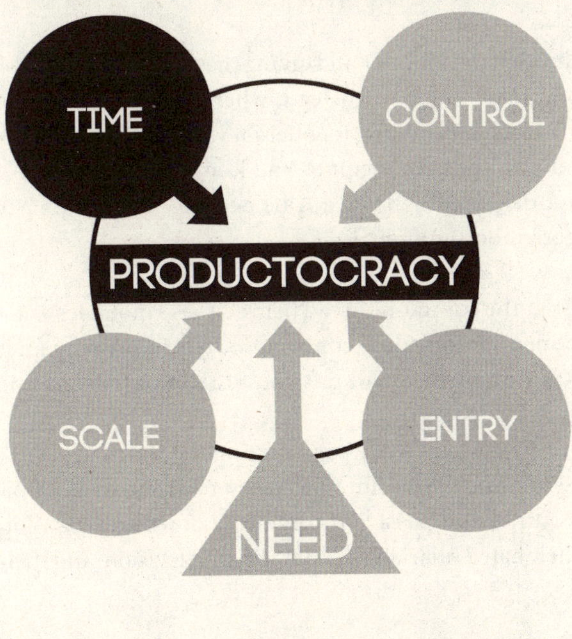

The Commandment of Time has two components. The first is *physicality*, where your value must exist in space-time separate from you. This book exists regardless of my existence. On the other hand, if you consult for a living, your income stops when you stop. There is no physicality.

The second is *detachment*. Eventually in your enterprise's evolution, you must detach from its physicality, effectively freeing your time and life. When this is accomplished, it puts you "on the clock" 24/7, giving you the ability to earn perpetually *THROUGH* time versus *IN* time. This is how you wake up and earn a day's wage before brewing the morning coffee.

Unfortunately, the Time Commandment is the most misunderstood and perverted CENTS Commandment. Instead of time being honored, it is worshiped. Why? Because it's the gatekeeper to every starry-eyed entrepreneur's wet dream: passive income.

<BEGIN RANT>

As I mentioned earlier, I have a love/hate relationship with my forum.

Most folks there are great people working toward great things. But the other minority need steel-toed-boot ass-kicking. Thankfully, these participants disappear as quickly as they arrive. I call them "drive-bys"—people who love this radical idea of "passive income" but don't care about value, contribution, or entrepreneurship. Time and time again, one phrase I hear echoed by drive-bys is "passive income."

- *What's the best way to earn passive income?*
- *Can I make passive income publishing 300-word eBooks on Kindle?*
- *If I YouTube myself picking my nose while eating a cheeseburger, can I make passive income?*

Reaching through the monitor and giving these dreamers a turd-basted knuckle-sandwich would make my day. Instead, whenever I read such nonsense, I hear Charlie Brown's teacher rambling incoherent wah-wahs in the background. Wow, that's great you want passive income! You know what I want? A billion dollars, preferably hand-delivered by Jessica Alba bearing wine and a penchant for hot-tubbing on a cool moonlit night.

Get real.

Take a guess at the common thread behind these inquiries and the other 4,000 like them? No mention of value, contribution, or improving anything. Just me, me, and me—as if the world will gift you $10K/month for doing abso-fuckin'-lutely nothing.

Once a drive-by discovers that tag-teaming the shortcut scam and the special scam doesn't work, they lash out. Once they realize a daily effort (the process-principle) is required and passive income isn't downloading WordPress, they're gone. Back to their hated salaried weekdays, their television, and their lottery tickets.

Behind the word "start-up," no phrase makes me grit my teeth and punch walls more than "passive income." The problem is many drive-bys read my first book (as well as others) and cherry-pick hyperpalatable concepts while discarding the rest. When they learn that the Commandment of Time is the pathway to passive income, every other Commandment is quickly forgotten.

THE MYTH OF PASSIVE INCOME

The passive-income lure sounds deliciously simple. Just upload an unedited four-page eBook to the Kindle store and, wham, watch the cash come pouring in! Unfortunately, such simplicity is about as complicated as a zero-calorie cheesecake.

For the unwashed, passive income is mystically clothed like free or easy money. It resonates like entrepreneurial welfare, where value is disrespected and money comes for nothing—no effort, no challenge, and no work. Nothing could be further from the truth. *The big irony of passive income is it's anything but passive.* Every single entrepreneur I know who enjoys passive income today exercised an extraordinary and committed process yesterday. Passivity? LOL. It played no role.

Passive macro-events (and action-faking) doesn't produce passive income. Launching a podcast, interviewing three people, and giving up a week later is not the path to passive income. Neither is uploading one badly programmed app to the Apple store and expecting thousands of downloads.

Satisfying the Commandment of Time (and getting to the point of a sustainable, life-altering passive income) takes months, sometimes years, of nose-to-the-grindstone effort. We're talking about ten-hour days six to seven days a week demonstrated by the process-principle. Or is your expectation in line with the event-driven, 4-hour crowd?

While I've enjoyed passive income for nearly twenty years, its road has not been passive. In my first business, it took me several years to create passivity. Ask any of my friends and they would confirm: I'd hibernate in my office for days and not come out except to reload on the Ramen and Red Bull. My publishing company and my forum? Again, years. When I started my forum years ago, I was the primary content creator because I had few users. **I literally commented on every thread created.** That's right, every thread. Sometimes I just talked to myself. Think that was time-consuming? Or do you think I just kicked my feet up on the sofa and smoked a cigar while daydreaming about the forthcoming passive-income avalanche?

Entrepreneurs who play this game with a foremost objective of passive income are delusional. And if I had to guess, lazy.

Your business bull's-eye is a productocracy and fiduciary entrepreneurship. Much like value is a predecessor to money, a systemized productocracy is a predecessor to passive income. Honor the Commandment of Time; don't collapse to your knees and sacrifice your firstborn for it. With a productocracy in your corner, passive income eventually comes knocking. <END RANT>

HONORING TIME: LEGACY VALUE CREATION

To honor the Commandment of Time, simply forget about it. Yeah, forget about it, but only in the short term. Instead, focus on *legacy value systems* (LVS) for the long term.

Essentially, an LVS is your personal slave that surrogates for time. Legacy value systems could be grown virtually from anything: a product invention, a game, a franchised restaurant, a smartphone application, a website, a human-resource system, a series of books, or any system that exists as a conceptual entity disconnected from your time.

If the Commandment of Time were a fruit tree, legacy value systems would be its seeds while its fruit would be passive income. When you focus on nurturing the legacy value's seeds, eventually passive-income fruit sprouts. And you can't enjoy the fruit without first caring for and cultivating its seeds.

For example, this book is a legacy value creation and falls into the category of a product system. Once I published this book into both digital and paper form, it existed as a tangible product sold through multiple channels, which aptly, are also systems. *Its physicality doesn't require my existence* or, hence, my time. I could be dead and my books would live on. Like doppelgänger robots, they work while I don't. At the precise moment you bought this book, I made a small amount of money. Who knows what I was doing at that moment: I could have been sleeping, exercising, or at the dentist.

Another example is the Internet company I founded. That system also worked for me 24/7, never shut down, complained about long hours, or called in sick. I've been long gone, and nearly ten years later, that system still exists. My entrepreneur forum? Another system, again, surfing perpetually through time and producing income on the same "round-the-clock" schedule. There are some days I "work" twelve hours and make $200. Other days I can work two hours and earn $2,000. Once you experience the power of legacy value systems and being "on the clock" 24/7, the idea of trading your time for money will seem as obsolete as dial-up Internet.

THE SIX LEGACY VALUE SYSTEMS

There are six legacy value systems, each capable of passive income. Some are more autonomous and hands-off, while others require more babysitting, sometimes for years. In order of legacy strength, they are:

MONEY SYSTEMS

Via the capital-principle, a *money system* is the kingpin system, and it's our *UNSCRIPTED* goal. Legacy strength and passivity are the strongest, although traditionally speaking, it isn't a business. Essentially, a money system is a capital rental business—regular and recurring income from your investments: interest, dividends, notes, option sales, and partnership income.

Within (TUNEF), the money system is our end goal because it is ridiculously, jaw-dropping passive. Much of my yearly income is derived through a money system. And if I wiped clean my entrepreneurial endeavors, my money system earns enough to live well, far beyond survival. Every month, without regular intervention, management, or oversight, I receive thousands of dollars in interest and investment dividends working around the globe. My management of these affairs amounts to hours per year.

Unfortunately, a money system and its corresponding instigator, compound interest, are not very effective at creating wealth or income unless leveraging a large sum. Remember, using compound interest as a wealth creator is a *SCRIPTED* tenet. The entire plan is theoretical because it dismisses life expectancy, economics, and market returns. However, we, the *UNSCRIPTED*, don't use Wall Street to fund our money system; we use our business.

My business and its large explosive income (as well as liquidation events) grew my money system, not stocks, bonds, or mutual funds. A money system leveraged against a tiny pittance is a limp dick in a whorehouse. With $1,000 and 5 percent interest, you couldn't pay half your cell phone bill. And yet, 5 percent on $10 million is a nice comfy $500,000 per year. That's right, a whopping $500K per year, and that's *without touching the principal*. When it comes to money systems, it definitely takes money to make money.

Compound interest doesn't take the stage until we've earned and saved a large enough amount to make it fabulously impactful. Every dollar saved NOW is a soldier fighting the fight of "fuck you" LATER, giving you the increasing probability that work remains optional and life is lived on your terms. In Chapter 48, I dig into money systems further.

DIGITAL PRODUCT SYSTEMS

The most popular systems for tapping into legacy value are *digital product systems*. Digital product systems fall into the category of content or information dissemination. Typically, they are the easiest to create and, henceforth, the most crowded of spaces. Some examples:

- eBooks, PDF reports, white papers
- YouTube videos, blogs, podcasts
- Website templates, skins, scripts

SOFTWARE/INTERNET SYSTEMS

The next popular legacy systems are *software/internet systems* designed to solve a problem, make something easier, or even provide entertainment. Software systems provide the most legacy bang as, once coded, management consists of upgrade and support. The software-system umbrella contains all the following:

- Software as a service system (SAAS: learning academies, analytics, social-media management)
- Internet websites and applications (social media, marketplaces)
- Mobile applications
- Enterprise software (software designed for a purpose, e.g., a dental patient management tool)
- Video games (computer, smartphone, social-media gaming)

PRODUCT SYSTEMS

A *product system* is any physical merchandise sold through a distribution channel. Because products are tangible and survive with minimal support, they are the third-most effective form of business legacy. In a product system, the product and its distribution represent the central executional challenge. Some examples of legacy product systems:

- Food products (Grandma's BBQ chicken soup recipe, gluten-free crackers, cookies)
- Clothing or jewelry
- Cosmetics (makeup, skin care, chemical-free deodorant/ toothpaste)
- Books (this one), board games, toys
- Inventions, gadgets, art, other creative endeavors

RENTAL SYSTEMS

A *rental system* is a form of a product system where the product is not bought but rented. The legacy occurs because both the product and its use through duration create income. Notably, the expiration of time becomes your ally. Some examples:

- Rental real estate (residential, commercial, Airbnb property)
- Rental services (cars, party tents, heavy equipment, bounce houses)
- Parking garages
- Licensing (rental of intellectual or brand property)

HUMAN-RESOURCE SYSTEMS

A *human-resource system* is a product (or service) system that requires people, or employees, for operation. It could be many people, as in the case of a restaurateur, or just you, as in a consultant. Delivering the product to the customer is contingent on someone's time. For example, if you design websites, your product can't be created without someone's time investment, either yours or your employee's.

Human-resource systems usually subordinate another system. For example, if you're considering a restaurant concept, it's technically a product system, but in practice, it's requires human resources to succeed. Since human-resources systems entail multiple tiers of execution beyond just the product, they are the most difficult to execute. Some examples are:

- Restaurants (either chains or franchises)
- Service businesses (consulting, accounting, copywriting, web development, SEO)
- Retail brick-and-mortar storefronts (fashion boutique, bookstore, hardware store)

Just to give you an idea how these systems work in an *UNSCRIPTED* life, here is a complete list of the legacy systems currently working for me:

- Digital Product Systems: eBooks, MP3 audiobooks (product sales)
- Software Systems: forum (advertising/sponsor revenue, monthly membership revenue)
- Product Systems: physical books, audiobooks (product sales)
- Rental Systems: foreign-rights licenses (royalties on international translations)
- Rental Systems: rental real estate (monthly rent)
- Money Systems: interest, dividends (monthly/quarterly payments)

All of these legacy systems work for me like little worker bees who never stop buzzing.

Unfortunately, in the *SCRIPTED* realm and in business, we're taught to operate under a zero-legacy mindset. Work directly correlates with income. If you don't work—fix the faucet, open the store, or finish the project—you don't make money. When you take the vacation, so does your income. Such businesses aren't different from a job. Instead of employer ownership, your business owns you. In fact, many employed, corporate sales reps who sell products with a residual component are more disconnected from time than many business owners. The consumption of time is indifferent to whomever eats it—sixty hours spent at a job or a business are still sixty hours gone. If income disappears because you disappear, you're in a bad marriage.

LEGACY STRUCTURES: HOW TO SELL WITHOUT SELLING

Another component of legacy value creation is *legacy structures. Legacy structures are other perpetual systems that support, promote, or market your LVS, also 24/7 and separate from your time.*

For example, as I write this paragraph, I have hundreds of legacy structures working for me infinitely in time. Floating around the Internet are dozens of podcast interviews that I've done, each *unlinked* from my time, and each sells books.

Back in 2011, I did a Smart Passive Income Podcast with the well-known Internet marketer and blogger Pat Flynn. The interview consumed about forty-five minutes of my time, and yet, more than six years later, people still message me, saying they bought my book because of that interview. That's legacy—not just with value creation but with your ability to reach people on a continual basis.

Another example of legacy structure is my forum and the hundreds of posts I've made over the years. These are continually readable in space-time like a neon light that never goes dark. Many times I hear, "Hey, I read your post about [whatever] and bought your book." Again, my doppelgänger never stops peddling and promoting for me while I'm off doing something else.

Similarly, the same legacy concept applies to posts made by others, not just by me. For instance, there's a forum post questioning the credibility of a certain unnamed guru. I can't count how many times someone has told me that they bought my book because of that thread. In a nutshell, the sales funnel goes like this:

1. **Search Google for background on guru.**
2. **Find and click my forum's thread via Google.**
3. **Read valuable information.**
4. **Read great word of mouth about my book(s).**
5. **Purchase my book(s).**

I'm guessing this thread has made me $25,000. That's right, other gurus and their market penetration is selling my book, thanks to my forum. And that's just one thread; there are 30,000 more.

Legacy structures also play a role in how I spend time. One example—one you shouldn't follow and I'm embarrassed admitting—happens a lot. I am often asked to be interviewed on radio. These interviews take about twenty minutes, and while they can garner good exposure for me and my book, I typically decline. Why? No legacy structure. These interviews aren't available anywhere except in one space of time. Once the interview is over, it evaporates like a fart in the wind. It does not survive time. Sure, I could sell more books, but since I dislike interviews and love my *UNSCRIPTED* retirement, I don't need to do them. Ahh, the beauty of "fuck you."

Nonetheless, if you're trying to grow a business or inspire a movement, I don't recommend declining interviews. Remember, *before you can do what you love, you have to do what you hate.*

To demonstrate legacy structure, I logged into my business bank account and recorded all the automatic deposits and their sources. The following chart highlights the legacy structures paying me regular bank deposits. There are more than twenty:

Google AdSense	VigLink
Google Play	Amazon (FBA/Seller Account)
Apple iBooks	Book Distributors (3 total)
Amazon (Kindle)	PayPal (Membership Revenue)
Kobo	PayPal (Sponsor Revenue)
Lightning Source (UK)	PayPal (Advertising Revenue)
Lightning Source (US)	Visa/MC (eCommerce sales)
Lightning Source (AU)	Vanguard
Barnes and Noble	T. Rowe Price
Rental Income from Tenant	TD Ameritrade
Foreign Publishers (10 total)	Fidelity

Again, each of these legacy structures effectuates my legacy value systems. My legacy system surrogates for my time, but so do the systems promoting it! An autonomous system sells the autonomous system. Who would have thought? My "cost" in these systems is the channel's administration time, usually amounting to minutes.

For example, the Amazon FBA fulfillment system sells my books. I timed how long it takes me to prepare and ship a case of books. Prep time and delivery to the corner UPS store take me seventeen minutes. Once I send it off to Amazon, it's out of my hair: no packaging, shipping, or further time required. With thirty-two books in each case at a six-dollar profit per unit, I make $192 for each case.

Now $192 dollars isn't impressive, but that isn't the point. The point is the return on time invested (ROTI) is impressive. Calculated at an hourly rate, my time is paid at $677 per hour ([60 / 17] X 192). Would you object to earning nearly $700 per hour?

THE COST OF LEGACY

Sleeping in and making money. $700 an hour. Regular checks for doing nothing. Yes, the dreampreneurs are salivating. Sadly, creating legacy isn't cheap. And I'm not talking about dollars. Legacy's price, ironically, is your time. If you can't say NO to what you want today—an easy unlearned ride—you won't be saying YES to what you want tomorrow. The problem as it relates to the Commandment of Time is thinking that time can be bought by not giving it time. You can't spend three hours writing a shitty book and expect to make oodles of passive income simply because that shitty book exists in perpetuity. Trash survives time as does gold. The only question is will someone want your creation? And tell others?

Don't be afraid to spend oodles of time building your system.

The fundamental truth underscoring this entire book is *we eventually want to be paid BOTH time and money.*

"Eventually" is the operative word.

Many business ventures, especially those in service, require undivided attention in the beginning. If you are creating a new organic-food restaurant with franchising as the long-term vision, legacy benefits won't vest for years until the system is perfect. Like seeds, legacy value creation requires cultivating before the seeds grow and sprout fruit. And when that fruit accumulates by the bushel, it's transferred into a money system.

> ***Your objective in creating legacy value through a business system is an immediate payment of MONEY, but an eventual payment of FREE TIME.***

WHY SELL A GOLDEN GOOSE?

If you own a golden goose that lays golden eggs, that goose can only live for so long before it must be replaced or rebirthed. Starve and neglect the goose (while still enjoying its eggs) and the eggs will diminish over time. Ignore the goose entirely and death comes early.

This scenario frames a common question I am asked: Why sell a company that yields a monthly six-figure income that's mostly passive? Why on earth would I do that? There are three reasons why, and all of them relate to the Commandment of Time.

First, I judged the goose's ability to lay future golden eggs and determined it was a depreciating and expiring asset. In order to solve that future challenge, a present challenge emerged: Put forth a huge time investment and additional employees to create a rebirth. This would extend and re-ensure passivity for another several years. Unfortunately, in the Internet space, technology moves so fast that permanent passivity is a misnomer. If you sleep too long and ignore your goose, competitors take over.

Unless you're Craigslist, you can't survive very long on shitty technology that looks like it was birthed in the late nineties. In this case, I had to recommit, and that commitment, whether it was learning new technology or managing new employees, would cost my time.

Second, I was ten years into the business and my role of "entrepreneur" withered away. In its place, I became a manager. Managing employees—or in the case of executive management, managing the manager—was not something I wanted any longer. I decided to change my identity to an author and a semi-retired entrepreneur.

The third reason is probably the most profound as it relates to the Commandment of Time: I wanted to upgrade a system that was semi-passive and expiring to become one that was fully passive and permanent. I transformed my Internet business system into a money system. Since my company had a multimillion-dollar valuation and I already made (and saved) millions, I knew a money system would allow 100 percent *UNSCRIPTION*—never needing to work another day in my life.

An UNSCRIPTED lifestyle should be challenged regularly. Whenever life gets routine or mundane, it potentially signals it's time for a new pursuit.

CHAPTER 37

THE COMMANDMENT OF SCALE: WIN LIFE & LIBERTY, NOT DINNER AND A MOVIE

Entrepreneurship is neither a science nor an art. It is a practice.
~ **Peter Drucker, Author**

SCALE: EXPLODING INCOME

A productocracy's fifth and final CENTS Commandment within the *Fastlane* structure is the Commandment of Scale.

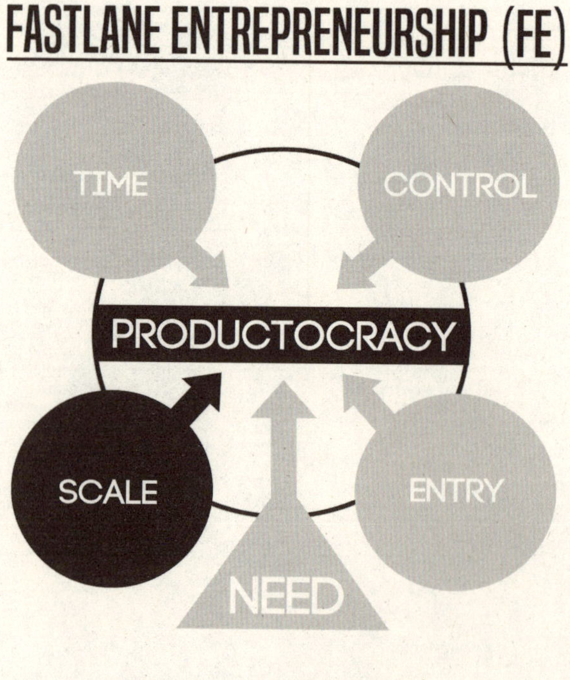

Scale instructs that legacy value systems must be replicated through *mass* or *magnitude* while making a profitable impact. The four definitive components are:

1. **Legacy value system**
2. **Replication**
3. **Mass or magnitude**
4. **Profitable impact**

First, your offering must eventually evolve into a legacy system in accordance with the four prior commandments.

Second, your LVS must be replicable, or easily copied into multiple units, locations or chains. Optimally, this replication should extend among hundreds or thousands, if not millions, of units. For instance, software is easily replicated. The same goes for a website service where increased users and traffic extend replication. My forum receives over 100,000 visitor sessions per month. In the ten years I owned my Internet company, I served a multitude of millions. Physical products like this book also offer replicative elements; my printer can print one million books as easily as 10,000. Replication turns one store into twenty, one duplex into a dozen, and hundreds sold to millions.

Third, replication must have either mass or magnitude. Most people think scale automatically equates to mass-market millions or operating in multibillion market size. However, scale can also be graced through *magnitude*, or the gravity of your impact. For instance, if you provide housing for twenty families (not mass market), you've scaled by magnitude and probably are doing well—housing is a magnitudinal endeavor. Sell ten restaurant franchises for your organic, GMO-free restaurant, and again, brute-force magnitude occurs.

As an example, a forum entrepreneur sources then negotiates industrial raw materials for both corporations and government. His enterprise is not mass but magnitude—a few repeat clients and he's rolling in the millions. Additionally, his clients are operating in mass, so by serving that market indirectly, he nudges mass. Aside from confirming the "do what you hate" theme, he touched on magnitude in a forum Q&A. He wrote:

> As far as the activities I dread, of course I still do things I don't want to do. I don't think this will ever change for anyone. This four-day trade show makes sense because almost every person attending has the power to pull the trigger on seven figures worth of product. I'm not going to waste my time.[101]

On the flip side, if you invent an eco-friendly, biodegradable food container, your magnitude is negligible per unit—the scale occurs through volume. Get one-quarter of all food manufacturers to use it, and well, you might join the three-comma club without grabbing a mention in Valleywag.

The fourth element in the definition is a **profitable** impact. The *UNSCRIPTED* business is about profits, not ten years from now but within your first year. Nowadays, too many businesses are labeled a success by virtue of growth or run rates. Many never make a profit for years and bleed cash like an Instagram playboy. Most start-ups birthed on the tech coast create value and make an impact. The problem is, they don't make a *profitable impact* for years.

Amazon is a great example of a company that makes a phenomenal impact but largely hasn't been profitable. Remember: Selling hundred-dollar bills for fifty bucks isn't what we want. "Bleeding value" might grow a company fabulously and have VC's drowning us in term sheets, but that's not our objective. Let the deep-pocketed sultans of Silicon Valley make those gambles.

Your goal is *UNSCRIPTION*, which demands profitability now, not later. And if you want to create the next hot start-up reveled on TechCrunch, the better bet is doing it *UNSCRIPTED* where "fuck you" opens up more possibilities.

As producers, we are in the business of serving consumers—not few, but many. However, before impacting the masses, we must first *impact one*—and do so profitably. If you can impact one profitably and your legacy system is replicable, congratulations, you've laid a scaling track.

For example, each book I sell makes me about six bucks. I only needed to sell a few hundred to break even. Thereafter, each book sold makes a profitable impact. Similarly, each new user at my forum is worth about a dollar. Each list subscriber, also worth about a buck. When I owned my Internet company, each new user represented a lifetime customer value of thousands. For every dollar I spent in advertising, four came back in revenue and nearly two in profit. Profitable impact.

The act of profitably impacting many is where your income (and life) makes quantum leaps. Optimally, your business solution should impact an industry large enough to impact your life. If you have a software solution appealing to hospitals, the appeal of magnitude scale exists. If any business owner could use your product, the appeal of mass scale exists.

Your market size is the ceiling which you limit yourself. If your solution sells for twenty bucks and your target customer is an Internet-savvy octogenarian who owns a Corvette, the ceiling is at your ankles. How big is that market; ten people in the world? You can't fill a pool with an eyedropper. Olympic swimmers don't train in bathtubs. Swim in bodies of water large enough to take you somewhere.

EXPECTED VALUE (BOWLING FOR BILLIONS, NOT HUNDREDS)

The mathematical construct behind the Scale Commandment is *expected value*. Expected value, or EV, is the expected outcome of many random occurrences.

E(x) = SUM * P(x)

EV is calculated by multiplying each occurrence's estimated probability and adding the result in a comparison metric. EV positive results are favorable to pursue while negative ones are not. Higher EVs are better than lower ones. For instance, say you are offered a ten-dollar raffle ticket for a chance to win a new car valued at $25,000. Only 5,000 raffle tickets will be sold. Is this a raffle you should enter? Not according to expected value.

Outcome #1:

Lose $10 (Odds of occurring 4999/5000) [-10 X .9998 = -9.998]

Outcome #2:

Win $24,990 (Odds of occurring 1/5000) [24990 X .0002 = 4.998]

When you sum the two values (-9.998 + 4.998), you get an expected value of negative five (-5). That means, if you play this raffle infinitely, you will always lose.

The world's casinos operate on the same principle, where odds are slightly EV positive, while for the gambler, EV negative. This is why the house eventually wins if you play long enough. As occurrences increase over time, expect a mean reversion to expected value.

In life, your outcomes (and consequences) are based on your EV plays, the opportunities and risks taken, and the ones avoided. For example, let's say you are considering two businesses in two markets. Business A is something you love—a laser-tag facility serving your local city. Business B is a software/gaming company educating millennial investors on financial planning through a unique video-game experience. The chart below represents the potential monthly profits and their estimated probability given a business investment of one year.

Business A (Laser Tag)	Odds	Business B (Software)	Odds
$26,000 loss	3%	$42,000 loss	7%
$6,000 loss	4%	$6,000 loss	14%
$1,000 loss	7%	$1,000 loss	22%
$1,000 profit	15%	$3,000 profit	39%
$2,000 profit	36%	$10,000 profit	14%
$3,000 profit	21%	$100,000 profit	3%
$5,000 profit	14%	$1,000,000 profit	1%

Which business should you pursue? Open a laser-tag facility and "do what you love"? Or the riskier software biz?

According to the chart, the laser-tag business has an 86 percent chance at profitability while the software company's is just 57 percent. Notably, your chances of failing in software are more than three times greater, 14 percent versus 43 percent. So is the laser-tag business and its higher success probability the better opportunity?

Nope, not by a long shot.

Business B, the software company, is the business to own, and expected value is why. EV marks the difference between entrepreneurs who own businesses that pay the bills for the month and businesses that pay bills for a lifetime. First is the best-case scenario.

Laser Tag, Best Case:	**Software Co., Best Case:**
$5,000/mo	**$1,000,000/mo**

While Business B's best-case scenario is low probability, its results are life-changing. Over time, large EV opportunities and their probabilities put big outcomes within your grasp. The gumball machine is packed with golds, and luck starts lurking around corners. Or, as Mark Cuban says, you only need to be right once. And as I say, hit for singles, but make sure you can hit a home run.

On the flip side, the best-case scenario for your laser-tag facility is $60,000 yearly profit, a nice middle-class paycheck that will make you the newest millionaire-next-door in about forty years. And it will jeopardize your love for the game.

The second reason the optimal choice is the software company is expected value, which is nearly ten times (10X) better than A.

Expected Value of A:	**Expected Value of B:**
+$1,110	**+$11,570**

Remember the gumball machines. Expected value is the machinery operating the luck spigot. If the gumballs are the potential business outcomes, you want machines packed with golds, big-win gumballs with life-changing outcomes.

If your overall vision is rolling into a construction site and selling burritos from a roach coach, I can say without doubt, no life-changing homers will occur in that endeavor. (Not unless you apply one of the strategies below.) Dial coins into big EV gumball machines where the best-case scenarios (and their EVs) change lives.

HOW TO KILL SCALE (AND EXPECTED VALUE!)

Expected value is the expected outcome of many occurrences. For EV to work, you need occurrences. In entrepreneurship, we call occurrences failure. Practically every day on my forum, I can predict entrepreneurial failure before it occurs.

These bulls ride into town with gleeful proclamations about starting a business, saying things like:

- *I just read the book and I'm going to give Fastlane a try!*
- *I've never been so motivated—I'm gonna take a stab at this!*
- *I'm so excited to give this a shot!*

Ahem. {clears throat} Uh, taking a stab? Giving it a shot? Please. Spare yourself the ride on the rainbow. *Fastlane* Entrepreneurship is not something you "try." Come to the game with that mentality, and sorry, failure is guaranteed. You see, "trying" or "taking a stab" or "giving it a shot" does not take advantage of expected value. Failing one web business and retreating back to your job diminishes the positive expected value of CENTS, which requires occurrences. "Taking a shot" is what you do when you play the Powerball.

In business, occurrences mean multiple swings at the plate: strikeouts, pop-ups, foul outs, and other musings of fail. If you're playing in big EV ventures, it will take multiple failures before hitting something substantial. For me, I had multiple occurrences banked before I struck something that gained traction. Occurrences are just part of the game. Expect it. Occurrences have their benefits, and that's our aim. As you move through the trials, your network grows, as do your skills and abilities, hence increasing your odds (and better expected values) at your next shot. Get expected value working for you: drive those occurrences higher.

WINNING THE LOTTERY: GRAND PRIZE? $100

Starting a business is tough. Owning one is tougher.

And no matter what business you own, let's be clear: It will work you silly. I don't care if you own a local landscaping company or a multinational software service, the life choice to be an entrepreneur can be rip-your-hair-out challenging. Obstacles and problems are all part of the process, requiring unrelenting commitment.

So with the cost of entrepreneurship so high, why on earth would you cheat your payoff?

Assuming everything goes your way—a little luck, great timing, and a banging execution plan—what stands to be the outcome from your best-case scenario? Will you be celebrating in a steakhouse, compliments of your great month? Or on a beach, celebrating how your life will never be the same?

In early 1997, I had an opportunity to buy a limousine service in Chicago, Illinois. Being the analytical type, I analyzed the opportunity and decided against it. I still remember my decision metrics, two of them being the best-case scenario and expected value (to be honest, I didn't know about EV back then but had empirical data as well as "industry averages" giving me a sense of EV). Both metrics indicated:

don't do this! The average limousine-company profit was unimpressive—even the best-case scenario sounded more like a worst-case scenario: seven-day workweeks, long hours, weather issues, etc.

Later that year, I opted to pursue an Internet company because it had better best-case scenarios, including a higher expected value. The decision proved correct, multiple times.

The point is this: You're going to have to work your ass off, and if all the cards flop your way, you want a big payoff. If you're going to scale a mountain, you want the jackpot at the top to be worthwhile, not a salad and breadsticks at Olive Garden. Seriously, would you buy lottery tickets if the grand prize was $250? You work crazy hours and your reward is a thirty-year mortgage in suburbia that you can barely pay? Play small and you shortchange a strong effort with weak rewards. Build a business that makes a difference in your customers' lives but, more importantly, yours.

PLAYING BIG DOESN'T MEAN FORGETTING SMALL

Scale, or playing big, is the forest among the trees. Playing small is the trees. And if you're not willing to plant one tree, you'll never grow the forest—one of the greatest scale misconceptions I'm responsible for. For years, I've been praising a law called *The Law of Effection*. It states: The more lives you impact in either scale or magnitude, the more money you will make. In other words, *impact millions to make millions*. If there ever was a "secret" to wealth, both monetarily and spiritually, "impact millions" are the only two words needed. The more you legitimately help in the value exchange, directly or indirectly, the more fulfilled your soul and bank account become.

Nonetheless, impact millions (or billions) for personal wealth is pretty straightforward, right? Not really. I've seen too many entrepreneurs corrupt this commandment and take "impact millions" too literally. As a result, great ideas get dismissed and the entrepreneur never starts.

Oh, that has no scale! That restaurant only serves my city! If I can't start a mobile app company, I ain't doing nothing! Brick-and-mortar business? That doesn't scale easily! Remember, our scale definition begins with profitably *impacting one*, not hundreds or thousands. Every established productocracy started with ONE SINGLE CUSTOMER!

Imagine if Steve Ells, the founder of Chipotle, interpreted "scale" as most entrepreneurs and ruled out starting a restaurant. There's no scale and it only serves the local neighborhood! MJ says that doesn't impact millions!

Your scaling long-game is helping as many people as possible. However, the short-game is like the Time Commandment: Forget about it. Impact one through a productocracy. Scale will work its way through by design.

THE THREE SCALING SYSTEMS

You can scale anything: a laundromat, a retail store, rental houses, your husband's secret mustard recipe, anything. The question is, how difficult will it be?

There are three basic scale strategies, each with their own internal challenges. They are:

- A customer strategy
- A chain/franchise strategy
- A channel strategy

#1) THE CUSTOMER STRATEGY

The most preferred scale method is a simple customer strategy. A customer strategy sells directly to your customer and in volume: foot traffic for retail stores, eyeballs for websites, users for software, or players for mobile gaming. A customer strategy is only limited by the market size and the available scaling economy.

Your Product -------> Your Customer

For example, a tennis website that sells tennis equipment theoretically has a maximum market size based on the total number of tennis players in existence. Its scaling economy is simply server capacity and bandwidth. On the other hand, a local shoe repair store on Elm Street has a maximum market size limited to people living in the local area AND those who need a shoe repair. The shoe business's scaling economy is also limited to staffing and how many soles can be fixed in any given hour.

Brick-and-mortar stores typically have challenging scale economies, while web ventures do not and, hence, are the most competitive. Nowadays, every teenager has some kind of app on the app store. Hot Internet start-ups find money easier than calling Geico and saving 15 percent. These enterprises with prolific scaling economies, namely digital-based ventures, attract the crowds and, therefore, are the crown jewel of pursuit. But don't be fooled: that doesn't make them better.

#2) A UNIT STRATEGY

Every so often, I'm asked, "Where are the best opportunities?" When I don't say something Internet or mobile related, shock follows. Within a private forum at *Fastlane*, we have a category for ideas needing executioners. Within this depository, entrepreneurs post their foregone ideas due to other commitments. I've posted a few ideas, and would you guess most have been brick-and-mortar based?

There is tremendous opportunity in local hardlines, brick-and-mortar businesses where many people (especially young people) don't consider because they don't dwell in a digital ecosystem. You pass on starting your entrepreneurial journey making $5K/month in the local community and instead chase after soured, low-hanging fruit based solely on a tantalizing scaling economy. I'm gonna start a mobile app promoting my fitness tips! Yippee!

Don't be the entrepreneur who overlooks a great local opportunity just because of a challenging scaling economy. Don't misinterpret expected value; it exists when you can see the brushstrokes that paint the picture. And that picture? It's a unit strategy.

A unit strategy is a local business iterated in multiple markets through replication, chains, network marketing, or franchising. It takes a singles playing field and unitizes it so homers can be hit. In our laser tag business, a unit strategy would *Fastlane* the business where challenging scaling economies are overcome. A unit strategy could be applied to products (network marketing/brands/licensing), real estate (replication), retail stores (chains), and restaurants (chains/franchising). Our laser tag facility would benefit from a unit strategy.

Your Unit -------> Your Product ----- > Your Customer

The unit strategy is one of the scale strategies I use to sell my books. Whenever I sell an international translation license, a unit is created. To date, I have over ten license units producing and selling my books in foreign markets: China, Korea, Italy, and more. On top of a license fee, I receive future royalties.

An example of a unit strategy in an *UNSCRIPTED* business comes from an idea I posted in the idea depository. I suggested a heavy-duty crate rental company. I uncovered the idea (a rental system) during one of my moves after I borrowed a stack of boxes from my sister. The boxes made my move so much simpler, and the landfill was saved from enduring another hundred cardboard boxes. Afterward, I thought, "OMG, what a great idea," and I posted specific details about its potential.

Soon after, a Maryland entrepreneur liked the idea and bought it. (When an entrepreneur likes an idea, it's removed from the depository for a fee.) As a write this, the entrepreneur has turned this little business into great potential. He's landed regular commercial clients, local media attention, and outside funding. He's garnered rave reviews from his customers. He's been on CNBC on a pitch show. And best of all, he's having trouble meeting the demand and is often sold out. Ahh, the problems of a productocracy! This business is now the seedling to life-changing enterprise if the entrepreneur can manage the growth. While the idea has a weak scaling economy, directed under a unit model it becomes incredibly potent. And some of the most potent brands in history start small in the same way but explode when unitized through a chain/franchise strategy.

Who would have ever thought that some innocuous coffee shop in Seattle would become the largest restaurant chain in the world? When Howard Schultz bought into Starbucks many moons ago, he saw the dazzling pen that would write the best seller—it was a chain strategy—a worldwide network of company-owned stores. Likewise, Fred Deluca grew Subway to over 37,000 locations by deploying a franchise strategy, but only after a chain strategy wasn't meeting his growth objectives.[102]

Lost within the herd mentality of those chasing a customer strategy in the digital domain is a local treasure trove of productocracies just waiting to be systemized and branded into a unit strategy. *A unit strategy is the fix to a poor scaling economy in a customer strategy.*

Once the local productocracy achieves profits, you then intentionally iterate it (cookie cutter) by adding distributorships, opening more locations via chains, or selling locations via franchises. In essence, you have two products requiring management: the unit and the product itself. This is how the world's most recognized brick-and-mortar locations become national brands. The point is: don't fear getting dirty in your local sandbox.

#3: CHANNEL STRATEGY

The final scale method is a channel strategy where sales occur indirectly through third-party distribution channels or retail outlets. Instead of selling directly to the consumer (a customer strategy), your product is sold to a channel, or a distribution center. With a channel strategy, your challenge isn't selling to your end user but selling wholesale to the decision-makers of the channel.

Your Channel -------> Your Product ----- > Your Customer

For example, in Chapter 34, I mentioned Sal Paola, who co-founded a painting-accessory company. His invention, The Paint Brush Cover, makes painting more convenient and less messy. His initial strategy was a customer strategy: selling direct on his website. However, he knew a channel strategy was where the explosive growth would occur. After a *Shark Tank* appearance and a subsequent deal, Sal's business exploded. Why? He added channels: Home Depot, Sherwin-Williams, and hundreds of paint/hardware stores around the world. Instead of selling ten units a month by a customer strategy, he boomed to thousands of units per month. Of course, having thousands of *Shark Tank* viewers on national television helped too.

Likewise, 99 percent of the sales of this book, and my last, come from channels—not my eCommerce website. Amazon, Audible, Kobo, Kindle, iTunes, book wholesalers, retailers, and a whole slew of channels sell this book as a legacy structure. My job as an entrepreneur and a marketer is to leverage those channels by igniting demand. If a productocracy exists, sales naturally accelerate.

Most inventions—foodstuffs, clothing, and other tangible goods—scale through a channel strategy. Executional challenges are finding channel gatekeepers and convincing them of your product's benefits. Will their customers buy it? Is the margin large enough? Does it deserve prized shelf space?

Such negotiations can be harrowing and take months, depending on the retailer. Whole Foods is particularly open to stocking local products, whereas if you walked into Barnes & Noble with your Lulu book and asked for shelf space, they'd laugh you out. Want to get into the retail giant Walmart? Beyond having a product that isn't considered "me too," you'll need to meet a multitude of requirements, from product liability insurance to having an official Dun & Bradstreet registration.[103]

Want to get your product on a shopping network? The Home Shopping Network and QVC are channels with competitive airing requirements. But don't let that stop you from trying—mega-millionaire successes have been launched on QVC. Joy Mangano launched a $150 million empire with the Miracle Mop and later had the tale told in a Hollywood movie, *Joy*. A struggling waitress just trying to make ends meet, Joy grew tired of getting her hands dirty from filthy water (notice the need language, "grew tired") and conjured up the idea for a self-wringing mop. She started selling her solution at local trade shows and in grocery aisles. In 1989, after intense negotiation, she persuaded QVC to give her a shot. Her first airing fell flat. However, in her next attempt, she took advantage of EV and occurrences: she did a live demonstration and sold 18,000 in a mere twenty minutes.[104] Great story, great channel.

While getting a foot into these channels is tough, the good news is there are other channels with minimal entry barriers. Sometimes gatekeepers don't exist—just an online form or a short approval process. You can sell virtually anything on Amazon, Etsy, or eBay. Walmart and Best Buy offer third-party sales channels. Find where your audience congregates, and then query the channel.

$2,740: THE MATHEMATICS OF SCALE

Question: Does $2,740 mean anything to you? Probably not. It's not life-changing, and it's certainly not something to jump up and down on the mattress about.

Or is it?

If there was ever a magic number, it's $2,740.

This figure represents the daily average profit you need for one year to earn one million dollars ($2,740 X 365 days = $1,000,100). And when you break down this number into its mathematical roots, you'll see that scale isn't as daunting as you think.

Back in Chapter 23, the frugality scam's polarizer was controllable unlimited leverage, or CUL. The Commandment of Scale is what brings CUL to life. It is your offense. I don't think the average person knows (or thinks about) how important scale is to wealth creation. For them, scale means buying more stocks or mutual-fund shares. Mention leverage and they think about risky loans or investment margin. None of this relates to scale and the unlimited mathematical possibilities as it relates to a CENTS-based business.

For example, let's say you created a great product and advertised it on Facebook using its awesome targeting options. (You can target very specific consumers on Facebook: e.g., "Show this ad to men over twenty-five who are divorced and live in Arizona.") Assume your profit margin on each sale is twenty-five dollars. If you sell 110 units in one day, congratulations! You just tickled the threshold of being a million-dollar earner—not over fifty years because of a 401(k), but in JUST ONE YEAR—all because you scaled value.

Think about that for a moment.

Neither 25 (bucks) nor 110 (units) is a large number. And yet these numbers are large enough to eek a millionaire pace in just one year. Even in my semiretired *UNSCRIPTED* wonderland, every so often, my business ventures go over the $2,740 number in one day, where it continually validates the *UNSCRIPTED, Fastlane* phenomenon. Don't misinterpret scale to be gargantuan numbers requiring a gargantuan payroll. *Before impacting millions, you must impact hundreds.*

Just like the Commandment of Time is perverted into "passive income," the Commandment of Scale is often molested into something worse: "get rich quick." Too many people dream about the millionaire mountaintop, making them blind to the molehill in front of them. Like college, you didn't take calculus until you passed trigonometry, which was after algebra. *You can't make millions if you don't learn how to make hundreds.*

Scale is a process, not an event.

So where does mindfulness and knowledge start translating into action?

The next step in the *UNSCRIPTED* Entrepreneurial Framework: *kinetic execution.*

The CENTS Commandments are long-game constructs. Near term startup processes can violate one or several commandments but eventually satisfy them.

In my first book, The Millionaire Fastlane, I go into a detailed mathematical analysis about how wealth is created through the power of scale.

If you have multiple business failures banked, try analyzing them under the microscope of the Fastlane Commandments to uncover the failure's source.

THE UNSCRIPTED ENTREPRENEURIAL FRAMEWORK

KINETIC EXECUTION (KE)

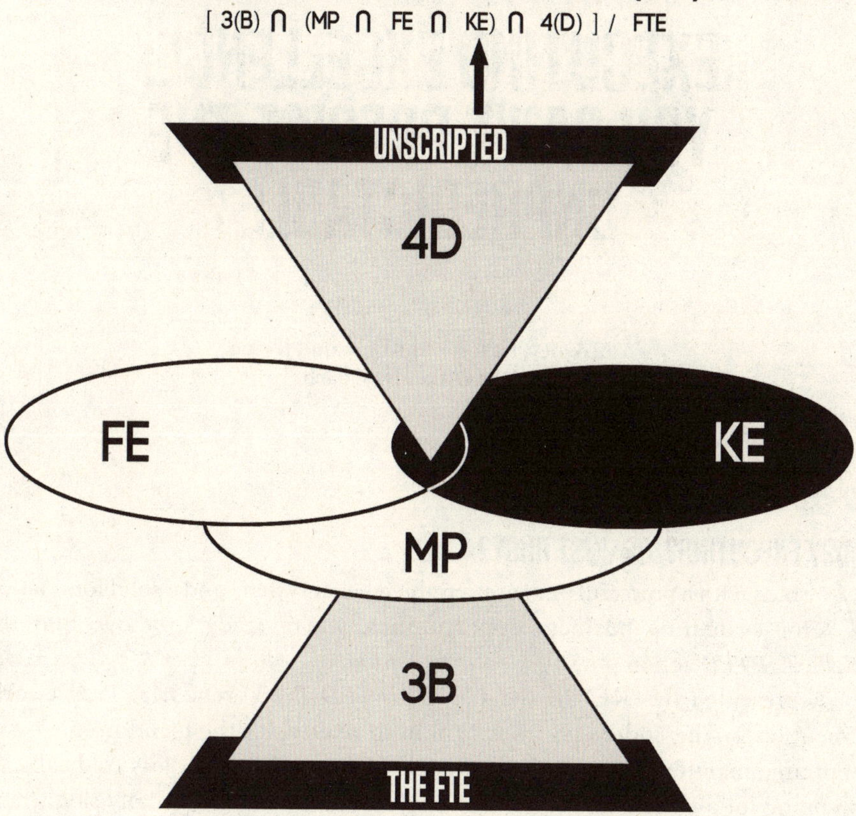

CHAPTER 38

EXECUTING EXCELLENCE: YOU CAN'T PREDICT THE UNPREDICTABLE

You're never a loser until you quit trying.
~ **Mike Ditka, Da Coach**

BUSY EXECUTING? OR JUST BUSY?

Armed with a powerful purpose, a righted belief system, and a solid foundation for evaluating business opportunities, you're ready to move into the *UNSCRIPTED* action phase—*kinetic execution.*

Represented by "KE" in the *UNSCRIPTED* Entrepreneurial Framework, execution is where ideas go from napkin to reality. It's the grind no one sees: Sourcing, manufacturing, learning how to code, enduring endless cold calls, or prepping for a trade show. It's where life jolts out of balance, a daily slog where friends complain they haven't seen you in weeks because you're backlogged in orders, emails, and other urgent to-dos.

In my first book, I stressed execution is king. Great execution shines dog ideas and makes them profitable while poor execution strips great ideas worthless. But what is execution? A reader once tweeted me, "What does execution mean?" A good question, but 140 characters isn't gonna cut it.

Tune in to any postgame press conference for a losing team and undoubtedly "execution" will be mumbled a dozen times. We lost because we didn't execute the game plan. OK, but what does that mean beyond taking the field?

Too many entrepreneurs *think* they are executing when, in fact, they're action-faking. A friend of mine has an acquaintance who's been an aspiring entrepreneur for a decade. Want to know his idea of execution? It's launching a new WordPress website in a new industry every two weeks, SEO the crap out of it, and "hope" something new happens. After ten years, I think he owns 1,000 websites—all of which make nothing, unless you count fourteen cents from Google AdSense something.

You see, execution is not business cards from Vistaprint with "CEO" emblazoned on them. It's not reading books. It's not learning Python or PHP with no basis for learning that code. We're confusing preparation, overanalysis, and busywork for execution. Sure you're busy, but not busy executing.

The problem with penning execution is no one knows what execution **IS** until you're deep in the trenches. And once you're there, the real game begins.

Execution wears many dresses, dependent on the dance. If you're opening a new sports bar downtown, execution is vastly different from executing a clothing line. Sure there are a lot of "best practices" and things you can learn, but the bottom line is, you won't know what needs to be known until you get there. *You will never be ready.*

Everyone faces the same challenge: you, me, and even the seasoned venture-capitalist with a million lapdog followers. *You don't know what you need to know until you know.*

EXECUTING ENTREPRENEURSHIP: THE HUNGER GAMES FOR BUSINESS

It's you against your opponent. You're in a clearing inside a dark forest. In the spirit of *The Hunger Games*, your objective is to kill your opponent. Knowing this day would come, you've prepared for two years. During this time, you've read dozens of books and have become a proficient marksman while learning jujitsu.

The gamemaster stands before you. You and your competitor are presented with a table of ten weapons: a crossbow, a ball-peen hammer, a samurai sword, a sniper rifle with unlimited ammo, a large suffocating plastic bag, a baseball bat autographed by Pete Rose, a serrated hunting knife, a tire iron, a canister of pepper spray, and a cattle prod. The gamemaster offers a choice: pick two weapons. Based on your recently learned skills, you logically decide on the knife and the sniper rifle. Strangely, your opponent chooses the pepper spray and the plastic bag.

The gamemaster nods and announces the game has begun. After saddling up your gear, you head north into the forest, your opponent south.

After an hour of walking (and strategizing), your trek is interrupted by an artificial hissing noise heard beyond the ravine ahead of you. You quietly drop to your stomach, taking a tactical position behind a piece of driftwood.

Armed with your sniper scope, you aim your sight at the source. It's your competitor and he's inexplicably spraying his plastic sheet with pepper spray.

Hmmm, that's odd. Nonetheless, it's your chance to take him out.

But before you can angle your body for the shot, you hear another noise—not a hiss but a buzz, subtle at first but intensifying by the second. You gather to your feet and look around. You see nothing, but the buzz crescendos louder. The sky darkens and it's not the clouds.

You crane your head skyward and see it: a black mass, swarming and large.

Oh shit. It's killer bees and they're heading your way.

You fire your rifle into the mass, hoping the noise redirects them. Nothing.

Shit! Find cover! A river! Something!

You sprint out into the ravine, knowing you have about eleven-seconds to find refuge. Unfortunately, eleven-seconds is faster than you.

The black cloud engulfs you.

Your hands flail in a frenzy, one of them armed with your knife. You strike a bee dead—but two billion remain. Every inch of your body rages as if being burned alive. You slump to your knees and crumple over in the fetal position as the suffocating venom invades. As everything fades to a burnt black, death welcomely arrives after an eternal minute.

Your comrade in competition?

He survives the swarm...*under the cover of a plastic bag that stinks of capsicum.*

***

The moral of this tale parallels the perils of execution: *you simply won't know what's needed until you need it.* The odds of picking the right weapons before they're needed are about as far-fetched as someone picking pepper spray and plastic for the forest. In the end, we confuse preparation and busywork for execution, when *the real mettle comes from entering the forest and experiencing firsthand what the game demands.*

Identify the problem or the challenge and then act.

Unlike the death forest, we can choose the tools needed based on the encounter. Unfortunately, I have no clue what your business is or might be. I can only offer a solid foundation and the best practices making your forested venture expected and manageable. The roadmap to the great executional unknowns within our *UNSCRIPTED* framework is called *kinetic execution*, or (KE).

When you are led by a need or a nagging problem urging to be solved, the often asked "where do I begin?" and "what do I do? " quickly comes into focus.

CHAPTER 39

KINETIC EXECUTION: EVERYTHING SIGNIFICANT STARTED INSIGNIFICANTLY

Perfection is not obtainable, but if we chase perfection we can catch excellence.
~ **Vince Lombardi, Coach**

GETTING SHIT DONE: KINETIC EXECUTION

My forum started with just one post in one thread. Now it has over a half-million messages. War and Peace by Tolstoy? A single word breathed life into a 587,287-word novel. No matter what the goal, getting shit done requires meaningful action, otherwise known as kinetic execution. Self-help porn, endless research, and Chamber of Commerce dally-whacking are not considered meaningful actions.

Represented by (KE) within the *UNSCRIPTED* Entrepreneurial Framework, *kinetic execution is meaningful action before answers, a method of situational and incremental problem-solving graduated to resolve a larger problem, which culminates into your business solution.*

If you're starting a business, kinetic execution is the quickest and least expensive path to your first customer.

If you already own a mature business, it's the quickest and least expensive path to a productocracy.

The model consists of three core elements:

1. **The Marketmind,**
2. **The 3 As, and**
3. **The 7 Ps of Process**

All together it looks like this:

KINETIC EXECUTION

THE MARKETMIND ~ THE 3 As ~ THE 7 Ps

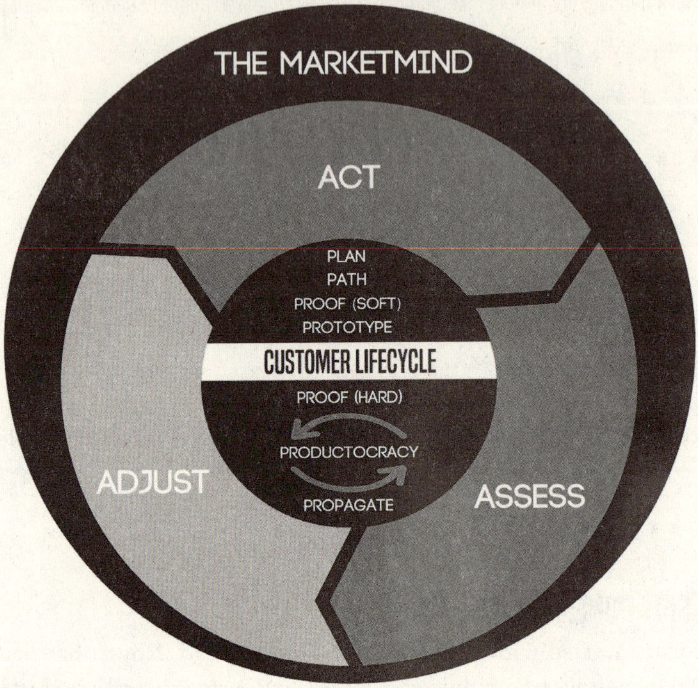

THE MARKETMIND

Kinetic execution's first component is represented by the outermost circle—*the marketmind*—an understanding that the market cannot be forecast, predicted, or tamed. No one can accurately say what challenges await in the forest until you arrive. The marketmind is like the stock market; no one can predict market movements—not Wall Street advisors, financial planners, and certainly not your average retail investor. As an entrepreneur, the best we can do with the marketmind is engage it.

This is why "business-plan competitions" are about as accurate as monkeys throwing darts at stock pages. Since markets can't be housebroken to predictions, why waste time trying to tame them in a 50 page dissertation? Gates, Dell, and Jobs never had a business plan. And neither did I, and neither does kinetic execution.

Peel away the business plan's colorful charts and graphs and what remains is a wild speculative gaggle scripted to paper, the business world's version of the Drake equation, plus more variables thrown in for laughs. It's the love child of guesswork and dreaming, an aggregation of unassailable market variables sugarcoated to constants. The truth is, when you take many unknowns and arbitrarily put them to numbers, you get a worthless road map to Wonderland. Seriously, your business plan is about as foretelling as Jim Cramer is at pinpointing the S&P 500's price next year. But hey, at least you spent six weeks on a cute little binder that looks great at the bottom of the filing cabinet.

Anyhow, a business plan is more action-faking than execution because the market is a collective mind representing millions. Nobody can predict how this collective will react to a given stimulus: your advertising, your product, your customers' use of the product, your customer service, your brand, your packaging, your everything! This unpredictable collective makes fools of its forecasters.

For example, sometimes I'll read a news story profiling a new business and I'll make a quick viability judgment. Because the marketmind doesn't give a shit about my solitary opinion, I'm quickly proven wrong. Example: Turo (formerly RelayRides.com) is a peer-to-peer car network where your car can be rented to a stranger. Personally, I'd never use it, and my impulse reaction is "no effin' way." And yet, it leaves me scratching my head because thousands use it all while funded to the tune of $48 million.

And of course, my favorite example is my freshman book, *The Millionaire Fastlane*. Several "publishing experts" said it would never sell, claiming it was too long and broad for a specific genre. Others in the mediocrity mob likened *Fastlane* to my opinion of *Fifty Shades of Grey*: the book is crap and belongs at the bottom of a birdcage. Ultimately, the marketmind proved them wrong, pissing on their opinion while I sold millions' worth. Loud critics from cheap seats can't dissuade the marketmind.

History is littered with stories of individual opinions being crushed by the marketmind. Stephen King's first book, *Carrie*, which later morphed into several movies, was rejected an astonishing thirty times. In fact, King thought it sucked so bad it ended up in the trash, only to be salvaged by his wife.[105] Likewise, before *Star Wars* was released, several actors including the production company's board of directors stated that they hated the movie.[106]

Even Steven Spielberg wasn't immune to individual opines as he was rejected by the USC film school, not once or twice, but THREE TIMES. Later, USC would award him an honorary degree subject to one condition set forth by Spielberg: his rejector had to sign it![107] How's that for a productocracy executing justice!?

I could write an entire book about similar stories where the marketmind suffocates individual opinions. Google "famous singers rejected" and you'll find hours' worth of reading. You see, the marketmind has the ultimate veto power, over singular opinions of empowered individuals, including mine. This unpredictability is why business plan authors cannot predict market responses, whether it's a new start-up or a closing stock price. The ultimate judge and jury of your ideas isn't your mom, friends, or colleagues—*it's the marketmind that reacts to them*. And as an *UNSCRIPTED*, *Fastlane* entrepreneur, your first execution task isn't speculating on how the market might respond; it's to engage it (as cheaply as possible) and find out.

THE 3 AS: ACT, ASSESS, ADJUST

Bruce Lee once said, "The stiffest tree is most easily cracked, while the bamboo or willow survives by bending in the wind." In business, you must be like the bamboo which is kinetic execution's next guiding principle; *act, assess, and adjust.* These 3 As steer effort like a propeller (action), a tachometer (assess), and a rudder (adjust direction). Remember, kinetic execution is *action before answers,* situational and incremental problem-solving graduated to resolve a larger problem, which culminates into your business solution. "Action before answers" means starting now—before you're ready, before the right timing, and before you know all the right steps. Again, kinetic execution is not business plans or blueprints outlining every detail. On the contrary, it's a dive into the abyss, expecting a gauntlet riddled with problems and challenges. Some might call it "winging it," and that's OK because the marketmind gives directional clues to where you should be headed.

> ***One week of real market engagement is more valuable than one month of market research and analysis.***

ACTION

"Action" is poking the finicky cat that is the market and seeing what happens. Most of the time, the cat ignores you; sometimes you'll hear a meow; and once in a great while, it's every entrepreneur's dream: the loud roar of demand.

Unfortunately, most never poke the cat. Too often, dreampreneurs stay dreamers because they're preoccupied with knowing every answer and every step. They peek into the dark forest and nervously cower, "Can you tell me exactly what to expect in there?" Remember, there is no freaking list, no paint-by-numbers plan, and no fairy god-mentor. As a result, these folks sit on their thumbs for years, reading books and armchair quarterbacking other entrepreneurs. For example, take this ridiculous forum post:

> I have a concept I'd like to try, but I have no idea about building websites, so I need advice on what to look for and where. My first question is, what is a good price to charge for advertising? And a good rate to charge for fresh leads?[108]

Aside from the "I'd like to try," get a laugh at the tail wagging the dog. Such an asinine question is like aspiring to be an actor and your first question is "What should I wear at the Academy Awards?" I'm ashamed when I see horseshit questions like these polluting my forum. The "give me all the answers before I start" or the "tell me the exact steps" questions are like clairvoyance—guaranteed failure preceded by a whole slew of mental masturbation. You see, if you postpone action until you have all the answers that pave execution, you'll never get started. NEVER.

For example, when I started my Internet company, I had little knowledge about best practices, web technologies, and how to sell customers. I learned based on the immediate objective in front of me, incrementally and gradually, each step dictated by continual improvement. Would you believe it started with learning HTML and the simple "hello world" code? Each step in the build process (and my personal build process) *I learned by solving only the problem that stood in front of me.*

How do I randomize directory output? Research, learn, solve.

How do I interact with a database? Research, learn, solve.

How do I streamline this cumbersome billing practice? Research, learn, solve.

How do I manage a hellacious employee payroll and the regulations surrounding it? Research, learn, solve.

With each solve, value improved, as did my experience and skill set. After ten years I probably solved over 1,000 problems. Had I suffered from the "big picture syndrome", spying the mountain summit while absorbing ALL of these problems and unknowns in aggregate, I would have been terrified and overwhelmed into inaction.

This "wing it," in essence, is kinetic execution.

Many great companies started the same way—with one line of code and no idea what lay ahead. Of course, this doesn't mean learning code or following in my footsteps is the right choice; it simply means to act on one problem, one challenge, one unknown at a time. The only real problem is the one in front of you. What needs to be done? Learned? Outsourced? Researched? Do it and move on to step two.

ASSESS

In early 2011, about two months after my book was released, it became painfully clear: my cover, which I designed and loved, sucked. At every turn—tweets, emails, FB—I heard it.

- *Great book, just ignore the hideous cover!*
- Fastlane *(despite the cheesy cover) is an awesome book!*

By the end of 2011, I knew I had a problem that needed fixing. My gregarious, Lamborghini-inspired, neon-orange-and-green book cover was a turd and turned away potential readers. Luckily, I buried my righteousness and heard the message.

After acting (putting a book into the marketmind), I shifted to ASSESSING.

Every action pushed into the marketplace comes with a reaction, or an orange or white gumball. Your job is to listen, *even if it isn't what you want to hear.* Within months of release, the negative comments about my horrific cover were about as regular as a Kardashian selfie. Whenever you interact with the market, two types of reactions are inevitable: (1) the most common, diffusion; and (2) the desired, echoes.

DIFFUSION (WHITE GUMBALL)

Diffusion is when the market absorbs or ignores your message/value proposition and chooses to do nothing. Despite this, it's still a reaction.

Anytime you're presented with a Facebook ad and choose not to click or read it, the reaction is *diffusion*. Anytime you drive by that new restaurant, uninspired by its signage and exterior decor, you react by tuning it out as an option.

Unfortunately, diffusion is not deposited into your lexicon and is only measured by data analysis. If 10,000 people viewed your ad and no one clicked or bought, the market reaction is 100 percent diffusion.

MARKET ECHOES (ORANGE GUMBALL)

On the flip side, market echoes (orange/gold gumballs) are the preferred reaction we want, assuming that gumball isn't red. *A market echo is direct feedback—a reflective, unbiased, and uncensored representation of the marketmind.* Of course, the ultimate market echo is a click, a sale, or a conversion. But oftentimes, it's something else: a complaint, a suggestion, a user-interface problem, or just an email seeking more information. Whatever echoes land in your lap, it is your job to HEAR them and then ASSESS them. Is this echo actionable? Problematic? Is it an opportunity to redirect or reevaluate your value proposition?

The number-one reason why I can grow my income into six- and seven-figure ranges is my ability to hear and react to market echoes. This concept grew my internet company: *morphing from what I thought the market wanted to what the market actually wanted.* In fact, study business success and you'll find that most businesses often evolve into figments of their former selves—it was our goal to sell X, but in the end, we sold Y.

Saturating the market with your action is great, but you've got to tune your senses and unwrap the gifts of echoes. Inside you'll find clues to where you should and should not be heading.

ADJUST

Action and assessment are worthless without ADJUSTMENT. The entire point of grinding the first two As is to uncover how to react. Recently, I've heard this concept gain fame from others who refer to ADJUSTMENT as a "pivot." Well, I started pivoting when most new entrepreneurs were playing T-ball. Whatever name you give it, adjustment is a strategy redirection based upon correlated and compounded market echoes.

The key to uncovering actionable feedback comes from recognizing *pattern echoes.*

I used to record all market echoes in a notebook, which I affectionately called my "black book." Whenever a pattern emerged, I acted on it. If several people think your UI sucks, you can bet the marketmind is thinking the same thing. For example, every new feature addition at your website should come from pattern echoes. When several people request something you lack, you can bet the marketmind thinks similarly. The same goes for products: if twenty customers ask about a certain color you don't offer, you've exposed a new opportunity and revenue pocket. Heed these echoes, add/subtract where needed, and you've skewed value for your market. And skewed value equals more value competitions won, which means more profit.

For myself, once I learned that my book cover was an abject failure, I lurched into adjustment: I had the cover redesigned, despite the 8,000 copies already in print. (If you have an old cover edition, hang on to it—it might be a collectible someday.) And guess what? Ever since that change, I NEVER heard another cover comment again. And more importantly, the book went from a few hundred sold to over 300,000. Thanks to action, assessment, and then adjustment.

? ***What business failures in your past can be held accountable by failing to ASSESS, then ADJUST?***

CHAPTER 40

THE 7 Ps OF PROCESS: GO FROM IDEA TO PRODUCTOCRACY

Happiness does not come from doing easy work but from the afterglow of satisfaction that comes after the achievement of a difficult task that demanded our best.
~ **Theodore Isaac Rubin, Psychologist**

EXECUTING A PROCESS TO A PRODUCTOCRACY

Kinetic execution's final sequence is represented by the innermost circle and the customer life cycle: the 7 *P*s of process. The 7 Ps are where shit gets done. They are:

1. **Plan**
2. **Path**
3. **Proof (Soft)**
4. **Prototype**
5. **Proof (Hard)**
6. **Productocracy**
7. **Propagate**

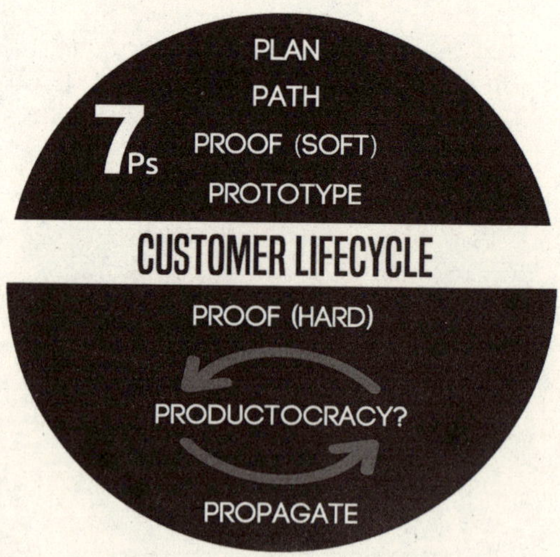

PLAN (BUT DON'T GO CRAZY!)

Kinetic execution is essentially "winging it" under the governance of act, assess, adjust. However, don't confuse this with ill-preparedness. The kinetic execution planning phase is relatively short and confirms the strength of your opportunity by a CENTS evaluation.

CONTROL

- ✔ Does your solution have any primary dependents for execution? Example: exclusively sold at Walmart, distributed at Facebook, etc.
- ✔ If so, what control risks can be mitigated?
- ✔ Does your solution have secondary dependents? Partners, suppliers, manufacturing, importers, channels?

ENTRY

- ✔ What are the entry barriers for your solution?
- ✔ What key resources, assets, or relationships strengthen, and can strengthen, your entry walls?
- ✔ Does your solution require substantial resource inputs and/or coordination for execution? Is the concept-to-launch two days? Or two months?
- ✔ How will your competitor(s) respond to your solution? And can you sustain their adjustment?

NEED

- ✔ Have you identified *ALL* the value attributes within your industry?
- ✔ Is your proposed skew strong enough to adequately firm a unique selling proposition (USP) relevant to your target customer?
- ✔ Can you effectively communicate this value skew to your target customer?
- ✔ How is your solution monetized? What are your primary and secondary revenue models?

TIME

- ✔ What resources, if any, are needed to dissolve your solution from YOUR time?
- ✔ What dependencies are needed to dissolve your solution from YOUR time?
- ✔ What are the future challenges for these requirements?

SCALE

- ✔ Are there existing mediums, channels, or partners that can reach large numbers of your target market?
- ✔ What is your solution's scaling economy and their resources—funding, infrastructure, and human capital—required to scale it?
- ✔ Are there any scale challenges in the cost structure and/or supply chain?

After your concept survives the CENTS wringer, it's time to prove its worth.

PROOF (SOFT)

Nothing sucks more than spending months and thousands of dollars only to discover the market doesn't want your product. Soft proof's objective is to verify your concept/idea with the marketmind before spending a fortune in resources. In entrepreneurial circles, the soft proof is often referred to as "validation." You can soft prove your concept, either indirectly or directly, using six different methods.

1. LANGUAGE PATTERNS

As mentioned in Chapter 35, language patterns are uncovered through observation. For example, if many Redditors complain about X, the market is hinting demand. My forum was born in this manner—a forum I frequented was rash with disgruntlement—so I created my own. *Any dislike voiced is the public square is an opportunity.* Multiple instances of irritation language ("I hate, I wish, I need") through multiple mediums (Twitter, Topsy, Facebook, forums) essentially confirm the seeds of need.

Unfortunately, just because someone "hates" something doesn't mean they will pay for its solution. My friend has had one such experience. He wrote:

> I once had a situation where 100 out of 100 people surveyed said something was brilliant, marketable, and provided value. When it came time for the item to hit the market (with no change in competition or value proposition) 0 out of 100 people bought it.[109]

Another helpful tool for exposing consumer shifts and possible emerging opportunities is Google Trends. For example, some years ago "gluten-free" emerged as a trend and still is a trend today.

2. CHANNEL RESEARCH

Another confirmation method is a channel investigation. Amazon is the best for this. Find a similar product being sold and check its sales rank and review quantity. If similar products have many reviews, say 500, you can presume there is both demand and need. For example, by the time you're reading this book, *The Millionaire Fastlane* will have nearly 1,500 reviews. Assuming one person reviewed the book for every 250 readers (.4 percent review rate), you can speculate that my book has sold around 375,000 copies. This verifies demand for its message and genre.

3. SEARCH VOLUME

The beauty of keyword, cost-per-click (CPC) advertising is that you can peek into the marketmind and quantify the search volume for virtually anything. While there are other keyword-driven search engines, Google is the best. Create an AdWords account and log in to their Keyword Planner tool. Enter your product, service, or solution, and find out how many people are searching for your visionary offer. For example, if you are looking into creating a unique wedding-planning tool, a quick review of the "wedding planning" keyword reveals it has 30,000-plus searches per month. Moreover, your target marketmind (couples getting married) is flush with searches, on average ten million per month.

4. ASK/INTERVIEW THE MARKET

Asking the market is as implied: Find a congregation of your target marketmind and expose them to your idea. For instance, Reddit has an immense variety of sub-forums, which cover virtually any topic or interest. Likewise, Facebook has incredible targeting options where marketminds can be nailed down into specific groups. Looking for females over thirty-five who have a garden? Facebook can do it: Place an ad; send them to a page; see what happens. If your idea pertains to a specific niche, say owners of exotic cars, find the related forum(s) for it and ask.

Other possible asking venues are Craigslist, Instagram, and Twitter, although these aren't guaranteed to hit your desired market. The predictive power of asking is directly related to how well you isolate your target customer in its congregation. If you asked my forum about a potential idea serving small business, you'd score great feedback because you hit the market exactly. However, asking a group of entrepreneurs what they think about chiropractic software would yield flawed data and not constitute soft proof. The ASK method does NOT involve nagging your social circle, even if they represent your target customer. These folks will not be honest or impartial. You want candid feedback from strangers who, frankly, don't give a shit about strangers.

The other alternative is solution-selling, discussed in Chapter 35. This approach involves talking to various business owners and professionals and specifically asking them about their problems, frustrations, and challenges. When problems are identified, you try committing them to a solution. For example, if you interviewed ten home inspectors and they revealed frustrations with contracts and paperwork, you confirmed a need. Probe further and you can peg an ideal solution and an estimate of what they'd pay for it.

Another variation of interviewing the market is to compel your target marketmind to complete a survey. Using one of the many survey tools, SurveyMonkey, you could target and incentivize your target customer by using any of the tools mentioned above. Of course, incentives and reaching your market via CPC advertising (Facebook, Google, Reddit, Instagram) isn't cheap, but the data obtained are worth its price.

5. MARKET SIMULATION

The final variation of soft proof is market simulation. Here, you present your product or service to the market as if it already exists. Market tests and their simulations can be costly and time-consuming, but the data gathered are second to none. The two types of market simulations are landing pages and mock prototypes.

SIMULATING THE MARKET: LANDING PAGE

The most effective soft proof is an email address evolving from a one-page sell sheet, commonly referred to as a landing page. Create a web page solely for the purpose of collecting email addresses or pre-orders. Your landing page sells—the email address (or the pre-order) is confirmation of user interest.

Another deviant method is creating a sales page that can't close. The objective here is to track clicks to the order page. If that happens, the buyer is presented with a "Sold Out" notice or some other explanation. While this is effective at proving soft demand, it pushes ethical boundaries and isn't something I'd try unless approached authentically.

Unfortunately, capturing order-button clicks or email addresses is NOT preeminent proof: It simply validates that the marketmind is interested in your offer. *Interest and commitment are not the same:* "Here's my email addy" and "Here's my money" are two different things. For example, before I released my first book, I captured email addresses from a pre-ordering landing page. By release, I had roughly 3,000 email addresses from folks who indicated buying interest. However, when it was time to open wallets and fork over cash, nearly two-thirds bailed. Captured email addresses are circumstantial soft proof; *cash is a verdict* and hard proof.

TESTING THE MARKET: MOCK PROTOTYPING

Similar to the landing page, mockup prototyping involves creating a nonfunctional, dummy version of your idea and exposing it to the marketmind. The goal of the mock version is to gauge a market response, using any "ask the market" methods above.

This approach has been used on Instagram with great success. If you had a product in the bodybuilding space, you could build a targeted following and then present a product to your audience. Or, you could buy an existing account and do the same. The objective is to gauge your follower's response to your product. Do they like and share? Comment with "OMG, where do I get one of these?" or "How can I order this?" If so, you're onto something.

Another variation of this technique is influencer marketing: Hire an influencer in your market to post your product and gauge the response. Manually find relevant influencers or get assistance from such websites as Intellifluence, Whalar and Klear. Most Instagram users with 500K+ followers pimp products for a small fee—you could reach thousands for, literally, pennies and instantly find out what the marketmind thinks about your idea. Once your idea is soft proven, you're ready to draft your process path.

THE PROCESS PATH

Congratulations, you've proven your idea's potential. Now we want to draft a nuts-and-bolts road map to your first sale. The process path is a "low-level" stair-stepped estimation at executing your idea to reality. A typical process path shows numerous bulleted action items, each representing a major laddering toward your first customer. Each bullet itself is not one action but represents dozens of subtasks. For example, let's say you are creating a new party game. Your process plan might look like this:

(1) SOURCE A GAME BOARD MANUFACTURER

- ✔ Secure product samples, cost estimates
- ✔ Negotiate pricing
- ✔ Evaluate financials, fixed and variable costs, margins, etc.

(2) CONTENT CREATION

- ✔ Graphic design, theming, and branding
- ✔ Card creation (Learn)
- ✔ Board creation (Learn)
- ✔ Humor testing
- ✔ Prototype

(3) OPERATIONS

- ✔ File paperwork for LLC
- ✔ Secure merchant account
- ✔ Open bank account
- ✔ Secure insurance (if necessary)

(4) WEBSITE CREATION

- ✔ Investigate and select hosting, CDN options
- ✔ Design website (Outsource)
- ✔ Mailing list software

(5) LAUNCH

- ✔ Disburse press releases (Outsource)
- ✔ Influencer outreach, research
- ✔ Marketing actions

In this example, the process path contains only five major elements. However, within each of those five elements are numerous subtasks, which could take weeks to complete. The subtasks could entail a variety of actions, from meeting with manufacturers to learning new skills to outsourcing expertise where needed. The key for an effective process path is to define the **major action blocks** and their requirements while eliminating unnecessary actions and their costs.

For example, can you get away with a logo you designed yourself? Or do you really need to spend $1,500 at the local design boutique? (If the path to your first customer doesn't involve face-to-face meetings with anyone, you have no business buying business cards. Seriously, save the custom-branded T-shirts and water bottles until IPO day.)

Another element of the process path involves self-reflection—knowing what things you can learn and what you cannot. For example, "learning to code" was a part of my process path years ago. I am very much a "hands-on" guy, so many of my process paths involve doing things myself. However, this "learn it" and "do it yourself" process path might not be right for you.

The truth is, not everyone can learn how to code. You might have a knack for communication and delegation, whereas outsourcing, partnering, or hiring is the better process path. *UNSCRIPTED* is not about *my way* as the best way. The best way is *your way*: the one that fits your personal strengths.

The process path's objective is not detailing every actionable nuance but breaking down execution into broad progress chunks, each with bite-sized actions that can drive Chapter 28's motivation cycle and spark the feedback loop. Remember, we're entering a forest and we won't know what's needed until we get there.

PROTOTYPING

After outlining the process path and confirming soft proof, you probably need a functional prototype. For digital services, this is your beta version.

Your objective in the prototype stage isn't a feature-rich masterpiece but something simplistic yet valuable and *economically demandable* to the marketmind. In the end, it must do what you claim.

First, expect a lot of prototyping actions to be learning, specifically *just-in-time (JIT) learning.* Just-in-time learning is learning based upon the challenge in front of you. In essence, it's jumping off a cliff and learning to fly on the way down. You don't learn PHP code unless the challenge in front of you: (A) warrants PHP, and (B) you can learn it. More than half the build stage probably involves learning something new. Expect it.

Second, build the right prototype. Optimally, it should be *reverse engineered from the solution you envision.* Specifically, start at the end. Begin at the customer experience. Visualize EXACTLY how you, as a customer, want your product to function, and then move backward using the act, assess, adjust model. What actions will put the solution into reality? What skill sets are needed, and can they be learned, hired, our outsourced? What challenges block the way? Focus only on the required actions for the necessary features. Bells and whistles can come later, and only if the marketmind signals for them.

"YOU SHALL NOT PASS!"

Pardon the Gandalf mention, but it needs to be said. The prototyping stage is the "you shall not pass" part of execution, a perennial graveyard for entrepreneurial dreams. Epitaphs read, "Here lies a great idea that never happened" and "His vision was real; his execution was not."

Because prototyping a product or a web service can take months, sometimes years, of lonely, hind-to-the-grind work, the risk of giving up is high. Seriously, I think prototyping is oddly similar to what happens to newlywed men: suddenly every attractive woman is flirtatious. The prototype stage is the valley within the *desert of desertion* where entrepreneurs are clubbed with shiny-object syndrome—every idea seems better (and easier) than the one they are working on. With no feedback loop—zero sales, emails, or market resonance—for months, the motivation cycle stalls and passion can quit us. This is normal. Expect a long and lonely walk. Mud through it and let the marketmind light the way.

THE CUSTOMER LIFE CYCLE

The next three stages within the kinetic execution model all occur within the customer life cycle, a transitional process where strangers are turned into prospects, prospects into customers, and customers into disciples. The life cycle has seven steps:

- AWARENESS: Exposing your product to the target customer. Example: Your target customer sees your product's ad in their Facebook newsfeed.
- EVALUATION: Providing your customer with enough information to make a decision—a website visit, a white paper, FAQs, an internet search. Example: Your target customer visits your website and reviews your offer.
- ONBOARDING: Converting strangers into prospects by securing them into your marketing ecosystem. Example: Your target customer provides an email address or signs up for a FREE trial.
- PURCHASE: Converting from a prospect to a customer. Example: Your customer converts from a FREE trial to paid premium or buys your product after being emailed free content.
- USE: Management and monitoring how customers use your product. Example: Most of your target customers renew or reorder your product; others ask for a variation of it that you do not have.
- ENGAGEMENT: Interaction and relationship building with your customer to foster retention and/or repurchase. Example: You send your customer a periodic email regarding trends or topics within your industry.

- DISCIPLESHIP: Creating loyal customers who become evangelists for your company, hence fulfilling the productocracy prophecy. Example: Your target customer shares and recommends your product on social media and in person.

Because customer life cycles vary based on products/industries, it isn't within this book's scope to explore them all. For example, onboarding for a restaurant (getting a customer into your building) is entirely different from onboarding for a software service (getting a customer to accept a free trial). Nonetheless, kinetic execution's next three steps are relevant for any business.

PUSHING PROOF (HARD)

Once the prototype or beta version is fully functional, seek a verdict. Will the marketmind pay for it? Your aim is hard proof which is a sale (or pre-order) and the receipt of moola. Hard proof is a market oscillation that says, "I like your stuff; here's my money."

Every so often, I'll get an email from a reader who experiences hard proof, and let me tell you, it's like having billionaire parents on Christmas day. Once the motivation cycle closes its circuit, affirming your offer though a sealed value loop, it's game over. Addiction. There's no going back to time clocks, nine to fives, and dismal Sundays. But more importantly, hard proof sparks the endorphinous feedback loop, inspiring passion, self-worth, and an overall feeling of accomplishment. Above all, hard proof is your first goal worthy of celebration.

AWARENESS > EVALUATION > ONBOARDING

Acquiring proof starts with the first three steps of the customer life cycle: awareness, evaluation, and onboarding. Rarely will all of these things happen at once (an event) but take weeks (a process). No matter which, everything starts with awareness and exposing your offer to the target audience. But where and how?

Well, the good news is you don't have to spend $5 million on a Super Bowl ad to reach a large audience. There are many venues to choose from. Amazon, Reddit, ESPN, Twitter, Craigslist, Instagram, Pinterest, Yahoo, and Bing are just a few mass-market websites with targeting functions and plenty of eyeballs. Post or advertise your product, send the customer an offer, and see what happens. If you have cash to throw at hard proof, my favorite mediums are Amazon, Google AdWords and Facebook ads, all of which offer enhanced audience targeting. No cash? Try Reddit, Craigslist, or targeted Facebook groups.

If your budget is drawn from a dishwashing job, social-media venues offer excellent opportunities for a targeted reach at minimal cost, and sometimes for FREE. For example, my friend owns a personal grooming business and sells a ton of stuff on Instagram—he posts high-definition product photos and captions them. Voila, every post generates sales.

If your product relates to dog lovers, you could create an Instagram page and build the account to attract dog lovers. You could find large accounts targeted to dogs and ask them to feature your product. Many users with large followings allow paid promotions on the cheap; for twenty-five bucks (or using your product as payment), you can get your product in front of thousands. One forum user used this exact method to launch his designer sunglasses company.

Another popular means to hard proof is reward/donation-based crowdfunding services, such as Kickstarter, Indiegogo, or RocketHub. Here you post a concept offer and accept funding donations in lieu of rewards, usually the finished product or some type of accolade. Because crowdfunding involves a money exchange, it can be considered hard proof. However, don't rush into these services unless you have a solid offer entailing good copy, a professional explainer video, and an expedited path to market. I recommend them for hard proof, not soft.

Other "old-school" mediums, such as radio and television, are also shockingly affordable as well as shockingly overlooked. For example, I used to advertise on local radio and it only cost me several hundred dollars to do so. Cable TV networks, such as HGTV, Velocity, and Speed, offer targeted audiences and are often cheaper to advertise with than you think. If your product or service lends itself to these mediums, they're worth investigating.

Once your product is exposed to your desired audience, onboarding or a sale is the next objective. *Onboarding is the conversion of a stranger to a prospect, usually involving the capture of an email address, a registration, or acceptance of a free trial.*

Onboarding is sometimes referred to as a "sales funnel" or "lead channel." Onboarding (and sales) results are solely dependent on the effectiveness of your offer. If your landing page conversion optimized? Does your copy promote benefits over features? Are the pictures sharp, or fuzzy? Have you demonstrated social proof?

You wouldn't believe the shit landing pages I've witnessed. If your primary headline is a Comic Sans "Welcome to XYZ Enterprises!" or "The greatest product ever!" expect zero sales and zero onboards. While onboarding and optimizing conversion rates aren't within the scope of *UNSCRIPTED* (entire books have been written about this stuff), they are essential to traction.

Prototype proof and moving through awareness, evaluation, and onboarding within the customer life cycle depend heavily on the act, assess, adjust modality. It is NOT act and then give up. It is NOT spend twenty-five dollars on Facebook ads and quit because you had zero conversions. Execution failures during hard proof are often premature due to misinterpretation. You see, any time you push your product out into the marketmind through any medium, your outcome is guaranteed to be one of three things:

1. **An echo (colored gumballs)**
2. **Diffusion (white gumballs)**
3. **A conversion (the sale or an onboard—gold, baby!)**

THE ECHO: THE MARKETMIND'S VOICE

Echoes are any feedback or measurable data that isn't a conversion. Essentially, it is the voice of the marketmind. An echo could be a question from your "contact us" form. It could be general feedback, such as "interesting, but I'll pass" or "lol" or "pretty cool." It could be tweets, Facebook comments, or website usage data. Whatever the echo, it is your job to analyze it. For example, were potential customers emailing product questions? Was there confusion about what your website did? Why did someone write "lol"? Did most of your users leave from the pricing page? Any echo should be assessed and then adjusted when needed.

MARKETMIND SILENCE: IS NOTHING REALLY NOTHING?

The second outcome for your awareness push is the most likely: The white gumball of diffusion. Nothing happens. No sales, just the stiff sound of silence and a lighter wallet. The "nothing" outcome is another execution fragility where most entrepreneurs raise the white flag and update the resume. If nothing is your result, don't overreact.

If you've soft proven your concept, nothing usually means there's another deficiency in your campaign and not that your product is a bust. Don't let a false flag end execution. Before you "fail fast" and move on to seemingly greener pastures, *confirm that nothing really is nothing.* You do this by checklisting your channel, reach, and message.

1. Checklist Your Channel:

Are you sure you're leveraging the right channel with the right targeting measures? Or is there a better medium to reach your audience? If you're advertising a facial cream on a Mustang forum, it's the wrong channel. If you're Facebook ads target "all adults over twenty-one", you're targeting the wrong audience. Before concluding a product failure, checklist your channel. You must constantly test varied channels and targeting options by acting, assessing, and adjusting. Your product might not suck, but your channel and your audience targeting do.

2. Checklist Your Reach:

The other failure of nothingness is a lack of reach. You might have selected the right channel and the right targeting, but you haven't reached enough of them. If your ad had only one hundred impressions or thirty-two clicks, you are drawing conclusions from an inadequate sample size. No matter what the industry, conversions need large samples. I don't care what the product is, zero response from thirty-two clicks isn't unusual, no matter what the offer! Just because you burned through one hundred dollars at Amazon and nothing happened, it doesn't mean failure. You might have failed reach. Check the sample size and ensure it's large enough to warrant conclusions about its data. I'd recommend at least 10,000 impressions and/or 1,000 clicks.

3. Checklist Your Message:

Probably the most common false flag is your message. Your offer is weak. Your copy sucks. Your call to action doesn't exist. Your design and UI look like they were done with GoDaddy's web tool.

Remember the cancer corollary: the greatest product in the world goes unsold if you cannot persuade the marketmind of its value. Kickstarter is a fantastic avenue for hard proof, but the fact is many great products die there because of flawed offers and poor presentations. In the end, you could hit the right medium and saturate the right reach—but a poorly constructed offer will kill success. *I'd estimate most launch failures are from failed offers, not from failed products!*

Put these three multivariate unknowns together—the wrong medium, the wrong reach, and the wrong offer—and do you see why failure is often interpreted when seeking hard proof?

The entire evaluative process of channel, reach, and message is likened to striking a piñata. Too many entrepreneurs poke and prod the piñata, only forcing a sway, giving up none of its goodness. To bust it open and get the bounty inside, you have to hit hard and multiple times. *Only act, assess, and adjust (followed by these three checkpoints) can flag a failure worthy of, "OK, this didn't work...next idea."*

THE MARKETMIND "YES": VICTORY

Pushing proof's third outcome is the desired: a sale! Congratulations. Light a cigar and toast the champagne, you've just proven the viability and value of your offer. Someone wants your product and is paying for it. You've just accomplished more than most entrepreneurs ever dream of.

Once the celebration is over, get dirty, and again, act, assess, and adjust. Is your marketing message as effective as it can be? Based on the sales, what is your customer acquisition cost and how does it relate to your cost structure? Did it cost you fifty dollars in advertising to generate twenty-five dollars in profit? Assuming a positive margin, your first sale segues into the next phase of kinetic execution: a productocracy.

PRODUCTOCRACY: USE > ENGAGEMENT > AND DISCIPLESHIP

A sale proves you have effectively communicated perceived value. Your marketing works. However, have you delivered actual value? Only your customer knows. This unknown establishes the contrast between a productocracy and a BRO-marketing scheme.

Some years ago, I befriended a respected "entrepreneur" I met on an exotic car forum. We shared a love for Lamborghinis. As I got to know this guy, I discovered that his business model was based entirely upon marketing and planned user forgetfulness. He was a value-cheater who dealt in perceived value, not actual value. His products merely surrogated the scheme. Ultimately, I learned that he was a slime bucket who deployed all the effective persuasion tools: powerful copy, fake testimonials, insinuated celebrity endorsements, and anything else that persuaded the customer to buy. After buying, the customer didn't know that their purchase included a continuity enrollment, of course nicely disclosed in a large block of text that no one reads.

If you're not familiar with continuity programs, that's when your credit card is automatically dinged every month for product refills or membership renewals. And yes, they're gold mines for entrepreneurs. But they often abused. Most people don't pay attention to their credit card statements, and when the client discovers the charges (and that the product sucks), several beefy monthly payments have already occurred. Worse, his refund and cancellation policy was like trying to navigate the IRS tax code. Let me be clear: If you have an entire department dedicated to chargebacks, you have a product problem—and probably a sleeping problem as well. Yet based upon his fleet of exotic cars, I'd fathom he was making a fortune, and he certainly wasn't going to win any awards for ethics.

Within the customer life cycle, *the productocracy stage covers use, engagement, and discipleship.* Your objective in the productocracy stage is to confirm gravitons—investigating if actual value is delivered (worthy of discipleship) over perceived value (worthy of nothing). If your customers aren't loving your product, the objective becomes to skew value until they do, establishing a productocracy. You can only do this by listening, observing, and engaging your customers. Are they complaining or not using your product as intended? Are they reordering, or is it one and done? Do they comment on your email blasts? Are they recommending your products on social media? The answers to these questions determine your potential product power in terms of transforming customers into loyal disciples.

Once again, act, assess, adjust comes into play. When I owned my Internet company, I made a mandated effort to reengineer the entire site every eighteen months. Why? I was proactively adding value to my service by adopting features uncovered by pattern echoes.

Quite possibly the most famous "pattern echo" comes from Instagram's meteoric growth. When Instagram was first started (back then it was called Burbn), founder Kevin Systrom and his programmer, Mike Krieger, noticed that no one was really using the "check-in" feature while everyone was engaging the photo-sharing feature. They acted, assessed, and adjusted, and bam—Burbn was dumped and simplified, and Instagram was born.[110]

Anytime you prod the marketmind, rise to full attention and see what's bouncing back to you. These three gravitons could be a sign of a productocracy:

1. **Reorders or renewals: both say, "Yes, you've delivered on your promise."**
2. **Private emails: Written accolades or testimonials signify success.**
3. **Public reviews or praises from strangers: a positive blurb (blogs/ social media) from strangers hints of a productocracy.**

HOW I FOUND A MILLION BUCKS HIDING IN MY FORUM

I launched my entrepreneur forum in the summer of 2007. As mentioned earlier, I started it because another forum I frequented was littered with schemers, self-promoters, and spammers. In need language, "I was tired" of the BS. My intent was not to make money (I was driven by the need as community building is incredibly difficult) but to provide a refuge for legitimate entrepreneurs.

Over the next few years, the forum grew to where it became beneficial to monetize the traffic with advertising. Most users didn't care. But others did. One publicly posted a thread and complained about the ads. A few others followed, voicing the same opinion. However, embedded in their complaints was an opportunity. The complainants said that they'd be happy to pay for an ad-free forum.

I thought the suggestion was ridiculous. Why? My personal bias interjected. It scoffed, "I'd never pay to view a forum ad-free, so why bother?" Despite my sentiment, I listened to my users and offered an ad-free version of the forum for a mere $7.99 a month. I spent about one hour implementing the plan and named the ad-free option "*Fastlane* Insiders."

On top of ad-free viewing, I also added several other benefits, including what many saw as most important: privacy and less dreampreneur noise. This one decision—merely acting, assessing, and adjusting to users—helped me find a fortune hiding underneath my forum pages. Over the life of my ownership, this simple decision should net out to over a million bucks. Additionally, the business move also increases the valuation of my property, should I sell it. Pummel piñatas; don't poke—watch how the beast sways as it reveals important clues into how your next swing should strike.

PROPAGATION: PENETRATE AND SCALE

The final *P* of kinetic execution is the money stage: *propagation*. This is where millionaires and billionaires are created. It's wild growth, scale, and exposing your productocracy to the masses.

The productocracy confirmation validates a self-replicating product, like fire, and propagation becomes an accelerant. A lacking productocracy distorts this relationship, where you're not dealing with fire but the short-lived spark of marketing and the churn of dissatisfied customers. If marketing stops, how long can your business survive? Or will it grow?

Only a productocracy can precede propagation. If it doesn't and cannot be acted, assessed, and adjusted into a productocracy, I discontinue. I'm not interested in being a push marketer who sells substandard products. For example, it took me nearly six months to determine if my first book was a productocracy. At first, many forum regulars mentioned they enjoyed the book. Some said it was the best thing they ever read. But I never considered them an impartial audience. It was only when strangers started recommending the book—tweets, Facebook shares, emails—that I realized, wow, this book is worthy of propagation.

Once disciples start evangelizing for your products, it forces an expansion loop, which in turn forces growth, expands margins, and fudges mathematics. Recommendations, shares, and word of mouth fires the growth engine. Marketing becomes not a necessity, but an option. While I'm not suggesting a zero-marketing strategy, *a productocracy survives one.*

Regardless of industry, propagating a productocracy is accomplished by reach expansion, channel expansion, and/or network expansion.

REACH EXPANSION

Once I discovered *TMF* was a productocracy, I went on a podcast tour for several years. My objective was reach expansion to expand product awareness. This can involve paid marketing and promotion as well as social-media initiatives. If fifty advertising dollars generate net fifty dollars in return, it pays to increase the ad spend. A net return on ad spend is a license to print money. And because you've proven a productocracy, your profit potential shifts from a linear to an exponential construct.

Another popular avenue of reach expansion is content marketing, where you provide valuable content for your target audience, free of charge. Writing contributor (or guest) articles on Medium, *Entrepreneur*, Quora, or any crowded venue delivers awareness in lieu of value. When people garner value from your contribution, they are more likely to hop "onboard" and eventually become your customer. With a productocracy, your product is a selling machine.

I once was roped into jury duty and knew the juror waiting room had a library. I slipped my book onto the shelves. I also offer books at cost for any insider who wants to resell them, give them away, or use them for educational purposes. Similarly, I also give away a ton of free books. For years, I've been giving away free copies to military personnel, ex-cons, the recently unemployed, and single moms. I sell more books than the prior year because I know that with each book unleashed into the wild, my expansion loop accelerates.

CHANNEL EXPANSION

For product-based businesses, channel expansion involves adding locations where your product is sold. If you're selling a home-improvement product, like Sal of The Paint Brush Cover, channel expansion is getting your product into Home Depot, Ace Hardware, and every hardware store on the planet. Every channel added accentuates your potential for SCALE and TIME, assuming the channel represents your target audience and maintains brand integrity.

For instance, if you've created a designer brand of purses where the average price of your satchels is $2,000, you might not want to celebrate a Target invitation. Stick to channels that enhance your brand and hit your audience.

A great example where channel expansion can backfire is the Michael Kors company. Originally considered a high-end brand, overexposure and brand dilution has hurt the company.[111] Sold in over 3,700 department and specialty stores worldwide, many consumers now perceive the brand as too ubiquitous. If you see a Michael Kors bag every time you walk down the street, how special will you feel paying a premium price to own one? What happened to Kors is the consequence of overcapitalism—instead of protecting the brand and the original mission, Wall Street pushes the impossible: infinite growth to appease shareholders.

In my world, channel expansion has done wonders for my bottom line, although I admit I've made costly mistakes. The *Fastlane* audiobook wasn't added to the Audible channel until 2015. That mistake cost me roughly over six-figures in lost sales. Likewise, Lightning Source is another channel I added, which serves markets outside the United States. Again, I didn't add this channel until three years after release. After adding it, sales poured in. Yeah, another six-figure mistake by acting three years too late. As long as channel expansion hits your audience, maintains your brand, and fits into your cost structure, add, add, and add.

EXPANSION OF NETWORK

In 2014, I noticed a fellow author was tweet-recommending my book. His name was Hal Elrod, who authored the book *The Miracle Morning*. In gratitude, I thought it would be nice to read his book, especially since mornings and I mix like water and the Wicked Witch. The book changed my life because it reframed my hellish perception of the morning. As a result, I recommend it often. While I can't put numbers on it, I'm sure my recommendation added thousands of dollars in sales for Hal. Likewise, his constant recommendation of *TMF* to his group of influence has done the same for me.

This relationship, one of many, is the final means of propagation, which is network expansion. Network expansion involves networking and partnering with others: business development, affiliate marketing, and win-win joint ventures. While some might call this "I'll scratch your back if you scratch mine," I don't.

Network expansion is finding partners who share a similar purpose and synergizing your effort. It is NOT about compromised principles or being disingenuous for the sake of making money. Had I not enjoyed Hal's book, I would have felt no obligation to recommend it. Without the productocracy, there is no back-scratching.

I bring this up because, in the book industry, it's common for authors to paste glowing reviews on their book covers from "thought leaders" who actually never read the book. Yes, those rave reviews from best-selling authors urging "this is a must read" for other best-selling authors are contrived. That's right, they're fibbing for the sake of network expansion.

For someone not selling a book, network expansion consists of joint ventures, affiliate relationships, and business development. For my friend who owns a box rental company, network expansion is partnering with corporate relocation firms and real estate agents. When I owned my Internet company, reach expansion constituted approximately 60 percent of my revenue, while network expansion constituted about 40 percent. I had affiliate partnerships with hundreds of websites in the wedding, travel, and nightlife industry. They offered my service, and whenever one of their users used it, I paid them a juicy commission. Some of my best affiliates made thousands of dollars; they got an additional revenue stream and I received a fixed customer-acquisition cost.

> ***"It's not WHAT you know, but WHO" is partly true but misleading. Having better WHATs (knowledge and experience) can open the door to better WHOs.***

So how do you expand your network if it can grow your business? The same way you would if you approached a mentor. Focus on value and what you can offer your potential partner. Take, for instance, this email I received. Its opening was this: "Hey MJ, I'd like to promote your book to 100,000 subscribers to my YouTube channel…this is what I'd like to do…."

Think that opening would strike my interest and initiate a new network contact? How about this opening? "MJ, I'd like to interview you for my new success podcast I'm launching next month. I don't have listeners yet, but I plan on interviewing many successful people and it should be cool. What time works for you?"

Not sure if you can see the difference, but Email A opens with a GIVE mentality, while Email B opens with a TAKE mentality. In fact, I'd guess that nine out of ten emails I receive regarding mentorship open with a TAKE and ignore the GIVE.

"Hey MJ, do you do any mentoring? I enjoyed your book, and I'd really like to get rich one day. I really can't stand my job, and my boss is a total ass. My girlfriend doesn't believe in me, probably cuz I don't have any skills or money, but I am willing to learn if you could just show me what to do. I love Lambos too."

I, I, I, me, me, me. No one cares. Well, I do, but I don't.

I get it—all of us are selfish. Unfortunately, your selfishness keeps you from success. If your opening email contains more than two *I*s and *ME*s, there's no chance. This simple concept of pushing aside selfishness and GIVING first, while TAKING later, is why networks don't expand, let alone why value-vouchers remain elusive.

FUNDING PROPAGATION

In 2007, after I sold my company for the second time, the new owners moved headquarters from Phoenix, Arizona, to a hot tech district in San Francisco. I'm sure the rent increased by $30,000 per month, not to mention the cost of labor and everything else from coffee to cubicles. Since I knew the inner workings of my old company, I never understood this reasoning, other than wanting to "look the part" of a technology company. I know Phoenix is not devoid of office space and talented people who know code.

Anyhow, it felt like déjà vu. You see, the first time I sold the company nearly six years earlier, the exact same thing happened: a fast move to San Francisco, increased costs, and an increased visibility on things that don't seem to matter. I know foosball tables and free Pringles in the lunchroom are good for employee morale, but you know what isn't good for employee morale? Layoffs, pink slips, and bankruptcy.

Sadly, years later, despite a different economy, a different team, and a different vision, the outcome would be the same: bankruptcy. My point, hopefully, is clear. *Cash is king when it comes to propagation.* Every dollar should go toward that effort. If it cannot grow the bottom line, it shouldn't be done. There's a difference between a $4,000/month Class-B commercial lease in Phoenix and a $50,000/month Class-A space in the San Francisco financial district. Auxiliary expenditures, such as marble floors, custom-branded mousepads, and that cool neon light of your logo, can wait. *Preservation of cash and its ultimate redirection into growth is the only thing that matters.*

When cash is tight, propagating a company is impossible. More sales, traffic, and users demand more resources. Every dime of revenue (and profits) should be reinvested into the company to fund whatever growth challenges await.

Your role as CEO is not to fly from New York to Los Angeles in business class. It is not a mahogany desk, but an Ikea desk that screams dorm-dweller. It is not a salary increase with every incremental increase in revenue. There will be a time and a place to reap rewards, but propagation isn't it.

And lastly, my advice for growing companies is to reject funding unless necessary. Why? Because funding typically shifts stakeholder priority from the customer to the investors. If you can finance growth while maintaining 100 percent control over your business, do it.

Another option is a different type of crowdfunding: equity crowdfunding. Whereas reward/donation-based crowdfunding rewards contributors with products or rewards, equity crowdfunding sells a piece of your company. Websites like Circle-Up, Crowdfunder, and Fundable give you the opportunity to actually secure equity financing, convertible notes, and other financing options for your expansion. However, be warned: These services are best deployed after concept proof and sales are growing. Equity crowdfunding is like an online *Shark Tank*: you don't walk through the doors with zero sales, an idea, and a dream.

CHAPTER 41

MAKE EXECUTION MATTER: 13 BEST PRACTICES

Great marketing only makes a bad product fail faster.
~ David Olgilvy, Businessman

#1) EXPECT DIFFICULTY AND DEVIATION

Two expectations outline kinetic execution: difficulty and deviation. Once they're expected, you won't be shell-shocked when they happen. And then quitting isn't an option.

The first is difficulty, the theme throughout this book.

Starting a business isn't a waffle cone and a stroll on the boardwalk. Value-vouchers aren't awarded for solving easy problems. Expect a challenge, whereas failures are merely market echoes, a false flag needing reassessment for what it is. In truth, there is only ONE *UNSCRIPTED* failure: giving up on your dreams and regressing to *SCRIPTED* mediocrity.

Everything is an echo and an opportunity to act, assess, and adjust. As I say, failure is the sweat of success. When you refuse to sweat, you can't expect guns of steel and washboard abs. The truth is, my past failures weren't real failures, but failures at acting, assessing, and adjusting. I failed channel, reach, and messaging. I nudged piñatas—I didn't break them.

Second, expect your initial business purpose to deviate. Once you learn acting, assessing, and adjusting, your original business intent will veer. When I started my Internet company, my vision wasn't lead generation, but I ended there. Had I continued to own the company, lead generation would have morphed into online reservations and ride sharing. *Market echoes steer the ship.*

Likewise, Amazon started solely in the book space. When PayPal first launched, its original intention was payment processing for eBay top sellers. eBay itself? Pierre Omidyar started it on a whim as a collectible auction site after he sold his laser pointer for an unexpected profit. In reality, he was looking to start Etsy nine years early, but instead eBay became the Internet's top destination for auctions. The point is, you may want to drive to Los Angeles, but the market might take you to San Francisco.

#2) BE FAITHFULLY MONOGAMOUS

Faithful monogamy is a characteristic storyboarding the launchpad for many top entrepreneurs. From Richard Branson to John Paul DeJoria to David Geffen—the world's most renowned entrepreneurs become renowned because of monogamy: *they commit to one business and one business only.* Then after striking it big, polygamy is often the result: diffusion into multiple ventures where passions are explored and capital allocated. Don't be fooled by these high-profile entrepreneurs who have twenty projects going on. You haven't sold a company for millions and you aren't Robert Herjavec.

Monogamy solidifies a great marriage. If your time and emotional support are being shared with six other partners, can you expect a good marriage? Will this type of relationship thrive, survive, or die?

Whenever I hear a young entrepreneur say, "I have six businesses," it's both sad and amusing. This is code for, "I have six businesses that suck." A productocracy is a money printing press—side businesses are either distractions or impotent business opportunities. Tethering yourself to multiple businesses is like trying to become a world-class violinist with one hand tied behind your back.

Monogamy must precede polygamy. You have one business or none. You can be a world-class anything—but it requires an unrelenting focus. Whatever your thing, you have to eat, sleep, and shit it. Execution is tough enough. Divert your focus and you'll get killed by the entrepreneur who isn't diverted. Work four hours a week and the entrepreneur working ten hours a day will shellac your biz behind the woodshed. You can't dismiss working hard by saying you'll work smarter. The *UNSCRIPTED* do both.

#3) BALANCE IS BULLSHIT

Good father? Fuck you! Go home and play with your kids.

This classic line from the movie *Glengarry Glen Ross* is a statement about balance. And it must be said: Beware of bloggers and self-help nobodies preaching balance. It's no coincidence that preachers of such baloney are relative unknowns. *The key to happiness is a balanced life! Seven tips for a balanced and stress-free life!* Blah blah blah.

Think balance is how Michael Phelps won twenty-three Olympic gold medals? Is balance how Michael Jordan won six NBA championships and four MVPs? Does that photo of Elon Musk give you fuzzy feelings of balance? The fact is, balance is another *SCRIPTED* trap. Think about balance in terms of a plank and a fulcrum, like a teeter-totter. How do you get the plank to balance? Why, you put it in the *middle*. Middle equals average and ordinary.

You see, balance is bullshit—unless you aspire for middle-of-the-road results. Today's top leaders lead anything but balanced lives. Once again, like many *UNSCRIPTED* tenets, the escape from conventional living is paved by doing the opposite of what conventional wisdom preaches. Great results come from great imbalances. *The incredible life I live today is not because of balance; it's because I meandered into the world of the obsessed.*

Periodic, huge life imbalances often precede success.

When I owned my web company, there were many instances of twelve-hour days, thirty days straight. And yes, some of my relationships suffered. When I wrote my first book, I checked myself into a beach condo and wrote for thirty days straight: eat, write, sleep, lift. **Balance was nowhere to be found.**

Scott DeLong, founder of the content aggregator ViralNova, which he later sold in a deal potentially valued at $100M in cash and stock, echoes the importance of temporary imbalance on his personal blog. He wrote:

> I spent 5 years completely obsessed with business. I sacrificed my social life and nearly lost the ability to even know how to have fun. It did, however, pay off and now I am getting back to enjoying life with a lot more freedom and a lot more money. Like anything difficult, it's worth it in the end. So obsess over your venture...if you find yourself thinking about it around the clock, it's almost impossible to fail because you clearly want it bad enough to do anything to get it. And that's what it's all about.[112]

Like Mr. DeLong, today I lead an incredibly balanced life, compliments of imbalance. Ahh, the great irony of long-term balance is short-term imbalances win it. If I want to grow another multimillion-dollar company, I implicitly know balance will be forsaken. Decide what's more important to you: permanent balanced mediocrity or temporary unbalanced exceptionalism?

#4) ENVIRONMENT IS EVERYTHING

I have three different gym memberships. Spattered about the Phoenix area, the closest one is minutes away. But I rarely go. Instead, I drive thirty minutes to the farthest gym, Lifetime Fitness. Why? *Environment is everything.*

In my hometown of Fountain Hills, Arizona, the median age is ninety-two. As you can imagine, the local gym is not a hot spot for hot bodies. Not only am I the youngest, I am the fittest. And since I'm not exactly GQ material, I'm not bragging about it. Anyhow, this geriatric environment is detrimental to my workout. When everyone around me is in worse shape than I, it isn't particularly motivating. In truth, I find it depressing. No, I'm NOT better than anyone there—I hope thirty years from now I'm still working out. It's just I don't need a reminder that one day this will be me: rolling into the gym with socks-and-sandals and a pair of sweats pulled so high you'd think I was wearing a unitard.

On the flip side, my workouts at Lifetime are incredibly fulfilling, and sweaty. Why? Everyone around me is in better shape than I. Bodybuilders, fitness models—the place is like a beauty pageant jointly sponsored by Lululemon and Under Armour. This environment motivates me to work harder.

This same concept applies to your work environment. I truly feel my life did not begin until I escaped dreary Chicago and moved to sunny Phoenix. I needed the environmental shift to succeed. Without it, this book wouldn't exist, and to be honest, I'd probably be strung out on Prozac due to a vitamin D deficiency. My point? *Find the environment that gives you your best workout.* Not just with fitness, but with life. Find that city, country, church, coffee shop, or band of new friends that supports and inspires you.

If *SCRIPTED* peers are holding you back and trolling your dreams, find new peers. Ditch them, or at best, keep them a few zip codes away. An optimum environment isn't one that nags and naysays! You know your optimum environment. If pizza and a Planet Fitness filled with undedicated part-timers gives you a better workout, go. You are free to choose—not choosing makes you a victim to circumstance.

#5) GATEKEEPERS ARE DYING; DON'T ASK FOR PERMISSION

Five-time Grammy Award winner Hillary Scott of Lady Antebellum auditioned for American Idol, not once but twice, and never made it past the preliminary rounds. As she told *Entertainment Tonight*, "I literally performed for the production assistants and the interns, and I just didn't make it."[113] Thankfully, she didn't let a few greenhorns roadblock her success. Instead of choking on a gatekeeper's verdict, she persevered and became part of one of country music's hottest bands. A music productocracy did the rest.

We live in an amazing time. The ivory towers, which once courted the esteemed grantors of permission, are crumbling. If you have the talent and the desire, approval is no longer needed. Permission, not required. The keys to the dream palace await in open pastures: YouTube, Instagram, Amazon, and any other medium with an audience.

Years ago, publishing a book meant begging a publisher or a literary agent with a cute cover letter and a manuscript. You sent dozens, perhaps hundreds, of these cute little hope packages. And then you waited weeks. Seasons. Years. Hoping and praying that someone, somewhere, would take a few hours to read your dream and give you permission to live it. And if someone did respond? Hope you're ready to sell your dream cheap. You'll pack the negotiating power of a fire ant underneath a seven-year-old's shoe.

But not today. If you have the initiative and determination to throw yourself overboard into the marketmind, you can bypass the gatekeepers. Let the market decide if you are worthy. If you're practiced and talented, you can't be ignored. Gatekeepers can suppress talent like a cork in a bottle, but talent pressurizes in the marketmind, eventually bursting.

Perhaps my favorite story of marketmind's exposing talent is the once homeless drug abuser, Arnel Pineda. If you haven't heard of Arnel, he is the lead singer of the legendary rock band Journey. After the original lead singer departed the band, a replacement was sought. After seeing Arnel's YouTube videos singing Journey tributes, band member Neal Schon contacted Pineda for an audition with the real band. After a long flight and a few days of auditions, Pineda was named the new lead singer. Since, he's gone on world tours, including a Super Bowl performance, and even had a documentary produced, chronicling the tale.[114]

Ever hear of Ted Williams? He was another homeless man whose dazzling voice was discovered on YouTube. How about Justin Bieber? I'm not a fan of his music, but I am of his story. Discovered on YouTube after singing Usher tributes, he's gone on to become fabulously rich as well as fabulously annoying.

Lindsey Stirling tried out for *America's Got Talent* and was told by Piers Morgan, "You're not good enough…to get away with flying through the air and trying to play the violin at the same time." Sharon Osbourne piled on: "What you're doing is not enough to fill a theater in Vegas."[115] LOL. Stirling went on to sell and make millions by simply hearing the marketmind, and not the gatekeepers.

My story also gives the gatekeeper the bird: Had I waited for an agent or a publisher to give me permission to publish my book, it would have never made it to market. I didn't let a stranger perched in a Manhattan skyscraper stop me.

You see, fear—not gatekeepers—is the only thing that conceals talent. If you sing, sing to the marketmind and see if it swoons. If you tell jokes, tell jokes and see if the marketmind laughs. To steal Nike's slogan, "Just do it."

#6) BUILD A BRAND LIKENED TO A PERSONALITY

Productocracies go hand in hand with a powerful brand image. Behind every disciple, a clear brand identity reinforces loyalty. If you want a business that grows and sticks, brand strategy needs to be a primary consideration.

Branding, however, is a tricky business—so tricky that people make careers of it. For amateurs, branding means a slick logo, a pithy slogan, and some gold-foil stationery. For experts, branding is more: *it is the art of personifying a business with human qualities and characteristics so that it reflects or affirms your own customer's identity.*

Think about that for a moment. A well-executed brand identity affirms your customer's identity and, as a result, becomes a core decision metric in the buy decision.

Consider the brand Harley-Davidson. How would you describe their core group of customers? Risk-takers or conservative "play-it-safe" types? If you live YOLO and carefree, would buying a Harley enhance your identity or damage it? How about Nike? As a highly recruited athlete, would spending a fortune on Nike clothing affirm your identity or weaken it? How about the person aspiring to get fit? The Nike brand becomes an extension of identity, either existing or desired.

The strongest brands link into the identities of their target customer. Think about how these brands weave into identity: Louis Vuitton, Apple, Wrangler, Ferrari, Volvo.

In fact, an interesting story of brand and identity happened in my life recently. A few years ago, I sold my Lamborghini because it no longer matched my identity. At first, the Lambo brand resonated with my *UNSCRIPTED*, *Fastlane* identity—there's nothing like driving a car that 99 percent of the population can't drive. It's different, radical, and skewers mediocrity. Unfortunately, it also boldly screams for attention. For me, grabbing unwanted attention and being "off the radar" outweighed my desire to be noticed with 550 horsepower. The brand identity of Lamborghini didn't change—mine did.

#7) CONSISTENCY BUILDS BRANDS

"Thank you for holding; your call is important to us..."

Really? I doubt it. If my call was really important, I wouldn't be twiddling my thumbs for the last seventeen minutes while listening to funeral music. My guess is nine of ten brands are *brand fakers*. Brand fakery is words over actions. You say one thing, "Customer satisfaction is our top priority"—and yet your corporate actions reflect the opposite.

Customer disservice is the leading culprit of brand fakery.

Remember the cute Microsoft paper-clip "help" character, which appeared in its programs? It would interrupt your book report and say, "What can I help you with?" Besides annoying the hell out of you, the paper clip further irritated you by being absolutely worthless. Ask it a question and its answer was some link to the Microsoft website, which was another jargon-filled heap of so-called help. The Microsoft paper clip is indicative of how most companies feign customer service. "Smoke and mirrors" is the service du jour. Ever notice how most websites fail to post a phone number? And those that do bury it in some hard-to-find back page?

Customer disservice.

And ever notice how difficult it is to talk to a human being about something, and only after you've pressed 1, *, 2, 2, 2, 1, 1, and 0?

Customer disservice.

The point is, brands aren't created by website words or walled mission statements—*a brand is earned*. It is a reputation arising from consistent action, much like an individual earns a reputation. You can repeat the same shit over and over again, but if you (and your employees) aren't doing it in the public eye, it's a brand fake. If your actions are consistently inconsistent and bordering on the devilish, no saintly statement engraved on a plaque changes the reputation.

Brand building starts with identifying how you want your company to be perceived.

If it was a person, who would be its friend? What does it stand for, and how will it conduct itself to reflect that persona? Don't confuse a brand with your USP, or unique selling proposition. Being the cheapest or the service with the most features isn't a brand. A USP is a part of the brand build like ties are to suits, but underneath the image there must be something more. *Your customer must feel you are different.*

After you identify your brand persona, identify the specific initiatives that would make it happen. Is it a no-time-limit, no-questions-asked, money-back guarantee? Is it the ability to talk to a human being without having to press a gazillion buttons? Is it eco-friendly with a portion of profits going to a nonprofit environmental organization? Consistency of brand action must always be congruent with operations, from you to your employees. If you want to be known as the "witty" company, but your company blog posts wouldn't inspire a match in a pail of newspapers, you fail the brand game and hinder the productocracy.

#8) SELL OR BE SOLD

Execution is the "act, assess, adjust" trio, but it also has another three-headed pilot: selling, marketing, and communication. If you're idea-empty while saddled to the couch, here's what you can do in the meantime: *learn how to sell.*

Selling and all of its cousins (marketing, copywriting, negotiation) are the most important skills, no matter what your business is. These skills can be banked for life.

Remember the cancer corollary. Having the best product in the world is worthless if you can't initiate sales. If you can't persuade the marketmind to buy in your seed stage, the productocracy's grass roots never happen.

The urgency of selling is everywhere. At every point in the execution process, there are potential stakeholders to be sold: investors, employees, suppliers, partners, regulators, advertisers, and most of all, angry spouses who need convincing your late hours are worth the effort. Here are some selling strategies to get your productocracy moving.

TELL A STORY

If you want to sell more of anything, give your product or company a story. People love stories because it's how we make sense of our world. Linking a story to your company or product gives the customer a chance to become part of the narrative. When the story resonates with your customer's identity, it strengthens your brand.

Remember the story about Arnel Pineda, Journey's lead singer? I was a casual fan. However, once I learned the captivating story behind Arnel, I went from casual to engaged—I searched for tickets and started buying songs. That's story's power.

Stories and their powerful effect on buying psychology has been proven. SignificantObjects.com is one such experiment that demonstrates how narrative can impact the perceived value of any object. At Significant Objects, common thrift-store items were purchased cheaply and then resold on eBay, except with one difference: *A powerful story was linked to the objects.* As a result, items purchased at an average of $1.25 resold for many times more, nearly $8,000 in total. A one-dollar jar of marbles, storied and sold for fifty dollars.[116] A one-dollar wooden apple core, storied and sold for over one hundred dollars.[117] And dozens more.

Another benefit of the story is it frames your brand.

Take for example Stur flavor enhancers (SturDrinks.com), which are natural water sweeteners. I originally found this company while addressing my pain point: I sweeten San Pellegrino mineral water but avoid doing it unnaturally. I've been reluctantly using the Skinnygirl brand, which is an obvious brand mismatch: I'm not skinny or a girl. Skinnygirl was the only flavor enhancer that didn't use artificial sweeteners and colors. In search of something stevia-sweetened and without artificial colors, I found Stur in my local supermarket. On the tiny bottle was a short story behind the brand. On their website, the story goes long form:

> Stur was born while my wife was pregnant with our twin girls. The doctor had recommended she drink 8-10 glasses of water a day— but like most Americans, she wasn't drinking even half of that! And she was getting dehydrated. So to help her, I started looking for healthy ways to flavor her water. I went to the store and searched the drink mixes, but found that they were all made with artificial chemicals that we didn't feel comfortable putting in my wife's body. Finally we started making them ourselves, using real fruit and stevia extracts. It took us over a year and hundreds of different combinations to land upon a blend that tasted better than most bottled sugary drinks! [118]

Using this story further, their website continues the brand strategy by apportioning sales to a nonprofit organization dedicated to water resources. Anyhow, notice how businesses are founded based upon real needs, not what's convenient, easy, or loved. The founder then explains how his friends reacted to his venture:

> When I first told my family and close friends about Stur, they told me I was crazy to launch a product in this category, competing with established, multi-billion dollar companies.

This powerful statement tells a potential Stur customer that their purchase helps a man with a family—not a faceless giga-corporation. Who would you rather do business with? Tell your audience WHY you are in business; be fiduciary about it. When they make the connection, they will choose you over the big bully on the block.

HUMANIZE YOUR CORPORATION

A big part of attaching a narrative to your company (or product) is that it humanizes it. Humanization is another double-pronged strategy that helps reinforce your brand AND sweeten buyers to top-of-mind. The fact is *people want to do business with relatable people they like, not mammoth corporations hidden behind a bureaucratic wall.*

The easy way to humanize your business is to put a face to it.

My first book's author page has multiple photos of me from grade school to forty-plus! I've done this because studies have shown that the "About Us" page (or in my case, the author page) is one of the most visited pages on ALL websites.

Make that page mean something other than just a bunch of bullshit buzz phrases like, "We synergistically enable visionary collaboration and idea-sharing among multiple native environments." Instead of sounding like an automaton stuck on a douche loop, say something meaningful. Funny. Show your personality. And yes, post some photos. If you have a team, post photos of them looking like humans: at their desk, playing with their dog, anything not resembling a statue in a stiff suit.

Another humanization strategy is to engage your audience on social media.

I don't hang out on Twitter very often, but when I do, I take time to respond to fans tweeting about my book. If they took five-seconds to contact me, I can give five back. Likewise, whenever someone emails, I try to respond despite the volume which has made it impossible. When readers hear back, they're shocked that I responded and not a hired VA from the Philippines. Such simple gestures can move the brand meter and further enforce discipleship.

And finally, if you have employees, encourage them to flower their personality as opposed to gagging it. For example, Southwest Airline flight attendants are very creative in their precautionary preflight presentation. Instead of hearing the same rabble the umpteenth time, travelers have heard it sung, rapped, and humorized. Instead of a corporate hammer banning such witticisms, they allow it, ultimately humanizing a large corporation. Rare indeed.

APPEAL TO SELF-INTEREST, MEANING, AND PURPOSE

The ultimate consumer doctrine of selfishness is *what's in it for me?* The quicker and cleaner your customer learns what's in it for them, the quicker the sale. Forget features, doodads, and sparkly accoutrements—*sell benefits.* If you skewed multiple value attributes in the value array, translate those attributes into direct benefits.

Tell your potential buyer **exactly** what you can do for them. Your campaign focus should always drill down into one core benefit. Don't let your customer draw their own conclusions.

It is surprising (and sad) that many entrepreneurs fail to do this. For example, my friend who owns a moving-crate company isn't effectively appealing to self-interest nor communicating benefits—he leaves the customer to do the work. His home page's garish headline says, "Studio Package." This is a service level within his business. Yeah, that's his headline, a zero-appeal, zero-benefit nonstarter.

A more effective headline centers on self-interest and benefit. Something like:

> Crush Your Moving Frustrations! Simplify And Speed Your Move With Our Eco-Friendly Rentable Moving Crates!

Is there any confusion why a customer should buy?

You have seconds to appeal to self-interest, and it all happens with your headline. Make it large, bold, short, but long enough to convey the core benefit. For example, here's the headline I've used for years for *Fastlane*: "Is There A Millionaire Entrepreneur In You?" The headline clearly establishes fast that my book is about money and entrepreneurship. No guesswork is required other than seeding the customer with the question, which must be pondered.

Another strategy is to appeal to your customer's meaning and purpose, or lack thereof. Much of industrialized humanity lacks a purpose other than paying bills and then dying. When a business model imbues social inclusion, it has an advantage over one that does not. Why? Because studies prove that social inclusion in humans is linked to meaning.[119] When we feel a part of a group or a subculture, it gives meaning to our lives. This is why professional sports teams and their athletes are worshiped: pro sports teams and their ravenous fans leverage a meaning appeal—it's why grown men feel perfectly comfortable wearing another man's name stamped on their jersey's backside.

Lives that lack meaning are given it. The same concept applies to political parties, colleges, and even some of the most powerful corporations on Earth, such as Apple.

If your product or service can inspirit meaning or purpose with your customer, you will do well. In truth, I'm hoping this book does something similar: tapping into your heartfelt desire for an *UNSCRIPTED* meaning-and-purpose.

PRIORITIZE SOCIAL PROOF

Try remembering the last three things you bought. For me, all of my purchases occurred not because of a slick sales pitch or an advertisement, but because of *social proof.*

The best sales secret isn't about sales at all. It's peer testimonials and reviews. It's the good word from your friends, family, and neighbors who have purchased in the past. In a digital "sharing" economy, *social proof is the primary method in the buyer's decision process, not advertising.* Behind every exponential growth company is social proof's expansion loop towing the productocracy.

Unfortunately, social proof's ROI cannot be measured, whereas traditional marketing initiatives can. This measurability is why there are thousands of discussions and books about marketing but very few on social proof. The only measurability social proof offers is a correlative benefit relating to acquisition cost. If it costs one hundred dollars in advertising to acquire a new customer, a social-proof customer saves this expense and, instead, expands the margin and the expansion loop. These expansions expand the profit.

For the productocracy, social proof is everything. Every day, I hear positive comments about my first book in every format. When I first received these years ago, I always replied with appreciation. However, I'd also PS a favor in my reply: I'd ask the reader if they could take a moment and review my book at their favorite website, which typically is Amazon. I never asked for a "good" review, just a review. Since the reader contacted me to say something positive, a good review is likely.

Similarly, whenever a new user visits my forum (usually from a web search on entrepreneur forums), they see my book being discussed, quoted, or cited in virtually every thread. Most find the forum valuable, so they infer that the book will be valuable as well. On my forum, there's a thread titled "I've read *The Millionaire Fastlane.*" Here, readers share their thoughts on the book. I do not solicit favorable comments. If a visitor dives into that thread, they'd disappear for three weeks: It is 125 pages long and 3,000 posts deep—and 99 percent of the posts are favorable. If the potential reader views this thread, they likely become a buyer. How convincing are 3,000 unsolicited raves from readers? Or would some intrusive banner ad be more effective?

If review shenanigans are suspected, a reader can do his own investigation elsewhere. Still, the result is nearly the same. For every armchair gasbag that hates *TMF*, ten others say it kicks ass. I've sold thousands because social proof is the driver, NOT advertising, shock blogging, or podcast interviews.

So whenever you receive your first positive echoes, jump for joy. And then save them. Use them in advertising, on your website, and in your promotional materials. If the raves come by private emails, ask permission to use them. If they're on public websites, link to them, cite them, get them front and center so potential buyers read them and become actual buyers. If someone tweets positives about your wares, favorite it. Even more powerful, Twitter allows tweet embedding, where you can immortalize positive comments on your website. Dozens of such tweets are embedded at my website, and they sell for me 24/7.

#9) SHELVE YOUR BIASES

Mark Twain once said, "What gets us into trouble is not what we don't know. It's what we know for sure that just ain't so."

Seems like every website you hit nowadays has one of those intrusive pop-ups asking for your email address. Get your free report! Free coupon! Free secrets of the universe! After nearly twenty-years of web surfing and probably 20,000 interrupting pop-ups, I can't recall EVER giving my email address. They don't work on me and I hate them. And yet, guess what? **I use them**. Despite my pop-up hatred, I use them at my websites *because they work*.

You see, when it comes to execution, your personal biases do more damage than good.

Years ago, when I did the research on list building, the evidence was clear: interruptive pop-up lightboxes are more effective than any list-building strategy. Evidence ran contrary to both my experience and my bias. And yet despite this, I implemented the technique because financial security was more important than my righteousness.

Remember my million-dollar discovery that people were willing to pay for an ad-free forum? Here were my personal biases before acting, assessing, and adjusting the echo:

- *I don't mind advertising.*
- *I would never pay money to view forum content free of advertising.*
- *I wouldn't pay money to be a part of a forum.*

Each one of these biases piled atop each other and said, "Why bother, MJ?" Had I allowed these biases to overrule my decision, I'd be poorer today.

Here's another story, one I found SMH worthy. Some years ago, a young lady sought the forum's advice. She was a successful six-figure fitness consultant who wanted to break free from temporal prostitution. While she earned a pretty penny, she was overworked doing email consultations that fell outside the scope of her consultancy. She asked the group for suggestions for automating and scaling her expertise while simultaneously reforming her clients' expectations as a fitness consultant and not as a therapist. Dozens of suggestions poured in, many good. Unfortunately for this young lady, her biases ruled her world and she let them dictate her actions, or I should say, inactions. *She flat-out rejected every suggestion,* preceded by an excuse why it wouldn't work. Here are some of the actual comments:

- *...that doesn't work with these women, as they will not post about those things...*
- *...women don't buy supplements as much as you think they do.*

- *...hiring an assistant will not work, as it will take too long to train someone to respond in a way I trust.*
- *...if I offer a money-back guarantee, all my clients would demand a refund, even after they made progress.*[120]

These were just a few biases revealed in the discussion. The thread went on for pages, where every suggestion was dismissed, countermanded, or excused away. Once I discovered this gal was unwilling to shelf her biases, I checked out—she was more interested in being right, than rich.

Look, business is hard enough. Don't make it any harder by letting your limited worldview corrupt the real world. Again, your perception is not the reality.

#10) TO HELL WITH SEO (SEARCH ENGINE OPTIMIZATION)

A popular mimetic in web circles is this concept of "SEO," or search engine optimization. SEO is a coding practice to foster highly ranked webpages in the search engines, namely Google. If you own a mortgage company in Denver, showing up on the first page of Google for "Denver mortgage" is immensely valuable, and profitable. Hordes of free traffic would flow your way. Profit margins expand and customer-acquisition cost moves to zero. In a sense, it mimics a productocracy because customer lists grow without charge. So how can this be so bad to warrant a "to hell with SEO"?

Here's why: *Free traffic and expanded margins compliments of SEO are entirely different from free traffic and expanded margins compliments of a productocracy.* While both produce profits, a productocracy can be managed and controlled; SEO cannot. Every year, Google changes their algorithm and imposes penalties for companies gaming the system. And every year it happens: it exposes those who can't survive without it.

Let me be clear: If your business can't survive unless your customer-acquisition cost is zero compliments of a great Google ranking, *you don't have a business.* If you insist on living by the SEO sword, you will die by it. Too often, entrepreneurs come blazing into my forum talking about this great idea, and when their primary strategy for customer acquisition is revealed, it's SEO. Yes, LOL-worthy.

Sorry champ, but gaming the Google lottery is not a strategy. Yes, SEO should be a consideration within execution initiatives, but it is NOT an execution strategy. An olive accents the martini; it does not make it.

Here's the great irony of SEO, which similarly responds like money. My forum receives millions of visitors a year and makes fistfuls of cash. A healthy portion of my site traffic comes from properly optimized pages, which rank well on the search engines. I know for a fact that my forum shows up number one on many searches. SEO, right?

Guess how much time and money I've spent on SEO?

Zero. Zilch. Nada.

Instead, I've focused on creating great content, and Google has rewarded me with a good search ranking. This SEO relationship oddly parallels money—once I focused on what attracts money and not money itself, the money flowed. Likewise, once you focus on what attracts good search-engine results—valuable content—the good SEO results follow. SEO is a great temptress of easy money and free traffic, but don't be fooled. Quit screwing with the olive and mix a better martini.

#11) AVOID FADS OR TRENDS (UNLESS YOU NEED EXPERIENCE)

Is a leg-warmer business a good business to start today? How about in 1982? The answer is no—it's a terrible business—in both cases. Why? Because it's a fad—and fads fade. If the fad fades, so does your business.

I bring this up because too many entrepreneurs waste their time in fad businesses that have questionable longevity. For instance, a popular ongoing fad (as I write this) is long lumberjack beards. As a result, we now have a glut of beard-oil businesses. I think there are two guys on my forum who are pursuing this trend, not to mention the dozens of others saturating the market. Unfortunately, these business have expiration dates likened to peeled fruit: all fashion trends die just like leg warmers, popped collars, and man buns. Don't waste your time in businesses that have the staying power of a sitting president with poor approval ratings. You cannot *UNSCRIPT* by bedding in a house of cards.

Fad businesses might be poor ventures to pursue, but they can provide valuable business experience, especially for those who are just getting started.

#12) AVOID POLITICS IN YOUR BUSINESS

In November 2016, Kelloggs, the multinational food company announced it would no longer advertise on Breitbart.com, a large conservative website with over 45,000,000 readers. Kellogg's cited that the website (and their readers) are not "aligned with our values as a company."

As a result, Breitbart campaigned vigorously for a company boycott and their readers responded in a furor. Subsequently days later, over 400,000 signed on to the boycott, #DumpKelloggs became a trending Twitter hashtag, and their Facebook page blew up with angry customers. Months later, they missed their earnings target.

Unless your business *IS* politics, never infect politics into your business as you risk alienating half your customers. Politics is the only thing that can threaten the cancer-corollary.

While I realize *UNSCRIPTED* implies some political issues (I'm a gun-owning capitalist who doesn't want to poison the environment) it must be said: I didn't write *UNSCRIPTED* to make a fortune. If making mortgage payments was my primary motive I would have sanitized this book to be perfectly apolitical.

#13) NOT EVERYONE LOVES COFFEE

Be warned: *You will be criticized.* Not everyone will like your product. Some will even waste their time attacking you. The fact is, anytime you put your creative works out into the marketmind, you are guaranteed to hear from haters, detractors, and people who don't like what you are doing. This is normal. The best you can do is assess, adjust, and act (if their criticism is legit) or ignore. If you fear criticism or "what people might say" about your effort, quit now and update the resume.

THE UNSCRIPTED ENTREPRENEURIAL FRAMEWORK

THE 4 DISCIPLINES (4D)

[3(B) ∩ (MP ∩ FE ∩ KE) ∩ 4(D)] / FTE

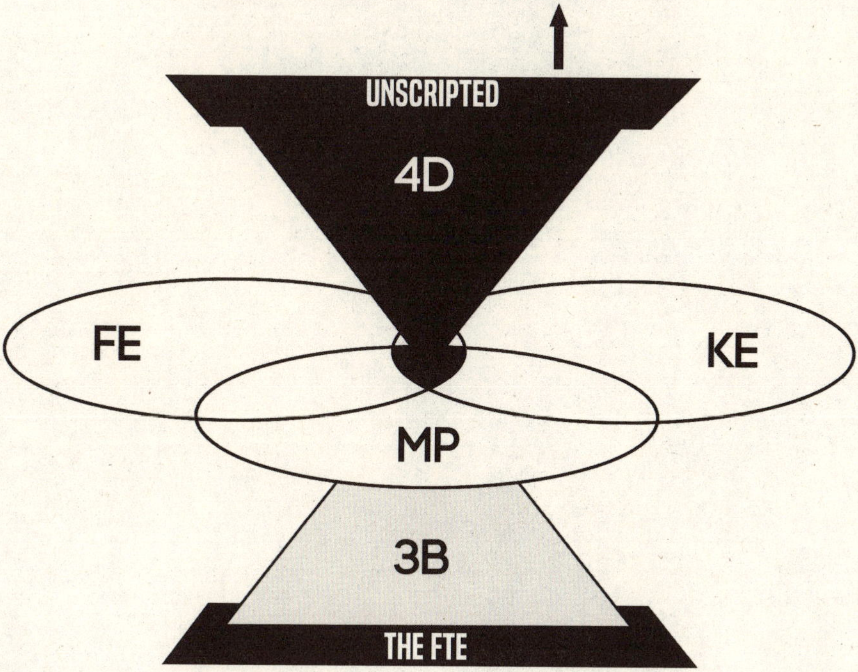

CHAPTER 42

THE 4 UNSCRIPTED DISCIPLINES: DESIGN, THEN INSURE YOUR FUTURE

> Some people regard discipline as a chore.
> For me, it is a kind of order that sets me free to fly.
> **~ Julie Andrews, Actress**

THE PRESTIGE: THE UNSCRIPTED MAGIC

In Christopher Nolan's 2011 movie, *The Prestige*, a magic trick has three parts: the pledge, the turn, and the prestige. The pledge is the audience offer: a deck of cards or an empty box. The turn is where something extraordinary is done with the pledge. However, the prestige is the hardest: it's doing something extraordinary on top of the extraordinary while leaving the audience dumbfounded about how you did it.

UNSCRIPTED magic is similar. Your business is the pledge. Your business's value given to the world is the turn. And the difficult prestige? It's managing the rewards of your business. It's doing the extraordinary when extraordinary happens.

Give the average paycheck-to-paycheck American $1 million, and after three years, they'll be back where they started: broke. Some will need only one year. Ever wonder how lottery winners always lose their winnings? The missing element in the riches-to-rags tales is the prestige: *discipline*. Making money is hard; keeping it is harder.

The *UNSCRIPTED* preamble, the final union represented by the upmost triangle, 4(D), in the *UNSCRIPTED* Entrepreneurial Framework is discipline: the tricky trick of getting to the prestige and staying there. Discipline completes the *UNSCRIPTED* penta-union, joining with belief, meaning, and an executed CENTS strategy. Once you accomplish a scaling productocracy, the four disciplines finalize the difference between lifelong *UNSCRIPTION* and fleeting success. They are:

1. **Comparative Immunity,**
2. **Purposed Saving,**
3. **Measured Elevation**
4. **Consequential Thought**

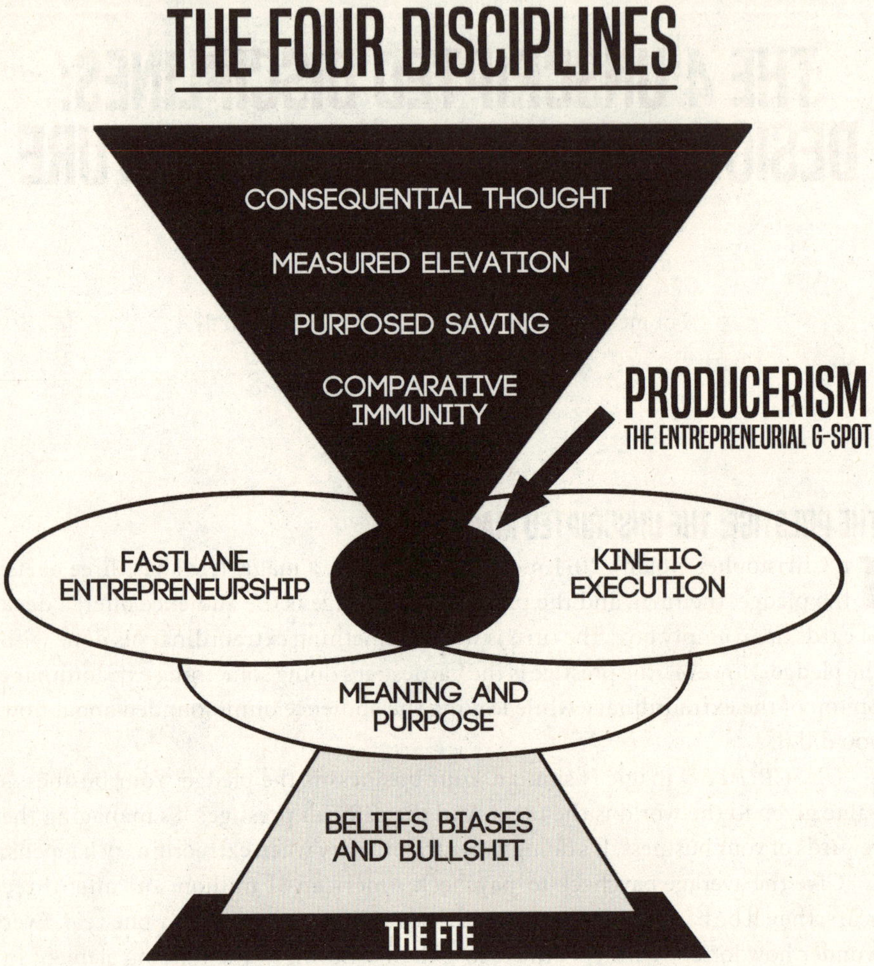

Like the prestige, the four disciplines are silently invisible, but they are as important to *UNSCRIPTED* as an offensive line is to a quarterback. Disregard any of them and one day you might be living large and the next, well, back to mowing lawns at the golf course.

CHAPTER 43

COMPARATIVE IMMUNITY: WELL-DRESSED SLAVES ARE STILL SLAVES

Materialism is the only form of distraction from true bliss.
~ **Douglas Horton, Clergyman**

SCREW THE JONESES

In the 2010 remake of *Wall Street: Money Never Sleeps*, the young trader asks the wealthy tycoon how much money he needs; what number is enough?

His response? *More.*

This is a favorite scene of some people I know. And it saddens me. You see, there is no exact formula for happiness, but there is one for unhappiness: *it's comparison—the drive for more when more isn't needed.*

The fact is there's always someone better off than you. The *SCRIPTED* media does a fabulous job reminding us of our peasantry, a daily smattering of success stories mastheaded on the front page of websites, giving us the constant nag of anxiety and inadequacy. And yet what you don't see is the other 95 percent—those poor souls living in abject poverty where hunger is normal, not the absence of the latest iGadget. Even if you are reading this crammed on an old lumpy mattress in a musty basement, there's someone in another country who's lying in a mud hut, struggling to find a dish of rice.

Every day, I could wake up and compare myself to someone else—someone younger, better looking, wealthier, with a faster car, bigger house, this, that—but I don't. Instead, I am grateful for what I have because I know persistent comparison rituals urging "more" is a one-way ticket to misery.

> ***Comparison is future-oriented and focused on what is missing, creating anxiety. Gratitude is present-oriented and focused on what you have, creating peace.***

Did you know halving something for an eternity, it would never disappear? Multiplication by half never meets zero. The problem with comparison and the ultimate drive for "more" is that they are similarly unattainable. *There is no finish line because the finish line always moves.* And that moving finish line will always be a source of antithetical apathy. Instead of being peacefully grateful for your gifts, you become entrenched in an unending race underscored by longing and inadequacy. Please don't confuse this for the "Kaizen Principle," which is continual personal improvement—being a better you is not the same as striving to own the most expensive house on the planet.

Your defense to "more" fuels the first *UNSCRIPTED* discipline: *comparative immunity. Comparative immunity is being at peace with your present pace while abstaining from the unwinnable game of comparison.* With comparative immunity, you're laughing at the Joneses for their idiocy; you pursue what's important while denying the rest.

For example, I could easily compare my entrepreneurial achievements to other entrepreneurs and conclude: I'm not as successful or high-profile as they are. "OMG, Johnny Entrepreneur just sold his company for $25 million! That's more than what I sold mine for!" These unguarded comparisons could force me into actions incongruent with my goals. My goals aren't theirs. My goal isn't to appease hecklers and haters who might say I need to create more "wins" when more wins isn't my goal. My goal is living *UNSCRIPTED*—not an *Inc. Magazine* cover. If I played the comparison game, appeasing opinions and "what other people think" becomes more important than appeasing myself. One pursuit is architected by the disease of comparison while the other is written by my soul.

INADEQUACY

Consumer culture is all about comparison. Comparative immunity doesn't care about image illusions because it acknowledges that a well-dressed slave is still, well, a slave.

For example, every once in a while, I find myself in North Scottsdale, an affluent Phoenix suburb. On this particular day, I visited my orthopedic doctor and got stuck in the waiting room. To pass the time, I picked up one of those local "lifestyle" magazines. Page after page was a hedonistic orgy of overpriced, consumptive temptations. As I thumbed through it, I felt sadness for the poor snobs sucked into faking affluence. Over three-quarters of the magazine was advertising for:

Plastic surgery
Your boobs are too small and your nose is crooked! Fix it and be happy!

Engagement rings
Give your fiancé a diamond ring that will be envied, not laughed at!

Personal effects: watches, cars, clothes, and shoes
Nothing screams success more than a $120,000 watch!

Imported furniture
This $30,000 coffee table will definitely be a conversation piece!

In my ten-minute pass of the $12,000 dresses and $42,000 chandeliers, the messaging of this "lifestyle" magazine was clear: *you are inadequate and your inadequacy can be solved by spending everything you earn on outclassing the other guy.*

It made me think.

While I can afford most of the overpriced garbage in this magazine, most people, even in North Scottsdale, cannot. Yet *somebody* is buying this stuff. And that's great news for us *UNSCRIPTED* entrepreneurs— the Joneses are always jonesing to spend.

With comparative immunity, you're free from comparison propaganda. You know you are adequate. You know your self-esteem and self-worth are not defined by a $1,000 pair of shoes made in an Indonesian sweatshop.

Let the fools fooled by the inadequacy messages succumb: debt, uncertain future, and work until death. Don't waste life's precious time adorning your coffin with diamonds.

? ***What part of your life is susceptible to comparison rituals? At the office? At the gym or in the club? In the school parking lot? And how have you reacted to it?***

CHAPTER 44

PURPOSED SAVING: PREPPING FOR LIFETIME PASSIVE INCOME

You can't try to do things; you simply must do them.
–Ray Bradbury, Author

#NEVERWORKAGAIN

When I was a I child I had a passbook savings account. Back in pre-computer days, the bank teller updated your little booklet (called the passbook) with entries showing your bank balance. One day I made a birthday deposit (thanks, Grandma!) and saw one additional entry. Stamped in front of my deposit was another deposit, one I did not make: *it was interest.*

While the dollar amount was terribly small, I vividly remember, "Wow, my money earned money, and I did nothing but let time pass!" It was fascinating and planted a seed that later sprouted a life-changing dividend. As I got older, I never forgot this simple concept—*money makes money while time passes.*

Unfortunately, once I graduated and real life's temptations hit, I neglected the money-system novelty and buried it behind a lot of feckless "feel-good" spending. I'm young! I'm going to live! Even after I sold my company the first time, lifestyle elevation ushered the money system idea to back-of-mind status. Knowing and doing became two different things.

And then the stock market collapsed. Once I saw the sale proceeds dwindle under the weight of hedonistic spending and falling tech stocks (so much for Wall Street being a safe investment, eh?), it was then that knowing became doing. I went from a free-wheeled spender to *a purposed saver.*

The second *UNSCRIPTED* discipline, purposed saving, is THE ONE that gates the promised land: the end of forced servitude, past-due electric bills, car payments, and price checking a box of Cheerios. The end of doing shit you hate for a paycheck you can't survive on. Never. Work. Again.

Your three objectives under the purposed saving discipline are:

1. **Lifetime passive income**
2. **Early "retirement" and dream pursuit**
3. **Tax relief**

#1. LIFETIME PASSIVE INCOME

While a business can spawn semi-passive income, a money system, regular monthly income generated from investments, is *numero uno* on the passivity scale. Unless you count regular royalties from *Seinfeld* syndication, the money system has no match insofar as regularity and "hands-off" management. Since you aren't Costanza, purposed saving, while growing your business, needs to be your go-to plan.

Recall our discussion on compound interest in Chapter 24. The mainstream errantly uses compound interest to grow wealth, which makes it pathetically slow, risky, and ineffective, akin to rearranging deck chairs on the Titanic. Growing your net worth is a job assigned to your business. The end game is the money system, which can be funded from two sources: (1) purposed saving from business income; and (2) a business sale, known as a liquidation event.

Regardless of how the system is funded, large sums of money transfigure compound interest from an impotent wealth creator to a potent passive-income machine. Remember, 5 percent interest on $10 million is a whopping $46,000 per MONTH for life—and that's without touching the principal! After fifty years, your $10 million is still there! Can you and your family survive on $46,000 per month? Or would you need to cancel HBO?

#2. EARLY RETIREMENT AND DREAM PURSUIT

I technically "retired" in my thirties. By retired, I don't mean I'm teeing off every morning at 6:00 a.m. and drinking champagne by midafternoon. Retirement can mean anything, but at its fundamental roots, it means that *working by force* is replaced with *working by choice*. Because of this freedom, you can do whatever you want without money's constraint or validation.

Remember, "doing what you hate" can beautifully lead to "doing what you love." If authoring a knitting book for MMA fighters is what you want to do, you can. When money is strained from the equation, suddenly market wants and needs become secondary. You just do it. My first two books exemplify this: I wrote them from my heart and not my pocketbook. I don't worry about commercial viability or how palatable the concepts are for certain "special-interest" groups. Yeah, I'm not expecting your financial planner—the one who makes a 3 percent front load on your mutual-fund investment—to recommend my books.

Anyhow, what's interesting about retirement and the money system fueling it is this: In the ten years since retiring, my net worth hasn't gone down; it's gone up. And that's in a horrific low-interest environment! Sure, I still own multiple businesses, but let's be honest: I treat them more like hobbies and mostly avoid "do what I hate" because I can afford to.

So the big question is what would you be doing if money wasn't a concern?

For many entrepreneurs, the answer is nothing different. They would start another business. Such is the addictive flavor of nourishing the world with value—it nourishes your soul.

#3. TAX RELIEF

Some years ago, a very successful entrepreneur visited my forum and told his tale of fortune and ruin. He owned an explosive business that made him money by the wheelbarrow. Naturally, hedonic adaptation followed: material excessiveness, periodic drug-induced partying, the weekend suites in Vegas—whatever came in, most of it went out. His downfall was something no one warned him about—not the recreational drugs or lavish extravagance, not a business failure or an economic collapse, not an industry shift: *it was taxes.*

I searched Google and found very little on this huge oversight that plagues many newly successful entrepreneurs. *It's the unplanned and unpaid taxation of business income that demands purposed saving.* For newbie entrepreneurs destined for success, pay close attention or suffer the same fate.

Let's assume you're an execution master. At year-end, your profit is a whopping $500,000. Congrats. During the year, you also paid yourself a nice, comfy salary of $60,000. Because you're smart and read *UNSCRIPTED*, you've also adopted purposed saving, or so you think. You've saved 20 percent ($100,000) of your $500,000 profit and spent the rest on a lake cabin, complete with ATVs and a speedboat. Smart? Not exactly.

By appearance, this might be perceived as purposed saving, but it isn't. Your $500,000 business profit will come with a tax bill at year-end. Technically, you should be paying the IRS quarterly tax payments as your profits occur. Many newbies forget to do so, which tacks on additional interest and fees. The IRS doesn't care if you "forgot" or "didn't know" and charges up to .5 percent per month plus interest on all failed tax payments.

Back to our example, with fees and interest, your $500,000 will be taxed approximately $200,000.[121] And this assumes they don't question your small salary relative to your profit. Yes, the IRS will send you a bill for 200Gs which must be paid IMMEDIATELY. Not tomorrow and not next month when more money rolls in. Get out your checkbook, champ, and learn how to write PAIN.

Oh shit. Looks like the 20% in profits you saved, $100K, isn't going to cut it. And now it's time to sell the Bayliner. Save purposely, or pay painfully.

FINANCIAL RECONSTRUCTION: PURPOSED SAVING

Your stage, page, or age in life is irrelevant. I don't care if you already own a business, want to start one, or are still drudging a job—you can be a purposed saver right now. A total financial reconstruction consists of five retooling phases. They are:

1. **Reframe**
2. **Reform**
3. **Reduce**
4. **Reallocate and Remind**
5. **Reward**

STEP #1: REFRAME

Reframing is changing your perception about money.

First, rename money as value-vouchers. Reread Chapter 21 if you need a refresher.

Second, see one saved dollar as a tiny passive-income machine that produces a nickel in lifetime passive income. A buck saved today is one you won't need to earn tomorrow. While passive-income yields fluctuate with economic conditions, money always creates offspring. In today's economy, one saved dollar generates around 3.5 to 5.5 cents per year. In history, it has been as high as ten cents per dollar saved. Once enough value-vouchers are saved, exceeding your monthly expenses, the need for work evaporates.

My favorite money reframe is approaching it as a ruthless conqueror: Each dollar saved is another freedom fighter added to your slave army. You army also procreates more soldiers. Altogether, your saved soldiers are fighting for your freedom. On the other hand, every dollar spent on the latest fad is one fighter killed.

STEP #2: REFORM

The second step is reforming expenses and cash outflow. This involves eliminating any expense that is not conducive to an *UNSCRIPTED* objective. You can say reform is about *temporary* frugality. That pile of magazines you never read? Cancel them. Is your McMansion precluding you from taking risks and allocating time and money to better yielding opportunities? Dump the house. Escalade too costly to maintain with insurance, repairs, and gas? Maybe it's time for a used Prius—or take the bus, ride your bike, or walk. Yeah, I know, none of that is cool or easy, but is discipline ever easy? Remember, *unearned luxury equates to earned suffering*. You can be the undisciplined 99 percent or hold yourself to the standard of the 1 percent.

STEP #3: REDUCE

The third step of attack is reducing debt, eventually paying back everything you owe. You must attack your debt and label it an enemy of the state. Here I urge pragmatism over fanaticism. Fanaticism is extreme frugality, settling for less and marathon coupon clipping. The pragmatic approach for attacking debt within a purposed saving mindset is that every dollar spent should fall into one of three categories: 1) *Business expenses;* net-worth acceleration is anchored by your business. Don't fear spending money here. If one dollar spent translates into ten dollars tomorrow, the risk and returns are worth it. 2) *Living expenses*; food, shelter, transportation, insurance—your household should be run like a fine-tuned machine. 3) *Debt reduction*; if it isn't needed for basic living expenses or can't be reinvested in your business, it should go toward repayments. Pay down credit cards or reduce the principal on loans, such as mortgages or student loans.

Debt attack's first step is to plug your financial hole from taking on more water. Paying an extra $200 on your credit card doesn't mean squat when next month you add $500. Stop freaking spending. And when you do spend, pay cash only, or carry a debit card or a "spend card" linked to a separate, budgeted bank account. This spend card is for discretionaries: drinks, dining out, entertainment, clothes, etc. Every month, give your spend card a budget, creating the proper financial environment for debt reduction. When the spend card's budget is gone, it's gone. Card declined. You might be embarrassed at the checkout register, but you stick to the program.

Another tactic is to carry no cash at all. The goal here is to put everything on a credit card that offers reward points, and then pay off the balance monthly. If you aren't disciplined, don't bother. This is a great strategy to rack up reward points for stuff you always buy. Everything I buy goes on my credit card, from utilities to groceries. As a result, I get a ton of free stuff (gift cards, trips) from the accumulated rewards.

From the conqueror mindset, debt is another army, except this one wages war against you! And yes, this army also holsters the interest weapon, procreating more fighters determined to trap you into a servitude system. The question is *whose army are you funding?* The one working to free you? (I saved $500 last week!) Or the one working to enslave you? (I charged a round of drinks on my Visa!)

If you're in jail, a KEY represents your freedom. If you're imprisoned by SCRIPTED dogma, careful stewardship of MONEY is your key to freedom.

STEP #4: REALLOCATE (AND REMIND)

Financial reconstruction's fourth step is to reallocate *something* into your money system every month, *even if it is only a few dollars.* Optimally, allocate any surplus income after covering your business and living expenses. And yes, even if you have to divert a few dollars away from debt repayment, do it.

When I started my purposed-saving journey, I went to Home Depot and bought some nails, a short two-by-four, and some vinyl number stickers, the kind used for labeling house addresses. After hammering the nails into the wood, I hooked the vinyl letters on the nails to form an interchangeable number, almost like something you'd see on *The Price Is Right.* This number represented my liquid money-system total: my total dollars saved. I then hung this makeshift meter on the wall above my desk. Every day, it reminded me what my purpose was. While this might seem neurotic, I was neurotically opposed to slaving at a job for 50 years in lieu of a gold watch and a two-week vacation. Believe me, I made sure this makeshift counter went up a few bucks every darn day.

Another reallocation trick I used was an empty coffee can. Here I deposited loose change daily. This always creates an extra $500 per year.

While none of these strategies makes more money, they help align your mind for a money-system goal. **The real magic happens when your income starts to explode.**

At some point in your *UNSCRIPTED* evolution, you will see your income rising to levels never experienced. When I eclipsed $100,000 per month in profits, I remember being excited with all types of temptations: multiple cars, second homes, new this, new that. This is when you need to clamp down and really flex your discipline muscles. Instead of spending, I save most of it. And no, it didn't involve frugality.

When your income expands into five or six-figures monthly, this is where your money-system can really ramp up. More importantly, it prepares you for the expected quarterly thunderstorm: the tax man. You'll find making millions is bittersweet; explosive income, hooray! Six-figure checks to the IRS? Ugh. Talk about burning a bag of cash.

In the end, a lifelong dividend of passive income needs to come from measured adaption and reallocation of cash from frivolous expenditures into savings. Once you realize that becoming a millionaire isn't this long tortuous process, saving becomes a breeze.

SCRIPTED sheep take a Slowlane to the slaughterhouse while *UNSCRIPTED* freethinkers drive the *Fastlane* of a CENTS business. The former creates millionaires timed by centuries—the other, years.

STEP #5: REWARD

Reward is the final phase of financial reconstruction for purposed-saving: giving yourself a gift for milestones achieved. This could be dinner at an expensive restaurant, a vacation, a fun gadget, any desire craved. For example, my first Lamborghini purchase was a reward for a financial milestone. Even today, while living within the *UNSCRIPTED* pinnacle, I reward myself with treats for new accomplishments: expensive gadgets, toys, and yeah, even hours of mindless television.

Besides business, living, and debt-repayment expenses, reward is the one exception to the three cash outlays described above. Of course, no reward should threaten the long-term goal of *UNSCRIPTION.* A speedboat is not a reward if it increases debt and living expenses and injures the reallocation phase of financial reconstruction.

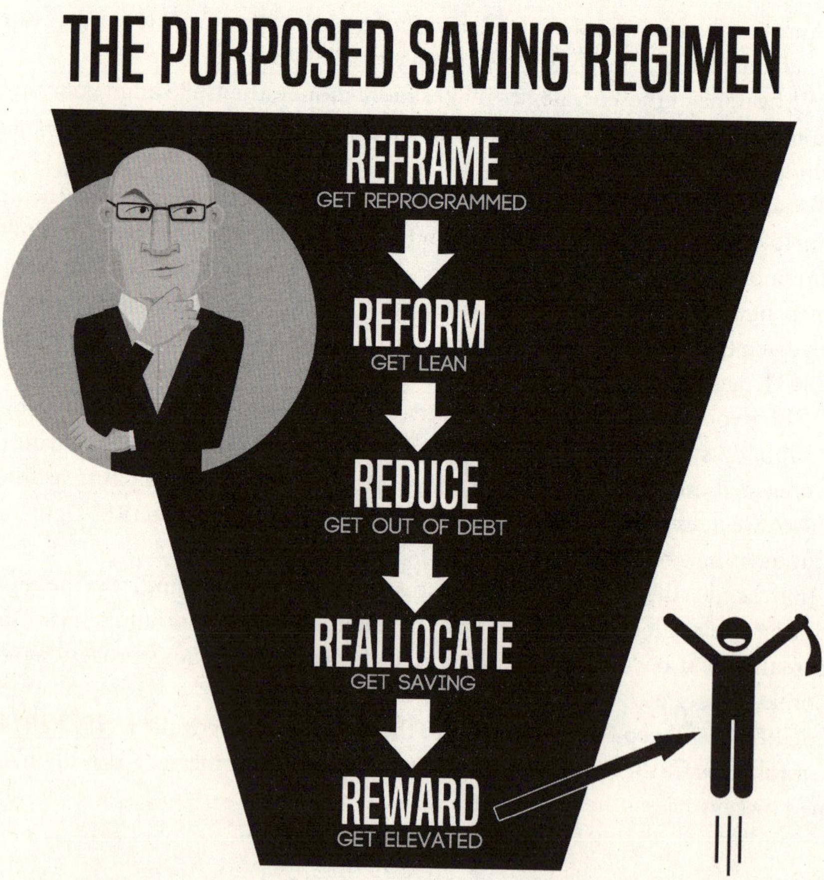

CHAPTER 45

MEASURED ELEVATION: REWARD AND ENJOY THE RIDE

For every disciplined effort, there is a multiple reward.
~ **Jim Rohn, Author**

LIVING LARGE WITHOUT MORTGAGING THE FUTURE

I've generally avoided statistical regurgitation in this book because people typically exclude themselves from the data. If a survey says, "93 percent of adults will be financially unprepared for retirement by sixty-five years old," we absolve ourselves and think, "That won't be me." *Unfortunately, without discipline, it will be you.*

One statistic bears this truth: According to a 2015 survey conducted by GOBankingRates, only 28 percent of Americans have more than $10,000 in savings.[122] Nearly 8 percent have nothing. Can you comfortably retire on ten-grand? Or will a bankrupted government program be your savior?

But wait, there's more.

I omitted one crucial detail about this statistical group representing the 28 percent: These polled savers weren't average Americans. *They were people who earn more than $100,000 per year.* Yup, six-figure earners.

The antithesis to this data is the disheartening truth: A whopping 72 percent of those considered "affluent" or "upper middle class," by all accounts, are a few months from broke. You see, beyond the white picket fence and the late-model Lexus in the garage is a rotten financial apple. Few people, even those making six-figures, possess the third *UNSCRIPTED* discipline: the fortitude for measured elevation. *Measured elevation is the discipline to raise your lifestyle disproportionately as your income rises.* In essence, measured-elevation is the successful management of the reward phase in the purposed-saving discipline.

Without measured-elevation, human nature takes over. And that nature is *hedonic adaptation*. Hedonic adaptation is your propensity to elevate your lifestyle in **direct** proportion to your income. All new income is rewarded with new stuff.

Wants suddenly morph into needs. You might *need* a reliable car to get to work, but do you need one that costs $70,000? Does your eleven-year-old kid really need a new iPhone? Do you really need a snowblower for your eight-foot driveway? Hedonic adaptation pushes bigger incomes into bigger spending: a faster car, a larger apartment, silkier clothes, a better this, a better that. Hedonic adaptation is why paycheck-to-paycheck Americans stay paycheck-to-paycheck, regardless of the paycheck's size.

Measured elevation's discipline is simple: You only limitlessly consume a fractioned amount of production. If you want something expensive, it's earned and then some. I mean, let's be serious: We all like nice things. Flying privately is better than being stuffed in economy next to the lavatory. Producerism produced by a productocracy sells enough of what OTHERS want so you can purchase whatever YOU want. You can live very well and still save disproportionately.

Your truth serum, however, is affordability: Anytime you do mental gymnastics over a contemplated purchase—sorry, you can't afford it. Cognitive debates about "why" you can buy something—"I'm expecting a raise," "I have a tax refund coming," or "The dealer is giving me a great financing rate"—are reality checks.

You can't afford it.

Like buying a loaf of bread at the store, affordability never carries conditions, worries, or justifications—you just buy it and it's forgotten. In the end, buying a $300,000 car isn't a problem if you happen to have a $15M net worth; it's a problem when you finance it because you can barely scrape together $50K.

For example, I can theoretically pay cash for ten Lamborghinis and rent a Beverly Hills mansion, instantly becoming an Instagram superstar worthy of scantily clad women with specious motives; however, doing so puts me at the financial redline, jeopardizes my freedom, and tatters my safety net. Remember, we aren't balancing production with consumption; we're outrunning it.

In the end, we don't dismiss hedonic adaptation; we control it.

Business booming? Great, reward yourself with something desired—but don't go overboard. By all means, measurably enjoy the fruits of your success, but don't endanger the goal: *UNSCRIPTION*—never needing to work another day in your life.

Having the choice and the financial wherewithal to buy whatever you want actually lessens the desire to follow through and buy the target of your affection.

Was there ever a product you desperately wanted to buy and when you could finally afford it, you passed on it? What changed?

CHAPTER 46

CONSEQUENTIAL-THOUGHT: PROTECTING YOUR KICK-ASS LIFE

Every action has a consequence, so always try to be good.
~ **Richard Eyre, Director**

HOW 2 MINUTES AND 20 SECONDS CAN DESTROY A LIFE

While the first three disciplines gate an *UNSCRIPTED* promised land, consequential thought is its lock.

In 2012, an Arizona medical-device CFO making $200,000 a year thought it would be cute to video himself berating a Chick-fil-A employee at a drive-through window.[123] The two-minute-and-twenty-second YouTube video went viral, stoking a national firestorm, which resulted in his immediate job termination. Besides his job, the smug man reportedly lost over $2 million in stock options and, as of March 2015, is now unemployed and on food stamps.[124]

One event can kill a process. A career. A marriage. A life.

The unfortunate reality of the event/process dichotomy mentioned in Chapter 18 is *UNSCRIPTION*'s final discipline: *consequential-thought—the foresight into the consequences of our actions and knowing that our choices are unfairly weighted toward the bad ones.*

Actually, "unfair" is understated—it's ridiculously uneven.

Good choices float like feathers while the poor ones sink like anchors. You could take two years to build your dream house, and all it takes is one carelessly placed cigar to burn it down. Process builds the events (I finally got my CFO dream job!) while an event (Let's berate this eight-dollar-per-hour employee!) rips the process apart.

Think about that for a minute.

Consequence inequity is where one impulsive decision (or mistake) has the staggering power to invalidate thousands of well-planned ones. *But the reverse does not apply.* One positive action cannot erase thousands of negative ones. Eating broccoli for one day won't help me lose fifty pounds. If this incongruity is unclear, let me explain.

I started accumulating a lot of value-vouchers in my late twenties. I was single, and … let's just say … engaging in some risky "YOLO" behavior. One of those behaviors was street racing. Nothing was more enjoyable than smoking a fart-can Honda in my nitrous-laced Viper. One evening after a few drinks (another bad decision), I thought it would be cool to race some tricked-out Mustang. The problem here, besides being young and stupid, was my unfamiliarity with my newly modified Viper. I over-throttled and spun into oncoming traffic. The oncoming traffic avoided my stupidity, but the innocent palm tree beyond the embankment didn't. Within seconds, my empty passenger seat was now the trunk of a date palm. Luckily, I survived unharmed.

You see, one reckless decision can ruin your life in an instant. Not just for you, but for innocent bystanders. I could have killed someone and been convicted of negligent homicide, spending the rest of my days in prison. I could have permanently injured myself. *One judgment lapse could have eradicated every good decision I made in my lifetime.*

Consequence-inequity is most visibly noted with professional athletes, some accidental, some incidental. Bill Buckner's successful baseball career has been overshadowed and mired by one game: He erred in the World Series. Thousands of at bats erased by one play. Another story, Pete Rose, banned from betting on baseball. Lance Armstrong, doping the Tour de France. Tiger Woods, crashing his Lincoln amidst a marital-infidelity cover-up. In each instance, an event spanning only minutes causes a lifetime of process to unravel, killing careers, relationships, and reputations. You can never, EVER underestimate the potential negative weight of one decision.

Consequence-inequity also plays a role with the relationships we choose. Every person who enters your social circle is a potential road. This road could be a road to ruin, or a road to winning. Question is, can you identify and remove potential people who are liabilities to your goals? Will you allow the negative inertia of someone take you to dark places? Or will you be a proactive CEO of your choices?

When I was sixteen-years old, I had an odd friend named Dave. Dave's oddity was he occasionally glossed over into a murderous expression, scaring the crap out of me. One day while I was at his house, he cursed at his mother, calling her "a dickless c*nt." I shit you not. His mother didn't discipline him; she simply shook her head and walked away. My eyes gaped like saucers. Later that same day, Dave caught a rat in the backyard and burned it alive on a leaf pyre. I objected in spirit but kept quiet, not wanting to be Dave's next burn victim. After the sick deed, I lied an excuse and left.

It was the last time I saw Dave. Why? *Because I decided it would be the last time.*

Even in my youth, I sensed something off. Disastrous. My intuition knew I didn't want to hitch a friendship to this guy. And sure enough, I was right. I read about Dave in the newspaper some years later: he murdered a police officer.

When I was eighteen, déjà vu. Rick was another oddball friend I had. A charismatic guy, Rick was a late-eighties version of Justin Bieber. Young girls swooned over him, making for a fabulous wingman at the under-twenty-one clubs. Like Dave, Rick also rolled with a dark and vacant look in his eyes that clued something was amiss.

Spoiled by his parents, Rick was birthday gifted a brand-new Trans Am GTA, an incredibly fast (and expensive) car for the period. Every so often, I'd find myself stuffed in the backseat of Rick's TA on the way to parties or whatever else teenagers muddy their feet with. Anytime we hit the freeway, Rick routinely sped, reaching speeds of over a hundred miles per hour. Each time, I'd beg him to "take it easy," and each time, my pleas deafened to the stereo sounds of Run-D.M.C. One night, during one of his 110-miles-per-hour jaunts, he almost lost control and struck a highway divider. I still feel the adrenaline from that night. While fearfully praying in the backseat of his car, it clicked. I decided that I would not put myself in this uncontrollable, life-threatening situation ever again. It was the last time I saw Rick, and while I don't know if he made murder headlines, I'm glad I wasn't there to find out. You see, you simply can't win life's game tethered to uncontrollable liabilities. Wipe them from your balance sheet so you have a chance to win.

> ***Negative influences or destructive people, no matter what their label (family, fraternity brother, coworker) shouldn't carry exemptions to excommunication.***

BECOMING A CONSEQUENTIAL THINKER

These stories highlight the perils and positives of consequential thought. A consequential thinker *thinks before acting.* Consequential thinking extrapolates outcomes and consequences. It assesses risk and probability and asks the following questions: What are the worst- and best-case consequences of this action and their reasonable odds? Are these consequences worth the risk I am taking?

Thinking these questions, or Worst-Case Consequence Analysis (WCCA), doesn't take hours; it takes seconds. A proactive mind initiates them. Once asked, catastrophic threats to your process can be exposed. If you're thinking about going into business with a partner who has two felonies and four bankruptcies under his belt, would WCCA be a wee bit helpful?

Hindsight might indeed be 20/20, but so is consequential thinking. But unlike hindsight, consequential thinking gives you ears to hear the cackling chickens before they aim to roost.

Choice is the most powerful asset we own. All of us have it, but few respect it. It steers our lives down an unending stream of outcomes. And those outcomes, good or bad, must be endured. Wherever you are today—free from the *SCRIPT* or imprisoned by it—face the uncomfortable truth: *You are exactly as you have chosen.*

You are the appointed CEO of your life.

And yet most people make their life's management decisions not as the CEO, but as a preschooler awaiting instructions on when to get their midday nap. Don't be one of the millions of adults who still live like children.

In decision moments, remember: Piss-poor choices have piss-poor consequences. Playing stupid games? Get rewarded stupid prizes. Don't join the legion of stupid-prize winners who are now whining and politicking that they've been dealt an unfair hand when the truth is, they deserve it. Play, but play smart.

MONEY CAN'T BRIBE DISCIPLINE

The four disciplines and their importance go beyond *UNSCRIPTION.* While a profitable business earning both money and freedom is the goal, neither can bribe discipline. In the end, the poor choices and their consequence inequalities will always prevail. For instance, if you struggle to live on $50,000 a year, you'll probably struggle to live on $500,000—except your struggle happens in a six-bedroom house. *More money doesn't solve money problems.* While a big income can postpone or hide consequences, eventually the consequences outlast the money. Chronic bad decision-makers are left nowhere to hide.

Like luck, it's about probabilities.

The more you partake in risky, stupid behavior, the more likely it will scar you for life. Just ask the once-famous millionaire athlete with six baby mamas, who now teeters on bankruptcy. If you are undisciplined in the disciplines, the consequences will outlast your cash.

? ***What risky "YOLO" behaviors are you (or your peers) engaging in that are invariably causing you to gamble with your future?***

PART 5

A NEW DAWN... NEVER WORK AGAIN

WHEN DEATH IS CELEBRATED

PART 5: Author's Objective:

LIFETIME PASSIVE INCOME

To stress the importance of all five *UNSCRIPTED* components while illustrating the technicalities of a money-system, and how you can create passive income for life.

CHAPTER 47

WELCOME TO "FUCK YOU"

The artist is nothing without the gift, but
the gift is nothing without work.
~ Emile Zola, Author

THE PROMISED LAND

Congratulations, you've arrived.

You are *UNSCRIPTED*. It's a new chapter. You might think it's a destination, an end, but it's really a beginning. It's where "fuck you" blooms: doing whatever you want, whenever, wherever. It's the official rite where life no longer lives you; you live it.

Thirty-year mortgage offered at 6 percent with two points in fees? Fuck you, I'll pay cash.

Warned your book will never sell because it's too brute force and not concept focused? Fuck you, I'm publishing it anyway.

Always wanted to own a Ferrari, despite its lack of utility? Fuck you, I'm buying it and paying cash.

"Fuck you" is a beautiful thing.

Composite the five unions: Belief, meaning-and-purpose, a *Fastlane* productocracy, execution, and discipline. Mix together and the concoction left behind is an empowered "fuck you" immune to the *SCRIPT*. No settling. No punching time clocks. No sardine seats on Southwest Airlines.

Unfortunately, fail to unionize one or more of the *UNSCRIPTED* components and *UNSCRIPTION* fails. All five components are like a cake recipe. You can't just say, "Meh, let's skip the sugar and see what happens." Deficiency in one ingredient (or more) and the outcome sours. Sorry, but the five *UNSCRIPTED* ingredients are not suggestions—*they're required.*

Dismiss any one and here is what happens:

THE COMPETENT SELF-DESTRUCTOR

Proficiency: Meaning, CENTS Business, Execution, Discipline
Deficiency: Belief

OUTCOME

While you're motivated with great ideas and have all the competencies to be a successful entrepreneur, your mind is your worst enemy. Through its multitude of flawed beliefs, biases, and bullshit, your ideas are quickly dismissed because of internally held untruths. While you possess the proficiency (intelligence and talent) to execute, your self-destructive beliefs stand in the way of results. The likely outcome is a job held for a lifetime, simply because your business ideas and actions never coordinate into an effective process. Or worse, you take an unethical, immoral road where success, money, and entrepreneurship are associated with a negative identity shift, a thought line that in order to succeed, you need to be greedy and/or scammy.

THE WANDERER

Proficiency: Belief, CENTS Business, Execution, Discipline
Deficiency: Meaning

OUTCOME

An *UNSCRIPTED* process void of meaning is deprived of initiative, motivation, and persistence. As a result, the entrepreneur fails the motivation cycle, gives up too early and fails to finish, namely because execution cycle was not exhausted. With an absent meaning, the entrepreneur might possess the knowledge, tools, and wherewithal to execute, but he doesn't sufficiently "beat the piñata" until it breaks. Obstacles bar progress. Difficulty goes unconquered. As a result, you get bored, distracted, or discouraged too easily, usually returning to a job or moving on to the next big idea, which again, is cursorily poked. A missing meaning quits shoveling three feet from gold.

THE "PAY THE BILLS" ENTREPRENEUR

Proficiency: Belief, Meaning, Execution, Discipline
Deficiency: A CENTS Productocracy

OUTCOME

The entrepreneur running an unqualified CENTS business struggles to create extraordinary wealth or freedom. While this entrepreneur might earn profit, net-worth acceleration and freedom expansion never happen. Because your business lacks the essential CENTS components, positive results are either short-lived or not very profitable. A golden goose isn't golden if you're married to it, if everyone has it, if the eggs aren't in demand, or if the goose is leased. The most common outcome here runs quite the gambit, but all of them are underscored by one theme: a lack of growth and profitability, ending in survival over thriving. *Your business might pay the bills, but it isn't going to buy your freedom.*

THE IDEA ENTREPRENEUR

Proficiency: Belief, Meaning, CENTS, Discipline
Deficiency: Execution

OUTCOME

Entrepreneurs lacking execution are idea guys.

These are the cooks who try competing with the chefs.

It's someone who has great ideas but rarely does anything about them. Instead, someone else makes the fortune executing the same ideas.

For the idea guy, great ideas come and go daily, but the willingness to act, assess, and adjust does not. As a result, idea guys are often found on forums, offering up their great ideas for millions in equity, just so long as you do the dirty work while funding it as well.

In rarer instances, an idea guy will attempt execution and be outclassed by competitors that aren't as executionally challenged. Or worse, they copy their competitors for the sake of copying, offering nothing unique or different. While they might have a fantastic product (or idea) that people need, few people know about it. And fewer buy.

Because they lack the necessary business skills, whether it's marketing, management, or operations, their business leaves a fortune on the table while more adapted players move in and take market share.

Typically, *idea guys are committed to the idea of wealth, but not committed to its realistic execution*. While they have a strong meaning-and-purpose, it is improperly focused, usually targeted toward idea-hopping, silver-bullets, and shortcuts. As a result, their strong meaning-and-purpose is channeled into endless action-faking; soliciting billionaires for mentorship, reading books, and buying expensive guru courses. Instead of blaming their execution, they blame their ideas—"It isn't 'disruptive' enough" or "Damn, someone else is already doing it."

Because idea entrepreneurs lack execution, they're often the "give me all the steps" type, seeking secrets and lists to tell them exactly what, how, and where to execute.

In the end, idea entrepreneurs don't have a problem entering the motivation cycle, they have a problem getting traction and connecting the value loop, the ultimate source of a continuation move.

THE GAMBLIN' ROCK STAR FALLEN FROM GRACE

Proficiency: Belief, Meaning, CENTS Business, Execution
Deficiency: Discipline

OUTCOME

You are a master business executioner and made a pile of money.

Unfortunately, as "gamblin' rock star fallen from grace," you are a poor decision-maker when it comes to your personal life, engaging in reckless behavior: screwing anything with a pulse, indulgent spending, sordid associates, drug abuse, or even your choice in a marriage partner.

Because of consequence inequity, your success walks the tightrope.

Some "rock stars" (like my acquaintance with the Lambos) push ethical or moral boundaries.

Others gamble with life itself.

Well known "falls from grace" usually occur in the entertainment industry.

Amy Winehouse, Kurt Cobain, and Heath Ledger are a few who come to mind.

In the business world, Felix Dennis, the flamboyant British entrepreneur who died young at 67, might be considered a rock star fall from grace. In his writings, he made it no secret he led a wild life consisting of multiple mistresses and illicit drug abuse. While we don't really know if his behavior correlated to his early death (he died of throat cancer) we do know that Felix lived YOLO—discipline was not his priority.

Whenever famous persons endure a "fall from grace," such tragedies are underwritten by disciplinary failures resulting in bankruptcy, a day of reckoning, or worse, an early death.

? *Do any of these entrepreneurial classifications currently describe your business modality?*

CHAPTER 48

YOUR LAST BUSINESS EVER (IF YOU WANT)

Riches are chiefly good because they give us time.
~ **Charles Lamb, Writer**

THE UNSCRIPTED MONEY SYSTEM

After my first book was released, many readers shockingly asked how a money system works. How do I earn interest on my money? Where do I go; what do I do? In fact, a friend of mine who consults high-net-worth business owners reported a similar perplexity with his clients: They knew how to accumulate large sums of cash, but they didn't know what to do with it once they had it. A million bucks is great. A million bucks sitting at Bank of America earning seventy-two cents every month is not.

While the intricacies of an *UNSCRIPTED* money system might seem somewhat "cart before the horse," I assure you, it isn't. Once you pack the know-how into turning money into a regular, recurring income stream, you'll see the big picture, fire your purpose, and be more motivated to make it happen. The moment passive-income investments exceed your current and expected living expenses, work becomes optional. And if you have no debt, mortgage, or car payments, this figure is surprisingly obtainable, even for those who don't want to accumulate fortunes.

First, the disclaimer.

The following is my opinion and should be viewed as such. IT IS NOT to be construed as financial, legal, tax, and/or any other professional advice. If you seek official advice in any of these fields, please contact a "licensed qualified professional," someone who can sell you a boilerplate plan of *SCRIPTED* hope-and-pray. Sad that I had to disclaim this, but the truth is, in some fields, reading textbooks and theory—not real-world results—qualifies someone to dispense advice.

Speaking of such, last year, "Kyle," a financial planner from one of my brokerage houses, called me to introduce himself as a part of the "Private Client Group"—a snooty name given to the folks who handle million-dollar-plus accounts. After a few niceties, he levied the close: "So can we talk about putting some of this money to work for you and growing it?" I found the question somewhat whimsical.

First, what qualified Kyle to give advice on how to grow money? Textbooks full of vacuum-packed theory based on the compound-interest scam? Or real-world results symbolized by his own huge portfolio, compliments of the growth advice he was about to dispense? Aside from a fancy degree from some fancy college, I suspect Kyle had zero real-world credentials about growing money. You see, Kyle—and millions of other people like him—is probably broke and tied to a job for life. He got up in the morning, fought traffic, answered to his boss, grabbed lunch at Subway at a predetermined time, cashed a paycheck, went home, went to bed, and will repeat this insanity for the rest of his life. And by following his own advice, his retirement will be codependent on a slew of uncontrollable variables: the economy, Wall Street, his health, and unpromised time.

So…

…should Kyle be calling me, or should I be calling him?

Second, the large sum of money parked into this account got there NOT because of Kyle's proposed investments (namely mutual funds) but because of *Fastlane* entrepreneurship via (TUNEF). Handing it over to "grow it" would be like replacing a printing press that printed dollars daily with one that printed pennies yearly.

Growth? Sorry, you and I have that covered—it's always a CENTS business. Anyhow, my point here is not to deride Kyle. He simply doesn't know any reality other than what the *SCRIPTED* machine has fed him. The bottom line? Think rationally and cautiously about who is giving you advice, especially about money. You never know if it's a book-smart college graduate with thousands in student debt who scored *A*s on *SCRIPTED* dogma, but scored *F*s in real-world results.

THE THREE POTS OF ALLOCATION

So let's get to the juice. An effective *UNSCRIPTED* money system is allocated into two pots and an optional third. The size of these pots is dependent on your lifestyle goals as well as your risk tolerance for each item they represent.

1. **The "fuck you" pot**
2. **The home pot**
3. **The paycheck pot**

Visually, the *UNSCRIPTED* money system looks like this:

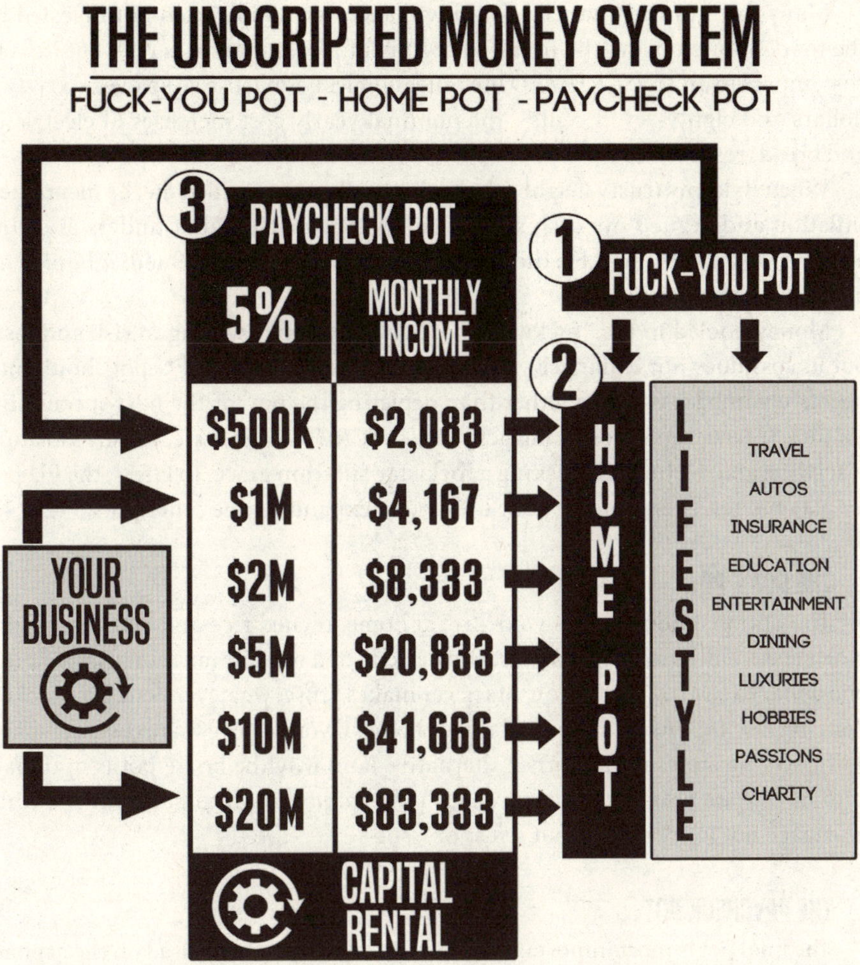

THE "FUCK YOU" POT

The "fuck you" (FU) pot is idle cash sitting in brokerages and money-market accounts, usually doing nothing, and yes, making nothing. The point of the "fuck you" pot is not about yields or returns, but about options, or *choices*.

For example, if you want to invest in start-ups, become an angel investor, or dabble in Las Vegas poker tournaments, the FU pot is where you do it. If your old high school pal is the founder of a hot new start-up and he's accepting equity investments, you can be the lead or the seed. If you want to dance Wall Street's waltz and buy a bunch of biotech stocks, hoping they explode to the upside, the FU pot is where you draw from. If your dream house comes up for sale and, lucky you, it's a foreclosure sale, the FU pot gives you the chance to steamroll the competition with a fast-close, cash offer.

Many folks in the financial world will sneer about idle cash not invested in the market, often using the inflation argument. Yes, inflation is real, but its real cost impact to an *UNSCRIPTED* life is negligible. I don't lose sleep over sixty-two dollars and eighty-seven cents—the nominal yearly cost increases of electricity and bread, respectively.

When Kyle, my trusty neighborhood financial advisor, called me, he mentioned inflation and argued my cash should be "working." He didn't understand this account was my FU pot. He didn't understand what it represented: *a liquid call option on opportunity.*

Money pooled in the "fuck you" pot is money you're willing to risk and lose, but its loss does not endanger your lifestyle. Losses from the FU pot should not negatively impact your life, other than depleting the pot for the next speculative venture. If catastrophic losses impact your *UNSCRIPTED* lifestyle, you are violating discipline and, technically, risking a rock-star fall from grace. In effect, the FU pot is "play money"—enhancing your lifestyle or expanding the other pots.

THE HOME POT

The optional home pot is your dream home, owned free and clear without a mortgage. While mortgage interest can be deducted on your tax returns, spending one dollar to save thirty-three cents never makes sense, whatever your tax bracket. Your biggest lifetime expense will be your home. If you remove this expense, money will never be an issue. The other alternative (and why the home pot is optional) is to have your next pot—the paycheck pot—*large enough* to pay your monthly mortgage nut (or rent) without stress or issue.

THE PAYCHECK POT

The final pot is most important to *UNSCRIPTION*, and it's based on the capital-principle referenced in Chapter 25. Whenever someone mentions a "money system," it's the paycheck pot they are referencing. The paycheck pot is the lead horse while the others are auxiliary. For the *UNSCRIPTED* entrepreneur, the paycheck pot is the end game—a passive-income system of financial instruments that pay your bills, fund your lifestyle, and throw off regular cash you can count on. Such financial instruments can be bonds, ETFs, options, stocks, bank deposits, investment trusts—anything that delivers a published, predictable yield. It could even be a low-cost mutual fund, and yeah, I just recommended mutual funds. My contradiction is absolved in our ends: purposed for income, not for growth. Once a 5 percent return on your paycheck pot is a large enough income to make you comfortably (or luxuriously) happy, you fund the other pots as you wish.

THE PAYCHECK POT (AKA: THE MONEY SYSTEM)

Contrary to what most believe, you don't need a king's ransom to start a business. I started my company with less than $1,000. Publishing my book, only a few thousand. Many hustlers on my forum resell Craigslist discards into new cash flow. Others spend countless hours in "learned" human capital, build great things, and go on to make thousands monthly. "It takes money to make money" is one of the biggest lies in the business of business. Unfortunately, in the business of money, it's true.

The transition from a busy entrepreneur to a semi-retired entrepreneur living off investment income via the capital principal is a fundamental operational switch—but still a business. Instead of managing the business of business, you manage *a business of money.* A money system is, in fact, a capital rental system. Like a real-estate investor who collects rents on his properties or an inventor who collects royalties on his licenses, the business of money rents capital. Instead of ceding control of a physical asset like a single-family home or a parking space in Manhattan, control is ceded to your money. In return, you expect more money as payment. For our paycheck pot, there are six primary instruments we deploy to effectively rent our money. They are:

1. **Stock Dividends**
2. **REIT Dividends**
3. **MLP Partnership Income**
4. **Bond Interest**
5. **Loan Interest**
6. **Managed Income**

STOCK DIVIDENDS

Dividends are corporate profits received from common or preferred stock ownership in a public or private company. Dividend-paying corporations "pass through" a portion of their profits to shareholders, usually quarterly. If you buy 10,000 shares of Johnson & Johnson (JNJ), which pays a quarterly dividend of three dollars per share, you should receive $30,000 in dividends per year. Publicly traded companies who pay dividends post their dividend histories and upcoming payments. Dividend-paying corporations do so voluntarily and are not obligated to pay future dividends, as such payments are influenced by cash flow as well as macroeconomic events.

Examples:

- SO (Southern Company)
- CVX (Chevron)
- MMM (3M)

REIT DIVIDENDS

Dividends received from REITs, or real-estate investment trusts, are an excellent income source for the *UNSCRIPTED* investor. Like stock dividends, REITs are corporations that manage and operate real-estate-related assets. Such assets could be tangible assets—such as apartment buildings, hotels, shopping centers, office complexes—or intangible assets, such as mortgage-backed securities. Several requirements exist in order for a corporation to be considered a REIT, namely 75 percent of their assets must be real-estate related. Moreover, 90 percent of a REIT's taxable income must be distributed to shareholders. This requirement makes their dividend yields higher than average and quite attractive.

Public REITs are traded on major exchanges, highly liquid, and give you a great opportunity to enjoy real-estate income without the hassles of real-estate ownership: broken air conditioners, busted water heaters, and unruly tenants.

Examples:

- AVB (AvalonBay)
- DLR (Digital Realty)
- EQY (Equity One)

MLP PARTNERSHIP INCOME

Master limited partnerships, or MLPs, are similar to dividend stocks, except their income is classified as partnership income and/or partnership distributions. Similar to REITs, MLPs are required to generate 90 percent of their income from "qualifying" sources, mostly related to the commodity space: oil and gas, energy production, pipelines, and transportation. Like their counterparts, MLPs are traded on the open market and offer attractive dividends and relatively favorable liquidity.

MLP partnership income is considered "pass through" in that their earnings are not taxed upstream to the corporation, but instead passed downstream to the partners as if you earned the income yourself. Dividends, or partner distributions, are classified as "return of capital" and not taxed when received. The varied distinction between partnership income and distributions can create some complicated tax implications for MLP unit owners. The IRS treats such income differently (K1 vs. 1099-DIV) and their proper accounting can be both messy and costly.

Examples:

- AB (AllianceBernstein)
- EEP (Enbridge Energy Partners)
- MMP (Magellan Midstream Partners)

BOND INTEREST

Bond interest is payment from loans or debt instruments issued by a government, corporation, or municipalities. For extending credit to a debtor, you get paid a "coupon," or an interest payment at a predetermined interval. For example, a hundred-dollar loan to ABC Corporation might pay three dollars a quarter for the next five years, yielding a 12 percent capital return. At the end of the five years, ABC returns your hundred dollars. The size, rate, term, and regularity depends on the bond offering. The following debt instruments allow you to lend money and earn regular interest payments, which is no different from receiving a regular paycheck, without the work:

- Corporate bonds: Corporations issue debt to arbitrage company growth, borrowing at a lower rate in hopes of achieving a higher rate of return through business operations.
- Sovereign debt: Sovereign debt, or government bonds and notes, are loans issued by sovereign nations to fund government operations.
- Municipal bonds or "munis": Local governments, counties, and municipalities borrow money to finance capital expenditures and public projects. While munis offer lower interest rates than corporate bonds, they are very attractive to high-income earners because their interest payments are exempt from federal taxes. Also, if you buy a bond issued within your state, the income is exempt from state and local taxes.

Unfortunately, buying individual bonds can be pricey, depending on their type and where you buy them. The bond markets aren't liquid, and as a result, the bid/ask (buy/sell) spreads can be a huge drain on your effective yield. Also, the market values of bonds inversely rise and fall with interest rates. If you have to dump a bond before maturity and in a rising rate environment, expect to receive less than face value, so much less that your entire investment could end a loss. Additionally, individual bonds carry default risk: if the issuer goes bankrupt, bondholders are after stockholders in terms of who takes the haircut.

LOAN INTEREST

Similar to bonds, loan interest is money received from notes (or IOUs), either from institutions or individuals. For banks, such loans are known as CDs, or certificates of deposit. In lieu of a lump-sum deposit and an agreed term and interest rate, you can loan money to a bank and receive regular interest payments. Unfortunately, the last time such an investment held attractiveness was the Reagan administration. Due to the laughably low rates offered by banks, CDs aren't a viable paycheck-pot investment vis-à-vis the systemic banking risk they pose. In the 2008 meltdown, over fifty banks, some large, went insolvent. Think a 1.1 percent return is worth this risk?

Another form of loan interest comes from peer-to-peer lending. Peer-to-peer lending is when you loan your neighbor money, except in this case, your neighbor is hundreds of miles away. The two big companies in the peer-to-peer space are

Prosper.com and LendingClub.com. Each offers loan opportunities diversified among many individuals. Loans to creditworthy borrowers can yield as much as 6 percent. For riskier borrowers, rates can balloon as high as 25 percent. The great thing about peer-to-peer lending is diversification. Because 1,000 different people are loaned twenty-five dollars, the default risk is diversified into the expected return. When several people flake out and don't pay, returns don't take a big hit.

MANAGED DISTRIBUTIONS

Managed distributions are payments evolving from a pool of financial instruments, professionally managed by a financial firm. Such funds can be exchange-traded funds (ETFs), mutual funds, closed-end funds (CEFs), or hedge funds.

For example, the Vanguard Dividend Appreciation ETF (VIG) consists of one hundred-plus dividend stocks, and its managed distribution comes as a dividend payment. Instead of buying one hundred dividend stocks, you could purchase the ETF and receive instant income and diversification.

Likewise, the iShares National AMT-Free Municipal Bond Fund (MUB) represents over 2,000 different municipal bonds. Own this fund and you will receive a managed distribution in the form of an interest dividend, while enjoying significant diversification among bonds without the expense of dabbling in the bond market.

Managed distributions are available from any asset pool you want: dividend-paying stocks, MLPs, bonds, REITs, long/short plays, option strategies, real estate—if you have the cash, there's a financial firm offering it. In lieu of a management fee from the fund sponsor, buying into these funds instantly diversifies your holdings amongst hundreds of assets pooled on a particular strategy. Many of these funds also use leverage to increase their payouts.

In terms of liquidity, managed distributions from ETFs and closed-end funds are easily bought and sold because they trade like regular stocks on the exchanges. You can trade them during market hours as well as monitor intraday price fluctuations. Mutual funds, however, are bought or sold at their net asset value (NAV), a market price determined after the close of each business day. Despite this, mutual funds are highly liquid depending on the fund sponsor and usually can be traded at the next prevailing NAV with just hours' notice. Be aware, however, that in rapidly declining markets, an ETF can be exited intraday at better prices over a mutual fund, which is transacted at a closing NAV.

Examples:

- PREMX (T. Rowe Price Emerging Bond Mutual Fund)
- FAX (Aberdeen Asia-Pacific Bond Fund)
- PFF (iShares US Preferred Stock Fund)

All of these financial instruments represent a capital rental business that establishes a paycheck pot, a system creating regular, recurring passive income for the rest of your life. However, before you proceed, no matter if you're investing ten thousand or ten million, there are seven rules I incorporate to ensure my principal is kept safe and the income flowing.

MY 7 PAYCHECK-POT RULES

RULE #1: THE RENT RULE

Consider this for a minute.

You buy an expensive piece of commercial real estate. A prospective tenant offers this: Instead of paying monthly rent, he offers a tiny ownership percentage of his new restaurant and its future profits when they arise. The exact duration and amount of these future profits are unknown and not guaranteed. Oh, and one more thing: these future profit payments are voluntarily, arbitrarily, and unconditionally decided by the tenant. A realized profit, or rent, could be months, decades, or never. In the meantime, the tenant tells you to sit tight and hope his restaurant succeeds so your ownership shares might be worth more.

Good deal? You probably don't think so.

And yet this is how people fund their retirement through stock market investing. They part with their money and, in return, hope to get a piece of future earnings or price appreciation. Neither is guaranteed.

In effect, any "investment" you make in a stock that carries an unstated return is nothing but a fifty-fifty coin flip. Stock goes up, you win; down, you lose. In truth, you are renting real estate, in this case money, and getting paid ZERO RENT. In lieu of rent, you are paid a hope and a dream—two things that do not pay mortgages or buy baby's new shoes.

For those of us who are familiar with stock options (puts and calls), the truth behind any stock investment is revealed in the mathematical delta of any at-the-money option. With stock options, the delta correlates the statistical probability of any option's chance of being "in the money" or higher than the strike price at which you bought it. For example, if stock XYZ is trading at forty dollars and you buy a forty-strike call option (at the money), your probability of having that option worth anything at expiration (in the money) is fifty-fifty. In other words, *the statistical probability of you making money on any stock purchase is exactly 50 percent*—a freaking coin flip. If you buy ten stocks, your chance remains 50 percent—while your chance at being profitable on every single one of them is 0.09765625 percent (.50 to the tenth power).

Yes, the entire *SCRIPTED* world has laid their retirement hopes on a series of coin flips. Ever hear the mainstream parrotheads admit this little fact? Of course not. This factoid brings us to our first rule of the paycheck pot: *the rent rule. The rent rule states that anytime you cede control over your paycheck-pot money, demand rent, not unconditional promises and coin-flip pipe dreams.*

As for the rent you should receive, it should come every month or quarter in any of the aforementioned income streams: dividends, interest, or partnership income.

RULE #2: THE SNAP RULE

When it comes to global economics and the central banking systems that manipulate them, nothing stays the same. A great investment today will be a bad investment tomorrow. For example, in several interviews I did years ago, I recommended Australian government bonds as decent investments. If you took that advice today, you'd be late to the party. When I did those interviews, the Australian dollar yielded better interest rates and possessed more purchasing power.

Since then, macroeconomics have changed. Advice spoken years ago has become questionable today. In other words, because global economies bend and flex, the right investments for creating a paycheck pot also bend and flex. I can't tell you a good from a bad investment because, by the time this book gets to print, a great investment will deteriorate into a sour one, and vice versa.

Economic flux is the methodology behind rule #2: *the snap rule. The snap rule requires that paycheck-pot investments must remain highly liquid, or recallable back to cash at the snap of a finger.*

The "snap of a finger" usually means a simple sell order at a brokerage firm and within twenty-four hours, sometimes within seconds, you're out of the investment and safely back to cash.

When the economics of an investment changes—and it will change—you want to be sure your principal is not at risk. Remember, our objective here is not to grow our nest egg but to "rent it" into a regular income. Without the snap rule in place, your principal investment can deteriorate into an "at-risk" position, where its income understates the assumed risk.

For instance, in 2008, when the real-estate boom started its slide south, everyone from the mailman to the dishwasher at Waffle House owned real estate. When "dumb money" got wind that the ship hit an iceberg and was taking on water, sellers flooded the market. Liquidity fled the scene, and the real-estate plunge drowned investors with it. Because real estate can take months to liquidate, investors could not "cry uncle" and had to endure the abuse.

Without a snap rule to recall your money, a good investment can tank, and when it does, you have to suck the rotten egg. In this case, some real-estate assets lost as much as 50 percent of their value, making bankruptcies and foreclosures the only alternatives. If only those real-estate investors could have snapped their fingers and been "out" once they saw trouble...trillions of dollars of personal net worth would have been spared.

The snap rule says that if a cash recall takes longer than a finger snap to initiate, liquidity could be an issue. Liquidity issues put your principal at risk in shifting markets. The rule saves you from asset price declines that significantly outweigh the income received from the asset. $10K in interest from a bond ETF that has declined $100K in value is not an effective investment, as it takes ten payment periods to recapture the lost asset value.

A recent snap rule example comes from one of my favorite dividend stocks, Southern Company, an electric utility in the southern United States. As I write, its dividend yield is nearly 5 percent. However, in late September 2013, the stock price accelerated from forty-three dollars to above fifty-three dollars just a few months later. On 10,000 shares (a likely investment amount for a $10M money system), this stock appreciation generated a $100,000 unrealized gain (not including the dividends) and posed a prime example of why you need to "get out" when the iron is hot. First, the $100,000 unrealized gain represented nearly FIVE YEARS in dividends. Why wait those five years when those gains could be captured now by selling? I snapped my fingers, pushed through a brokerage sell order, and it was done. Years of dividends in a matter of months (although I wish I owned more and picked the top, I was close enough to be happy).

And then guess what happened a few weeks later? Hear that sucking sound? That's the stock retreating to the mid-forties where, once again, I bought. I will repeat this scenario until I die, or at least until Southern Company gives me a reason to believe they cannot sustain their dividends.

Similarly, in the summer of 2015, I started to liquidate my bond holdings as the chatter of interest-rate hikes picked up. When interest rates rise, the value of bond funds (managed distributions) decline. A 1 percent rise in rates could translate to a 10 percent decline in asset values. Instead of waiting for it to happen, I preemptively took action and moved out of my bond positions. While I wasn't right on the timing, I'd rather sit in cash earning nothing versus risking ten to make one.

RULE #3: THE APOCALYPSE RULE

American Greed on CNBC is one of my favorite shows. The hour-long program chronicles some of the nation's worst financial frauds. Ponzi schemes, investment frauds, money laundering—every scant of financial malfeasance makes a cameo. Using empiricism, notwithstanding witnessing the nth grandma swindled out of her life savings, including her Cadillac, I noticed a familiar pattern: In all the cons, the company perpetrating the fraud is always a small boutique company that grows from the power of a sham productocracy. Uncle Joe tells Uncle Bob that Lustig's Investment Fund is paying 20 percent yearly, and wham, the company grows.

This pattern underscores rule #3: *the apocalypse rule. The apocalypse rule holds that the only catastrophic threat to your principal investment has to come from a global financial apocalypse.*

I consider a financial apocalypse to be hyperinflation of our fiat currency or the collapse of our banking system. On the contrary, a bankruptcy or a financial fraud perpetrated by a small company is not apocalyptic to the banking system but apocalyptic for the investor. Such events might not make the evening news but could headline a financial failure that imperils the rest of your life.

The apocalypse rule means your investments should only be trusted to largely recognized megalithic companies subject to considerable governance and rules of transparency. The phrase "too big to fail" comes to mind as a criterion. And if such a failure does occur, we're looking at a total collapse of the world banking system. At this point, we're no longer talking about a financial apocalypse but a real apocalypse where societal hyperrealities fall apart.

For example, here is the list of institutions that hold my cash and/or paycheck-pot assets:

Fidelity	**TD Ameritrade**
Vanguard	**Charles Schwab**
JP Morgan	**T. Rowe Price**
Bank of America	**Blackrock**

Notice that none of these is a tiny, unknown company small enough to be shielded from public scrutiny. Each of these entities is large enough where a failure (or a large-scale fraud) in any of them would inject systemic risk into the world banking system. In other words, if Vanguard's umbrella of shareholder-owned companies fails, I know we're looking at a worldwide failure in the banking system and, perhaps, an event so large that the world will never be the same.

When you trust your entire nest egg to Donald Lapre at a boutique firm working out of a 1,200-square-foot office in Hoboken, you aren't afforded such protection. I invest in peer-to-peer lending, but the apocalypse rule keeps my investment under six figures because the concept is too new and too untested. A fraud or failure in these companies might be worth thirty seconds on CNBC's *Squawk Box*, but for the wronged investor, the impact could last thirty years.

RULE #4: THE "3 YEARS IN 3 MONTHS" RULE

When Southern Company's stock moved from forty-three dollars to above fifty dollars in a few short months as mentioned above in The Snap Rule, another rule is what compelled me to sell. It's called *the three-three rule.*

The three-three rule says that *if any of your investments, whether they be stocks or bonds, appreciates unrealized gains greater than or equal to three years in dividends in any three-month period, SELL and take the profits.* Consider this appreciation a compressed dividend advance where, instead of waiting three years to receive the money, you can take the cash now by selling. Money today is better than money tomorrow. Here are the mathematics behind this rule, using two different asset classes: Southern Company (SO), a dividend stock; and The Aberdeen Asia-Pacific Income Fund (FAX), a closed-end income fund.

SOUTHERN COMPANY (SO)

- Current Dividend: 5%
- Share Price Cost Basis: $43.00
- Shares Purchased: 1,000 ($43,000 principal)
- Annual Dividends: $2,150 (.05 X $43,000)
- Three-Year-Rule Scenario: If SO appreciates to $49.50 within (3) months, you should sell and take the $6,450 (3 X 2,150) gain, which represents 3 years of dividends.

THE ABERDEEN ASIA-PACIFIC INCOME FUND (FAX)

- Current Dividend: 8%
- Share Price Cost Basis: $5.00
- Shares Purchased: 10,000 ($50,000 principal)
- Annual Dividends: $4,000
- Three-Year-Rule Scenario: If FAX appreciates to $6.20 within (3) months, you should sell and take the net $12,000 gain, since the $12,000 (3 X 4,000) threshold was breached.

While appreciation is not our objective within the paycheck pot, asset appreciation happens. When it does, the three-three rule is a guideline for turning unrealized gains into compressed dividends. If, after selling an appreciated asset, it reverts down, I use a 66 percent mean reversion as a potential rebuy flag. Assuming the company's financials have not changed, the 66 percent criteria is a guideline, not a rule.

For instance, in our Southern Company scenario, a fifty-dollar stock sale (a move from seven dollars from forty-three dollars) might be worth rebuying in the forty-five-dollar range (66% of $7.00 is $4.62 [$50 - $45.38]). The 66 percent reversion flag is based on mean reversion, which is the statistical probability that stocks mean revert back to averages as opposed to shooting straight to the stars or down to zero. I dance this little rhythm of buy-sell-rebuy quite often. It sounds like a lot of work when, in reality, it only requires a daily ten-second peek at your paycheck-pot investments.

RULE #5: THE ADMIRAL ACKBAR RULE

Ah, the old saying, if it's too good to be true, it probably is. The same goes for paycheck-pot investments. If the S&P 500 yields 2.5 percent a year and that oil refinery MLP suddenly advertises dividend yields of 18 percent yearly, picture Admiral Ackbar trumpeting, "It's a trap!". In the finance world, they call these stocks *dividend traps*: alluring investments that ping your radar NOT because of a great balance sheet, but because the dividend yield is eye-poppingly tempting. The Ackbar rule is the classifying identifier between an income investment and a speculative one. The rule is not disqualifying (although I avoid them) but qualitative—such "investments" don't belong in the paycheck pot but in the speculative "fuck you" pot. A closed-end fund with an advertised dividend of 21.5 percent is speculative, not an income investment. The paycheck pot should be boring like C-SPAN on a Monday afternoon.

The danger of dividend traps is widely known. In finance, it is one of the few things that are predictable, more so than a coin flip. For example, on December 19, 2015, Linn Energy, a publicly traded LLC, traded down to $12.24 from almost $22 less than a month earlier. At that point, its advertised annualized dividend was a beefy 22 percent. For an uneducated income investor, a 22 percent dividend yield might be as tempting as rotting meat to a fly doing a dumpster buzz-by.

However, for the educated *UNSCRIPTED* investor familiar with overly obvious *Star Wars* generals, these investments have enough red flags you'd think you were at a Chinese military parade. You see, the farther you get from the yield of the S&P 500, the larger the risk. At some point, the teeter between risk and reward totters to the risk side. Not that the investment can't succeed, but more than likely, it turns into a ticking time bomb ready to blow out your principal.

In the case of Linn Energy, had you invested in this company at the time it boasted its 22 percent dividend, you would have faced an announcement several weeks later: due to declining oil prices and a subsequent decline in cash flow, Linn Energy suspended its dividend payment. Your salacious 22 percent dividend went to zero. And the real travesty? In a few short months, the stock tanked from twelve dollars to just under two bucks. A $122,000 investment would have lost more than 80 percent of its value. No "winner winner, chicken dinner." This is not income investing; it's gambling. Remember, shiny big yields shine bright like the neon lights on Las Vegas Boulevard: they're exciting and grab your attention. Unless you're ravaging your FU pot, such investments shouldn't grab your cash.

RULE #6: THE 1% RULE

By the time you reach the *UNSCRIPTED* pinnacle, you will be a part of the 1 percent. Even if you aren't the richest 1 percent in terms of monetary wealth, you will be in time. Thus far, the rules are designed to protect your principal investment, which protects your 1 percent standing. Besides asset devaluation, there's another threat to your money that isn't so obvious: *management fees*.

Since we're not in the business of making Wall Street and Billy Bankers rich, we find ourselves with another rule: when dealing with managed distributions from managed funds, avoid any fund with a management fee greater than 1 percent, excluding interest charges.

This rule means you should avoid any investment where the total management fees, including commissions, front loads, and/or 12b-1 fees exceed 1 percent. This 1 percent, however, should be exclusive of interest fees, which is common with funds that use leverage. For example, if ZZZ bond fund has total fees at 1.2 percent, but half this fee, or .6 percent, is an interest expense, this fund would still meet our 1 percent rule.

In any case where fees, net of interest, are larger than 1 percent, you can scream NEXT! There are simply too many other alternatives. We're not interested in funding some financial dude's home in the Hamptons. Personally, I like to shoot for less than .5 percent, but sometimes I dabble in funds that creep near the 1 percent threshold. I also avoid any investment that carries a front load or a commission.

Once you remove the +1 percent funds, many options and asset classes remain. For example, here are some paycheck-pot investments I use now, or have used in the past. (The stated management fees are as of December 2015 and may be different at print time.)

- T. Rowe Price Emerging Market Bond (PREMX), Fees: . 97%
- Vanguard High-Yield Corporate Bond (VWEHX), Fees: .23%
- Vanguard GNMA (VFIIX), Fees: .21%
- Vanguard Dividend Appreciation ETF (VIG), Fees: .10%
- Fidelity Municipal Income Fund (FHIGX), Fees: .47%
- BlackRock Income Trust (BKT), Fees: .88%
- Putnam Managed Municipal Income (PMM), Fees: .86%

RULE #7: THE OSTRICH RULE

In the middle of May 2012, RadioShack, the long-time strip-mall electronics retailer, sported an attractive 11 percent dividend.[125] At the time, the stock was trading around five dollars. If you skipped the Ackbar rule, hopefully you won't skip the next rule: *the ostrich rule*. Both can save you from calamitous financial ruin.

The ostrich rule states that you should avoid investments where the business no longer jives with either the cultural or economic climate. Don't bed yourself to a dividend yield while ignoring the jaguar sleeping next to you. In RadioShack's case, the stock had been falling for years, creating the plump dividend. Moreover, anytime I visited a RadioShack, it was like walking into a mortuary. RadioShack was clearly dying because retail was transforming; their products were sold online and cheaper. Despite stock propping attempts through buybacks, RadioShack filed bankruptcy in 2013, costing investors millions.

With the ostrich rule, you steer clear of potentially troubling investments. This includes dinosaur investments (RadioShack, Kodak) or fads (Crocs, Krispy Kreme). For market awareness, here are some questions which cornerstone the ostrich rule:

- ✔ Is the company's industry dying? (RadioShack, Kodak)
- ✔ Is the company's industry being disrupted? (Barnes & Noble, Blackberry)
- ✔ Is the company's industry going through a cyclical shift that could endanger the underlying asset? (Linn Energy, Chesapeake Energy)
- ✔ Is the company likened to a fad or a trend? (Crocs, Krispy Kreme, Mossimo)

Again, *paycheck-pot investing is boring.* If the investment is "hot" or the dividend is "fat," you're probably playing a shell game with a suit who has a big parachute. Clamoring after fat yields ultimately will have you clamoring after a box of tissues.

BUYING PAYCHECK ASSETS

If you're following the snap rule, buying paycheck-pot assets is a breeze. First, open an account at a major financial firm. Keep in mind the apocalypse rule and stick with larger companies. You shouldn't be depositing millions with some dude claiming to be a financial advisor who just started his company eighteen months ago. My preferred financial providers are as follows:

- Vanguard (vanguard.com)
- T. Rowe Price (troweprice.com)
- TD Ameritrade (tdameritrade.com)
- Charles Schwab (charlesschwab.com)
- Fidelity (fidelity.com)

Once your account is established, start researching paycheck-pot assets. A good starting point are the in-house funds that many firms offer. Vanguard, by far my favorite, has a wide variety of managed distribution funds with extremely low fees. T. Rowe Price and Fidelity also have a large selection. Keep in mind the 1 percent rule, as well as any "redemption fees"—fees charged for shares sold after a short period of time. For example, T. Rowe Price's Emerging Market Bond (PREMX) has an annual yield of 5.6 percent paying monthly with fees less than 1 percent. It also has a 2 percent redemption fee. This fund is an acceptable paycheck-pot asset, but only if you don't sell within two months of buying.

If you are actively trading your way to paycheck-pot assets through a brokerage account, such as TD Ameritrade, E-Trade, or Schwab, focus on ETFs, REITs, MLPs, dividend stocks, and closed-end funds (CEFs).

In addition to the seven rules above, here are some simple guidelines (notwithstanding any economic conditions) I use to target the right assets:

EXCHANGE TRADED FUNDS (ETFS)

- ✔ Daily trading volume averages in excess of one million shares, ensuring liquidity and tight bid/ask spreads
- ✔ Should be offered by a notable sponsor with over $50 billion in assets. As of print, that's BlackRock (iShares), Vanguard, State Street, and Invesco (PowerShares)

DIVIDEND STOCKS (NOT INCLUDING REITS AND MLPS)

- ✔ Dividends must be stable or rising, preferably with a three-year history.
- ✔ Dividend yield should not be unrealistically high; pay close attention to the Ackbar and Ostrich rules.
- ✔ A dividend payout ratio, the percentage of profits paid to shareholders, in excess of 50 percent

REAL-ESTATE INVESTMENT TRUSTS (REITS)

- ✔ Must not be a new offering; preferably three years or more trading history
- ✔ Dividends must be stable or rising.
- ✔ Funds From Operations (FFO) must be stable or rising. If this metric is not easily obtainable, use Net Margin.
- ✔ Daily trading volume of at least one million shares
- ✔ Prefer REITs with physical assets over paper (notes), which can be more volatile and subject to asset price declines.
- ✔ Dividend yield should not exceed five times S&P 500 dividend.

MASTER LIMITED PARTNERSHIPS (MLPS)

- ✔ Should have at least a three-year operating history.
- ✔ Distribution history preferred to growing, or minimally, stable.
- ✔ A healthy distribution coverage ratio, which is distributable cash flow divided by distribution to partners. Your selection universe should be anything greater than 1 with a preference toward 1.25 and above.

CLOSED-END FUNDS (CEFS)

- ✔ A tight bid/ask spread or a daily trading volume of at least 100,000 with the exception of state municipal bond funds
- ✔ Price is trading at less than a 1 percent premium to net asset value (NAV), or better, at discount to NAV.
- ✔ Follow 1 percent rule.

THE PAYCHECK POT: A REAL EXAMPLE

A paycheck pot and its income are snapshotted on the next page.

This asset portfolio was put together in December 2015 and is only representative of that time. When you're reading this, the asset values and their income will be different. The point of this exercise isn't to recommend any of these securities, but to show you how you can receive regular monthly income—for life—based upon a large lump-sum investment.

To restate, nothing in this book is a recommendation for any one security or basket of securities. Neither I nor my publishing company is in the business of recommending financial instruments: this example is for illustrative purposes only. With that behind us, assume a paycheck pot of $10 million.

For simplicity, our asset diversification will be limited to dividend stocks only. We will only consider established companies with stable or increasing dividend histories. Each company pays quarterly dividends, and each group is allocated so **that income is received every single month**.

Group 1: Pays dividends in January, April, July, and October.
Group 2: Pays dividends in February, May, August, and November.
Group 3: Pays dividends in March, June, September, and December.

Other assets can be added for diversification, such as ETFs, bonds, closed-end funds, and mutual funds.

Using data taken in the middle of December 2015, here is how a simple mix of corporate assets can give you monthly passive income for life:

$10,000,000

GROUP 1: DIVIDENDS PAY IN JAN/APR/JUL/OCT

DLR, Digital Realty Trust:	10,000 shares	@ 73.87 (3.4% Yield)
WPC, WP Carey Inc.:	10,000 shares	@ 60.97 (6.33% Yield)
HEC, Holly Energy Corp:	30,000 shares	@ 30.19 (7.49% Yield)
BNS, Bank of Nova Scotia:	12,500 shares	@ 40.97 (5.35% Yield)
KHC, Kraft Heinz Company:	7,500 shares	@ 74.63 (3.4% Yield)
Your Dividend Paycheck per Quarter:		**$46,256.25**
Yearly Dividends:		**$185,025.00**

GROUP 2: DIVIDENDS PAY IN FEB/MAY/AUG/NOV

SO, Southern Co.:	15,000 shares	@ 44.21 (4.91% Yield)
ABBV, Abbvie, Inc.:	10,000 shares	@ 80.29 (3.30% Yield)
T, AT&T:	12,500 shares	@ 56.38 (4.04% Yield)
BNS, Bank of Nova Scotia:	20,000 shares	@ 34.03 (5.52% Yield)
EEP, Enbridge Energy:	25,000 shares	@ 20.40 (11.4% Yield)
Your Dividend Paycheck per Quarter:		**$45,850.00**
Yearly Dividends:		**$183,400.00**

GROUP 3: DIVIDENDS PAY IN MAR/JUN/SEP/DEC

CVX, Chevron:	10,000 shares	@ 90.54 (4.73% Yield)
PFE, Pfizer:	15,000 shares	@ 60.97 (6.33% Yield)
KSS, Kohls Corp.:	11,000 shares	@ 30.19 (4.5% Yield)
D, Dominion Resources:	10,000 shares	@ 67.54 (3.83% Yield)
TGT, Target:	10,000 shares	@ 72.33 (3.1% Yield)
Your Dividend Paycheck per Quarter:		**$32,775.25**
Yearly Dividends:		**$131,100.00**

ANNUALIZED TOTALS

Principal investment:	$9,964,910
Total dividends:	$499,525 per year
Portfolio yield:	5.01%
Monthly income:	**$41,627 (average)**

In this example, you receive (on average) about $41,000 a month. Sell some covered calls on the positions and you could easily stretch that 5–6 percent, receiving another $100K annually. Of course, your principal investment will be subject to market fluctuations but, theoretically based on our coin-flip truth, should remain within the $10M neighborhood.

Additionally, dividend stocks owned longer than four months receive favorable tax treatment (Google qualified vs. ordinary dividends). So not only do you get passive income for life, you get special tax treatment. Sounds almost too good to be true, eh?!

Want to see how the investment income changes with a change in principal? Simply divide the figures by the change in principal. With a $20M portfolio (twice the principal) just multiply by two: instead of $40,000/month, you'd receive $80,000/month and $1M per year. With a $1M portfolio, divide the results by ten: instead of $40K per month, you'd live comfortably passive on $4,000/month and nearly $50,000/year.

Now imagine for a moment how your life would look at ANY of these income levels. Even at $50,000 year—with no house payment and no debt—how would your life look and feel? Remember, this is monthly income without doing anything other than peeking at the assets periodically to determine cataclysmic or cyclical threats. How would you live on $40,000 a month? And even better, what would you do with your free time, knowing bills were paid and you already lived lavishly? Maybe write a book on how to do the same? Maybe expose the scam-sham known as the *SCRIPT*?

With a money system, money works for you *through* time without your attachment to it. And we aren't exhausting our capital—we can do this for decades, shuffling assets around here and there, and at the end of the day, your principal is still there.

My friend, this dream exists.

It's out there.

I'm proof of it and I'm nobody special.

Refocus your grind into the right system as opposed to the wrong system and it's yours for the taking. I remind you: When I got started, there were plenty of people in this world who worked far harder than I did. I simply channeled my effort into a system where results could be unlimitedly leveraged versus limitedly capped.

While in cash-accumulation mode, I did not change my investment style and invested according to the capital-principle: I saved for income, not for growth.

Basic financial awareness is a required UNSCRIPTED skill, as important as sales and communication. Apply the KAIZEN principle in these areas.

CHAPTER 49

#UNSCRIPTED

I know the price of success: dedication, hard work and an unremitting devotion to the things that you want to see happen.
~ **Frank Lloyd Wright, Architect**

THANK YOU

The many hours you've spent reading this book mean a lot to me. Probably more than you know. Because time threads our human experience, neither renewable nor returnable, giving me yours is a heartfelt privilege. I thank you for trusting me with it.

I hope you found *UNSCRIPTED: Life, Liberty, and the Pursuit of Entrepreneurship* a valuable visionary blueprint for how to reclaim your life and its dreams. An entrepreneurial career is more than a job without a boss; it's a life loved daily, not postponed until Saturday and hibernated Monday through Friday. It means living free from the soul-destroying death cult of peer conformity, media-mandated mediocrity, and *SCRIPTED* cultural conditioning. But most of all, it means *you own you*: your choices, your time, and your life.

Honor this book as your connective dots: flexible guideposts, not written in the ink of devout absolutism, but written in erasable ink and connected by your own experience of act, assess, and adjust.

Ultimately, I cannot connect your dots; I can only spotlight them as landmarks for improving probability. I can only light the chasm between them, while cautioning; their crossing will be trying and transformative, but incredibly rewarding.

Going *UNSCRIPTED* starts as a simple seed planted in your mind. It's cultivated with resolve and wisdom that you aren't a slave to a car, a television, or a government. Bloom that seed into a lifestyle and you'll find abundance and happiness as its flower, no matter how you define it.

In the end, we all share a humanity that cannot be rewound. Some write the story of that experience, while others allow the *SCRIPT* to steal the pen. Our primordial pages of time don't care if you acknowledge the universal truths of our civilization. It bleeds unceremoniously, only becoming ceremonious when a terminal health diagnosis arrives, or worse, it's gone, leaving nothing but a funeral.

Don't be that person.

Don't be the person dreaming of a do-over.

Your time machine is here and it's telling you to change the history of what may become. Start now, not tomorrow, not next week after you get paid, and not after you get that great idea.

My friend, this is the first day of the rest of your life. It is precious and IT IS YOURS. Don't give the *SCRIPT* the deed to your life—claw it back, rip it up, and rewrite your own *UNSCRIPTED* story.

Good luck and may God, Jesus, Allah, Yahweh, Buddha, advanced ETs, random coagulating amino acids, the Oprah New-Age Karma God, or whoever has engineered our brief existence on this tiny dot in the universe bless your journey.

#TimeMachine

#StartToday

#RipUpTheScript

#*UNSCRIPTED*

#TheEnd.

:-)

**If you enjoyed *UNSCRIPTED*™
and would like to learn more
about the *UNSCRIPTED*™ philosophy,
please check out my first book,
The Millionaire Fastlane,
or visit TheFastlaneForum.com!**

<u>Ready to roll?</u>

**Tweet me a message @MJDeMarco
#UNSCRIPTED #Entrepreneur #Fastlane
or email me at mj.demarco@yahoo.com!**

NOTES

CHAPTER 2

(**1**) Ben. S, User. "Progress Thread - Why I'm Dropping Out Of College." The Fastlane Forum. February 22, 2016. Accessed June 15, 2016. https://www.thefastlaneforum.com/community/threads/why-im-dropping-out-of-college.66365/.

CHAPTER 5

(**2**) Merriman, Paul A. "How Time Can Turn $3,000 into $50 Million." MarketWatch. December 28, 2015. Accessed June 15, 2016. http://www.marketwatch.com/story/how-time-can-turn-3000-into-50-million-2015-12-02.

CHAPTER 7

(**3**) User: Solrac. "Relying on Hope Set Me Back Further from My Goal." The Fastlane Forum. November 7, 2014. Accessed June 15, 2016. https://www.thefastlaneforum.com/community/threads/relying-on-hope-set-me-back-further-from-my-goal.56276/#post-412985.

(**4**) User: Dknise. "Slowlane - Just Heard a Dad Tell His Son to Go the Slow Lane to Get a Lamborghini." The Fastlane Forum. November 10, 2012. Accessed June 15, 2016. https://www.thefastlaneforum.com/community/threads/just-heard-a-dad-tell-his-son-to-go-the-slow-lane-to-get-a-lamborghini.43575/.

(**5**) User: El_hombre123 "What's Love Got To Do With It?" The Fastlane Forum. February 3, 2016. Accessed June 15, 2016. https://www.thefastlaneforum.com/community/threads/whats-love-got-to-do-with-it.65982/.

(**6**) Kurtz, Howard. "College Faculties A Most Liberal Lot, Study Finds." Washington Post. March 29, 2005. Accessed June 15, 2016. http://www.washingtonpost.com/wp-dyn/articles/A8427-2005Mar28.html.

(**7**) Owens, Eric. "Grade School Field Day Flyer Warns Parents: 'Competitive Urge To Win Will Be Kept To A Minimum'" The Daily Caller. May 23, 2014. Accessed June 15, 2016. http://dailycaller.com/2014/05/23/grade-school-field-day-flyer-warns-parents-competitive-urge-to-win-will-be-kept-to-a-minimum/.

(**8**) Owens, Eric. "School That Banned Honors Night For Being Too "Exclusive" Decides Not To Be National Laughingstock." The Daily Caller. May 21, 2014. Accessed June 15, 2016. http://dailycaller.com/2014/05/21/school-that-banned-honors-night-for-being-too-exclusive-decides-not-to-be-national-laughingstock/.

(**9**) Fitzsimmons, Emma G. "Condoleezza Rice Backs Out of Rutgers Speech After Student Protests." The New York Times. May 03, 2014. Accessed June 15, 2016. http://www.nytimes.com/2014/05/04/nyregion/rice-backs-out-of-rutgers-speech-after-student-protests.html?_r=0.

(**10**) Maranjian, Selena. "Average Retirement Income: It's Grim, but You Can Beat It -- The Motley Fool." The Motley Fool. December 1, 2014. Accessed June 15, 2016. http://www.fool.com/retirement/general/2014/12/01/average-retirement-income-its-grim-but-you-can-bea.aspx.

(**11**) "Lobbying Database." Opensecrets RSS. Accessed April 22, 2015. https://www.opensecrets.org/lobby/.

CHAPTER 8

(12) "Hyperreality." Wikipedia. Accessed June 15, 2016. https://en.wikipedia.org/wiki/Hyperreality.

(13) Diaz, Daniella. "Poll: 10% of College Graduates Think Judge Judy on SCOTUS." CNN. January 19, 2016. Accessed May 17, 2016. http://www.cnn.com/2016/01/19/politics/judge-judy-supreme-court-poll/.

retrieved May 17. 2016

(14) YouTube User: Politechttu. "Politically-Challenged: Texas Tech Edition." YouTube. October 28, 2014. Accessed June 15, 2016. http://www.youtube.com/watch?v=yRZZpk_9k8E.

(15) Cole, Marine. "11 Ridiculous College Courses You Won't Believe." The Fiscal Times. September 4, 2014. Accessed December 15, 2015. http://www.thefiscaltimes.com/Media/Slideshow/2014/09/04/11-Ridiculous-College-Courses-You-Won-t-Believe?page=7.

(16) "Critical Theory and Social Justice." Occidental College, Accessed May 25, 2016, http://www.oxy.edu/critical-theory-social-justice/courses

(17) YAFTV. "Students Unaware of 9/11 Anniversary, but Able to Name Celebrities Involved in Nude Photo Scandal" September 10, 2014. Accessed December 9, 2015. https://www.youtube.com/watch?v=VHVZAAuDrQI.

(18) Rao, Leena. "Here's How Much Kim Kardashian's Hit Game Has Made." Fortune Heres How Much Kim Kardashians Hit Game Has Made Comments. February 18, 2016. Accessed June 15, 2016. http://fortune.com/2016/02/19/kardashian-game-revenue/.

(19) GuestUser112. "Drop the Bad (Internet) Habits!" The Fastlane Forum. November 19, 2014. Accessed June 15, 2016. http://www.thefastlaneforum.com/community/threads/drop-the-bad-internet-habits.56473/#post-415762.

(20) Unknown. "Only 2 Fans Welcomed the Cardinals Back to Arizona after Their Loss to the Panthers." Accessed January 28, 2016. http://www.theweek.com/speedreads/601373/only-2-fans-welcomed-cardinals-back-arizona-after-loss-panthers.

(21) Paton, Graeme. "CSI Fuels Forensic Science Degree Rise." The Telegraph. October 19, 2009. Accessed May 17, 2015. http://www.telegraph.co.uk/education/6348107/CSI-fuels-forensic-science-degree-rise.html.

(22) Ley, Tom. "Floyd Mayweather Claims That His Reality Show Is Completely Fake." Deadspin. September 23, 2014. Accessed March 11, 2015. http://deadspin.com/floyd-mayweather-claims-that-his-reality-show-is-comple-1638115038.

(23) Erb, Kelley P. "Widow Loses House Over $6.30 Tax Bill." Forbes. April 29, 2014. Accessed June 15, 2016. http://www.forbes.com/sites/kellyphillipserb/2014/04/29/widow-loses-house-over-6-30-tax-bill/.

(24) https://www.treasury.gov/services/Pages/auctions_index.aspx (Retrieved December 2014)

(25) "January 20, 2011 Clip: Corporations Are Not People." HBO. January 20, 2011. Accessed January 28, 2016. http://www.hbo.com/real-time-with-bill-maher/episodes/0/234-episode/video/corporations-are-not-people.html?autoplay=true.

CHAPTER 14

(26) El-Erian, Mohamed. "Father and Daughter Reunion." Worth. January 7, 2014. Accessed December 22, 2015. http://www.worth.com/father-and-daughter-reunion/.

(27) "Henry Ford Quotes - The Henry Ford." Henry Ford Quotes - The Henry Ford. Accessed August 22, 2015. https://www.thehenryford.org/collections-and-research/digital-resources/popular-topics/henry-ford-quotes/.

(28) Saharaaaa111222. "Ashton Kutcher Acceptance Speech - Teen Choice Awards 2013." August 12, 2013. Accessed November 23, 2016. https://www.youtube.com/watch?v=zuBSRC1zpHw. (Start at 1:59)

CHAPTER 15

(29) Searvogel, Kurt. "Kurt's Bio." Tarzanrides. Accessed March 21st, 2016. http://www.tarzanrides.com/kurt-bio.php.

(30) "Self-Actualization". Wikipedia. Accessed March 10, 2015. https://en.wikipedia.org/wiki/Self-actualization

CHAPTER 18

(31) "The U.S. Weight Loss Market: 2015 Status Report & Forecast." The U.S. Weight Loss Market: 2015 Status Report &. January 2015. Accessed May 18, 2016. https://www.bharatbook.com/healthcare-market-research-reports-467678/healthcare-industry-healthcare-market-research-reports-healthcare-industry-analysis-healthcare-sector1.html.

(32) Burkitt, Laurie. "But Wait, There's Still More." Forbes. August 12, 2009. Accessed May 19, 2016. http://www.forbes.com/2009/08/12/telebrands-infomercial-cmo-network-pitchmen.html.

(33) Lindner, Melanie. "What People Are Still Willing To Pay For." Forbes. January 15, 2009. Accessed May 22, 2016. http://www.forbes.com/2009/01/15/self-help-industry-ent-sales-cx_ml_0115selfhelp.html.

(34) "U.S. Weight Loss Market Worth $60.9 Billion." PRWeb. May 9, 5. Accessed June 15, 2016. http://www.prweb.com/releases/2011/5/prweb8393658.htm.

CHAPTER 19

(35) Kaufman, Scott Barry. "Learning about Learning: An Interview with Joshua Waitzkin." SharpBrains RSS. January 21, 2009. Accessed July 11, 2016. http://sharpbrains.com/blog/2009/01/21/learning-about-learning-an-interview-with-joshua-waitzkin/.

(36) Morehead, James. "Stanford University's Carol Dweck on the Growth Mindset and Education." OneDublin.org. June 19, 2012. Accessed October 24, 2016. http://onedublin.org/2012/06/19/stanford-universitys-carol-dweck-on-the-growth-mindset-and-education/. AND (https://www.youtube.com/watch?v=NWv1VdDeoRY)

(37) Popova, Maria. "Fixed vs. Growth: The Two Basic Mindsets That Shape Our Lives." Brain Pickings. January 29, 2014. Accessed Nov 17, 2015. http://www.brainpickings.org/2014/01/29/carol-dweck-mindset/.

(38*) TEDtalksDirector. "Carol Dweck: The Power of Believing That You Can Improve." YouTube. December 17, 2014. Accessed Nov 17, 2015. https://www.youtube.com/watch?v=_X0mgOOSpLU. (At 2:03)

(39) Reviews for the the Cheat Master 5000, Apple App Store, Nov 23, 2015.

(40*) TEDtalksDirector. "Carol Dweck: The Power of Believing That You Can Improve." YouTube. December 17, 2014. Accessed Nov 17, 2015. https://www.youtube.com/watch?v=_X0mgOOSpLU. (At 2:57)

(**41**) Mcardle, Megan. "Why Writers Are the Worst Procrastinators." The Atlantic. February 12, 2014. Accessed April 16, 2015. http://www.theatlantic.com/business/archive/2014/02/why-writers-are-the-worst-procrastinators/283773/.

(**41a**) User: amp0193. "This made me so mad" The Fastlane Forum. Dec 20, 2016. Accessed Dec 21, 2016. https://www.thefastlaneforum.com/community/threads/this-made-me-so-mad.71785/#post-579242

CHAPTER 20

(**42**) Merzer, Martin. "Poll: More Americans Expect to Be in Debt Forever" CreditCards.com. December 9, 2014. Accessed December 3, 2015. http://www.creditcards.com/credit-card-news/debt-forever.php.

(**43**) Bartlett, Jeff. "Car Financing On Rise | Loans and Leases - Consumer Reports News." Car Financing On Rise | Loans and Leases - Consumer Reports News. September 6, 2013. Accessed June 15, 2016. http://www.consumerreports.org/cro/news/2013/09/car-financing-on-rise-loans-and-leases/index.htm.

(**44**) Ahn, Jeanie. "Former NBA Star Antoine Walker: Life after Losing $110 Million." Yahoo Finance. December 5, 2014. Accessed June 15, 2016. http://finance.yahoo.com/news/former-nba-star-antoine-walker--life-after-losing--110-million-214644672.html.

CHAPTER 22

(**45**) Gunther, Marc. "BUSINESS IS TV'S NEWEST BAD GUY VILLAINS OF PRIME TIME - July 7, 1997." BUSINESS IS TV'S NEWEST BAD GUY VILLAINS OF PRIME TIME - July 7, 1997. July 7, 1997. Accessed May 21, 2016. http://archive.fortune.com/magazines/fortune/fortune_archive/1997/07/07/228626/index.htm.

(**46**) Weil, Dan. "Competitive Enterprise Institute's Smith: Entertainment Industry Vilifies Business." Newsmax. November 19, 2014. Accessed August 2, 2015. http://www.newsmax.com/Finance/Smith-entertainment-industry-business/2014/11/19/id/608319/.

CHAPTER 23

(**47**) Wiseman, Richard. "The Luck Factor." RichardWiseman.com. May/June 2003. Accessed January 4, 2016. http://www.richardwiseman.com/resources/The_Luck_Factor.pdf.

(**48**) Wiseman, Richard. "Be Lucky - It's an Easy Skill to Learn." The Telegraph. January 9, 2003. Accessed January 5, 2016. http://www.telegraph.co.uk/technology/3304496/Be-lucky-its-an-easy-skill-to-learn.html.

CHAPTER 25

(**49**) Johnson, Angela. "76% of Americans Are Living Paycheck-to-paycheck." CNNMoney. June 24, 2013. Accessed October 05, 2015. http://money.cnn.com/2013/06/24/pf/emergency-savings/index.html.

(**50**) Morris, Patrick. "Warren Buffett Tells You How to Turn $40 Into $10 Million." The Motley Fool. Jan 7, 2014. Accessed October 11, 2015. http://www.fool.com/investing/general/2014/01/07/warren-buffett-tells-you-how-to-turn-40-into-10-mi.aspx.

(**51**) Swanbrow, Diane. "Stock Market Participation Has Dropped Most among Small Investors | University of Michigan News." Stock Market Participation Has Dropped Most among Small Investors | University of Michigan News. September 8, 2014. Accessed June 15, 2016. http://ns.umich.edu/new/releases/22365-stock-market-participation-has-dropped-most-among-small-investors.

(52) McMahon, Tim. "Cumulative Inflation since 1913." U.S. Cumulative Inflation by Decade since 1913 :InflationData. June 18, 2015. Accessed March 3, 2016. http://inflationdata.com/Inflation/Inflation/Cumulative_Inflation_by_Decade.asp.

(53) "AIER - EPI Component Levels." AIER - EPI Component Levels. Accessed April 15, 2016. https://www.aier-charts.org/charts/prop/epi_CL.html.

(54) DeSilver, Drew. "For Most Workers, Real Wages Have Barely Budged for Decades." Pew Research Center RSS. October 09, 2014. Accessed April 14, 2016. http://www.pewresearch.org/fact-tank/2014/10/09/for-most-workers-real-wages-have-barely-budged-for-decades/.

(55) "SEC Charges Radio Personality for Conducting Misleading Investment Seminars." Investor.gov. May 9, 2012. Accessed April 29, 2016. http://investor.gov/news-alerts/press-releases/sec-charges-radio-personality-conducting-misleading-investment-seminars.

(56) "Capital Markets Definition | Investopedia." Investopedia. November 18, 2003. Accessed February 19, 2016. http://www.investopedia.com/terms/c/capitalmarkets.asp.

CHAPTER 26

(57) "Contemporary Reaction to Ignaz Semmelweis." Wikipedia. Accessed February 24, 2016. http://en.wikipedia.org/wiki/Contemporary_reaction_to_Ignaz_Semmelweis.

(58) Sellers, Patricia. "Warren Buffett's Secret to Staying Young: "I Eat like a Six-year-old."" Fortune.com. February 25, 2015. Accessed February 25, 2016.

(59) McNichol, Tom. "Be a Jerk: The Worst Business Lesson From the Steve Jobs Biography." The Atlantic. November 28, 2011. Accessed March 3, 2016. http://www.theatlantic.com/business/archive/2011/11/be-a-jerk-the-worst-business-lesson-from-the-steve-jobs-biography/249136/.

(60) McRaney, David. "Survivorship Bias." You Are Not So Smart. May 23, 2013. Accessed March 5, 2016. http://youarenotsosmart.com/2013/05/23/survivorship-bias/.

(61) Wald, Abraham. "A Reprint Of 'A Method Of Estimating Plane Vulnerability Based On Damage Of Survivors' BY ABRAHAM WALD." July 1980. Accessed June 15, 2016. http://www4.ncsu.edu/~swu6/documents/A_Reprint_Plane_Vulnerability.pdf.

(62) Ghilarducci, Teresa. "Our Ridiculous Approach to Retirement." The New York Times. July 21, 2012. Accessed December 26, 2016. http://www.nytimes.com/2012/07/22/opinion/sunday/our-ridiculous-approach-to-retirement.html.

(63) "Bringing Reality into Conventional Economics." Retirement Account Balances by Income: Even the Highest Earners Don't Have Enough. July 3, 2012. Accessed June 15, 2016. http://www.economicpolicyresearch.org/guaranteeing-retirement-income/528-retirement-account-balances-by-income-even-the-highest-earners-dont-have-enough.html.

CHAPTER 29

(64) User: JasonR. "Jason's How to Build Wealth & Golden Nuggets." The Fastlane Forum. May 13, 2014. Accessed June 19, 2015. https://www.thefastlaneforum.com/community/threads/jasons-how-to-build-wealth-golden-nuggets.52268/#post-362266

(65) Carlson, R.Neil and Heth, C.Donald (2007). Psychology the Science of Behaviour. Pearson Education: New Jersey. (https://en.wikipedia.org/wiki/Overjustification_effect)

(66) User: Developmental. "My Firsthand Example WHY You Should Never Do What You Love; and It's Not What You Think." The Fastlane Forum. Nov 17, 2014. Accessed June 26, 2015. http://www.thefastlaneforum.com/community/threads/my-firsthand-example-of-why-you-should-never-do-what-you-love-and-it%E2%80%99s-not-what-you-think.56464/

(**67**) https://twitter.com/pmarca/status/471367634655510528

(**68**) https://twitter.com/pmarca/status/471368638935465984

(**69**) Cuban, Mark. "Dont Follow Your Passion, Follow Your Effort." Blog Maverick. March 18, 2012. Accessed July 21, 2015. http://blogmaverick.com/2012/03/18/dont-follow-your-passion-follow-your-effort/.

(**70**) https://www.commonlit.org/texts/steve-jobs-stanford-university-commencement-speech/student-pdf

(**71**) PragerUniversity. "Don't Follow Your Passion." YouTube. June 06, 2016. Accessed June 16, 2016. https://www.youtube.com/watch?v=CVEuPmVAb8o.

(**72**) Kim, Leonard. "Why Do Some People Choose to Write on Quora over Writing on a Blog?" Leonard Kim RSS. December 24, 2015. Accessed June 16, 2016. http://leonardkim.com/choose-to-write-on-quora-over-writing-on-a-blog/.

(**73**) Satran, Joe. "Steve Ells, Chipotle Founder, Reflects On McDonald's, GMOs And The First 20 Years Of His Chain." The Huffington Post. September 12, 2013. Accessed August 11, 2014. http://www.huffingtonpost.com/2013/07/12/steve-ells-chipotle-20th-anniversary_n_3583927.html.

CHAPTER 30

(**74**) Knight, Kathryn. "Billionaire Who's Proof That Money CAN'T Buy Happiness: He's a Mobile Phone Tycoon with Money to Burn - and a Lifestyle to Make Your Jaw Drop. But What's That worth When Your Family's in Turmoil?" Mail Online. October 2, 2014. Accessed October 12, 2015. http://www.dailymail.co.uk/news/article-2778696/Billionaire-s-proof-money-CAN-T-buy-happiness-He-s-mobile-phone-tycoon-money-burn-lifestyle-make-jaw-drop-But-s-worth-fmaily-s-turmoil.html

(**75**) Lubejewsky, Sonya. The Myths of Happiness Have to Belief, External Locus of Control, Accessed April 17, 2015. http://themythsofhappiness.org/discover-happiness/

(**76**) Allure, Louis; Guenther, Stacey; Lucas, Nance; Oliveri, Sara; Polly, Shannon; Rogers, Brandi, Thurston, Mark. "The Happy Movie Higher Education Instructor's Guide", Page 12. Accessed April 22, 2015.

(**77**) Fischer, Ronad; Boer, Diana "What Is More Important for National Well-Being: Money or Autonomy? A Meta-Analysis of Well-Being, Burnout, and Anxiety Across 63 Societies" Journal of Personality and Social Pyschology, 2011. Accessed June 10, 2016. http://www.apa.org/pubs/journals/releases/psp-101-1-164.pdf

(**78**) Li, David K. "New York, America's Unhappiest City." New York Post New York Americas Unhappiestcity Comments. July 22, 2014. Accessed June 16, 2016. http://nypost.com/2014/07/22/new-york-americas-unhappiest-city/.

(**79**) Ryan, Richard, and Edward L. Deci. "Self Determination Theory and the Faciliation of Intrinsic Motivation, Social Development and Well-Being." January 2000. Accessed May 2, 2015. http://selfdeterminationtheory.org/SDT/documents/2000_RyanDeci_SDT.pdf.

(**80**)(**81**) Salmansohn, Karen. "The No. 1 Contributor to Happiness." Psychology Today. June 30, 2011. Accessed April 16, 2016. http://www.psychologytoday.com/blog/bouncing-back/201106/the-no-1-contributor-happiness.

(**82**) "CareerBliss Happiest and Unhappiest Jobs in America -- 2015." Career Bliss. March 11, 2015. Accessed April 16, 2015. http://www.careerbliss.com/facts-and-figures/careerbliss-happiest-and-unhappiest-jobs-in-america-2015/.

CHAPTER 33

(**83**) Hester, Sammy Jo. "How Provo-based MLM "WakeUpNow" Failed." Daily Herald. February 18, 2015. Accessed May 2, 2015. http://www.heraldextra.com/business/local/how-provo-based-mlm-wakeupnow-failed/article_c56901a2-f064-5e21-affb-ff8ddcdc6585.html.

(**84**) User: Paul David. "Here's Why You Should Never Forget What The C Stands For In Necst" The Fastlane Forum. May 19, 2015. Accessed May 4, 2015. https://www.thefastlaneforum.com/community/threads/heres-why-you-should-never-forget-what-the-c-stands-for-in-necst.60352/

(**85**) User: LeungJan. "CENTS, A tale about Control." The Fastlane Forum. Oct 28, 2013. Accessed May 4, 2015. http://www.thefastlaneforum.com/showthread.php/48682-NECST-A-tale-about-Control?p=309130#post309130

(**86**) Berzon, Alexandra. "U.S. Alleges Poker Site Stacked Deck." September 21, 2011. Accessed May 6, 2015. http://www.wsj.com/articles/SB10001424053111904106704576582741398633386.

(**87**) "Icahn Enterprises - May 2015 Investor Presentation." Scribd. May 2015. Accessed May 5, 2015. http://www.scribd.com/doc/265935665/Icahn-Enterprises-May-2015-Investor-Presentation.

CHAPTER 34

(**88**) User: Likwid21. "Progress Thread: The Paint Brush Cover." The Fastlane Forum. April 16, 2011. Accessed May 11, 2015. https://www.thefastlaneforum.com/community/threads/insiders-progress-thread-the-paint-brush-cover.30969/ (Private Insider Thread)

(**89**) User: Vick. "My New Project: 8 Eyewear." The Fastlane Forum. May3, 2016. Accessed July 26, 2016. https://www.thefastlaneforum.com/community/threads/insiders-my-new-project-8-eyewear.45203/page-61#post-535473 (Private Insider Thread)

CHAPTER 35

(**90**) User: InLikeFlint. "The Inside Out Technique" The Fastlane Forum. March 9, 2013. Accessed May 5, 2015. https://www.thefastlaneforum.com/community/threads/the-inside-out-technique-getting-started.43781/page-2#post-269682

(**91**) Fisher, Jay. "Jay Fisher - World Class Knifemaker." Knife Anatomy, Parts, Names by Jay Fisher. Accessed June 1, 2015. http://www.jayfisher.com/Knife_Anatomy_Parts_Names_Definitions.htm#Knife_Component_Illustrations_with_Descriptions.

(**92**) User: 1step. "2015 Resolution: Provide More Value." The Fastlane Forum. Dec 27, 2014. Accessed May 5, 2015. http://www.thefastlaneforum.com/community/posts/425272/

(**93**) Hamblin, James. "A Brewing Problem." The Atlantic. March 2, 2015. Accessed May 15, 2015. http://www.theatlantic.com/technology/archive/2015/03/the-abominable-k-cup-coffee-pod-environment-problem/386501/.

(**94**) "Utah Man Makes His Living Selling Tumbleweeds." Fox 13 Now. March 17, 2014. Accessed June 16, 2016. http://fox13now.com/2014/05/16/utah-man-makes-his-living-selling-tumbleweeds.

(**95**) Murray, Sarah. "Fixing the Fashion Industry." NRDC. January 05, 2016. Accessed March 27, 2016. http://www.nrdc.org/business/design/denim.asp.

(**96**) Moss, Hilary. "Lucrecia Lovera Makes Handbags Out Of Old VHS Tapes (VIDEO)." The Huffington Post. February 1, 2011. Accessed June 16, 2016. http://www.huffingtonpost.com/2011/02/01/lucrecia-lovera-makes-han_n_817161.html.

(**97**) "Road Debris." Wikipedia. Accessed December 16, 2015. https://en.wikipedia.org/wiki/Road_debris.

(**98**) User: JAJT. "0 - Billionaire Without Creating Anything

" The Fastlane Forum. Dec 27, 2014. Accessed July 8, 2015. http://www.thefastlaneforum.com/community/threads/0-billionaire-without-creating-anything.61315/#post-470884

(**99**) Wheatley, Jon. "I Bought An Apartment To Rent Out On Airbnb | Need/Want." Need-Want I Bought An Apartment To Rent Out On Airbnb Comments. October 28, 2015. Accessed March 27, 2016. http://needwant.com/p/buying-apartment-airbnb/.

(**100**) "How to Win as a First-Time Founder, a Drew Houston Manifesto." First Round Capital, Accessed March 28, 2016. http://firstround.com/review/How-to-Win-as-a-First-Time-Founder-a-Drew-Houston-Manifesto/.

CHAPTER 37

(**101**) User: Kak. "Fastlane 201: How I Went From Employee to Self Sustenance"

The Fastlane Forum. Aug 5, 2015. Accessed Aug 18, 2015.

https://www.thefastlaneforum.com/community/threads/ama-fastlane-201-how-i-went-from-employee-to-self-sustenance.61838/page-3#post-476518

(**102**) "History of Subway." Sub Sandwiches. Accessed February 2, 2016. http://www.subway.com/subwayroot/about_us/history.aspx.

(**103**) Souza, Kim. "The Supply Side: The 'adventure' of Doing Business with Wal-Mart - Talk Business & Politics." Talk Business & Politics. May 18, 2015. Accessed June 16, 2016. http://talkbusiness.net/2015/05/the-supply-side-the-adventure-of-doing-business-with-wal-mart/.

(**104**) Nguyen, Lan N. "Joy Mangano Invents Her Way to Success." AOL.com. January 1, 2010. Accessed February 4, 2016. http://www.dailyfinance.com/2010/01/01/joy-mangano-invents-her-way-to-success/.

CHAPTER 39

(**105**) Reilly, Lucas. "How Stephen King's Wife Saved 'Carrie' and Launched His Career." Mental Floss. October 17, 2013. Accessed February 6, 2016. http://mentalfloss.com/article/53235/how-stephen-kings-wife-saved-carrie-and-launched-his-career.

(**106**) "Star Wars Execs Were Nervous the Film Wouldn't Be a Hit." NewsComAu. December 09, 2015. Accessed June 16, 2016. http://www.news.com.au/entertainment/movies/star-wars-memo-from-1976-reveals-studio-executives-were-nervous-the-film-might-not-be-a-hit/news-story/33bcc01b7912ec2676301cdbe2c46abf.

(**107**) Luzi, Evan. "The Steven Spielberg Three Step Guide to Rejection." The Black and Blue. April 05, 2011. Accessed February 7, 2016. http://www.theblackandblue.com/2011/04/05/the-steven-spielberg-three-step-guide-to-rejection/.

(**108**) User: srjjames. "Seeking Advice" The Fastlane Forum. February 24, 2012. Accessed July 25, 2016. https://www.thefastlaneforum.com/community/threads/seeking-advice.37556/

CHAPTER 40

(**109**) User: Vigilante. "Prince Has Thousands of Songs in the Archive" The Fastlane Forum. May 2, 2016. Accessed May 2, 2016.https://www.thefastlaneforum.com/community/threads/prince-has-thousands-of-songs-in-the-archive.67676/#post-535260

(**110**) Garber, Megan. "Instagram Was First Called 'Burbn." The Atlantic. July 2, 2014. Accessed June 16, 2016. http://www.theatlantic.com/technology/archive/2014/07/instagram-used-to-be-called-brbn/373815/.

(**111**) Kapner, Suzanne. "Popular or Overexposed? Michael Kors Walks Thin Line." WSJ. August 1, 2014. Accessed March 3, 2016. http://www.wsj.com/articles/popular-or-overexposed-michael-kors-walks-thin-line-1406911371.

CHAPTER 41

(**112**) DeLong, Scott. "The Keys to Success According to Me." Nearly Nomadic. May 31, 2012. Accessed March 11, 2016. http://www.nearlynomadic.com/the-keys-to-success-according-to-me/.

(**113**) "Hillary Scott (singer)." Wikipedia. Accessed Mar 12, 2016. https://en.wikipedia.org/wiki/Hillary_Scott_(singer).

(**114**) F4BBEST. "Trailer: "Don't Stop Believin': Everyman's Journey" YouTube. March 09, 2011. Accessed June 16, 2016. https://www.youtube.com/watch?v=ISqCjjoOrfw.

(**115**) Wikipedia. Accessed June 16, 2016. https://en.wikipedia.org/wiki/Lindsey_Stirling#2010.E2.80.9312:_America.27s_Got_Talent_and_debut_studio_album.

(**116**) Ehrenreich, Ben. "Jar of Marbles by Ben Ehrenreich | Significant Objects." Significant Objects. November 2, 2009. Accessed June 16, 2016. http://significantobjects.com/2009/11/02/jar-of-marbles/.

(**117**) Julavits, Heidi. "Wooden Apple Core by Heidi Julavits | Significant Objects." Significant Objects. April 3, 2010. Accessed June 16, 2016. http://significantobjects.com/2010/04/23/wooden-apple-core-heidi-julavits-story/.

(**118**) "Our Story" Accessed June 19, 2015. http://www.sturdrinks.com/our-story.html

(**119**) Lambert, Nathaniel, Tyler F. Stillman, Joshua A. Hicks, Shanmukh Kamble, Roy F. Baumeister, and Frank D. Kincham. "To Belong Is to Matter." To Belong Is to Matter. May 2013. Accessed Mar 22, 2016. http://psp.sagepub.com/content/39/11/1418.

(**120**) User: MEAH. "$120k+ Online Coaching Business to Autopilot w/o Ceiling"

The Fastlane Forum. April 24, 2015. Accessed May 22, 2016.

https://www.thefastlaneforum.com/community/threads/120k-online-coaching-business-to-autopilot-w-o-ceiling.59883/

Chapter 44

(**121**) "Tax Calculators - Jackson Hewitt Tax Service." (Single Filer) Tax Calculators - Jackson Hewitt Tax Service. Accessed Mar 25, 2016. http://www.jacksonhewitt.com/Resource-Center/Tax-Calculator/.

Chapter 45

(**122**) Kirkham, Elyssa. "62% of Americans Have Less Than $1,000 in Savings, Survey Finds | GOBankingRates." GOBankingRates. October 04, 2015. Accessed June 16, 2016. http://www.gobankingrates.com/savings-account/62-percent-americans-under-1000-savings-survey-finds/.

Chapter 46

(**123**) YouTube User: Brandnew9er. "Adam M Smith at Chick Fil A Drive Thru." YouTube. August 02, 2012. Accessed June 16, 2016. https://www.youtube.com/watch?v=VFdPBtxzT6k.

(**124**) Diaz, Joseph, and Lauren Effron. "Former CFO on Food Stamps After Controversial Viral Video About Chick-Fil-A." ABC News. May 25, 2015. Accessed June 16, 2016. http://abcnews.go.com/Business/cfo-food-stamps-controversial-viral-video/story?id=29533695.

Chapter 48

(**125**) "RadioShack." Wikipedia. Accessed June 16, 2016. https://en.wikipedia.org/wiki/RadioShack.

Additional Credit

(*38),(*40) Compiled from YouTube, Excerpted from MINDSET: THE NEW PSYCHOLOGY OF SUCCESS, by Carol S. Dweck, PhD., © Copyright 2006 by Carol S. Dweck, PhD.. Used by permission of Random House, an imprint and division of Random House, LLC.

INDEX

A

B

D

E

F

G

H

I

J

K

L

M

N

O

P

R

S

T

U

V

W

Y

Z